THAT MYRIAD-MINDED MAN

THAT MYRIAD-MINDED MAN

a biography of
George William Russell
"A.E."
1867–1935

Henry Summerfield

ROWMAN AND LITTLEFIELD
TOTOWA, NEW JERSEY

First published in the United States 1975
by Rowan and Littlefield, Totowa, N.J.

Library of Congress Cataloging in Publication Data

Summerfield, Henry.
That myriad-minded man.

Includes bibliographical references.
1. Russell, George William, 1867–1935—Biography. I. Title.

PR6035.U7Z83 828'.8'09 [B] 74–2161

ISBN 0–87471–536–9

Produced in Great Britain

To
ALAN DENSON
for his devotion to AE
and to the arts

Contents

Illustrations

Preface

To readers of Anglo-Irish literature, the signature 'AE' is familiar as the pen-name of George Russell, poet and discoverer of poets, mystic and patriot, and proponent of a more humane social order. Russell is remembered not only for his place in literature, his role in the co-operative movement, and his success in combining the practice of contemplative mysticism with an active life in the modern world, but for the extraordinary affection and hero-worship which he inspired in the most diverse persons. He makes frequent appearances in the memoirs of his contemporaries, for his prophet-like ardour for social reform was combined with the power of enabling others to share his own sense of the reality of the invisible world, so that even a chance acquaintance could find himself carried, astonished and enchanted, into a realm in which he had never before believed. There has long been a need for a full-length biography of this man who developed from a shy and inarticulate dreamer into a public figure who was consulted by two British Prime Ministers and an American Minister of Agriculture.

The publisher of this book plans to issue an edition of AE's Collected Works in which separate volumes will be allotted to the poetical, literary prose, political and economic, mystical, and editorial writings. Besides bringing such valuable books as *The Candle of Vision* back into print, this enterprise will rescue from rare and obscure periodicals the articles in which most of AE's best prose appeared.

The author of a biography is dependent on the kindness and co-operation of many people. Throughout my undertaking my greatest debts have been to the late Mr. Diarmuid Russell, AE's younger son, and to Mr. Alan Denson. Mr. Russell gave me every encouragement, answered all my questions, and graciously allowed me to quote from his father's books, articles, letters, and manuscripts and to publish photographs of his paintings. Mr. Denson's dedicated bibliographical research and editorial work have alone made possible any serious study of AE. With unlimited generosity, he has permitted me to use his published and unpublished work and has given me very extensive personal help. Since completing his volumes devoted to AE, he has compiled and published Bio-

Bibliographies of AE's friends James Cousins, John Hughes, Padraic Colum, and Herbert Palmer, and editions of Cousins' correspondence, plays, and writings on the theatre (all obtainable from their author, c/o Messrs. Colin Smythe, Ltd.).

I owe an especial debt of gratitude to Dr. Monk Gibbon, who most kindly allowed me to use his doctoral thesis and make public for the first time much valuable information contained in it. His thesis corroborated my own conclusions, reached before I had seen it, about AE's courtship. From an early stage in my work, I have benefited from the criticism, encouragement, and continuous assistance of Dr. Ann Saddlemyer. Mr. James A. Healy of New York invited me into his home to enable me to consult important letters by AE in his fine private collection. Dr. Colm McDonnell showed me AE's Theosophical paintings and later allowed me to have them professionally photographed. Major Richard Gregory has permitted me to quote a statement by Lady Gregory. Among the many people who have given me useful advice and information are Mr. Roger Beck, the late Padraic Colum, Miss Dorothy M. Emerson, Miss Irene Haugh, Mr. Gerald Heard, Dr. S. W. Jackman, Mr. Peter Lundt, Dr. Charles Milligan (in whose journal the *Iliff Review* some passages of this book have appeared), Dr. Kenneth Moss, Dr. Clyde Pope, Mr. Arthur Power, the late Constance Sitwell, Dr. A. H. Somjee, and my father, Mr. J. S. Summerfield. I am also heavily indebted to a Theosophist of profound insight who prefers to remain anonymous. In 1961 I visited Sheep Haven, Donegal, and learnt much about AE's holidays there from Mrs. Mary McGinley, Mrs. Stewart, Mr. Agloe, Colonel and Mrs. Law, and Mrs. Hall. My wife, Marian, and my colleagues Dr. Norman Alford, Dr. Mike Doyle, Dr. Patrick Grant, and Professor Robin Skelton have read the typescript of this book in whole or in part and made valuable suggestions.

I owe much to librarians and members of library committees. In particular I would like to mention Mr. T. G. F. Paterson and Mr. D. R. M. Weatherup of the County Museum, Armagh, Mr. Alfred MacLochlainn of the National Library of Ireland, Miss D. Jordan of the Plunkett Foundation for Co-operative Studies, Oxford, Dr. Richard Cary of Colby College Library, Waterville, Maine, Mr. Thomas E. Ratcliffe and Mr. Richard G. Smith of the University of Illinois Library, Mrs. Lola L. Szladits and the late Dr. John D. Gordan of the Berg Collection, New York Public Library, Dr. C. L. Cline, Dr. Gordon H. Mills and Mrs. Mary M. Hirth of the University of Texas, Miss Alison Maude and Mr. Howard Gerwing of the University of Victoria Library, and the staffs of the British Museum Library, the Houghton Library, Harvard, the Lilly Library,

Bloomington, Indiana, the Lockwood Memorial Library, Buffalo, New York, the general collection of New York Public Library, the State Historical Society of Wisconsin, the University of Wisconsin Library, and Yale University Library.

Colby College Library and the Library of the University of Texas have allowed me to quote from important unpublished letters and manuscripts in their possession. The poem 'I've no exotic deity' appears by permission of the Harvard College Library. Many passages from letters and manuscripts are published by consent of the

Henry W. and Albert A. Berg Collection.
The New York Public Library.
Astor, Lenox and Tilden Foundations.

December 1974 Henry Summerfield

I

A Seer Born (1867–1890)

Of all the outstanding men of the Irish Renaissance, George Russell – AE – was least concerned to accomplish a great work in a single field. His lifelong friend William Yeats was determined from early youth to be a poet and through years of dedicated self-discipline he surpassed all others of his time. James Joyce, with supreme confidence in his own genius, endured exile and poverty to raise the novel to new heights of artistry. Others, outside the literary movement, earned their places in history as labour leaders, reformers, patriots, and statesmen. AE's greatness is rooted in his renunciation of the singlemindedness which offers the man of genius the most promising path to fame.

So far as is now known Russell's earliest ambition was to become a painter. He was turned aside from this purpose over a period of several years by an influence which was then acting powerfully upon many distinguished minds whose spiritual needs were left unsatisfied by their traditional faiths. To such people Madame Blavatsky's Theosophical Society offered an immense and intricate body of mystical teaching, which purported to be a large segment of the ancient knowledge underlying all religions but preserved in them only in fragmentary and distorted form. Yeats, rebelling against his father's non-belief, was drawn after a period of wavering into the new movement. AE hesitated longer, but his assent, when given, came from the depths of his being, and his loyalty to Madame Blavatsky, though not to the organisation she left behind her, lasted for the remainder of his life.

Having abandoned his artistic ambitions, AE devoted seven years to purely spiritual endeavour, of which composing poetry was a minor portion half guiltily indulged in for higher purposes. When the semi-monastic community which had become his home broke up, he turned to the service of his country and his countrymen, and joined Horace Plunkett's movement for the advancement of Ireland's backward farmers. After travelling and working among them, he was appointed editor of the movement's weekly journal and was able to develop a political philosophy in its columns without neglecting the agricultural causes and technicalities it had been founded to publicise. Meanwhile he had returned to painting as a hobby and had continued to write and publish poetry, for which he was now famous. When Ireland, having helped Britain to defend the rights of small nations, won her own independence, AE was called upon to edit a review which would assemble expert opinion on all questions of national importance. With consistent sanity the mystical poet proposed rational approaches to problems obscured by passion – approaches which his over-emotional compatriots often found hard to accept. He was highly regarded abroad and when his last illness overtook him he was travelling in the United States to advise the Department of Agriculture on rural problems.

Some of AE's activities made important contributions to the life of the early twentieth century and none of them was insignificant. Nevertheless no résumé of his achievements does justice to him or explains why he was for many years one of the best loved men in Ireland. His greatest accomplishment was the creation of his own character. A gently mocking humour, an inexhaustible appetite for ideas, a benevolent courtesy extended to all comers, and a knack for handling statistics and obtaining results from committee meetings were underlaid and supported by an inner tranquillity which the pressure of external events could rarely cloud. To those sensitive enough to perceive it, this tranquillity, won by spiritual effort, was the clearest outward sign of his genius.

Yeats, whose authoritarian temperament eventually brought him into conflict with the more democratic AE, realised that the latter suffered inferior minds gladly because his genius was essentially religious.[1] AE, a visionary artist akin to Blake, also had affinities with those saints whose boundless love of their fellows is nurtured by an austere self-discipline. Unlike Blake, who is said to have seen visions in infancy, he was not marked out in childhood by any special gifts, and he resembled Mahatma Gandhi in that his personality was not transformed by a sudden conversion but moulded by the patient exercise of willpower over many years.

In adult life AE was not inclined to attribute any aspect of his spirituality to the religious training of his upbringing. He attached little importance to family background and did not talk about his parents or brother even to intimate friends. Once when he was walking with the Gaelic scholar Osborn Bergin, he greeted a man in passing then turned to his companion and said, "Do you know who that was? That was my brother. He is too fat." But for this chance encounter Bergin, who saw AE regularly, would never have known that he had a brother.[2] Information about his parents and early life remains meagre.

George William Russell was born on 10 April, 1867, in the small Ulster town of Lurgan. His father, Thomas Elias Russell, came either from County Tyrone or Drumgor in Armagh, and was a book-keeper employed by Bell and Co., a Quaker firm of cambric manufacturers. His mother, Marianne Russell (née Armstrong), belonged to the Armagh countryside and had worked in a general dealer's. Dr. Monk Gibbon, commenting perceptively on a photograph of the couple, remarks on the earnestness and idealism reflected in the bearded face of the husband, beside whom the wife appears undistinguished.[3] Thomas Elias Russell was a highly respected, gentle, cultured and pious man. Though he and his wife were devout members of the Church of Ireland, he had strong evangelical leanings and used also to attend Primitive Methodist services. George was the youngest of three children. His sister, Mary Elizabeth, died at the age of eighteen; his brother, Thomas, predeceased him by only a few years.

During the first decade of George's life the family remained in Lurgan, a market town which was surrounded by fertile countryside and which possessed a flourishing linen industry established more than a hundred and fifty years before. In 1868 the Mechanics Institute built a new hall, which provided a centre for cultural activities. Here Thomas Russell must have attended concerts, but his love of music was not passed down to George, who later confessed he could not tell the difference between one note and another.[4] The population included Roman Catholics, Presbyterians, Quakers and members of the Church of Ireland, and Lurgan had an unenviable reputation for religious fanaticism. All his life Russell remembered how 'at any time a chance word might provoke a battle, and a whole horde of wild fanatics lying in ambush might rush out of the doors at a signal given, and in the name of God try to obliterate His image on each other's faces.'[5] Once a bigoted but courageous old Orangeman beat his drum and uttered his war-cry alone in the Catholic quarter at three o'clock in the morning.[6]

George Russell was born in William Street, which runs downhill in a straight line from the town centre and even today quickly reaches the countryside. Soon after his birth the family moved to a cottage just within the entrance of Lord Lurgan's grounds. The three children attended the Model School, where George, who first entered in February 1871 when he was not quite four years old, did well in writing and drawing.[7] According to one of his friends, a master told him fairy stories which made a lasting impression,[8] while at Sunday School he was taught about the wickedness of Roman Catholics, and the prizes consisted of books on the Inquisition and the burning of Protestant martyrs.[9] In later life he remembered having been a quite ordinary child,[10] who took pleasure in spending his own money when he reached the age of five or six,[11] and who enjoyed a thrill of surprise when the gift of a chocolate cow put the finishing touch to a perfect Christmas day while black-faced mummers were dancing in the street.[12] He acquired a boyish taste for penny dreadfuls about the Wild West[13] and afterwards confessed to 'an early childhood made lurid by pirates and highwaymen and detectives and Red Indians.'[14]

When Russell became a Theosophist he practised a retrospective meditation, which enabled him to bring back into memory certain forgotten incidents of childhood. To two of these he ascribed the fundamental impulses of his life. When he was about four or five years old he wandered into a park and lay stretched out on the grass overcome by the loveliness of the daffodils. Soon after, he read a child's story and was almost mesmerised at the mention of a magic sword with silver hilt and blue steel blade. All the spring evening he wandered around repeating the words 'blue and silver!' This marked the birth of his sense of beauty, and as primroses, lilac and other objects enchanted his sight new hues were added to the original harmony of two colours. In his meditation he seemed to recognise that the choice of those colours he would most cherish was prompted from a profound level of his being. Not till later did he learn the meaning of the word 'magic', which had vibrated strangely in his mind.[15]

It was also while he was living at Lurgan that he heard of a dying woman who wept a quarter of an hour before she died because she could not leave her bed to help a sick neighbour. An answering selflessness seemed to rise within him, and though the mood was only transient a spiritual aspiration had been awakened. But because the love of beauty had appeared first it always took predominance over the ethical impulse.[16]

In 1878 Russell's father accepted an offer of employment from his friend Robert Gardiner, who had a partnership in a firm of accountants, and the family moved to Dublin. Looking back Russell wrote, 'I was born in Lurgan . . . and have never been sufficiently grateful to Providence for the mercy shown to me in removing me from Ulster, though I like the people I cannot breathe in the religious and political atmosphere of the North East corner of Ireland.'[17] From time to time he returned to Ulster on holiday. According to his friend Carrie Rea, who met him just after he left school, he spent a fortnight in Armagh City every two years, but in the alternate years he may have stayed on his maternal grandparents' farm at Drumgor, which it is known he also visited.[18] Drumgor is between Lurgan and Portadown and in the neighbourhood of Lough Neagh where the local people have a rich stock of legends passed down by word of mouth. Armagh, a small but beautiful city where Russell stayed with his father's sister in her home at Shiels Almshouses, is the Canterbury of the Church of Ireland. The somewhat squat yet dignified Protestant cathedral overlooks the residential area from the top of a steep hill. Armagh is only a short distance from Emain Macha, capital of the kings of the Red Branch in Ulster's Gaelic past. It is difficult to determine whether Russell, who was unimpressed by Irish Christianity and who always insisted that he was ignorant of Celtic tradition in his early youth, was sensitive to the rich heritage of Armagh. His aunt is said to have been an intelligent woman, and it may have been of her that he was poignantly reminded by the kindly, peace-making mother in St. John Ervine's play *Mixed Marriage*.[19] While still a boy he read aloud beautifully and old people in Armagh loved to listen to him.

On one of his early holidays with his aunt, Russell made a decision which foreshadowed the future course of his life. He was walking along a country road at about the age of fourteen when he began to consider the problem of divine retribution, and within a few minutes he passionately concluded that God had no right to punish him for not doing what he had never promised to undertake.[20] This event was probably associated with a waking dream that he describes as the fountainhead of his lifelong sympathy with revolt. He was lying on his bed when he came to imagine himself as one of the Children of Light in a primeval paradise troubled by a rumour that there also existed Children of Darkness who were utterly abhorrent. Wandering alone into space, he felt the presence of one of the latter beside him and heard the gentle whisper, 'We of the Darkness are more ancient than you of the Light.' With this he renounced his former allegiance and felt a great yearning to lose himself in the Divine Darkness.[21] It would be interesting to know whether he had then read Milton.

The mental rebellion on the road in Armagh sounds like the reaction of a sensitive child to a harshly repressive image of the Deity. Russell's friend Katharine Tynan, a devout Catholic, assumed that this was at the root of his Theosophy, but Henry Goodwillie, who knew him from his schooldays, remembered his parents as being very far from stern and puritanical,[22] and what other evidence there is supports him. Russell acknowledged no debt to the religion of his youth, but Dr Gibbon notices the strain of other-worldliness and mysticism in the evangelical tradition to which his father was attracted, while Eglinton draws attention to the Biblical phraseology which pervades much of his prose,[23] and indeed scriptural quotations always came readily to his pen. A writer on *Song and Its Fountains* who preferred the content to the style regretted AE's addiction to the language of the Salvation Army.[24] It was, however, only in late adolescence that he developed an interest in the mystical experiences of St. Paul, who was acclaimed as an initiate by Madame Blavatsky.

In moving from Ulster to the South, Russell made an unobtrusive entrance into the life of the metropolis where he was to become famous. Dublin, being a centre of commerce but not of industry, was free from the hustle and bustle of grimier and more modern cities. With the sprawling Phoenix Park nearby, the shore within easy reach, and mountains visible in the distance, its inhabitants were never very far from the countryside and the sea. The compact city centre, adorned with elegant Georgian architecture, was surrounded both by middle-class suburbs with pleasant gardens and working-class slums which formed a natural breeding ground for revolution. Nationalist politics and Catholic piety flourished and sometimes clashed under the shadow of Dublin Castle, from which the Sovereign's representatives ruled Ireland on behalf of the Protestant and Saxon people to whom the Russells belonged. Already rich with centuries of history, the city contained all the ingredients for the cultural and national revival which was to make it the centre of events as tragic as any in its past, and victories that contradicted the experience of seven hundred years.

Russell's family first lived at 33, Emorville Avenue, a few minutes' walk from the city centre; in 1885 they moved a little more than half a mile south to 67, Grosvenor Square, in the suburb of Rathmines. He attended first Dr. Power's school in Harrington Street,[25] close to his new home, and while there showed sufficient talent to be sent to evening classes at the Metropolitan School of Art from March to May of 1880. Early in 1882 he entered Rathmines School whose headmaster was Dr. Benson, not a strict disciplinarian but a teacher devoted to the intellectual and moral welfare of his boys and, in spite of his earnestness, the possessor of an individual sense of humour. Russell was afterwards proud that the School had fostered another heretic, Father George Tyrrell, who was expelled from the Jesuit order for his unorthodox theology, but had no recollection of having known him.[26] Russell's quip 'I learned nothing at school being quite clever enough to evade knowledge by seeming to possess it'[27] must be balanced against the fact that from 1883 to 1884, while he was in the Lower Sixth, he won prizes for mathematics, French, Classics, English and handwriting, and far outdistanced the remainder of the perhaps small class.[28] In later life he was almost ignorant of French and admitted that he had forgotten most of the little Latin and Greek he had once known, partly because he had never been able to adjust his ear to the melody of classical verse, and it was only through its poetry that he could learn a language.[29] Dr. Gibbon, however, recollects him stumbling through a passage in the Greek text of the Gospels in middle age.[30]

As a Sixth Former at Dr. Benson's, Russell was a happy and high-spirited schoolboy, who did not appear to be fundamentally different from his fellows, though he was unusually talented and bore the nickname of 'The Genius.' While his greatest passion was for art – in October 1883 he resumed his evening classes t the Metropolitan School – he was able to find satisfaction in friendships deep enough to outlast his schooldays with two youths very different from himself: Henry Goodwillie, a distinguished athlete, who became a banker; Henry Chester Browne who was to spend his life as a clergyman. The trio went on country walks together and on some of these expeditions Russell would paint by the side of the River Dodder. They also engaged in much good-humoured merriment and Browne recollected of Russell:

> In school he was quickly recognised as having literary and artistic instincts of an order not usually found amongst boys, and he had to put up with a little playful ragging, from me as well as from others, in consequence. A lampoon of mine, done of him in 1883, describes him as 'the special artist and literary critic of Rathmines College.'[31]

Browne sketched him at the age of seventeen staring at a cast of 'The Dancing Faun' in an art shop window while a man with a wheelbarrow ran into him. Comic drawing as well as serious painting was a pastime of Russell's too, and surviving examples of his sketches illustrate the sorrows of an examiner tearing his hair and exclaiming, 'If I caught the young lunatic who wrote this, I'd – I'd –,' and a candidate who 'looked first at his paper and then began to study the ceiling.' One series, drawn in June 1884 on the annual expedition to Holyhead, where the boys visited the lighthouse and Lloyd's signal-station, depicts the agonies of sea-sickness, the pleasures of surreptitious smoking, and the troubles of bad-tempered sailors confronted by unruly boys.[32] It was probably at this very period that Russell underwent a remarkable spiritual awakening, the first effect of which was to dispel his easy gaiety and turn him into an indrawn, selfconscious and socially awkward young man, though it was eventually to provide him with the faith and inspiration that moulded his life. He was both dazzled and bewildered by intimations of other, more ethereal forms of life, imperceptible to the physical senses, so that he alternately withdrew inwards to brood on the visionary images which haunted him and then rebounded outwards to indulge in the playfulness of a schoolboy. 'An age of the spirit,' he wrote, 'would fall upon me, and then I would come out of reverie and be the careless boy once more.'[33]

In spite of his admirable scholastic record, Russell was sharply critical in later years of the education he had received, though he may have been thinking of the Model School and of Dr. Power's more than of Dr. Benson's. He deplored the painful teaching methods which had given him a lifelong distaste for the nation that had produced Latin poetry,[34] and remembered his burning indignation at the blows of a master who would strike out with his cane at random 'not because of any special wickedness . . but only because he was sure there was a vast amount of unpunished mischief about.'[35] Worse still (though he should probably have blamed the British authorities for this), there was not the least attempt to create even a rudimentary consciousness of national identity:

> The editor of this paper enjoyed in his youth a liberal education completely divorced from life and from country. Looking back on it, it seems now as if the system had been thought out amid the aether and interstellar spaces by someone who was doubtful as to what planet or country it might be worked in . . . Luckily we met at that period a young Russian who was much interested in Irish questions, and his excited analysis of what was going on here set our mind on a path which finally landed it in an Irish movement.[36]

The Russian boy gave a stirring account of a society where students 'sat up to all hours at night discussing everything from God down to the Russian prisons, which were as near hell as was possible for anything earthly to be . . .'[37]* Russell's new sense of national identity was forgotten for a time when he came to devote himself almost wholly to Theosophy, but ultimately another influence arrived to awaken his dormant patriotism for a second time.

While Russell would allow his education none of the credit for his intellectual distinction, he early developed a voracious appetite for fiction. From the penny dreadfuls of his childhood he advanced to such substantial romances as Dumas's novels of D'Artagnan, of which it seemed to Eglinton that he remembered every word.[38] At the time of his spiritual awakening he had read principally 'such tales as a boy reads'[39] and his youthful love of the exotic and miraculous is reflected in a nostalgic review of a book on alchemy: 'I was naturally of the stuff of which alchemists were made. I read of them in mediaeval romances in my childhood, and not a speck of scepticism marred my perfect belief in the Elixir or the Stone.'[40] His taste in fiction was permanently fixed at this early age, and he continued to prefer the ancient art of the story-teller, found in Kipling and in the *Arabian Nights*, and imaginary characters of supernatural prowess to the subtle realism of the modern novelist. He discovered the sister art of poetry when his father, at some unknown date, gave him a copy of

*But these discussions resemble some which AE mentions in *Ideals in Ireland: Priest or Hero?* (Dublin, 1897) that he has read about.

Tennyson.[41] Parts of the waking dreams which came to him in adolescence bear a distinct resemblance to the cosmic happenings of *Paradise Lost*.

From the time he left school at the end of 1884 until he joined the Theosophical community in 1891, Russell continued to live at his parents' home.[42] While his father appreciated his artistic gifts, his mother was puzzled by his uncommon personality and would exclaim when his talents were praised, 'If George would only eat his food.'[43] He seems to have had little in common with his brother Tom, who used to tease him about his slimness.[44] His ambition was to become an artist, but, as he recollected, 'my people were poor and I did not like being a burden to them as I knew it would be many years before I could support myself by painting so I went into an office . . . '[45] For some years, however, he clung to his ambition and he continued with the evening classes he had begun to attend in October 1883 at the Metropolitan School of Art in Kildare Street. It is probable that, on leaving Rathmines School, he indignantly rejected on moral grounds the job that his father and brother had obtained for him at the Phoenix Brewery where they themselves worked,[46] and then found intermittent employment until he took a more permanent post as a clerk at Pim's, a large Dublin drapery store, in August 1890. It is certain that this was not his first job as he wrote to Carrie Rea on obtaining it, 'I have got work again.'[47] In the letters written from 1886 to 1888 he makes references to his lack of spare time, alludes to the uncongenial routine in which he has become trapped,[48] and mentions that he is much handicapped by want of money.[49] During this period he was intensely preoccupied with painting, writing, and spiritual exploration in such time as he had available.

While Russell was studying art he began to write verse and shortly afterwards he was spellbound by a new student who arrived at the Metropolitan School in May 1884.[50] This youth, two years older than himself, was slender, dark-haired, and carelessly dressed; he looked and talked like a poet, and it was not long before his conversation was full of stories about Madame Blavatsky and her centuries-old Himalayan Masters, whose beards trailed down the mountainsides for birds to nest in.[51] Russell and his new friend, William Yeats, were soon writing in competition under the influence of the arch-rebel Shelley on such subjects as a magician who uttered resounding heresies from a throne in Asia.[52] Russell delighted in the delicate rhythms and spiritual fantasy that his friend was to bring into Irish poetry; once, walking down Leinster Road, he heard Yeats' first plot for *The Shadowy Waters* – a tale of magic and the immortal world. The enchantment of this early friendship lingered in Russell's adult memory and he never reconciled himself to the later revision of poems he had grown to love. Yeats, for his part, was overjoyed to find a powerful ally in his revolt against the materialist beliefs of his father. Russell's faith in the unseen was stronger than his own and did not need the external support of the séance and planchette. When Yeats, much disturbed by inner conflicts, was fascinated by Russell's drawing of a man on a mountain top staring in astonishment at his huge shadow cast on the clouds, the latter's surprise soon gave way to an understanding that the concept of divided personality reflected something fundamental in his friend's nature.[53] In the evenings he used to visit the Yeats family at 10, Ashfield Terrace, where he was known to the poet's sisters as 'The Strayed Angel.'[54] The two young men would discuss such subjects as the nature of the cosmic sounds that stimulated the growth of mushrooms. When the household had retired for the night they would withdraw into the kitchen, cook a late meal, and recite their poems. The family upstairs thought they were trying to escape from their bodies. John Butler Yeats, the poet's father, was a well-known artist whose brilliant, fanciful talk and delight in the variety of human nature appealed to Russell, but he was a firm agnostic and disapproved of his son's new friendship. To his mind Russell was not only a mystic but at the same time something of an Ulster Protestant: 'I used to tell him,' he wrote, 'he was still a *Portadown* boy . . .'[55] The friendship was equally distressing to Russell's churchgoing parents.[56]

At the Art School Russell was Blake-like in his spurning of the outward creation. While Yeats and the other students laboriously drew from the model, he would turn aside to paint the irrepressible images which rose before his imagination, producing such compositions as a 'St. John in the Wilderness.' His friends were awestruck at the facility with which he worked as well as at his simplicity and innocence and his chaotic speech, half revealing and half concealing mysteries; but at least one pupil noticed the excessive fluency which was to be a lifelong handicap in his practice of both art and literature, and whispered, pointing to a figure, 'That is too easy, a great deal too easy!'[57]

At this time Dubliners had little opportunity to see great paintings, especially by modern artists, and Russell sought in the illustrations of such books as Gilchrist's *Life of William Blake* what he could not find in galleries. In the publications of the 1860's, produced before illustrating in black and white had declined into a business, Russell discovered drawings in which the artists seemed to have embodied an imaginative vision usually to be expected only in large paintings. 'They dreamed over their drawings,' he wrote later. 'I think Rossetti spent a month over one.'[58] A few years afterwards he was eagerly praising Jack Yeats's small sketches of the characters in the west of Ireland.

Russell made a number of friends at the Art School. To an eccentric student who would often wear a daisy chain as a necklace he lent the small Theosophical book *Light on the Path*. It was returned with the ominous comment, 'You will drift into a penumbra.'[59] He tried to influence Edward Corbett, 'a dreadful little materialistic Roman Catholic,' without speaking directly against his religion, and was proud to find that he became a Theosophist several years later.[60] But his most important friend, apart from Yeats, was John Hughes, whom he was later to acclaim as a sculptor of genius. Hughes and Russell went for walks outside Dublin and one night they encountered an old soldier, 'the remains of a magnificent human being,' newly returned to Ireland after forty years of exile. 'Over those hills,' he exclaimed, 'I wandered forty years ago. Nobody but myself knows what happened under the thorn tree forty years ago. The fret is on me. The fret is on me. God speaking out of his darkness says I have and I have not. I possess the heavens. I do not possess the world . . .'[61] The story of this incident excited Yeats, who made from it the early version of his 'Lamentation of the Old Pensioner.' Russell himself was set searching by this spontaneous poetic speech for beauty in other unselfconscious revelations of the soul's experience in time.

In the summer of 1885 Russell left the Metropolitan Art School and enrolled in evening classes at the school attached to the Royal Hibernian Academy where the atmosphere, according to Yeats,[62] was more vital. He was, however, highly critical of the teaching provided; twenty years later he told a Parliamentary Committee about the four Visitors who supervised the students' life studies:

> One Visitor, Mr. Duffy, is an excellent landscape painter, and I have a great admiration for his work. Another was Mr. Gray, who painted bulls and cows; the third was Mr. William Osborne, who painted cats and dogs, and the fourth was Sir Thomas Farrell, who did not paint at all. These gentlemen, not one of whom painted figures, were put there to assist us . . . They never put their fingers on the students' work – which was probably the best thing they could have done under the circumstances.[63]

It was during his studies at the Academy that Russell's attention became partly deflected from art, though the inadequate teaching is unlikely to have been a cause.

Several years after his childhood rebellion against the religion of his parents, Russell underwent a spiritual awakening which began while he was on holiday in Armagh.[64] If his own accounts are to be relied on, this must have occurred shortly before his meeting with

Yeats in mid-1884. At this time he was a sensitive boy, devoted to art, troubled by adolescent sensuality,[65] and uninterested in his inherited creed. Quite suddenly he began to experience waking dreams of astonishing power and vividness which seemed to be thrust into his consciousness by a mind which was not his. Images of cosmic happenings and other worlds overwhelmed him with a majesty far removed from anything of which he was aware in his own being. 'I remember how pure, holy and beautiful these imaginations seemed,' he wrote in later years, 'how they came like crystal water sweeping aside the muddy current of my life . . .'[66] He became conscious that a self strange to him was seeking to enter his body or, already present in some realm of his mind shut off from waking consciousness, was trying to enter that consciousness to reveal to him the true meaning and purpose of his life. It was not itself pure and ethereal, but a being that had accumulated experience over many ages, and had base and noble desires, an arcane wisdom, and, somewhere within it, an incorruptible spark of purity which longed for reunion with God, or the Spirit, from which it had come. Later he suspected that this greater self, the psyche, was not a single entity but a multiplicity of beings, which might by spiritual effort be brought into a unity.[67]

While this immortal self illuminated his mind from within, he became aware that it had companions without who shared its immortality. Nature had become translucent, a vast composition of beautiful forms on which he could perceive but not yet decipher the cryptic signs which told of the beings they tenuously concealed. He knew that these spirits were akin to his newly discovered self; he felt their presence and that they were about to reveal themselves; at moments he was almost rapt into their eternity.

> As I walked in the evening down the lanes scented by the honeysuckle . . . I felt that beings were looking in upon me out of the true home of man . . . The visible world became like a tapestry blown and stirred by winds behind it. If it would but raise for an instant I knew I would be in Paradise.[68]

Two effects followed from this first awakening. His old self, the person he had always thought George Russell to be, was incited by vanity to claim this vision of nature as a personal possession, and not as a gift bestowed from without. If such a thought arose in his mind at the time of a visitation, his sense of communion with something beyond mortality would immediately dissolve. More happily, he discovered himself celebrating his new-found joys in verse which rose into his consciousness of its own accord.

It is hardly surprising that under the pressure of these experiences Russell was transformed from a carefree schoolboy with a sharp eye for the amusing foibles of those about him into the shy and diffident youth who smiled benevolently but silently when Yeats took him to Katharine Tynan's parties,[69] stuttered when he tried to express his ideas to fellow writers,[70] and attempted to sell pamphlets at a Theosophical function while innocently unaware of the price.[71] With Yeats, a kindred soul, he could feel at ease, and the poet's sister remembered him arriving at their home full of vitality and enthusiasm, with his overcoat flapping loose, to exchange poems and ideas and talk far into the night.[72] He began to have fears that he would lose the power of coherent thought and his speech at the Art School was apt to seem like a confused rigmarole shot through with fragments of beauty and wisdom. He once spent three days wandering alone on the Dublin mountains during the hours of sunlight for fear that he would not be able to talk intelligibly and he did not entirely outgrow his shyness and timidity for many years.[73] He ascribed to the immaturity of his conscious mind the fact that he was able to write verse with ease when he could not express his thoughts in orderly prose, though a friend pointed out to Yeats the irregularity of Russell's early poems. His supposed inability to handle prose was probably exaggerated. By 1886 and 1887 his letters, in spite of occasional contorted sentences, are on the whole well written. When, in 1887 he was unable to compose an intelligible article on the intuitive language, the intricacy of the subject was to blame. 'I can't write Science,' he explained to a correspondent.[74]

The miracle which finally turned Russell into a seer of visions occurred on a summer day as he lay on Kilmasheogue, one of the hills just south of Dublin. He was relaxing in the sunlight making no attempt to exert his willpower, when he felt with great intensity the presence of supernatural beings and heard their music passing into the earth. Then, in his own words,

> . . . the heart of the hills was opened to me, and I knew there was no hill for those who were there, and they were unconscious of the ponderous mountain piled above the palaces of light, and the winds were sparkling and diamond clear, yet full of colour as an opal, as they glittered through the valley, and I knew the Golden Age was all about me, and it was we who had been blind to it but that it had never passed away from the world.[75]

The gift of seeing radiant and majestic visionary beings remained with him throughout his life and their clear and distinct forms are preserved in many memorable sketches. It was probably when he became interested in Celtic tradition in the mid-1890's, that he first gave them a specifically Irish interpretation, though his enquiring mind never reached final certainty as to their nature.

In 1885 Russell began the intellectual study and deliberate fostering of his spiritual experiences that dominated his life for the next twelve years. He was drawn, very slowly at first, into a complete commitment to Theosophy, of which both his parents disapproved. When he lent Madame Blavatsky's *Isis Unveiled* to a friend, his father lent the same youth the Christian *Lux Mundi* to counteract it.[76]

About the time he was at the Metropolitan School Russell attempted to portray in several series of paintings the myths which his newly creative imagination was fashioning. One of these shows the gradual evolution of primitive forms into the human image within the mind of God. This image took embodiment in the world of matter as the first man, but the latter's descendants gradually decayed into minute beings; Russell loved to paint the last man sitting on the gigantic skull of one of his forbears watching the universe relapse into its original chaos. One picture of the series showing the image of man newly born in the Divine Mind especially haunted him. During a holiday in Armagh he once lay awake at night seeking a name for it. His concentration was intense and his mind dilated; it seemed that something beyond himself was about to speak and at last came the whisper: 'Aön.'* Next day, or a little later, as he walked on the country roads, he was mentally fondling the strange syllable when he experienced one of the waking dreams which entered his consciousness from without. An emanation of the Divine Spirit, unable to endure any superior in its pride, rebelled against the Deity and falling into chaos made the earth and became its god. To this spirit he applied his new word. About two weeks later he was back in Dublin and, while he was in the National Library in search of an art journal, his eye caught the definition of 'Aeon' in an open book: it was the name the Gnostics gave to the earliest beings separated from the Deity. This was the first hint that his imaginations could be anything more than fantasy. His discovery suggested to him the possibility of pre-existence and his excitement soon drove him back to the Library, where he asked for an account of the Gnostics. He was handed a volume of Neander's *General History of the Christian Religion and Church,* which provided his first introduction to the literature of mysticism. Here Gnosticism is described from the hostile viewpoint of that Christianity against which he had already rebelled. It is said to be a mixture of oriental Theosophy and Greek philosophy, and certain elements of both are adumbrated. Here Russell must have encountered the use of the word 'theosophy' in the general sense of knowledge of divine things acquired through

*Cf. AE's contemporary account of this event: 'I was thinking of what would be the sound for the most primeval thought I could think and the word "aön" passed into my head. I was afterwards surprised at finding out that the Gnostics of the Christian Era called the first created beings "Æons" and that the Indian word for the commencement of all things is Aom.'[77]

inner illumination. And he read with wonder the Sabean myth of a glorious spirit revolting against the Deity and seeking to create an original world in the abyss – a myth similar to his own but with added intricacies.[78]

The whisper of the word 'Aön' led Russell to brood on a new question, the possibility that component sounds of speech were not arbitrary or accidental, but that they corresponded to some spiritual realities perceived intuitively by early man. Recognising both the human psyche and external nature as manifestations of the one Divine Spirit, he felt that when man was able partly to rise above the personal self of the waking consciousness he could perceive elements of his kinship with the created world and affinities imperceptible to the unaided reason. He was beginning to read the signs which he had at first been unable to decipher. For each vowel and consonant he sought a related concept, colour, and form. Wandering the streets at night he would murmur these sounds over and over to himself trying to evoke by intuition their affinities in his mind. After having had, as he thought, some success in relating sounds to the elements, he opened a book in the library seemingly by chance and came upon the Upanishads where he read:

> From the self (Brahma) sprang the air, from the air fire, from fire water, from water earth, from earth herbs, from herbs food, from food seed, and from seed man.[79]

This suggested that he search for some order among the sounds which might correspond to this sequence of the related elements, and he began to arrange them, proceeding from those produced in the throat to those made at the lips. The results encouraged him to continue his experiments but he never obtained a complete set of correspondences.

It was Russell's opinion that such early languages as Coptic, Sanskrit, and Hebrew, though not their 'artificial' modern descendants, probably embodied the inherent meanings of the sounds. Though he abandoned certain early conclusions, such as his interpretation of the word 'Æon' (A = the Deity, Æ = the first emanation from the Deity, o = static continuance for a certain time, N = change – hence the spirit returns into God),[80] he retained his belief in a primal language and in 1918 suggested that it could be objectively verified by linguistic study. He claimed that the Aryan roots provided much corroborating evidence.[81] It may be noticed that the languages he refers to are highly developed rather than primeval. A. R. Orage, an intellectual and a friend of Russell in old age, noted the many contradictory occult attempts that had been made to interpret sounds and concluded that Russell's speculations were guesses and nothing more.[82]

The chance reading of a passage from an Upanishad gave Russell his first introduction to the sacred literature of India. Soon afterwards he was waiting for a friend in a lodginghouse when he fell into conversation with a stranger who shared his new and passionate interest in these scriptures.[83] The stranger was Charles Johnston, a recent schoolfellow of Yeats and a brilliant classical scholar. The meeting took place in 1885[84] and for the next three years, until Johnston went to India as a civil servant, he and Russell carried on their spiritual explorations side by side. Through this friendship. and the study of the Upanishads and the Bhagavadgita, Russell began to construct an intellectual framework for his experiences.

Johnston had been converted to Theosophy in 1884 through reading A.P. Sinnett's book *The Occult World*. Sinnett's second book, *Esoteric Buddhism*, excited the interest of Yeats at Easter 1885. In the June immediately following[85] Johnston started the Hermetic Society for the study of eastern religion and kindred subjects, and Yeats became its chairman. Russell, whose approach at this time was less bookish, did not join.[86] In the second half of the year,[87] when an Indian Theosophist named Mohini Chatterjee visited Dublin to address the Society, Russell met him and was greatly impressed. Though it is unlikely that, as Moore claimed, the encounter marked a turning point in Russell's life, the latter remarked wryly fifteen years later: 'Mohini has I think a halo of glory given him by distance but he was a very wonderful fellow. Now, alas, a very corpulent Brahmin who has a good practice as a lawyer at Bombay. The glory has departed.'[88]

In 1885 Johnston visited London and heard Madame Blavatsky denounced as an impostor who had rigged psychic phenomena to dupe credulous disciples. The experience only increased his zeal in the cause of Theosophy and he and two friends started an official Dublin Lodge of the Society in the following year. Once again, Russell preferred to remain outside the organisation.[89]

Charles Johnston was the son of William Johnston of Ballykilbeg, a fanatical Orange M.P. with an incongruous underlying gentleness which enabled him to tolerate the odd friends his children brought to the house – even Nationalists and Catholics. Charles and his sister, Georgie, were wholehearted in their Theosophy, being vegetarians, teetotalers and non-smokers, and they dragooned their less enthusiastic brother, Lewis, into conforming with their strange habits. Extraordinarily handsome, Charles Johnston was very clever and rather vain. He liked to assume an air of sophistication and the dress and manners of a dandy. His impudence amused Katharine Tynan, but it was his serious side that impressed Russell, who observed, '. . . he has got the most determined firm face I ever saw,'[90] though he later came to suspect that his surface brilliance might after all conceal no great depth of character.[91] While Russell was primarily a seer drawn into Theosophical interests through his experience of a transcendent self, Johnston was an intellectual and a scholar with much less of the poet in his nature. His new enthusiasm led him to turn from the Greek and Latin at which he excelled to the study of Sanskrit.

Russell and Johnston met when both had just reached the stage of youthful enthusiasm when life suddenly appears full of endless possibilities and no hope seems too extravagant.

> On such a day as this, rejoicing in the sunlight, we lay on our backs in the grass, and, looking up into the blue, tried to think ourselves into that new world which we had suddenly discovered ourselves to inhabit. For we had caught the word, handed down with silent laughter through the ages, that we ourselves are the inventors of the game of life, the kings of this most excellent universe: that there is no sorrow, but fancy weaves it; that we need not even knock to be admitted, for we already are, and always were, though we had forgotten it, within the doors of life.

So Johnston wrote ten years later of the joy they shared at the time of their first meeting, adding, 'there was a gaiety and lightness in the air then, a delight of new discovery, that I do not think we shall find again.'[92]

An identity of aspiration enlivened by a mild collision of temperaments characterised the new friendship. On one occasion Johnston dissuaded Russell from attending a séance out of curiosity.[93] He became interested in Russell's theory of the inherent meaning of sounds and urged him to write up his conclusions in an article for the Madras *Theosophist*, but Russell approached the task in an disorganised manner and reduced his material to chaos. This infuriated the scholar, who insisted on rewriting the article himself, and it was published under both their signatures as 'The Speech of the Gods' in December 1887. Madame Blavatsky told Johnston that she was charmed with it.[94]

Russell and Johnstone were fellow travellers in search of the infinite, but they were also boys with a lively sense of fun and mischief. Johnston was more severely intellectual and less emotional than most of the Theosophists and he found an exquisite pleasure in deflating his friends' pretensions. For months Russell sought revenge for the good-natured taunts at his 'butterfly wisdom.'[95] Eventually he lured him into sympathising with his gushing remarks about the heavenly bodies, and Johnston admitted in an unguarded moment, 'I used to lie on my back on the grass for hours and gaze up at the moon.' To his astonishment he was calmly asked, 'Did you ever catch cold?'[96]

The most eccentric of Russell's friends at this time was a devoted but naive and fanatical Roman Catholic whom he regarded as a true poet and mystic, and mentally invested (at least in retrospect) with a certain heroic stature. He met Philip Francis Little one evening on a country road near Dublin and they were drawn together because each aspired to merge his individuality into the Spirit as It is manifested in nature.[97] Little was entirely uncompromising in matters of conscience. He tried to persuade Russell to live with him in a derelict truck so that they could preach to the people. When Russell was not quite able to conceal his amusement, he charged, 'You smile. You never saw me smile.' His relations were understandably reluctant to live with him for, as he explained, '. . . whenever I think anything, something says to me, "You think so! Why didn't you say so? You are a coward! You are a damned coward!" and I say"I am damned if I am" and out it comes. And just because of this my people are paying me a hundred and fifty a year to live away from them. I think it should be two hundred. Don't you?' Only once – and evidently at a later date – Russell was able to gain the moral victory in an argument. 'Philip,' he said, 'when you write poems for your fellow creatures you use all your power to create original imaginations, and all your art to find the new[,] beautiful and fitting words. But when you speak to God you pray to Him in an outworn language, and I do not think God will be pleased . . .'[98] They did not in fact share the same saints and heroes, and Little once denounced Russell loudly in the street for an incautious remark. For a while he even ignored him but was later reconciled; Russell believed at the time he had forgiven him, but decided in retrospect that he had been lonely.[99] The friendship persisted in some degree throughout Little's life and as late as 1924 or thereabouts the latter read his still unknown poetry to his now illustrious friend.

Though Russell admired Little's courage and willpower, it is likely that the principal effect of his companionship was to warn him against spiritual eccentricity. In 1887 he wrote to Carrie Rea,

> I was speaking to my friend Little a few days ago and he was so full of eloquent and musical reveries about the soul seeking after God thro orb after orb and world within world and at last springing out into the mirth of his morning, that he did not see people almost holding onto the railings with laughter at his self-forgetfulness in the streets. I do not mind this myself but it is a pity that so much religious truth should be lost to people through want of a little earthly wisdom.[100]

Though Russell's conception of the cosmos and scale of values were essentially pre-scientific – Yeats observed to Katharine Tynan that he was 'not so much a theosophist, as you call him, as a mystic of mediaeval type'[101] – he had even at this stage a complementary modern side to his character. For him the wholly contemplative life was incomplete. 'A man cannot,' he wrote, 'by any private devotion to his Maker escape the consequences of his neglect of his duty to his fellow-man. Such folk are spiritual blacklegs, with no policy of loyalty to their kind. They profess to love God. In reality, as St. John suggests, they are passionately in love with themselves.'[102] In forming this conviction, which was a root principle of his life and not a concession to modernity, Russell may have been influenced by the beautiful tradition of the Buddha's compassionate turning aside from the bliss of *Nirvana* to enlighten those still entrapped in their attachment to the world. Madame Blavatsky held up this archetypal renunciation as an example to her disciples and Russell's story 'The Midnight Blossom' is based on her treatment of the subject in *The Voice of the Silence*.

Much of our knowledge of Russell's early life is derived from his letters to Carrie Rea, a young Ulster woman two years his senior. The Rea children and the Russell children originally met when both families resided in the North and their aunts lived in adjacent dwellings in the Shiels Almshouses.[103] Carrie remembered playing childhood games with George in his aunt's house,[104] but they really became friends in 1885 when Russell came to Armagh on his holidays. He had been told of her fondness for books and quickly found that she shared many of his interests and aspirations, while her outlook differed sufficiently from his to provide a stimulus and a challenge. She was unusually spiritual and almost resented the existence of her body. Russell, who remarked that she seemed to take in nourishment through her fingertips she ate so daintily,[105] wrote in reply to her questioning, 'The body whose being you cannot understand is the lowest point of evolution from which we will rise to more spiritual things hereafter.'[106] Though the local people were sure they would eventually marry, their friendship was Platonic in more than the obvious sense. They went for long walks together during which Russell expounded his ideas, acting as her spiritual guide, while she was his not always submissive disciple. As a committed Christian she feared lest his Theosophy lead her into apostasy. In long letters and during his holidays he urged her not so much to adopt his position as to pursue truth fearlessly for herself. 'I was willing long ago,' he wrote, 'to take my chance of condemnation after death, I said I am seeking for truth if for this I am punished then I can bear it, for the Paradise of such a deity would be a place beneath me to dwell in . . .'[107] He drew a sharp distinction between the popular Christianity preached by most of the clergy and the New Testament teachings, which, if correctly understood, were identical with Theosophical beliefs. His own esteem for the Bible, especially the Old Testament, and for natural science declined sharply as his explorations advanced. Some time after 1893, where the surviving part of the correspondence ends, Carrie Rea became a Theosophist; she married Robert Coates, a member of the Dublin Lodge, and remained in the Society till the end of her life.

The letters are not confined to spiritual matters. Carrie Rea wished to become a writer and Russell guided her reading, recommending scientific and literary works, including Darwin and most of the Romantic and Victorian poets, as well as spiritual books like Edwin Arnold's *Light of Asia*. He enjoyed the unaffected style of her letters and advised her not to adopt an artificial vocabulary for fiction – 'Now if you were writing to me you would not call the sun Phoebus, do not do so in your story.'[108] As a fellow enthusiast for ideas, he warned her to spread them thinly when writing for the public, citing Shorthouse's novel *John Inglesant* as an example. When she wished to leave Armagh, he made enquiries about possibilities of employment in an English market garden, and advised her, while she was in London, to hear Stopford Brooke, a clergyman and man of letters whose liberal ideas had led to his exit from the Church of England. He sent her books continuously, on loan and as gifts.

There is an engaging freshness and youthful enthusiasm in Russell's letters to Carrie Rea. His otherworldly experiences had recently burst upon him when the correspondence began and his beliefs were in their formative stage, while the counterbalancing vein of worldly sense, which is so marked in the mature man, had not yet appeared. In his devotion to nature he deplored the fact that men insist on disfiguring it with buildings – 'Thank heaven the birds do not build their nests in accurate cubes among the green leaves'[109] – and was 'afraid no amount of exhortations and common sense added, would make men leave off their houses just at present. It is a thing I hope for and which I believe will come to pass . . .'[110] He showed an amusing fear of his aunt's preaching and asked that his letters be kept private: 'I would not like auntie to be holding prayer meetings over me if I ever went to the North again as she certainly would if she heard any of my opinions, and I would not like to be bored by them.'[111] His ardour and earnestness are perhaps his most striking qualities as he urged his friend to pursue truth at all costs and to aspire to

> the sense of something cool pure and infinite within something like clear glass or calm water to radiate the starry influences, the cosmical design. Oh Carrie Rea get that above everything else for it brings everything else along with it in the end, having it we may

indeed fall through weakness but the end of the fight is certain.[112]

At the very outset of his spiritual awakening, Russell was quite alone and without the guidance of books on the interior life or of friends familiar with the concepts and discipline of any mystical tradition. His boy's mind was faced with an overwhelming and inexplicable experience and his response was simple and natural. With his artistic leanings he was attracted by the aesthetic aspect of his new experiences and he sought to create in his imagination a fantasy world shimmering with a paradise-like richness of light and colour. He had read of someone whose dreams formed a continuous series night after night and, brooding lovingly over his creation on his evening walks, he willed himself to see it again in sleep. Instead he dreamed of an ape perched on a bank of cloud watching the earth spinning below and trying to mould another globe out of the mist: with a warning grimace at the dreamer the animal vanished.[113]

From such childlike beginnings Russell passed on to books and friends who helped him to find a deeper meaning in his mental adventures. He discovered the Upanishads and met Charles Johnston and learnt that he had unknowingly stumbled into a realm of experience which had been explored by mystics throughout the ages. By 1885 he was on the threshold of his own search for truth, and art had a serious rival for his attention. He was more cautious than Johnston or Yeats in accepting dogmas on the authority of ancient or modern writings. This attitude persisted and he always valued those who knew things from their own psychic experience above those who learnt them from books or even from intuition;[114] he urged his disciples at the Hermetic Society to practice concentration and meditation for themselves rather than relying solely on study.[115] Looking back at this period after many years, he wrote (taking sixteen as the age at which he had left school): 'The inspiring influence in my life between sixteen and twenty was I think myself. I was rather a solitary and went on long walks to the mountains and lay there for hours letting what would come out of myself.'[116]

Early in 1886 Russell, thinking of himself as an advanced student of mysticism, embarked on a nine-month period of spiritual investigation without the aid of books or friends in an attempt to discover 'the truths of the world';[117] as a consequence he began to neglect his art. At this time he had read little about mysticism and was endeavouring to embody his own theories in short prose tales. Some of his ideas were markedly naïve, such as his shortlived belief that God was not eternal but had had a beginning. By the end of the year he reported to Carrie Rea his good fortune in having met a Theosophist who had saved him from the extreme danger of black magic – the use of psychic powers for selfish or evil purposes – towards which he had been tending. The same letter reflects his excitement at having come to understand that the apparent self – the personal emotions, traits of character, reasoning power, and memories – are no more the real 'self' than is the physical body, but that behind this mental facade is the spirit, uncreated and indestructible, and that this spirit within every human being is identical with God. As he phrased it, with a touch of naiveté, soon after:

> . . . our intellects and bodies are not our real personalities our real personality being the spirit within us, and if we could rise to this high level of consciousness there being but one spirit through all, we could not distinguish between ourselves and anyone else.[118]

To his surprise and excitement he was discovering that the beliefs to which his experiences were leading him were similar to those held by mystics of many ages and lands: St. Paul taught that within man is Spirit transcending the body and individual soul, and the conceptions of the Rosicrucians of Europe and sages of Tibet coincided with his 'first crude guess . . . about the nature of God.'[119] He had just begun to read Boehme and there too had found his own ideas, though seen from another standpoint. Besides this conception of Deity, he had already absorbed the Hindu belief in *Karma,* a universal inescapable justice meting out good and evil as impersonally as the law of gravity, and this too, he claimed, was confirmed by Jesus and Paul.

At the end of 1886 Russell had read only two specifically Theosophical books, *Light on the Path* and *The Idyll of the White Lotus,* both by Mabel Collins, but he explained, 'I call myself a Theosophist . . . because all of us believe in the principle of internal illumination.'[120] From the short treatise *Light on the Path* he learnt the first rules of 'the Secret Doctrine.' This book, which is based on the belief in the universal Spirit present in every man, teaches an austere doctrine of complete self-conquest, including the annihilation of all ambition and sensual or personal desires, as comprising the first hard steps on the road to spiritual enlightenment, while it holds out the promise of a divine state utterly beyond normal human conception but ultimately within the adept's reach. *The Idyll of the White Lotus* appears to be a mediocre historical novel without distinction of style or characterisation, despite Russell's assertion that many of its sentences are as rhythmically beautiful as those of the Hebrew prophets. It tells of a young boy in ancient Egypt who is dedicated to the service of a Temple. When he sees a pure and lovely goddess, the corrupt priests discover his gift of vision and seduce him into acting as their intermediary with an evil spirit who gratifies the inmost personal desires of her worshippers. After a long period he breaks free from his servitude to these black magicians and is entrusted with the sacred doctrines of *Karma,* the Spirit, and the unlimited possibilities latent within the immortal part of man – doctrines which he must preserve in the coming time of darkness. Russell was rather surprisingly overwhelmed when he read this book at the end of his nine-month quest and abruptly burnt his manuscripts, deciding to write no more until his knowledge, which he had much overestimated, was greatly increased.

The idea of pre-existence had flashed into Russell's mind when he first learned that the word 'Aeon' was not of his own invention. He had now a faith in reincarnation, which allows for spiritual development over many ages, and he believed that he was able to remember some of his own past lives. In one previous incarnation, he thought, he had been an Assyrian and in another he had been a friend of Blake, but in his mystical reveries and pursuit of beauty he had shunned action and weakened his will, which he had now to strengthen.[121] The demands of *Light on the Path* for an almost superhuman degree of self-control certainly reinforced his belief in the intense cultivation of will-power. It was this belief that led him a year or two later to renounce painting, though this was only temporary.

At this time Russell was working on two experiments. The first, the investigation of the intuitive language, occupied him during most of 1887 and was of his own devising; the other, which was less original, involved the separation of his physical and astral bodies, the latter being the tough etheric double which according to Theosophy is the mould of the former. What success he had in his project of travelling over the planet on the astral plane is not recorded.[122]

By the middle of 1887, Russell had at least some acquaintance with the Upanishads and the Bhagavadgita and was overwhelmed by the majesty and truth of these Hindu scriptures, which seemed, as he wrote to Carrie Rea, to 'contain such Godlike fullness of wisdom on all things that I feel the authors must have looked with calm remembrance back through a thousand passionate lives full of feverish strife for and with shadows, ere they could have written with such certainty of things the soul feels to be sure.'[123] In the same letter he tells how he has been haunted for a week by the phrase 'A Magician of the Beautiful' and is seeking its meaning. The phrase later became his usual term for the Logos, the Second Person of the Christian Trinity regarded as the Creator.

In May, Yeats and his family moved from Dublin to London and Russell clung to Johnston's friendship all the more, as he considered these two the only Theosophists in Dublin with ideas of their own. (Like himself, Yeats had not yet taken the decisive step of joining the Society.) Russell and Johnston, who lived within five minutes' walking distance from each other's homes in Rathmines, practised thought transference, they supposed with success. To begin with they used simple forms like stars, crosses, and flowers. Russell quipped, 'It will save me the trouble of calling on him.'[124] At this time he expressed belief in all of the New and most of the Old Testament, and was still, at least on occasions, a churchgoer. He maintained, too, the truth of the Darwinian theory of evolution and delighted in showing sceptical fundamentalists a statue in the Dublin Museum two thousand years older than Adam. His Theosophical pursuits were, however, drawing him away from practical life and he declared,

> I am afraid that I will never be of any use in this Western World. I will try sometime to go out to India to become a pupil of the adepts. My dreaming propensities would not be so much out of place there but to dream is delightful, it is the only thing which makes me happy for even a short time. I seem to rise higher within myself and come to a white circle of consciousness where I feel blind with joy as if I was united with an existence greater than my own . . .[125]

When this was written he was still acquainted with only two Theosophical books, but during the coming months he extended his reading considerably. While Madame Blavatsky's *Isis Unveiled* appealed to him, he was apparently unable to afford it, and he was most excited by *Man: Fragments of Forgotten History* written anonymously by two *Chelas* (disciples) in the Theosophical Society, one of whom was, in fact, Mohini Chatterjee. From this brief survey of the intricate system taught by Madame Blavatsky, he learnt to reject Darwinism as distorted and materialistic in favour of the Theosophical theory of evolution. He explained how modern man's ancestors in Atlantis had been superior to him fifty thousand years ago, but because each evolutionary regression was followed by an advance to a hitherto unattained height, he would eventually surpass the Atlanteans. He also examined Sinnett's *Esoteric Buddhism*, which had so excited Yeats, and concluded that it was only partly authentic. (Madame Blavatsky, on the other hand, claimed that it was more accurate than *Man*.)[126] By now he was recommending Carrie Rea to read only certain books of the Old Testament – Psalms, Job and the Prophets – and he warned that Genesis could only be appreciated if its esoteric meaning was understood. By the end of October he claimed that there was more religion in *Light on the Path* than in the whole of the Old Testament, and encouraged her to persist in her spiritual endeavours in the knowledge that the Masters – the perfected human beings risen to a higher state, who, according to the Theosophists, watched over mankind – would be with her whenever she was troubled or perplexed, whether or not they chose to appear visibly. The goddess in *The Idyll of the White Lotus,* was, he held, such a master.

It is clear that by this time Russell had adopted most of the beliefs of the Theosophists, though he still regarded himself as somewhat outside their circle: 'I have not read much of their books. I call myself a Theosophist because I believe in internal illumination . . . and because I have found that my intuitions about things agree in the main with theirs.'[127] A year later he wrote to Madame Blavatsky in her capacity as co-editor of the Theosophical journal *Lucifer.* The issue for October 1888 contained an announcement that an Esoteric Section of the Society would be formed for the deeper study of arcane philosophy, and an article, 'Lodges of Magic,' delivered a stern warning against the insidious desire for tangible phenomena and for that impossibility, a short cut to adeptship. In his letter, published two months later, Russell applauded and expanded on this caveat.[128] He expressed both satisfaction and regret that he was not formally a member of the Society, for he believed that any human organisation was certain to degenerate, but more urgently he insisted that the pursuit of magical phenomena was a powerful temptation all too likely to deflect the spiritual seeker from his primary aim of union with the Absolute. Was not the Esoteric Section, he asked, likely to fall into the very trap described in 'Lodges of Magic.' Madame Blavatsky replied that it would merely train the most ardent disciples in self-discipline and self-purification; there was no question of entrusting them with occult powers. Yeats joined the new Section, making certain mental reservations as to his interpretation of the pledges he was required to sign. For the time being Russell remained outside the Society.

During the later part of 1887, while he was studying Theosophical books, Russell was also extending his reading in general literature and in particular he lauded Whitman's *Leaves of Grass* with an enthusiasm almost as great as he showed for the Indian scriptures.

> From reading his poems I look upon Whitman as the greatest friend I have. He is the new evangelist of love and of universal brotherhood . . . He does not dream of the Past or of individuals who were famous long ago. He is full of hope for the future and he believes in the greatness of life at present.[129]

Whitman's lifelong appeal for Russell was many-sided. His love of the earth and his call for universal brotherhood were accompanied by a subtle sense of the immortality of all life and of an all-embracing spiritual unity, but it was probably his boundless optimism and his faith in the potentialities of man – individual, social, and divine – that constituted his strongest attraction. Whitman's teachings formed a bridge between Russell's conflicting aspirations, and his belief in democracy later influenced Russell politically. Possibly Russell's messianic faith, his expectation that an Avatar – an incarnation higher in the scale of being than man – would appear in Ireland during his lifetime had its seed in the prophecies of Whitman as well as in the teachings of the Theosophists, whose belief that a higher race was destined to emerge in America may have encouraged him to acclaim the intuitions of the poet. He expressed his hopes and longings in a letter to Carrie Rea:

> Sometime in the years when some man has gained for himself a diviner wisdom than was known in the world before men will begin to find what possibilities they have in themselves . . . I become impatient of the slow passing years when I know what will happen and that I will be a sharer in the new order of things.[130]

By the end of the summer Russell dared to exalt Blake even above Whitman as being more spiritual and subtle but not less enthusiastic and determined; he did not, however, penetrate deeply into the Prophetic Books other than *Thel* in spite of Yeats's enthusiastic talk about the Zoas.[131] In October he contrasted Whitman with Emerson, finding the latter an inferior poet but a subtler writer and 'the healthiest mind of America,' a man whose books were 'pure Theosophy.'[132] Blake was an inspired visionary and unyielding intellectual rebel whose life was devoted to poetry and painting, and when he escaped the wild confusion which was apt to beset him he achieved a depth and beauty quite beyond Russell's artistic powers. Emerson, an outwardly mild man, expounded beliefs similar to Russell's and related them to the experiences of common life in a terse, aphoristic prose. While Russell took pleasure in his kinship with both these authors, it is likely that he was far more profoundly affected by Whitman, who brought him something which he did not already possess by showing him how to unite contrary aspects of his personality.

About the end of the year Russell became excited over a new discovery, his own formulation of the way in which *Karma* or cosmic justice operates in the individual's life, though he soon found that it had been known to Emerson before him. 'Everyone with whom you are brought in contact,' he wrote to Carrie Rea, 'has some affinity for you and you get just as much of their companionship as you deserve . . . I think that this law which I have found is a thousand times better to know than any primeval language however curious.'[133] According to Russell's law of spiritual gravitation, a man has no need to search for books or friends or the fulfilment of any of his needs. The external world is not hostile or indifferent but malleable and responsive to the desires and aspirations of the human mind. Everything in a man's character, good or evil, draws its likeness towards him. So it was that he was led to the Upanishads and met Yeats and Johnston and Carrie Rea. A man's friends and enemies are equally brought to him by what is in himself. For the remainder of his life his belief in this law gave Russell the certainty that he, and no other, was the creator of his environment and his destiny.

Our knowledge of Russell's social life in the years immediately after he left school is not great. Outside Theosophical and artistic circles, he maintained his friendship with his former schoolfellow Browne, until the latter left Dublin in 1891.[134] During 1886 he enjoyed the companionship of a Russian adventurer named Lipman, who claimed among English socialists to be a nihilist, posed as a wealthy aristocrat in America, and in Dublin courted Yeats and talked about Russian literature. Russell found him likeable, clever, and unscrupulous, a man of excellent moral principles which he failed to practice, and when he absconded from Dublin with his friends' money was good-humoured about his small losses.[135] In December of this year,[136] Yeats introduced Russell to Katharine Tynan, a young woman who had already published a volume of poems and who was immediately intrigued by him and his ideas. She noticed the mixture of awkward shyness, benevolence, and genius which seemed to characterise him, together with his hero-worship of Yeats and Johnston, and decided that he was another Blake. Soon he was painting visionary figures for her and attending the Sunday parties at Whitehall, her father's large house outside Dublin, where her own intellectual guests kept quite apart from her sister's sporting friends. At first he would only smile silently at these parties, but he talked to his hostess when they were alone and once told her some of the stories he had made up in his head. Katharine Tynan was a Catholic well satisfied by the marvels of her own religion, and she looked with a certain amused detachment on the credulities and austerities of modern heretics. Russell, who was serious about his attempts at thought transference with Johnston, could see the humorous side of Yeats' excursions into the occult and wrote to Katharine Tynan about his intention of communicating with him by telepathy.

> No doubt he will have imagination enough to think he is receiving messages from me and whenever I write to him about these airy conversations I will use expressions which will suit his conversation at any time. 'Your poem is splendid' 'Your paradoxes are getting more startling every day' and 'You should not say such hard things of your friends.' These remarks will convince him more than ever of my occult powers . . .[137]

Once Yeats was pacing round a room carrying a sword and uttering solemn spells, but each time he passed a dish of plums he would pause to take one. 'Yeats,' Russell rebuked him, 'you cannot evoke great spirits and eat plums at the same time.'[138] The Theosophists were enthusiasts for the celibate life and there was much horror when Charles Johnston married Madame Blavatsky's niece in 1888. Russell, who was genuinely dismayed, vowed that he would never again make anyone his hero and lamented to Yeats how Miss Tynan would crow over him.[139] On another occasion Russell, Yeats and Katharine Tynan were fellow victims of an underhand writer. A lady novelist spent a Sunday at Whitehall, pumped them for their opinions, and held them up to ridicule in a lampoon. Johnston took Russell for a walk and enjoyed his discomfiture as he read the article to him without a smile.[140]

In spite of his faith in the law of spiritual gravitation, Russell could not always find congenial companions in Dublin. About the middle of 1887, he returned from his holiday in Ulster and discovered to his horror that his three best friends had left and were apparently not returning.[141] Yeats had moved to London in May and Johnston had probably gone away temporarily. The third may have been John Hughes, the sculptor. It took all Russell's willpower to keep him from despair. In October 1888, Johnston and his wife sailed for India.[142] By this time Russell was attending many of the meetings at the Theosophical Lodge, though he had intervals of absence lasting some months,[143] and it may have been from this period that Dr. Best, the Dublin librarian, remembered him as a shy, dreamy, bearded youth trying to sell pamphlets at a Theosophical meeting without having the least idea of their price.[144] At the same time or a little later he used to visit the London Headquarters of the Society[145] where he occasionally met Madame Blavatsky and was deeply impressed by this Russian woman, who was to some a profound scholar and messenger of the semi-divine Masters and to others a charlatan in search of power and adoration. The image of her imprinted in his youthful memory remained unaffected by any later development of his personality or judgment. 'I was too immature – too small,' he said in old age, 'and she too remote – a Cosmos in an ailing woman's body.'[146] He told Dr. Gibbon that he had seen her do wonderful things.[147]

It is clear that during these years Russell's aspirations attracted him in contrary directions. He had set out to become an artist and was intermittently writing verse, but personal fame had soon come to seem an unworthy and foolish object.[148] He had an intense love of mystical reverie and thought of becoming a disciple in India, and yet believed that action was a necessary part of even the spiritual life and that he had suffered in a previous existence from ignoring this fact. More and more he was drawn to the Theosophists and their leader, but Johnston had betrayed the ideal of celibacy and the danger of fascination with peripheral phenomena was ever present. Inspired by Whitman's vision of a new humanity, he longed to go in search of its fulfilment in the New World. Meanwhile he passed his twenty-first birthday without settling on any definite course of life.

At the beginning of 1889, Russell was planning to wander over the United States on foot and it was rumoured that Hughes was to be his companion.[149] The project fell through and it was probably in this or the next year that Russell gave up attending the Art School[150] and formally joined the Theosophical Society. His desire to follow the path of mysticism had prevailed and he renounced artistic pursuits, telling Yeats that they would weaken his will, which was the only thing given to man as his own.[151] At the beginning of August 1890, while he was staying on the coast at Sandycove, Russell obtained employment as a clerk in Pim's, a large Dublin drapery store.[152] The acceptance of this humdrum and uncongenial work gave him a modest but secure livelihood during the seven years which he devoted to searching for the primeval glory of the unfallen man.

II

A Mystic Trained (1890–1894)

Early in September 1890, having returned to the city to take up his new employment, Russell embarked on a four-month period of assiduous attendance at the Theosophical Lodge, round which his life was to revolve as long as he remained at Pim's. Twice near the end of the year he even took his father to meetings on evenings when open discussion was invited, and on 3 December he read a paper entitled 'One Page from an Occult Book.'[1] Six days later he was admitted to probationary membership of the Esoteric Section, about which he had originally been so guarded. He had now realised and accepted the fact that he, like Blake, was 'born with a different face'; the early struggle described in *Song and Its Fountains* lay behind him:

> I at last realised with a kind of anguish that I was becoming a solitary, that a gulf had widened between myself and normal human life, between myself and home and love, the things in which most find a rich content. In the house of dream I entered there was neither home nor love, but beyond me in its labyrinths were intimations of primaeval being and profundities like the Pleroma.[2]

George Russell, the artistic son of an Ulster Protestant businessman, had become AE, the spiritual seeker who aspired to communicate his vision of the unseen through poetry and painting. Recalling their early companionship in the Theosophical Society, Pryse reminded AE of when

> you penned
> Your earliest poems, but forebore
> To write your name, and sought to sign
> The name of Man when yet divine.[3]

'AE' – originally 'Æ' – is the first sound in 'Æon,' the mystic word which came to Russell at the beginning of his spiritual journey. In writing to *Lucifer* at the end of 1888, he substituted this name for his own, and the printer, able to read only the block capital, split the dipthong for convenience and the signature appeared as 'A.E.' When Russell began contributing verse and prose to the *Irish Theosophist,* he used the dipthong as his pseudonym, and it is as 'AE' that he became famous. He himself preferred the joined form and was annoyed that printers persistently divided it,[4] but eventually he fell into the habit of using the separated letters for his own signature. The name 'George William Russell' came to signify for him his superficial, personal self, a transient creation of this life, while 'AE' represented the Logos incarnated in human form, his immortal self passing from body to body with its sheath of accumulated desires and experiences, and destined to be ultimately reunited with the Spirit.[5] To the Gnostics, too, the word 'Aeon' signified a being emanated from the Godhead. On his admission to the Esoteric Section Russell must have learnt of the sacred significance of these letters to Theosophists. It was only from February 1893 that he used them regularly as a pen-name.

AE's resolve to devote himself unflinchingly to the fulfilment of his highest aspirations was intensified when he read a short essay by the American Theosophist 'Jasper Niemand' published in the *Path* for February 1891. 'I was keyed up,' he recalled, 'to meet its intensity and I felt I could not write poetry or mystical thought if I could not hold on to its truth in the face of death.'[6] This tract, 'Purposes of Soul,' presents a moving portrait of a man beset by the hardly recognised but insidious pressures of society and only upon his deathbed realising that he has allowed himself to be turned aside from the high aims for which his psyche took incarnation. The author implores the spiritual aspirant to search with all his strength for the One Absolute underlying and manifested in the diversity of life, that he may learn to distinguish the impulses which It radiates into his consciousness from delusive counter-impulses, and remain faithful to It in the face of every temptation. She warns especially against the tendency of the aspirant's loved ones to hold down both him and themselves by imprisoning him in life on the personal level. Her doctrine that each should act from his own will and centre became one of the most crucial tenets of AE's philosophy.

Now that his life had taken a clear and definite course, he settled into a regular routine. The long days of drudgery at Pim's appeared to be the price he was paying for the joy of sharing his leisure hours with fellow mystics, a happiness that came in retrospect to seem greater than any other he had known; ironically, the business skill that he was reluctantly acquiring would later enable him to perform the task closest to his heart. Pim's was a large drapery shop in an austere commercial block on South Great George's Street adjacent to Dublin Castle. AE made an able and conscientious employee in spite of a quaintness in his behaviour reflecting his immaturity in worldly matters. He may have had previous experience in book-keeping, since he used the phrase 'my office' in a letter written in the first weeks of his employment[7] as well as in subsequent correspondence, but whether he shared this room is not clear. By contemporary standards, conditions of employment were harsh. His working day lasted from 9.0 in the morning to 6.30 or 7.0 at night and sometimes later, and he was free only on Sundays.[8] His salary was £40 a year.

At first he suffered deeply, imprisoned for so many hours in stuffy, gaslit rooms among overstrained people caught up like himself in a soulless, mechanical organisation, and he felt a special compassion for the exhausted draymen sitting slumped up after many hours of driving.[9] In a few months, however, he came to realise that there was gain as well as loss in his new situation. 'I think I have deepened,' he explained,

> in a good many things since last summer. What was worst to me in this overwork is what happens now and then in the hot room, the sudden flashes of recollection, or looking out for a moment at the sunlight over the houses, golden white, the blue ether, the distance, the haze, then it *all* comes over one, the sense of some divine thing missed, swift like a lightning flash incapable of analysis only leaving a blurred impression on the mind as the lightning does on the retina of the eye.[10]

Katharine Tynan and Yeats have left descriptions of AE at this time. In 1917 the former remembered him as 'a tall weedy, gentle boy with the light on his face which is there today.'[11] The latter tells in his essay 'A Visionary' how AE, still a shy youth living half in and half out of the world, visited him in his lodgings and denied that a winged figure he saw there was projected by the thoughts of a living person. Speaking of his verse, Yeats praised it for its fine passages, but detected in it 'the vast and vague extravagance that lies at the bottom of the Celtic heart.' Sometimes a waking dream would interrupt AE in Pim's and he would lay his work aside for a few minutes to let a poem that accompanied it flow freely into his consciousness. For the last year or two, however, he had been wavering uneasily, trying to resolve on a final renunciation of writing and painting in order to concentrate on strengthening his will and cultivating non-attachment. 'I was indeed in love with colour,' he remembered in old age, 'and terrified by the richness of emotion it evoked . . . '[12] Though the firm determination with which Gerard Manley Hopkins gave up poetic composition was not for AE's gentler temperament, he seems to have felt none of the obstinate hankering after fame which made the Jesuit's sacrifice the more painful, and he forbade Yeats to name him in his essay as he was sedulously courting obscurity. In spite of his shyness, uncommon characters interested him, and people burdened with remorse chose him as their confidant, while on Sundays he still wandered over the mountains and talked with primitive peasants.

As AE became accustomed to business life, he acquired considerable influence over some of his fellow workers and at times rebuked them effectively. He found that his occupation had real if not very substantial compensations and was surprised to find a touch of spirituality in unexpected places. A shrivelled old clerk, interested only in his pipe and his newspaper, once told him that the night before he had suddenly woken to find another and greater self pacing back and forth in a moonlit avenue full of images. On one occasion AE asked a sympathetic senior employee, who expected a business question, 'Miss Ellis, have you ever really *seen* a fairy?' This lady was able to enter into some of his interests, and they would often walk round Mountjoy Square together after work, while AE recited poetry and talked of eastern philosophy. She carefully preserved the quotations from various scriptures which he copied out for her. Other colleagues were less sympathetic. Speaking to his friend John Eglinton of a bullying supervisor, he declared: 'Sometimes I think I will blaze out at that man and scorch him up.' He seems to have been attracted for a while to a girl who could see only his immaturity and laughed at him when his back was turned.[13]

In April 1891, the month before Madame Blavatsky's death, Frederick Dick, a Scottish engineer, and his wife Annie, rented number three of a row of five elegant Georgian terrace houses which lined the west side of a short cul-de-sac near Stephen's Green. This street, Upper Ely Place, was cut off at the south end by an imposing mansion, while a colourful orchard garden occupied the east side, and railings and a gate divided it from Ely Place proper to the north. The Dicks put their new home at the disposal of the Theosophical Society and not only housed the Dublin Lodge but also a resident community of young disciples. Besides themselves, the members included AE, who at last left his parental home, Edmund King, a medical student, Daniel Dunlop, a Dublin shopkeeper, and Malcolm Magee, whose brother William became a well known writer under the pen-name John Eglinton. The composition of the community, which came to be known as the Household, was not constant and at different times Arthur Dwyer, James Nolan, Charles Johnston's sister Georgie, Violet North, and James Pryse lived in the Lodge.[14] AE shared a room with Magee and later with Dwyer, but on at least one occasion he left to reside for a time at his parents' new home in Monkstown and visited Upper Ely Place on Monday and Friday evenings.[15] During the six years which followed the establishment of the Household, AE experienced both the ecstatic happiness of companionship in faith and the deep misery of daily exile from nature. The smallness of his income in no way troubled him: though he 'had to look at the soles of his boots before venturing on a long walk . . . he felt a Croesus or Rockefeller as far as ideas were concerned'[16] and Yeats was aware that he managed to reserve a substantial part of his earnings for charity.

AE came very slowly to maturity. In his middle twenties he in many ways resembled a brilliant, charming, affectionate and often naive undergraduate. His remarkable mind was gradually developing its powers, sharpening itself on the subtleties of philosophy while learning to grapple with the details of business. At the same time he was acquiring the tact necessary to make his benevolence effective and the powers of self-expression in speech and writing that would enable him to exert his influence throughout Ireland and beyond. He never regretted having missed a university education for he knew than his life in the Lodge had more than taken its place.

> The seven years I lived there were the happiest in my life. How fortunate I was to be drawn into companionship with six or seven others all as I think wiser and stronger than I then was.[17]

He recalls the 'companionship going deep far beyond external intimacy, in that thought would flash from mind to mind and often be apprehended before it was uttered.' Gradually he felt his weaknesses and uncertainties beginning to fall away, and

> seeds born in me began to blossom in that gracious air, and what before was but flickering of a mystic communion (?) began to glow to almost steadfast light. Out of this companionship came all that was best in my poetry, every delicacy of perception had its growth among these friends of my youth.[18]

An otherwise blank page in the notebook containing these passages bears the single sentence:

> My youth *was* blessed.

The responsibility for the housekeeping fell on Mrs. Dick, a beautiful, delicate, and rather nervous young woman, who looked after her large spiritual family quite selflessly. Her husband's dry, precise, scientific intellect was the antithesis of AE's romantic imagination. Though kind and generous, he was absolutely rigid in matters of dogma and liable to take serious offence when faced with opposition.[19] At one period, according to Yeats, the two men quite unconsciously led rival factions within the Lodge. AE was intensely irritated by the engineer's way of thinking and, being a student of the Indian philosopher Patanjali, he attempted to overcome this weakness by meditating on him with benevolence. For a while gusts of anger disrupted his concentration, but after a month of effort he felt only affection for Dick, who, it turned out, had been meditating on him in the same way.[20] Malcolm Magee later remembered how much AE idealised his companions, ever eager to see good in others and to overlook their limitations.[21]

Evidence that the Lodge could be socially attractive comes from a contemporary article by O'Leary Curtis, a young man who visited the Theosophists somewhat apprehensively about June 1893 and was surprised to find the sort of exquisite décor and refined and cultured conversation he would have expected in a small Paris salon.[21a] Even AE, however, in spite of his later nostalgia for the happiness of this period, could see in retrospect that the life of the community as well as his own character had had a lighter, indeed a fantastic side. Occasionally a misfit appeared in the Household. Yeats remembered a girl from a wealthy family who had run away to devote herself to art and poetry and had been found by Dick in a state of semi-starvation. Another girl was suspected of running after one of the young men and AE undertook the delicate task of correcting her.[22]

For about a year he was a vegetarian and he afterwards recalled how well he had thrived on his meals of fresh vegetables. At the end of this period, when he boasted to Philip Francis Little of the moral superiority of this way of life, the latter rebuked him: 'You with your crust of bread are as great a glutton as Nero with his banquets.' AE, who was trying to cultivate non-attachment to the senses, admitted the justice of this remark, and returned to a more conventional diet.[23] He felt, however, a definite revulsion at the idea of killing any animal, for he told Katharine Tynan how he had once caught a fish and the memory of it turning over in its death throes had been sufficient to prevent him from ever taking life again.[24] Madame Blavatsky advocated vegetarianism, and Charles Johnston's sister was enthusiastic enough to start a vegetarian restaurant in Dublin. It remained open for several years and AE, like other Theosophists and writers, often ate there.

The records in the *Irish Theosophist* show that, apart from the work of the Esoteric Section, the serious activities of the Lodge centred on the weekly study groups for beginners and advanced disciples held on Friday and Monday evenings respectively. Except during the summer, there were public lectures followed by discussions on alternate Wednesday nights. As well as doing his share of lecturing, AE served at various times as Librarian and Vice-President of the Lodge, and, together with his fellow businessman Dunlop, at least once certified the annual accounts.[25]

It is evident that the meetings open to the public, which were intended to spread interest in Theosophy, could be both deeply moving and wildly entertaining. A visitor to the meetings long remembered AE's performance on those occasions:

> After a few others had spoken AE would follow and those speeches were wonderful. As he went on, he seemed to become inspired,

rapt into some mystic world. I have never since heard anything like them; even AE himself in later years did not seem carried away by his subject, as in those early days.[26]

Ella Young, too, was deeply impressed by the 'tall, slender, bearded man' who rose at the back of the room and who 'did not seem to be human, but rather the vehicle through which some Being, rainbow-hued and unearthly, manifested itself.'[27] H. F. Norman always remembered how 'AE was *aflame* with Theosophy then, a red hot missionary.'[28] Occasionally his enthusiasm took a form that amused his companions. On 30 December, 1892, an At Home was held at the Lodge and it was recorded that 'In one corner Bro. Russell discoursed to an attentive group in tones "strange and mystical" . . .'[29]

The Theosophists were well aware that their public meetings were not always conducted on a level of high seriousness. In one number of their magazine an announcement of coming lectures is followed by the further information, 'and for the future, for those desirous of more wisdom and less hilarity, Friday evening will be set apart for the study of *The Secret Doctrine*.'[30] At one time a Christian zealot, secretly fascinated by their strange ideas, would regularly implore the Theosophists to return to the Bible lest they incur eternal damnation, and there was frequent debate with the materialists of the local Ethical Society.

The house in Upper Ely Place served as a social centre for non-resident Theosophists and the friends of members. Yeats and Eglinton came often, Katharine Tynan occasionally.[31] AE found that such spare time as he had was much occupied with casual callers,[32] though frequently on returning from Pim's, he would take refuge in the study of *The Secret Doctrine*, the thought of which sustained him during the hours of work. Study and companionship went hand in hand and he constantly interrupted his reading to discuss some points that had excited him. In their less exalted moods, the residents would enjoy listening to Dick playing the piano, while AE, who was unmusical, drew on the walls.[33]

In later years acquaintances of AE, misled by his habit of constantly repeating a few favourite quotations, assumed that he only had a smattering in philosophy and mysticism, but his contributions to the *Irish Theosophist* and his surviving spiritual diary show that his studies were surprisingly wide and deep. He read not only the Indian scriptures and Hindu philosophers of every school, but a broad range of Theosophical, secular and sacred literature, including Plato, the Hermetic writings, and the Chaldean Oracles.*

*In a letter of 10 May, 1932, to Miss Grace Emily Jameson, AE mentions that he read Plato when he was 23 or 24, as far as he remembered in Jowett's translation.[34]

Either at this period or later he developed a special love for Lao Tzu and for the God-intoxicated poetry of the Sufis. Norman records that he was a constant student of Du Prel's *Philosophy of Mysticism*, a scholarly treatise on dreams and related phenomena.[35] One of his favourite literary forms was the aphorism in which thinkers like Patanjali, the Chinese philosophers, and Blake embodied a profound insight in a few brief phrases. He would often ponder over one of these sayings for weeks at a time endeavouring to fathom its deepest meaning.[36] To an Indian who later complimented him on his insight into Hindu thought, he replied: 'There is nothing to be surprised at. I've had to sweat for it.'[37]

The urge to write and paint continued to trouble him, despite his periodic resolutions of mental austerity. Early in 1891 he sent Carrie Rea 'the last verses I wrote or am likely to write' and more than a year later he informed her:

> I go in for hard thinking, for scientific demonstration of laws as I think they are best after all. Now and then the old passion overtakes me and I write – anything – for the sake of getting rid of the temptress.[38]

By the summer of 1892[39] he had begun to paint the murals which captured the attention of all future visitors to the Lodge; they seem to have been completed some time before O'Leary Curtis viewed them in mid-1893. Extensive portions of these fantastic pictures still survive, their beautiful colours and Blake-like clarity of line unfaded. They appear to be at once delicate and majestic, showing a sense of form and an ability to design visual patterns on a large scale for which the smaller canvases by which AE is better known gave no scope. The giant and diminutive figures, both human and divine, and the planets, stars, flowers, and serpents undoubtedly have precise Theosophical significance, for AE told O'Leary Curtis that the paintings would be nearly incomprehensible to anyone unfamiliar with philosophical doctrines; their detailed meaning was apparently unknown to Yeats himself.[40] Ignorant rumours must have been spread about these murals as AE laughingly complained to Curtis, '. . . it was even said when these pictures were first painted that we worshipped them, said prayers before them . . . '[40a] Partly conjectural interpretations of some sections are given in the next chapter.

P. E. Jackson, a frequent visitor to the Lodge, saw a great deal of AE and was sometimes with him when he was happily absorbed in working on these designs. He would begin a sketch on the wall, stare at it for a long time, and eventually step back to examine it from the opposite side of the room. It was then time to turn his attention to his pipe, which had usually gone out. (Smoking was perhaps the only indulgence of the senses he did not avoid.) When Jackson questioned him about the meaning of his work, he would give a radiant smile and talk in a general way about the light from the One – the Absolute – manifesting itself as thought or beauty.[41]

It was probably about August 1892 that Jackson suggested the Dublin Lodge issue its own periodical. At first most of the members felt that the project was too ambitious and some feared that it would swell the number of Theosophical publications unnecessarily. However Jackson, who had worked for the Dublin *Freeman's Journal,* was able to reassure them that the scheme was practical. Printing equipment was purchased and installed at the home of two members, John and Robert Coates. Daniel Dunlop edited the paper, which was named the *Irish Theosophist* and was issued monthly from October 1892 to September 1897. Besides the Coates brothers, his main associates were Malcolm Magee, Dick, AE, and Jackson himself, who operated the machinery, but while printing was in progress other helpers called, as well as those who only came to watch. Jackson draws an amusing picture of himself hard at work setting the type, while two of the inner circle find room to sit on Robert Coates's bed, Yeats orates on some occult subject, and Dunlop arrives with his arms full of books and papers and calls out, 'Do ye work or play?'[42]

It has been mentioned that not all the visitors to the Lodge were committed Theosophists, and, even apart from Yeats, AE had friends who were outside the fold. In particular he conceived a great affection for Charles Weekes, a businesslike and kindly youth whose intellectual interest in Theosophy was tempered by a strong element of scepticism and an attitude of amusement rather than respect towards Madame Blavatsky. In 1893 AE publicly challenged Weekes's posture of doubt in the correspondence columns of the local *Ethical Echo,* and as late as 1932 he sadly warned his old friend that he deserved a better fate than the place of dreamless sleep or posthumous bewilderment that he was preparing for himself between his present life and his next incarnation. Around the time that the Household was established, Weekes pointed AE out to John Eglinton at Howth and the three soon formed a trio who enjoyed each other's company on long country walks. Eglinton, a short, red-haired Ulsterman with a round freckled face, was British rather than Irish in his sympathies and more interested in literature than in the Theosophy which attracted so many of his friends. Kill-o'-the-Grange churchyard was a favourite meeting place for Eglinton and AE, and sometimes the former, on returning late at night from his work in the National Library, would find himself coerced into going there when his train stopped near AE's Monkstown home. They often sat on a tombstone till nearly midnight, while AE talked and smoked. On Sunday afternoons they met regularly and were often joined by Weekes. On one occasion AE was indignant that Eglinton should allow his Christmas dinner to disturb this routine and with his usual unconcern for family bonds spoke of such a festive gathering as truly a tragedy. Even at this early date Eglinton was greatly impressed by AE's talk, which was sometimes interrupted for hours at a time by periods of depression and silence. His subjects ranged from funny stories about incidents at Pim's to the magnificence of Tennyson's anger in 'Locksley Hall Sixty Years After,' his dislike of Shakespeare and Lamb, and his visions of higher worlds from which man in his present state was exiled. The breadth of his reading, especially in fiction and poetry, and the retentiveness of his memory, astonished Eglinton.[43]

Not all AE's friends were as strong-minded in resisting his missionary efforts as was Weekes. O'Leary Curtis, who claimed that hundreds shared his impression that AE was 'of a very rare type of man,'[43a] is said to have undergone an instant conversion after listening to him for a few minutes in the Dublin Lodge. Soon afterwards he gave a muddled description of his Theosophical beliefs to a churchman and returned to his former Catholicism.[44] A firmer, indeed lifelong adherent of the new creed was H. F. Norman, who met AE about the time that he joined the Dublin Lodge in 1894 and became his devoted friend. Norman was a gentle but tough-spirited young man whose character and career were curiously like AE's. He gave up his chance of a musical training to spare his parents the expense, became an ardent Theosophist, and devoted his life to working for his countrymen in Plunkett's movement while writing music criticism for Dublin periodicals. Plunkett considered him a saint. When he first knew AE he was very downcast, and the latter wrote his poem 'Comfort' to reassure him that the very longings which tormented him were evidence that his true self was immortal and divine.[45] Norman was struck by the contrast between AE's outer modesty and his breathtaking claim that if men saw themselves as they really were they would know that they were gods. He told Norman, who must have been cultivating the intellect rather than the imagination: 'You think too much. Brood and dream.'[46]

While he was a member of the Household, AE made one acquaintance who was even more eccentric than Philip Francis Little. When he visited this friend, a Dublin businessman named Fitzpatrick, the brother-in-law of Dunlop, he had to listen to lavish praise of Keats. He protested that the latter's verse tended to be over rich, whereupon Fitzpatrick leaned back in his chair and screamed. Six or seven years later AE again found himself in Fitzpatrick's lodging, a meagrely furnished room in Wicklow Street. After refusing a whisky and soda, he read one of his host's sonnets and mildly remarked that the last two lines were not as good as the rest. Unfortunately those lines contained the author's discovery that Shakespeare was a reincarnation of Christ and that the Apostles had now returned to earth. Believing himself to be Peter, Fitzpatrick was seeking the rest. 'You are one,' he said to his visitor, who replied, 'If that is so, then I must be Thomas.''[47] In 1895 AE wrote his first book review: the subject was a volume of verse by a poet named R. H. Fitzpatrick.

During the course of the 1890's a change began to come over AE's relationship with the friend who had shared his discovery of the spiritual world. He and Yeats started to diverge in their approaches to this realm of experience and it became apparent that there were fundamental differences between them. AE was a mystic, one who attempted to subdue the personal self or natural man, to annihilate, in Blake's phraseology, his selfhood, in order that the Spirit might act unimpeded through him. Yeats, who, to AE's indignation, scorned Plato and found the Upanishads unreadable, became an occultist, one who sought to purify and strengthen his individual ego and to acquire supernatural power and knowledge. The occultist practises elaborate rituals involving chants and symbols, through which he hopes to attract to himself arcane images and forces. He runs the risk of developing a displeasing and dangerous pride, of imagining he can command spirits, and of coming to resemble the arrogant mage of tradition. While AE retained an almost unquestioning faith in Theosophy throughout his life, Yeats, having angered Madame Blavatsky, left the Society in the summer of 1890 and concentrated on the occult practices of the Hermetic Students of the Golden Dawn, an English order he had joined a few months before. Both men believed in the theory underlying the use of symbols, that just as the mention of a word like 'Pyramid' will cause the hearer to think of ideas associated with it, so ancient symbols can evoke appropriate images or powers in the cosmic mind.[48] For a time AE experimented with the Indian Tatvic series, but one of his visions conveyed the warning that powers acquired through ceremonial magic could easily vitalise the unpurged evil within the magician, and he thenceforward followed only the safer path of meditation.[49] According to Joseph Hone, he thought that the kind of magic practised by the Golden Dawn, which involved the imposition of one's will on men or spirits, was unethical,[50] and he was later of the opinion that Yeats mistook symbolism for mysticism and was not in any real sense a mystic at all.[51]

Despite their disagreement on spiritual subjects, AE continued to be an intimate friend of Yeats, and while the latter's experiments in magic sometimes amused him, he was impressed by the images which certain very ordinary people saw after the poet had given them symbols.[52] He himself once painted a Celtic symbol he believed would be unknown in England and sent it to Gerald Balfour, President of the Society for Psychical Research, who passed it on to a medium. On first holding it to her brow, this woman had a vague impression of water; on repeating the experiment she again saw the water, this time with reddish fruit dropping into it from overhanging boughs. The symbol represented Mananan MacLir and the Nuts of Knowledge.[52a] In 1891, as their correspondence shows, AE and Yeats were co-operating in the investigation of clairvoyant visions involving members of the Golden Dawn, and after Yeats began, about 1896, to construct a ritual for a Celtic occult order, he enjoyed his friend's enthusiastic help for several years. They experimented with appropriate symbols and by trial and error discovered the details of form and colour which had the power to call up visions of the various Gaelic gods.[53]

While AE was not completely opposed to this kind of occult practice, he was, like most Theosophists, hostile to spiritualism, holding that when a genuine manifestation did occur, it was a transient shell composed of the basest elements of the deceased that spoke through the medium. He told a correspondent that he preferred to investigate spiritual matters by other means, and he did not believe that disembodied spirits could move material objects.[54] Astrology interested him as illustrating the harmonious interlocking structure of the universe, but although he arranged to have a horoscope cast for his newborn son in 1899,[55] he later came to feel that the practice was dangerous and that it was wiser not to draw charts for living people.[56]

During his years with the Household, AE's training and self-discipline centred on his study of the book that may be described as the bible of Theosophy. In *The Secret Doctrine: the Synthesis of Science, Religion and Philosophy,* Madame Blavatsky attempted to produce a work of immense erudition which would clearly show that all the religions of the world, both living and obsolete, had their origin in an ancient Secret Doctrine embodying the whole truth about man and the universe. This doctrine, she claims, appears with varying degrees of distortion in all scriptures and in the classic works of mysticism and mystical philosophy, and throughout human history there have been initiates of all religions who were secretly aware of it and who embodied it incompletely in their writings.

AE entirely accepted and never discarded the Theosophical explanation of man and the universe, an account which turned upside down some of the most widely accepted axioms of cosmogony, evolutionary theory, and history to create a modern substitute for the unified world-picture of earlier centuries, which had been shattered by the scientific revolution. It is clear from the late verses 'To One who wanted a Philosophy from Me' in *The House of the Titans* that he did not always realise the degree of his own Theosophical orthodoxy: in only a few minor details was he ever at variance with Madame Blavatsky's teachings. The starting point of her system is the ancient Indian belief that time is cyclic and that the creation is not a unique but an eternally recurring phenomenon, since the universe is outbreathed by the Deity at the dawn of each cosmic day and indrawn with the onset of cosmic night. The cycle of complete manifestation and withdrawal occupies a period so immense that Hindus were not startled by the vast time scale of modern astronomy. Madame Blavatsky further taught that the visible earth, like each of the other planets, is but one of a chain of seven interpenetrating globes. The evolution of the human souls inhabiting the earth-chain involves a descent from an etherial state of bodily and mental spirituality to a nadir of physical and psychological materialism, and a re-ascent to a plane higher than that from which the process began. All this necessitates an immense pilgrimage of seven Rounds, each including a period of development on every one of the seven globes, and on each globe seven great Root-Races have to evolve. We are said to be now in the Fifth Root-Race of the Fourth Round and having passed the nadir are on the upswing. We have not yet, however, equalled the greatest civilisations of the past, the remains of which were buried beneath the sea or destroyed by cataclysms, leaving only fragmentary and now unrecognised remnants. These civilisations were founded by exalted beings who took incarnation as royal sages for this sacred purpose. Accordingly, primitive men are considered to be the degenerate descendants of civilised ancestors, and folklore and superstitions are regarded as the distorted remnants of great religions. Thus AE asked in the *Irish Statesman*:

> Is it not . . . likely that the world has seen civilisation after civilisation appearing and disappearing times beyond calculation, and that what we know as myth and folk tale is not primitive at all, but the decayed fragments of once mighty religions or literatures . . .[57]

Later, writing to a friend, he was able to exclaim less cautiously:

> The prehistoric horses are fine. Who talks about primaeval savage man! He was always civilised and always painted and made poetry and 'sculpt', if there is such a word, and that is civilisation.[58]

Madame Blavatsky claimed that she was fulfilling a sacred mission entrusted to her by the Masters (the Tibetan Arhats), men who, having reached a stage where they were no longer subject to rebirth, had postponed their own further evolution towards reunion with the Absolute to watch over humanity and guide the course of history.[59]

On 11 October, 1893, AE lectured at the Lodge on 'The Seven Races'[60] and he sometimes wrote on similar subjects, but the details of Theosophical evolution were of less interest to him than doctrines more immediately related to man's present and potential state. The foundation of his faith was the Indian concept of the division between Reality and Illusion or, more accurately, between Absolute Reality and Relative Existence. Only the One or the Deity can be said without qualification to exist. Though properly speaking It is formless and without attributes, It may be characterised by the Sanskrit word *Satchitananda* – Being-Consciousness-Bliss; It is therefore not personal, but, being infinite, It transcends the limitations inherent in the concept of personality. All else belongs to the realm of *Maya,* or Illusion. This includes not only inanimate objects, plants, animals, and men, but also more exalted spiritual beings, the Hindu or Gaelic gods or the angels who correspond to them in the Judaeo-Christian system, as well as the heavens and hells where the soul enjoys and suffers between incarnations, according to its virtues and vices during life on earth: all these have only the phantom existence of visual images which tantalise the traveller in a desert mirage. A human being, held in a prison of which the windows are his five senses, perceives phantoms and not reality, the Many and not the One. In his story 'The Cave of Lilith,' AE shows how insidious is the all but infinite power of *Maya* to hold the human mind in the grip of her illusion: personified as Lilith, she proclaims that the soaring imagination of Dante never escaped from her, even in his *Paradiso*.

There are two standpoints from which one may speak, the absolute and the relative. From the relative standpoint, the One appears to have become divided into the Many which comprise all that exists in the realm of *Maya,* but from the absolute standpoint the One remains undiminished and unchanged in eternal bliss, though to the deluded soul which imagines itself to be separated, the entire universe and the heavenly hosts seem to have been spun out of Its substance. Imagination or belief about oneself is the key to this philosophy. The great secret which the Upanishads proclaim is that the apparently individual soul of man is in reality identical with the Absolute: 'Thou art That.' By identifying himself with the physical body or the outward mental personality, man condemns himself to imprisonment in the material world; by his attachment to this world he is drawn back again and again into rebirth. Only by annihilating all bodily and worldly desires, can he come to know who and what he is, that his inmost self is identical with God, and so destroy the force which binds him to the earth. Reabsorption into the Absolute should not be thought of as an abrogation of individual life but as an expansion of consciousness until it becomes infinite.

It is held that the moral government of the phenomenal universe depends on the impersonal law of *Karma*. A man's good and evil thoughts and deeds inevitably bring good and evil consequences upon him, if not on earth, then in a hell or paradise. AE formulated his law of spiritual gravitation to describe the operation of *Karma* in the life of the individual, and his faith in this law made him certain that he could never lose the friends or fate that were rightfully his. He believed that every man travels from life to life with a group of friends who reincarnate together to continue their spiritual adventures;[61] occasionally he would refer to the nation or family as such a group,[62] but more often he maintained that physical relationships rarely coincided with kinship at a deeper level.

The consequences of thoughts and deeds, whether already experienced or still to come, are called *Karma*. But any *Karma*, whether good or evil, will draw the soul back to life on earth. It was therefore taught that while a life of moral action producing good *Karma* was immeasurably superior to a life of immoral action producing bad *Karma*, it was only by refraining from action completely and stilling the stream of thoughts in the mind through meditation, that one could avoid the generation of *Karma* altogether and so escape from the cycle of rebirth. The Bhagavadgita, a scripture written after this doctrine had been propounded, offers another solution to the problem. By acting without any desire of reward, by making of all one's action a sacrifice to the Lord – a possibility only with deeds that are morally pure and selfless – one can work without attachment to anything in the realm of *Maya* and so one's deeds will produce no *Karma*. For this reason one should renounce the desire of reward, earthly or heavenly. Moreover, it is argued, action must be performed, or the frame of things within which the individual can seek salvation will fall apart. The Bhagavadgita was AE's favourite scripture – 'the essence,' he called it, 'of human wisdom'[63] – and the chief inspiration of his work for Ireland as it was of Mahatma Gandhi's devoted labours for India. Its teaching lies behind even such a simple saying of AE as 'Let the joy be in the doing and not in the end.'[64]

For most people religious belief largely consists of faith in the unseen. For AE, though he once declared that he and his fellow Theosophists 'accepted these truths, even as intuitions which we were unable intellectually to justify,'[65] belief was rooted in his own mystical experiences. The first of these came to him spontaneously, but at an early date he came to feel a longing for some control over the flickering and uncertain gleams of his vision. In his quest for this power he was persuaded to take instruction in techniques of concentration and meditation long current among Hindus and Buddhists. By the spring of 1893, he was already recommending exercises in concentration to Carrie Rea.[66]

To begin with, AE tried to cultivate the power of concentrating intensely upon a simple geometrical form. Holding a triangle or other shape in his imagination, he sought to exclude utterly all other images and thoughts. The extreme difficulty of this task can soon be discovered by anyone willing to attempt it. Only after he had practised continuously for a period of months or even years rather than weeks, did he find himself able to maintain control over his own mental processes for even a few minutes.[67]

When AE first attempted deliberately to withdraw his mind from contact with the outside world and cut off the influx of sense perceptions, all was darkness and emptiness, but hitherto dormant faculties began gradually to awaken and an awareness of his own mysterious inner being flooded his consciousness. He found that a newly discovered energy, which he confronted with both fear and wonder, was at the service of his will, and the *Chakras* – the hidden spiritual centres of the body, which, according to Hindu tradition, lie principally along the spinal cord and in the brain – began partially to open. There appeared within a world of far greater beauty than any of his senses could have perceived externally. 'I attribute,' he wrote,

> to that unwavering meditation and fiery concentration of will a growing luminousness in my brain as if I had unsealed in the body a fountain of interior light . . . at times in meditation there broke in on me an almost intolerable lustre of light, pure and shining faces, dazzling processions of figures, most ancient, ancient places and peoples, and landscapes lovely as the lost Eden.[68]

AE's earliest exercises in concentration were designed to strengthen the willpower which he believed he had neglected in his previous life. The will itself is morally neutral and its cultivation is only a step to further achievement, either good or evil. In *The Candle of Vision* he implies that the energy he evoked vitalised the worst as well as the best that was in him, and that he had to contend in lonely agony with desires and hatreds of an intensity he could not hitherto have imagined. Meditation without moral self-discipline led, he believed, to an inflation of the personal self instead of its transcendence on the mystic's journey towards the Spirit, and he told his son that three steps should be taken in self-perfection for one in knowledge.[69] According to Indian doctrine, anger, attachment to possessions, and desire of enjoyment through the senses are the great hindrances to spiritual progress. These emotions churn the surface of the mind, which should be like a motionless and transparent pool in which the Spirit can be reflected without distortion. Like Mahatma Gandhi, though with less remarkable success, AE made a deeply sincere effort to realise this high ideal of non-attachment to the body and the world. In 1894, when his hero Judge was accused of dishonesty, he felt able to protest: 'I confess to greater sins than he is charged with; to years smothered with sensuality, lurid with anger, wrinkled with meanness, dark with fear . . .'[70] and at the end of his life he could write, 'I who have been angry and sensual.'[71] It is evident that he judged himself with the severity of those who are truly spiritual.

Having acquired some power of concentration, AE devoted all his strength to meditation upon the inmost Self, the Self of all beings, and strove to identify himself with Its attributes of beauty, power, and compassion. Spurning a false humility, ('We do not kneel to It as slaves,' he wrote, 'but as Children of the King we lift ourselves up to that Glory . . .'),[72] he sought to realise himself as a part of all Its manifestations in mankind and in nature: 'We have imagined ourselves into forgetfulness, into darkness, into feebleness. From this strange and pitiful dream of life, oh, that we may awaken and know ourselves once again.'[73] A man is slowly transformed, he believed, into whatever he thinks of intently, becoming nobly like what he loves and ignobly like what he hates, and this psychological law operates as certainly for a nation as for an individual. He therefore held it wrong to hate even when one's moral sense impelled one to struggle against evil, though to his sorrow he never overcame his own tendency to lapse into impersonal anger at wrongs inflicted on others or on his country.

According to Hindu tradition, there is in every human being a vast reservoir of dormant spiritual energy which can be awakened through such ethical and mental disciplines as AE imposed upon himself. This power, the *Kundalini,* is pictured as a coiled serpent lying at the base of the spine. When roused in meditation through an intense focusing of the will, it moves upwards, vitalising the *Chakras* on its way, until it reaches and opens the Third or Divine Eye 'in the hollow of the brain,'[74] the Eye which can see the presence of the infinite in all things.[75] In his state of trance the mystic finds that light and sound have become interchangeable.[76] Only by thus evoking the *Kundalini,* with which the Theosophists equated the Christian Paraclete or Holy Spirit, can man be resurrected from his bondage to matter and reassume his spiritual nature. AE describes how he once experienced in meditation the full force of this awesome power:

> . . . it ran up like lightning along the spinal cord, and my body rocked with the power of it, and I seemed to myself to be standing in a fountain of flame, and there were fiery pulsations as of wings about my head, and a musical sound not unlike the clashing of cymbals with every pulsation . . .[77]

But he thought of the danger which besets the man who, insufficiently purified, calls forth the divine fire, and he forbore to open the Eye 'by which, when it is fully awakened, we dead shall be raised . . .'[78] Twice, according to one of his friends, he delivered a speech when he was possessed by this force and he could hear voices and see light imperceptible to others, but he could not afterwards remember what he had said.[79] More often, he believed, the power manifested in him in a weaker form as 'a steady light in the brain,'[80] bringing him mental inspiration for all his activities. Eventually, mindful of the moral and physical peril involved and even fearing madness, he gave up the meditation on the power which draws the *Kundalini* into consciousness.[81]

One of the most remarkable systems of mental discipline which AE adopted took the form of a retrospective meditation. To begin with, each night he would rapidly visualise all the events of the day and then those of the preceding days, until gradually, with continual practise, he became able to review his life over many years as though a film were being very swiftly rewound in his mind. Long forgotten happenings – some, as has been mentioned, even from infancy – re-emerged into his consciousness. It seems likely that he succeeded in bringing an area of the memory which is normally unconscious under voluntary control. In this way he developed the phenomenal memory for which he became famous; he not only knew by heart the whole of his own verse but seemed able to recall with only slight verbal errors any passage of verse or prose he had ever read.[82] In a letter to Carrie Rea written in 1887 he quoted a few fragments from a poem by Katharine Tynan and apologised for not remembering the rest.[83] Such a limitation is inconceivable in the mature man. His extraordinary mnemonic power, however, was confined to a limited field: he explained to Yeats that he remembered ideas because they interested him, but had difficulty with dates and events in his own or others' lives, though he might be able to recall them by deliberate concentration,[84] and he was not spared the annoyance which most people suffer on forgetting an important address.[85]

The underlying purpose of AE's retrospective meditation was to relive the past, destroying the evil in himself that he had once been too weak to overcome and tracing his impulses at least part of the way towards their origin in the Spirit, where all things, however perverted they might have become, had their ultimate beginning. 'You should discover,' he explained to Carrie Rea, 'where the ray became deflected which caused you to be angry, where gentleness becomes weakness and will passion,' and having identified 'this spot of deflection a past thought, we should think again, think it over in the true way, and so that false byeway which perverted the pure stream perishes . . .'[86] He believed, moreover, that his meditation enabled him to penetrate beyond his present incarnation to hitherto inaccessible memories of previous lives in both male and female bodies; at times he would speak of riding out to battle as a Christian soldier in a Spanish army of the ninth century, of undergoing an initiation in ancient Egypt, and of living in Chaldea, in pre-Columbian America, and more than once in Gaelic Ireland. (He had a strong feeling that Spain and Ireland had the greatest reservoirs of idealism and humanity in Europe.) In later life he once defended his interpretation of the sharply detailed images of places and people he had never seen against the scepticism of Julian Huxley. The scientist admitted that they could not have been physically inherited from his ancestors and after sitting up all night failed to find a flaw in AE's argument. It will be noticed that this recollection of mediaeval Spain contradicts his assertion of 1887 that he had last lived in Assyria. If the belief in reincarnation is accepted, doubt may yet arise over the origin of particular images or mental pictures, as he admitted in a letter to a correspondent who questioned him about the meaning of her visions.[87]

For AE, memories of former lives were not the only source of vision into the past. Theosophy teaches that the antecedent of matter is the *Akasha* or *Aether*, the grossest form of which is the all-pervading Astral Light in which every thought and deed is recorded and preserved. AE believed that the sight of a ruin, an antique object, or even a sentence or picture in a book, was often sufficient to call up before the inner eye related scenes from this World Memory and that they could even be evoked at will by intense concentration – concentration of a degree that he himself only rarely attained. Visiting the remains of a chapel in Ulster, he saw the worshippers who had once prayed there, and noticed how the fervour of a kneeling red robed woman contrasted with the pompous vanity of the altar boy and the proud detachment of an onlooker. At prehistoric mounds, he was able by deliberate effort to conjure up visions of the Gaelic past, and to see clearly the material details of its crude civilisation. It was probably soon after he had begun to work at Pim's that he first saw a fleet of majestic airships bearing beautifully robed passengers over the mountains; five or six years later one of the mysterious vessels reappeared and passed so close to him that it was within arm's reach. At the time he thought they came from one of the civilisations which, according to Theosophy, flourished before Atlantis, and, as he recalled,

> I cried out in my heart in a passion of regret for romance passed away from the world, not knowing that the world's great age was again returning and that soon we were to swim once more beneath the epic skies.[88]

AE experienced a comparable sorrow for long forgotten glory in a vision or waking dream which came upon him during his earlier years at Pim's. Suddenly he found himself a child in ancient India among happy companions of his own age; yet his mind was only half with his friends, for he saw the gods or *Devas* in the air and longed to be with them. Then he was rapt in grief for he knew that the last Divine Incarnation who would appear for many centuries had died and the Iron Age, destined to engulf mankind for more than four hundred millenia, had begun. When AE came to himself he understood that what he had seen had taken place five thousand years before, in 3102 B.C., the traditional date of Krishna's death. The belief that we are living in the Iron Age had a lifelong influence on his thought, perhaps partly due to the impact of this vision.[89]

Before he published his first book of verse in mid-1894, AE had another waking dream which he felt to be of great importance. He was walking along an ancient shore with a woman whom he loved, and withdrawing into himself, he sought union with her on the level of spirit, but instead entered a trance in which he moved towards infinite being; suddenly the trance was broken and he no longer felt close to his beloved, but alone and outcast and an exile from Deity. At the time of this vision, AE had never been in love, at least in his present life, and he took the visitation as a warning that he should avoid romance. At the end of 1893 he published a story carrying the message that romantic love is the hardest of all temptations to renounce and that it inevitably turns into bitterness.[90]

Some of the mental phenomena over which AE pondered with such curiosity belong to the field of telepathy. He was certain that if one's consciousness were emptied of thought, ideas and images from other minds could stray into it. Once, sitting in his office beside a colleague who was writing a letter, he suddenly found himself looking at an old man handling papers behind the counter in a small, dark shop, while a red haired girl watched him from the rear; a few moments' conversation revealed that he had seen his companion's father and sister. Mr. Diarmuid Russell testifies that his father sometimes showed he knew facts about people he could not have discovered by normal means, and Yeats tells how a young woman complained to him, 'Oh, Mr. Russell, I am so unhappy,' and blushed when he replied, (he could not afterwards explain why) 'You will be perfectly happy this evening at seven o'clock' – the exact time at which she had an appointment with a young man.[91]

AE drew a careful distinction between telepathy, which involves no emotional identification with another person, and what he thought of as the intersection of minds. He later came to feel that as the body, through the organ of sight, can perceive extremely distant parts of the universe, so the psyche is capable of making contact with all humanity, and the spirit, the highest element in man, mirrors the images in the Divine ideations. His poem 'A Summer Night' was, he believed, the result of his briefly taking on the identity, memories, and emotions of a statesman who had sacrificed his childhood love of nature for a worldly career. Such men of genius as Shakespeare and Balzac, AE suspected, had, unknown to themselves, innumerable experiences of this kind, and many of their characters were in fact living people and not, as they supposed, the work of their imagination. He concluded that the individual consciousness was but a tributary of the collective consciousness of humanity, a thought that he expressed in one of his early poems:

> And all my thoughts are throngs of living souls . . .

In the whole body of his verse, he said, this was the line that carried most meaning.[92]

The corollary of AE's belief in the invisible unity of mankind was the conviction that by intense meditation one could deliberately enter into communion with one's fellow men and do them incalculable good. He assured Carrie Rea,

> You will find yourself much closer to humanity in your inner nature than in your material contact with them. I felt this some few evenings ago when within myself and far away the stir of the long imprisoned souls of men seemed to reach me.[93]

In his story 'The Meditation of Ananda,' he tells how by mental effort an ascetic impelled a king to release his enemy, a child to relieve the loneliness of a prisoner, and a teacher and his disciples to consort with an outcast leper.

The Theosophist attaches great importance to experience and endeavour on this plane, since he believes that they can help to bring about the brotherhood which is the goal of the Society. He distinguishes, however, between consciousness on this – the psychic – level and those highest moments in life when the transient personality comes nearest to the Spirit, the Absolute within the individual. It is the aim of the mystic to bring the personal self into abeyance in the stillness of meditation, allowing the Spirit to radiate Its inspiration undistorted into the waking consciousness.

According to AE, not only Yoga discipline but devout brooding over whatever one wishes to be illuminated on will be rewarded by a visitation of the divine in the form of poetry, music, conscience, or the flash of intuition by which the scientist sees into the mysterious workings of nature. That brooding AE regarded as a sacrifice, and he expressed his faith that it would be answered in his saying 'As our aspiration so is our inspiration.'[94] He explained the psychology of the process by describing how ideas and speculations pass from the conscious mind through the psyche and upwards towards the Spirit; where inner and outer meet, and at what he came to call the Mount of Transfiguration, they are miraculously remoulded, and thence they return suffering a greater or lesser degree of distortion according to the condition of the psyche. In *Song and Its Fountains* he accounts in this way for the poet's inspiration.

The active members of the Dublin Lodge learnt and taught simultaneously. AE began his career as a writer with the numerous essays, stories, and poems which he published in the *Irish Theosophist* to instruct and exhort his companions and especially those less learned than himself. Unlike some of his fellow contributors he eschewed as far as possible technical terms and set out to appeal to the imagination and emotions as well as to the intellect of his readers. Almost from the beginning he had two distinct prose styles – one matter of fact and lucid, the other deliberately poetic and affectedly simple. When dealing with a complicated, intellectual subject, he wrote well:

> From these quotations it will be seen that the occult teachings as to speech are directly at variance with the theories of many philologists and evolutionists. A first speech which was like song – another and more developed speech which is held sacred – and an esoteric side to speech in which the elements of our conventional languages (i.e. the letters) are so arranged that speech becomes potent enough to guide the elements, and human speech becomes the speech of the gods – there is no kinship between this ideal language and the ejaculations and mimicry which so many hold to be the root and beginning of it.[95]

The competence with which AE, even at such an early stage, handled language disappeared when he self-consciously attempted to produce 'literature':

> Agathon the husbandman went away and bent tenderly over his fruits and vines, and he loved each one of them more than before,

and he grew wise in many things as he watched them and he was happy working for the gods.

Then spake Damon the shepherd, 'Father, while the flocks are browsing dreams rise up within me; they make the heart sick with longing; the forests vanish, I hear no more the lamb's bleat or the rustling of the fleeces; voices from a thousand depths call me, they whisper, they beseech me, shadows lovelier than earth's children utter music, not for me though I faint while I listen . . .'[96]

A number of themes recur in AE's contributions to the *Irish Theosophist*. Many of his stories treat of man's potential divinity and the snares which lie in wait for him along the path of spiritual progress. The age-long renunciation, after the example of the Buddha, of the reward within reach when freedom from rebirth has been won, the tempting distraction which visions constitute for the disciple, and the urgent necessity of strengthening the will are among his favourite subjects. He writes of the fate that befalls the mystic who allows the intense ray of his concentrated thought to dissolve in pleasing reverie and his sharply focused will to disintegrate in desire, but when he thinks of man at his most ill-starred or most corrupt, he finds solace for him in the inexhaustible love of God, which, breathed out through His emanation, the Mighty Mother, invisibly surrounds and embraces all beings. This love is paradoxically the cause of pain and suffering as it overcomes the evil within the man whose actions violate the law of the universe, and because pain teaches and corrects a hidden sweetness is found within it. Perhaps most significant of all, AE proclaims his conviction that every human soul abdicated its heavenly station of its own free will, descending into the world of matter to remould it in a more heavenly pattern and simultaneously to acquire through suffering the experience which alone could make its own being richer than before its descent:

They are but the slaves of light
Who have never known the gloom,
And between the dark and bright
Willed in freedom their own doom.[97]

Following Madame Blavatsky, AE looked with adoration on the crucified Christ and the suffering Prometheus as types of the Spirit imprisoned and tortured in the human body, which it entered for a transcendent purpose and in full knowledge of the agony before it.[98] His faith in this heroism of the soul enabled AE to reverence even the most mean and wretched. It was fundamental to his conception of the ideal of human brotherhood, which was probably the aspect of Theosophy that always meant most to him. His first prose contribution to the Lodge's magazine[99] showed how the other functions of the Society contributed to its realization, and many of his visions and psychic experiences were closely related to his belief that all individual human minds are parts of a greater whole: he once saw how the apparently separated souls of men were contained in that greater soul, the Logos, which he often called the Ancestral Self.[100]

The activities in which AE's commitment to Theosophy involved him were not confined to mysticism and teaching. The society, founded by Madame Blavatsky, Olcott, and W. Q. Judge in 1875, was aiways racked by internal politics, and since the struggles for leadership of the 1890's it has never been a united body. After Madame Blavatsky's death, Olcott and Judge were left as the Sectional leaders in Madras and New York. The former distrusted the latter, and in December 1893 he produced evidence which persuaded Annie Besant, the forceful English Theosophist and orator, whom AE knew personally,[101] to join him in charging that Judge had forged the handwriting and signatures of certain messages supposed to have been inscribed by one of the Masters. Judge's devotion to his late leader's memory and ideals was absolute, while Olcott was not convinced that her teachings were perfect or final. To the many Theosophists who held what may be called orthodox views, the charge against Judge was a betrayal not only of the Society but of mankind, for they believed that the Masters had brought human history to a crucial turning point by the mission they had laid on Madame Blavatsky. In March 1894, when the time for the official assessment of the accusation was approaching, AE published a leaflet entitled *To the Fellows of the Theosophical Society* in which he defended Judge with an earnestness and urgency that prefigured the more public appeals of his mature years. No man is able, he argued, and every Theosophist ought to know that no man is able, to judge the action of another solely on material evidence. Who but a profound occultist could know whether the will that guided the hand – if it was indeed Mr. Judge's hand that wrote – was the will of the human writer or of a Master? To demand that the advanced soul reveal the secrets behind his deed or else forbear to act, is a denial of the freedom every individual must enjoy; to condemn on the basis of surmise is a denial of that human brotherhood which is the fundamental principle of the Society.

The case was decided by the Judicial Committee which met in London on 10 July. Judge, a bearded lawyer of dignified, gentlemanly appearance, had produced an ingenious defence a few days earlier. Theosophy was not intended to be a religion in the ordinary sense: membership of the Society was open to followers of every faith and was not conditional on the acceptance of any dogma whatsoever. Judge argued that to pronounce him guilty or innocent would by implication commit Theosophists collectively to a belief in the existence of the Masters. On this ground the case was dropped. Two days later the decision was reported to the Third Session of the European Convention, which also met in London, and in the evening the assembly heard Annie Besant praise Judge and largely exonerate him from the charge. At this gathering AE felt that he saw for the first time the real greatness of his hero, the sound of whose name had profoundly moved him before he had seen the man or read his writings:

> As he sat there quietly, one among many, not speaking a word, I was overcome by a sense of spiritual dilation, of unconquerable will about him, and that one figure with the grey head became all the room to me.[102]

It seemed as though the adherents of Judge had won and the general of the opposing forces had surrendered, but the matter was not to be so easily disposed of. Far from heeding the call to resign, which now arose in many quarters, Judge attempted to deprive Annie Besant of the joint leadership of the Esoteric Section, which she shared with him, and charged that she and Olcott were unconsciously acting as the instruments of evil Adepts. The Theosophical press was soon full of propaganda on either side. Mrs. Besant replied vigorously to her accusers in the issue of *Lucifer* dated 15 February, 1895, and on the following day AE wrote to the magazine appealing to her on ethical grounds to refrain from attacking or even defending herself against a fellow Theosophist.

The climax of the struggle came at the end of April, when the American Theosophists meeting in Boston declared themselves an independent organisation, the Theosophical Society in America, and elected Judge as their permanent President. The impact of this action on the other side of the Atlantic became clear when the European Section met on 4 July in London under the chairmanship of Olcott. The majority of the English members were on the side of Mrs. Besant, but the Irish delegates and some others indignantly withdrew and assembling separately proclaimed themselves the Theosophical Society in Europe. In the afternoon of the next day they met again to hold what they called their First Annual Convention, and with the enthusiasm of fervent devotees they elected Judge as their President by acclamation. The Irish team then chose the officers for their national division – Dunlop for President, AE for Vice-President, and Dick for Secretary.[103] In the *Irish Theosophist* Dunlop declared that the meeting of July 5 had been 'like one grand apocalypse.'[104]

AE's preoccupation with the conflict between Annie Besant and Judge coincided with his first venture into authorship. Most of his early friends long remembered how he chanted in his mellow Ulster accent the poems which he published in the *Irish Theosophist*, though their opinions of their merit varied. John Eglinton was not at first impressed, but found after a few years that they lingered strangely in his mind. Charles Johnston, now back from India, did not appreciate them. 'My dear fellow,' he remarked to Eglinton, 'you have no notion how many people can write like that!'[105] Weekes, whatever reservations he had about AE's beliefs, had no doubts about the quality of his verse. In 1894, newly returned from England where he had published and then withdrawn a collection of his own poems, he set to work to cajole his friend into being less shy of the public than he had been. When his persistence was rewarded and AE agreed to compile his first book of verse, Weekes started a very small publishing firm for which he chose the name of Whaley. The final preparation of the manuscript occupied the whole attention of the two men for some days[106] and the book finally appeared in June, a tiny, paper-covered volume delicately printed by the Chiswick Press in London and entitled *Homeward: Songs by the Way*.

The initial reception of this book was in the main encouraging. Yeats was profoundly impressed and, regarding it as an important contribution to Irish letters, was anxious that it should be well publicised. He later came to consider it AE's most perfect book. Edward Dowden, the distinguished Dublin scholar, reviewed it appreciatively, with a slight reservation as to its oriental bias. A review copy sent to O'Leary Curtis's paper was followed by the author's disarming request: '. . . deal with it as you please. – Praise or blame.' AE was well satisfied by Curtis's article, which he felt made a pleasing contrast with the notices of English reviewers, who showed no understanding of mysticism.[107]

In discussing his methods of composition, AE usually emphasised the way in which his poems rose up spontaneously in his mind and critics have interpreted his statements literally. His manuscripts show, however, numerous corrections, and in 1917 he explained that in revising he had always taken particular care over quality of sound, trying as unobtrusively as possible to make deliberate use of assonance, alliteration, and various metrical devices. Often, at least in later years, he would make many drafts of each piece, and every draft would be a little longer than the one which preceded it, as though he were struggling to complete the poem and the creative part of his mind would not co-operate. Evidence about his early work is less abundant, but even in the 1890s he took care to improve upon the first product of inspiration. An unrevised version of 'Childhood,' for example, survives in one of his letters, and Eglinton prints what appears to be an early version of a stanza of 'The Golden Age.'[108]*

Homeward was published without AE's real name and he later blamed Katharine Tynan for making the secret of his identity public.[109] His resolve to shun the temptations of fame gradually weakened, and he came to hope that he would be remembered for his poems.[110] In spite of this ambition, his verse is very uneven in quality, and collectively it does not convey the uniqueness of his personality as do *The Candle of Vision, Song and Its Fountains,* and the selection of his journalism assembled by Dr. Gibbon in *The Living Torch.* He himself was well aware that his verse was far inferior to that of Yeats, a great poet who dedicated himself to perfecting every line and phrase.[111] The latter has long since found the worldwide audience he deserves, but AE, having been at one time over valued, is now unduly neglected. Scattered through his several volumes, among much that is second-rate, are poems in which precise images, tightly controlled rhythms, and unforced diction come together to communicate the emotions and experiences of the man who wrote as a preface to his first book:

> I moved among men and places, and in living I learned the truth at last. I know I am a spirit, and that I went forth in old time from the Self-ancestral to labours yet unaccomplished; but filled ever and again with homesickness I made these songs by the way.

To some of AE's contemporaries, *Homeward* brought a revelation of a new world, but at first acquaintance the modern reader may find in it only the record of a sensitive response to nature in her most tranquil moods. The delicate handling of rhythm is not always matched by an equal command of diction. AE is often content with the conventionally poetic vocabulary of such phrases as 'pearly fleece,' 'mystic bowers,' and 'the tresses of the twilight,'[112] and his visual images tend to be both indistinct and repetitive, especially when, as is so often the case, they involve colour. One of the early readers of *Homeward* noticed the overabundance of diamond and amethyst.[113] At the end of his life AE admitted to the young poet F. R. Higgins that he had allowed a 'Puritanism of the imagination' to soften the impact of his verse, and added: 'I was as easily melted as you but put all out of my poetry and made it pale. However the harvest of the poetically sensual eye I did not reap remained for you . . .'[114] Only rarely does he achieve such a precise image as in the lines

> Each chimney's vapour, like a thin grey rod,
> Mounting aloft through miles of quietness,
> Pillars the skies of God.[115]

---

*Early drafts of some poems in *Homeward* also survive at the University of Texas.

In another letter to Higgins he explains:

> You see I am primarily a dealer in ideas, and you so far are primarily a dealer in carven images . . . I only want my images to be like a dim tapestry behind my clear cut idea, and I don't want people to look at my tapestry and not listen to me . . .[116]

For AE, the thought always took precedence over the style, and a careful reading of his verse usually reveals that beneath the decorative surface there is an intellectual core. In expressing his mystical thought he felt himself handicapped by the limitations of the English vocabulary with its comparatively few words for spiritual concepts and states of consciousness.[117] His ideas, moreover, were the product of his extraordinary experiences, the nature of which it was impossible to convey in a late Victorian poetic style; unlike Hopkins and the later Yeats, AE did not succeed in creating his own idiom. The august powers of which he was continually aware are not brought to life in his poetry. A number of the poems in *Homeward*, however, are not open to these criticisms and achieve real distinction. In the two brief stanzas of 'Desire,' with its stately rhythm and austere phrasing, the poet moves from the abrupt opening to smoothly flowing lines as the mystic's awakening to the memory of his divine origin is succeeded by an all-absorbing yearning for the infinite. The description of the intense fire of sunrise passing into the scattered light of day in the lyric 'Dawn' represents the movement from unity into multiplicity through the symbolic image of pure white light dividing into the rays of the spectrum. The breaks in the sense are again skilfully arranged to accentuate the theme, and in the last stanza the poet's descent from ecstasy into the commonplaces of life parallels the fate of the first sunlight. Perhaps best of all are 'Symbolism' and the beautiful prelude 'Oh, be not led away.' The former contrasts the attraction of home and family for the mortal part of man with the power of the divine world to draw his immortal element to itself. Ultimately 'the loved earth things' are made into symbols of their heavenly counterparts to wean the soul gradually from its earthly attachments. The drawn out, winding rhythm of the latter reflects the poet's hope of turning aside from the sensuous beauty of the world to a perception of the Spirit.

> Oh, be not led away,
> Lured by the colour of the sun-rich day.
> The gay romance of song
> Unto the spirit life doth not belong:
> Though far-between the hours
> In which the Master of Angelic powers
> Lightens the dusk within
> The holy of holies, be it thine to win

Rare vistas of white light,
Half parted lips through which the Infinite
Murmurs her ancient story,
Hearkening to whom the wandering planets hoary
Waken primeval fires,
With deeper rapture in celestial choirs
Breathe, and with fleeter motion
Wheel in their orbits through the surgeless ocean.
So hearken thou like these,
Intent on her, mounting by slow degrees,
Until thy song's elation
Echoes her multitudinous meditation.

Weekes was able to reprint *Homeward* at the beginning of 1895 and the following year it was republished in London by John Lane. A pirated American edition also appeared in 1895, issued by the not ungenerous Thomas Mosher, who voluntarily paid a royalty of two per cent.[118]

From 1891 to 1894 the main object of AE's life, as his letters to Carrie Rea show, was to spread far and wide the eastern teachings embodied in Theosophy, and he employed his powers of speech and writing to this end. At the same time he was extending his own knowledge by careful study of the Indian scriptures, mystical philosophy, and *The Secret Doctrine*. Occult researches in such fields as the meaning of colours and sounds enabled him to explore the harmony that he believed to pervade the universe, the sevenfold pattern repeated on every plane from the periodic table of the elements to the highest order of archangels. He continually practised meditation and concentration, seeking the power that he knew man could attain if he shunned a false humility; at the same time he sought to realise the invisible links that bound the whole human race together on the psychic plane, endeavouring to labour for brotherhood by this means as well as externally by promoting the work of the Theosophical Society. In 1895 two new influences entered his life, influences which intensified and broadened his efforts. He began to receive instruction from the American mystic James Morgan Pryse whom he was always to regard as his greatest teacher, and he discovered for the first time his Celtic heritage.

III

The Disciple Becomes an Irishman (1894–1897)

During the early years of the Household, AE advanced far into the austere realm of the mystic, and, somewhat reluctantly, developed his poetic art. At this time, as he afterwards liked to say, he was so little aware of public affairs that he could not have named the Lord-Lieutenant.[1] The seed of national consciousness sown long before by his Russian schoolfellow was, however, restored to life by a book which nourished the patriotic pride of many writers of the Irish Renaissance. In 1878 and 1880 a Unionist barrister named Standish O'Grady had published two volumes of a *History of Ireland* largely consisting of the story of Cuchulain, greatest of the legendary Gaelic warriors, told in what amounted to a prose pastiche of the traditional epic style tricked out with archaisms, inversions, epic similes, and formal speeches. Beneath the gaudy surface there was real feeling for the heroic and chivalrous ideals embodied in the archaic lore, and it is easy to see how the rediscovered world of the remote Gaelic past made young Irishmen of artistic disposition feel that their own nation had a literary heritage comparable with that of Greece.

Intoxicated by this work, AE began to interpret the Gaelic gods and heroes in terms of eastern mysticism, and his own vision in terms of the Irish deities; soon he was convinced that the Druids had been the Brahmins of ancient Ireland. The first datable evidence of his interest in the Celtic past consists of a rather technical article, 'The Legends of Ancient Eire,' published in the *Irish Theosophist* in March and April 1895; and by June he was welcoming the spiritual character of the literary renaissance.[2] 'The Legends of Ancient Eire' contains the germ of his rapidly growing belief that his own country was as sacred as India or Tibet, and that it was one of the pivots on which mankind's spiritual destiny was to turn. In the coming years he worked out in some detail the philosophy he believed to be embodied in the Irish myths.

AE, who detected spirituality even in Dumas' stories of his musketeers,[3] was deeply moved, too, by the chivalry and love of truth which played a part in the old legends, and in later life he would continually hold up to his countrymen the examples of Cuchulain and Ferdiad pausing in their combat to embrace, and of Queen Maev praising the magnificence of the enemies who were arrayed against her. The modern Christian seemed too often to fall below the level of his pagan ancestors.

So enraptured was AE with his new found belief in the Druid wisdom that one Sunday afternoon while walking along the seafront at Bray, he threw off his customary shyness, climbed on the wall, and began to harangue the crowd. By a curious coincidence O'Grady himself was among those who heard the slender, bearded young prophet extol the Gaelic gods and acclaim Eire as a land not less holy than Palestine.[4]

Soon afterwards the two men met. AE had relapsed into his usual diffidence but O'Grady's dignified courtesy charmed him. In the subsequent years he came to see a strange duality in the older man, a contradiction between a comparatively superficial, even dull outer mind, and an inner nobility manifesting itself as literary genius. Thus O'Grady was a Unionist in politics but also a lover of Celtic traditions, a gentle character with an 'old warrior'[5] tucked away inside him, a writer with fewer ideas than AE[6] and less art than Yeats or Synge, but with an innate spirituality that was all his own. 'I was assured by my philosophy,' wrote AE, 'that underlying all diversities there was the unity of the spirit, that it was in others as in myself. But what was in my mind was not in my being. O'Grady without any philosophy at all would instinctively think about others as if they were of the same divine household . . .'[7]

The impact on AE's life of O'Grady's message from the nation's past was accompanied by another, more personal influence that came to him from within the Theosophical Society. Even in his last years he revered Madame Blavatsky and W. Q. Judge, but he had little acquaintance with them and his personal teacher was James Pryse, an American Theosophist eight years older than himself. Eglinton remembered Pryse as a shabby and unimpressive little man with a strong Yankee accent, who used to smile wryly and say of AE, 'He can do the sidereal all right!' He seemed to acquire an almost mesmeric power over his pupil; inscribing a circle round AE, he would defy him to leave it. Malcolm Magee, too, was disappointed in Pryse when he met him years afterwards, and Yeats referred to him disparagingly in his autobiography as an American hypnotist, which may account for AE's dislike of that book.[8]

AE first met James Pryse during his visits to the London headquarters of the Theosophical Society, where, as an expert printer, the latter ran Madame Blavatsky's press. At the beginning of 1895 Pryse and Violet North, a young English Theosophist with literary and psychic gifts, moved to Dublin bringing the press with them.[9] Pryse remained in Dublin, where he took up residence in the Household, until December, when he returned to the United States.[10]

His books show him to have been a man of unusual intellectual power and some literary sensitivity.

It was AE's belief that the greatness of a truly spiritual person is not to be perceived in his transient body or outer personality.[11] His relationship with the superficially undistinguished Pryse was that of a disciple with his master, and his reverence remained undiminished throughout his life. In middle age he acclaimed him as the only author to have written on mysticism from real knowledge since the death of Madame Blavatsky, and as late as 1930 he addressed him as his *guru* or honoured teacher.[12]

When Pryse arrived in Dublin he found that AE was depressed because his poetic inspiration seemed to have faded. He perceived that the young man's mind was full of new but unassimilated philosophical ideas, and he tried to persuade him that once he had absorbed these and made them his own the inspiration would return. As an encouragement, though he had composed no verse since his teens, he undertook to write poems alternately with AE for the *Irish Theosophist,* and the latter's abilities soon revived.[13]

The two men co-operated on the production of the *Irish Theosophist,* and taking advantage of Pryse's knowledge of colour printing they published reproductions of AE's visionary paintings.[14] Pryse was a vigorous and efficient worker and his disciple at first found it quite uncomfortable to have to give up his pleasantly easygoing ways.[15] It seems to have been around this time that AE began to shed the diffidence and social awkwardness that had encumbered him since he had left school. 'When I was about twenty-eight,' he wrote, 'I began rapidly to adjust myself to the life about me, to lose the old confused timidity, and to talk with easy assurance to others.'[16] He always felt, however, that his lack of self-confidence in 1895 had retarded his spiritual progress under Pryse's tutelage.[17]

Pryse was a Greek scholar and he instructed AE in the inner meaning of the New Testament, a subject on which he afterwards published several books. He identified one figure whom they both saw in vision as St. John. Under his influence AE began a rendering of the fourth Gospel into English verse, but he paraphrased St. John's meaning at such length that only one of his friends recognised his work as a translation and he abandoned the project.[18] A comparison of the published fragment with Pryse's own incomplete translation reveals much about the underlying meaning of some of AE's favourite terms. A number of his phrases usually understood as vaguely poetic have in fact precise philosophical meanings.

Indian teaching, Kabbalism, and the various philosophies derived from Plato expound the apparent division of the One into the

Many, the seeming descent of the Absolute through successive planes into Its final prison or grave in the world of matter. According to Pryse and Madame Blavatsky, the first emanations from the Deity are the coeval Logos and Archaeus. The Logos is the Divine Mind containing the images which are the originals of all separated beings and things, while the Archaeus or World Soul is the first spiritual form of that which becomes the *Akasha* or *Aether* and is eventually manifested as the Astral Light and the matter of the physical universe. The Logos in its unmanifested form is the Father and the Ancient of Days of AE's writings, and may be associated with the First Person of the Christian Trinity.[19] It contains innumerable Logoi, spiritual beings of divine power and glory. These beings and the subordinate Logoi in turn emitted from them are the emanations from the Godhead which were termed Aeons by the Gnostics. AE referred to their pure and exalted realm, the plane of illusion and multiplicity nearest to the Absolute, as the Pleroma. The true self of man is a Logos or Aeon; falling into physical existence and taking on a burden of noble and ignoble desires it becomes the reincarnating psyche or soul. Collectively the Logoi comprise the manifested or Second Logos, which is identical with the Word of Christian theology, the Second Person of the Trinity, termed by AE the Lamp of the World, the Ancestral Self, the Magician of the Beautiful, Brahma, and the Shepherd of the Ages. (The name the Light of Lights he applied sometimes to the manifested, sometimes to the unmanifested Logos.)[20] So close is the relationship between the primeval emanations from the Deity that Pryse, like Madame Blavatsky, found it difficult to distinguish clearly and consistently between them; he explained that the First and the Second Logos are in one sense identical, and described the Logos and the Archaeus as existing within one another and radiating the Light of the Logos, itself a form of the Archaeus.[21] The Light of the Logos is the Christian Holy Spirit, the Third Person of the Trinity, and the omnipresent force underlying and shaping all phenomena. When AE wrote of the Mighty Mother, 'the first spiritual form of matter,'[22] he was referring to the Archaeus; occasionally he used alternative names – the *Anima Mundi* or World Soul, and Madame Blavatsky's term the Great Deep, but confusingly he would sometimes employ this last designation as an alternative to the Divine Darkness or the Holy Sepulchre for the Absolute Itself.[23] The Light of the Logos, the divine energy, he spoke of as the Great or Holy Breath, while he regarded the earth as one of the forms assumed by the Mighty Mother, the Archaeus, and at the same time as the outer body of a Planetary Spirit.[24] This Spirit, one of the Logoi comprising the Second Logos, is the Ancient One[25] of his poems 'The Fountain of

Shadowy Beauty' and 'The Feast of Age,' and the Earth Spirit of *The Interpreters* and *The Avatars;* it may perhaps be represented in anthropamorphic form in his Ely Place murals where an awe-inspiring, god-like figure sits in majesty silhouetted against a great light, while beside and smaller than it a spinning planet is encircled with a luminous ring carrying two diminutive humans through the various stages of spiritual evolution.[26]* In certain regions and at certain times AE was able to see the Light of the Logos jetting forth from sacred places in great fire-fountains, from which spiritual beings drew sustenance, and he termed this form of the power the Earth Breath, a phrase he chose as the title of his second volume of verse. In prose he could write of a steppe-like landscape seen in vision, 'The earth-breath streamed from the furrows,' and in that manifestation of spirit he saw 'a ploughman lifting himself from his obscure toil' to 'stand with lit eyes as if he too had been fire-smitten and was caught into heaven as I was, and knew for that moment he was a god.'[27]

In *The Secret Doctrine* Madame Blavatsky drew upon most of the world's mythologies in her attempts to show that this elaborate cosmogony underlies them all. She seems, however, to have known little of Celtic tradition, and by the beginning of 1900 AE, his imagination captivated by O'Grady's *History,* had started to follow her example, though with less subtlety, by interpreting the Irish mythology as yet another ancient version of her account of creation. Lir, the God of the Ocean, he identified with the Absolute, and Mananan, Dana, and Angus with His primal emanations – the Logos, the Archaeus, and the Light of the Logos. Having followed closely the teaching of *The Secret Doctrine,* he was confident that he had rediscovered the lost meaning of Irish mythology, but A.R. Orage, who was sceptical of the explanation of the origin of language in *The Candle of Vision,* felt that the Gaelic scholarship of the time was too rudimentary for his interpretation to be more than speculative.[28]

The pattern of creation found in the cosmos is held to be repeated on every plane of existence and especially in man, the microcosm. The Great Breath, which gives life to the earth, is also present within the human body, where it normally lies dormant but may be awakened and manifested through the *Chakras,* the centres lying along the spinal cord and in the brain. It can rise from the head and is

*Alternatively, the human form prostrate before the seated giant may be the man bowing before a material deity of whom AE spoke to O'Leary Curtis; if so, the figure above this man represents his inner spirit ascending to a higher realm. Curtis also records that the diminutives on the planetary ring are Day pursuing Night, while above the globe a soul is imaged poised between powers of good and evil.[26a]

present in latent form in the aura which surrounds the human body and is perceptible to the visionary. AE drew many figures with such manifestations. Sometimes he was charged with having derived his forms from the head-dresses of American Indians, but he denied this and argued that the Indians were able to see the radiance and honoured their chiefs by adorning them with the likeness of an aura.[29] Pryse had lived with an Indian tribe and was convinced of their spiritual gifts.

The apparent transformation of the One into the multiplicity of the heavenly hosts and the created universe is often represented as the emission of a primal Ray, which divides and redivides to constitute the whole hierarchy of spiritual beings, including the souls of men. This image is a favourite with AE and other Theosophists, who frequently speak of the soul's quest to rediscover its identity with its parent ray and thence climb stage by stage back to the Absolute.

Among the first manifestations of the One in the world of form is a sun associated with the Light of the Logos which is so dazzling that the material sun is only its pale shadow. This heavenly sphere radiates an all-pervading light imperceptible to the physical eye but visible to the seer. Sometimes while lying in the sunshine AE would be caught up in a vision of this light and when he returned to normal consciousness the sun seemed dark.[30]

In Its apparent descent to the lowest plane, the Spirit seems to enter the inanimate, material realm and over long ages to evolve upwards through plants, animals, men, and gods. During the early years of his spiritual awakening AE believed that he saw in vision the emergence of animal forms:

> I saw the trees waving their arms not wind blown but consciously, then two great trees began to writhe knotted arms about each other and at last one was rooted up and flung afar off, but the full life moved in it still and it formed itself into an animal gradually . . . [31]

Much later he explained to Clifford Bax how all earthly life was moving upwards, the human body being the nearest form on the physical plane to the most perfect of all forms, that of the gods (or angelic beings) in the Heaven-world, and they in turn were aspiring still higher and 'trembling on the verge of no form.'[32] H. F. Norman records that AE was intensely aware of the presence of the Spirit in vegetable life and that through deep concentration he attained the power spoken of by Patanjali of comprehending sounds beyond the normal reach of human understanding, in his case the voices of lowly plants. Even his fellow Theosophists were at first astonished: '. . . we asked ourselves: is there indeed a true clairaudience in these heard protestations of the blossoming weeds, or is all this wilful phantasy?' But they themselves came to seek the power of hearing these voices as a goal of their meditation.[33]

In Its descent and return the Spirit passes through different planes. Below the God-world of the Logos (invisible even to the seer) is the Heaven-world, the Gaelic Tirnanogue, the Many-coloured Land or World of Immortal Youth. Between the Heaven-world and the Earth-world is the Mid-world, the Gaelic World of the Waters. It is to the Mid-world and the Heaven-world that AE assigned the visionary beings he saw – sometimes with his eyes closed for they were never perceptible to the bodily senses, though he and other psychics occasionally saw the same figure at the same time and place. He used to distinguish between two races of spirits. When the power of seership first came to him he saw only those he afterwards referred to as shining beings, inhabitants of the Mid-world, of similar stature to men but far more beautiful. These spirits enjoyed an extraordinary purity and freedom from passion, but they seemed also to be without freewill for a motion made by one was made by all and they would bend together to draw life from the fire-fountains. AE identified them with the elementals and with the nymphs and dryads of classical writers. At a later period his vision extended to a higher race consisting of self-luminous beings of the Heaven-world, who were much taller than men and appeared to be rulers in their sphere. When he saw them for the first time he was lying on the sand on the west coast of Ireland:

> Now and then the silvery sound of bells broke on my ear. I saw nothing for a time. Then there was an intensity of light before my eyes like the flashing of sunlight through a crystal. It widened like the opening of a gate and I saw the light was streaming from the heart of a glowing figure. Its body was pervaded with light as if sunfire rather than blood ran through its limbs. Light streams flowed from it. It moved over me along the winds, carrying a harp, and there was a circling of golden hair that swept across the strings. Birds flew about it, and over the brows was a fiery plumage as of wings of outspread flame. On the face was an ecstasy of beauty and immortal youth. There were others, a lordly folk, and they passed by on the wind as if they knew me not or the earth I lived on. When I came back to myself my own world seemed grey and devoid of light though the summer sun was hot upon the sands.[34]

This is a description of Angus Og and the lordly race who were the Tuatha de Danaan, the gods of ancient Ireland. By the time he talked to Evans-Wentz, about 1911, he had seen so many that he no longer identified them with individual deities, but believed only that they were of the same class of beings as the Irish gods and Indian *Devas*. He attributed to them certain characteristics of the latter, holding that they were not immortal, though their lives were much longer than men's, and that anyone who saw them often and thought of them constantly would enter their world after death.[35]

AE's Heaven-world is identical with the Theosophical *Devachan,* the plane of being where the soul, having painfully and temporarily shed its base desires in *Kama-loka,* enjoys the results of its good *Karma* before it is reborn. The dreaded *Kama-loka* is one of the several levels of the psychic realm or Mid-world, and AE once saw for himself what he took to be its horrors, 'not by any folly of spiritualism but by the alert concentrated psyche rising out of the cell of the brain.'[36] Another, the beautiful and alluring faery world of the elementals, appears to be the subject of one of the Ely Place murals. A Theosophical writer points out that AE has painted a delicate arrangement of nature spirits between a majestic *Deva* of the Heaven-world and a human figure seemingly crouched on the surface of our globe.* Appropriately, beside the spirits is a winged angel representing the *Augoeides* or overshadowing daimon of Yeats, the poet of their world. (Dr. Gibbon observes that the name 'W. B. Yeats' beneath this figure is not, as has been supposed, a signature, but is inscribed in block capitals.)[37]

Despite the aethereal loveliness of many elementals, others proved to be sinister or even evil. AE told Evans Wentz that he dreaded contact with those he called water beings, as they seemed to drain away his vitality. One of his disciples records his story of a haunted house, formerly the headquarters of the Hell Fire Club, where he and other writers used to meet early in the 1890's. Soon he became aware of a repulsive spirit, an elemental, which once prevented any of them from climbing a certain stairway. When he challenged it, it thrust him back making him feel the chill of its clammy presence and filling him with loathing by its touch on his hand. One of the writers, apparently Yeats, performed a ritual involving the burning of a chemical mixture which released so foul a smell that even the spirit could not stand it and never returned.[37a]

Though inborn mysticism was the fountainhead of AE's energies and ambitions, the artist's love of colour and form, and the thinker's questioning intellect, formed a part of his complex make-up. These led him to dwell upon his visions, perhaps to the detriment of his progress towards the Spirit, which he recognised as his ultimate goal. 'I often wish,' he wrote to Yeats, 'I had some of your prodigal rich imagination, which makes the fairy world more beautiful than the spiritual,'[38] and in verse he proclaimed:

The Fount of Shadowy Beauty throws

*AE told Curtis that the *Deva* was Brahma rising from a lotus, while the crouching figure stepping from one globe to another represented a cycle in man's spiritual evolution.[36a]

Its magic round us all the night;
What things the heart would be, it sees
And chases them in endless flight . . .
We will not follow in their ways
Nor heed the lure of fay or elf,
But in the ending of our days
Rest in the high Ancestral Self.[39]

The three worlds are not places but spiritual planes superimposed upon one another. Thus AE declares that 'the earth is not at all what the geographers suppose it to be . . . we live like frogs at the bottom of a marsh knowing nothing of that Many-Coloured Earth which is superior to this we know, yet related to it as soul to body' and quoting Plato he proclaims the reality of the Heaven-world with its 'temples wherein the gods do truly dwell . . . '[40] He saw the dwelling places of the Tuatha de Danaan within the solid hills on what he regarded as sacred ground, and during his last years at Pim's he visited such sites as the temple of Angus Og at Newgrange and the coast at Sligo, where he found it easy to see the Gaelic gods.[41]

The threefold division of the visible worlds beneath the fourth, transcendent plane is repeated on many levels. Both mind and matter exist in three conditions or *gunas* – *tamas, rajas,* and *sattva,* or sluggishness, fieryness, and tranquil harmony. The mystic seeks to overcome *tamas* and *rajas* and to rise through *sattva* still higher to reunion with the Absolute. Profoundly interested in the *gunas,* AE discovered a penetrating exposition of them in *The Dream of Ravan,* a philosophical masterpiece of singular literary charm, published serially in the *Dublin University Magazine* from 1853 to 1854. When Weekes refused to republish it,[42] AE persuaded the Theosophical Society to undertake the task, and he introduced the book as a subject of discussion at the Dublin Lodge in 1895.[43]

Human consciousness, too, functions on three planes – waking, dreaming, and dreamless sleep; in the last, the mental faculties are dormant and the inner being flies towards the Absolute, only a thin veil of illusion remaining to separate the individual from God. Dr. Gibbon observes that AE's Dublin Lodge murals include a representation of this nightly resurrection: a Blake-like figure is hunched up in darkness while a radiant, star-crowned being emerges from it with outstretched arms.[44] The fourth and highest state, spirit-waking, is identical with reunion with the Absolute. In its three normal states of consciousness, the mind is borne on three different vehicles, the physical, psychic, and spiritual bodies. Around the pattern of the last, the *Kundalini* eventually fashions the golden and transparent solar body with its many-coloured aura and the initiate is there upon freed from subjection to rebirth. This solar body, said to have been written of by St. Paul[45] and symbolised by the New Jerusalem of the Apocalypse, is related to the *Augoeides*, the direct projection, symbolised by the letters 'AE', of the Spirit or *Atman*. Pryse's description of the psychic body coincides with AE's account of many of the shining beings of his visions,[46] and it is clear that his opalescent self-luminous beings exist in solar bodies.

It is evident from AE's books that a coldly objective psychology or cosmogony was alien to his thought. The central philosophical concepts of *The Secret Doctrine* were not mere abstractions to him. His own poetic names for them constantly recur in his verse and prose, and in *The Candle of Vision* he protests at the way in which modern Christians have robbed their fundamental theological terms of any meaning that the imagination can seize on:

> . . . those who read do not know that the Mighty Mother is that Earth on which they tread and whose holy substance they call common clay; or that the Paraclete is the strength of our being, the power which binds atom to atom and Earth to Heaven: or that the Christos is the Magician of the Beautiful and that it is not only the Architect of the God-world but is that in us which sees beauty, creates beauty, and it is verily wisdom in us and is our deepest self; or that the Father is the fountain of substance and power and wisdom, and that we could not lift an eyelash but that we have our being in Him.[47]

AE's lifelong belief in Madame Blavatsky and *The Secret Doctrine* was the consequence of his visions and spiritual discoveries and was wholly distinct from blind faith. According to Indian tradition spiritual knowledge should not be taken on trust, but should be acquired from three sources, each of which confirms and supplements the others. These are reasoning, the scriptures, and the personal experience of the enquirer. It is held that by following the correct procedures every individual may rediscover for himself the existence of Brahman or God, which is also susceptible to logical proof and is abundantly testified to in the sacred books. When AE came to write *The Candle of Vision* about 1917 he followed all three methods, reasoning on the basis of his own and others' experience, quoting the Old and New Testaments as well as the Upanishads, Shankara, and Plato, and presenting to the reader an account of his own rich inner life. He is least convincing when he attempts to support his position by logic. This is partly because some of the basic concepts which he has to handle, such as that of consciousness, still have no satisfactory scientific definitions, and perhaps partly because his conclusions are so often doctrines of Theosophy, as when he tries to show the need to posit the existence of a body more subtle than the physical to account for our dream experiences. Occasionally, however, his arguments are distinguished by remarkable ingenuity; he ably supports his startling suggestion that all material things are continuously casting off subtle three-dimensional images of themselves into the ether which constitutes the medium of the World Memory. At other times an unmistakably modern note creeps into his exposition. He admits that he does not know whether a single self is responsible for our good and our evil thoughts, and explains that he has never been able to decide whether the mysterious airships of his visions are creations of some entity in his own mind, images of the past in the World Memory, or forms in the eternal mind which will enter the consciousness of future engineers. Mahatma Gandhi's admission that he could not prove that a voice he had heard commanding him to fast was the voice of God, though he himself believed it beyond the possibility of doubt, similarly betrays the influence of the scientific age.[48]

AE was able to absorb philosophy from many books and companions, but Pryse alone could admit him to a kind of spiritual initiation which was made possible by the psychic abilities of both men. Pryse had had other disciples but few of equal aptitude, and sometimes he had resorted to hypnotism to call up visual images before the pupil's inner eye, which was never necessary with AE. He records how when they were together in the evening he would say, 'George, I saw something while meditating the other day,' and AE, without a further clue, would visualize it and make a crayon sketch.[49] Frequently Pryse would hold up images in the Astral Light and his pupil would perceive them. It was in this way that AE first saw the human body in transparent form with the *Chakras,* crest of fire, and flaming wings – manifestations of the Holy Spirit or the Great Breath. By the same method he was shown initiation scenes in which the descent of Spirit deep into matter and the division of the One were reversed in the emergence of the spiritual man from the physical body and the return of the psyche into the Spirit, of the Son into the bosom of the Father. 'A good deal of what he wrote in the Interpretation of the Apocalypse,' he remarked of Pryse, 'he showed me in the "glass" '.[50]

AE's spiritual diary for July 1895 to July 1896 has survived, and much can be discovered about his mystical experiences during and just after Pryse's residence in Dublin. In the later part of 1895 he was preoccupied with initiation scenes, sometimes involving the occult potency of symbols. On 19 July he saw in vision an initiation scene in which the candidate was shown a series of symbols representing the development of the individual from the entirely phallic to a highly spiritual level. Thereupon his hidden eye opened and his solar body rose full of radiance to be reunited with the Divine

Darkness of the One.[51] Visions of this kind appeared to AE continually. The initiations occurred in holy places, which included temples cut out of the living rock and hills become transparent like those inhabited by the Tuatha de Danaan with which he had long been familiar. In such chambers, he held, the ancients had seen 'images of gods and immortals in a clear, immovable and blessed light' – a light known to St. Paul – during the performance of the Mysteries.[52] In *The Candle of Vision* he gives a moving description of a ceremony at which a soul, returned from its pilgrimage in human form, realises its own divinity and, resurrected into the solar body, enters the brotherhood of the Adepts. He believed that to behold such scenes out of antiquity exalted and strengthened the visionary and brought him a certainty of his own immortality, and he told in the *Irish Theosophist* how in the ancient mysteries the initiate returned into the Spirit:

> The poor dead shadow was laid to sleep in forgotten darkness, as the fiery power, mounting from heart to head, went forth in radiance. Not then did it rest . . . The dim worlds dropped behind it, the lights of earth disappeared as it neared the heights of the Immortals. There was One seated on a throne, One dark and bright with ethereal glory. It arose in greeting. The radiant figure laid its head against the breast which grew suddenly golden, and father and son vanished in that which has no place nor name.[53]

Pryse gave AE some help in the interpretation of visions; he explained that certain places which they both saw were sacred cities, *Chakras* on the body of the earth. Indian, American Indian, and Greek figures appeared in the scenes they witnessed, and a member of the red race seemed to be protecting the Dublin hills. After Pryse's return to America, the text of *The Secret Doctrine* helped AE to determine the meaning of what he saw. The fellowship of equals within the Household was also of great importance. The members adopted the practice of communal meditation often used by weaker and less advanced disciples to strengthen their power. About the time of Pryse's departure they evoked visions together and AE noted that the achievement of each member of the group was increased when their individual capacities were thus united.[54]

On Sundays a number of Dublin Theosophists would often spend the day on the nearby mountains – Kilnashee* was a favourite spot. All week, during the spiritually dessicating hours in the office at Pim's, AE longed to return to his true home in nature. On Sunday morning he would set off to walk to the hills, gradually casting aside his worldly cares and fears as the hope grew that the veil which hid

*Mentioned in the article cited in note 55, but perhaps an error for Kilmasheogue.

the secret life within the earth would again be lifted.[55] In the evening he used to return to attend the meeting of the Esoteric Section, of which Frederick Dick, Violet North and Daniel Dunlop were also members. Although Madame Blavatsky only revealed to the public the preparatory and purificatory aspect of the Section's work, phenomena often occurred at these meetings; AE and his friends frequently heard spiritual sounds and once a head ascended from the floor.[56]

Late in 1895 Judge became seriously ill and in December Pryse returned to the U.S.A. to conduct the affairs of the Theosophical Society. He was forced to leave incomplete his initiation of AE into the Lesser Mysteries, which involve moral purification and the awakening of the psychic (though not the higher, spiritual) faculties, leading the disciple to a perception of the hidden forces within the material forms of nature.[57] This introductory training is the first of a series of initiations culminating in the birth of the solar body. AE looked forward to a more fruitful resumption of their work together when they returned to earth in a future life.[58]

Judge died on 21 March, 1896. For the members of the Dublin Lodge, a misunderstood hero, martyred and crucified, had completed the labours for which he had taken incarnation. AE refused to sorrow but urged his companions to persist in their spiritual endeavours in full confidence that other leaders would appear to guide them. Simultaneously he warned against the danger of depending on teachers or on the Masters instead of on one's own efforts and one's faith in the Absolute – 'the One whose love a fiery breath never ceases';[59] he was to spend more than a third of his life trying to persuade Irish farmers of the virtue of self-reliance.

Meanwhile the Theosophical Society in America sought a successor to Judge. Mrs. Katherine Tingley, a former Spiritualist medium who had recently won his confidence, quickly gathered support. Having been appointed Head of the Esoteric Section she embarked on a world lecture tour and proved a formidable rival to Annie Besant. At the Second Annual Convention of the Theosophical Society in Europe, held in the Antient Concert Rooms in Dublin at the beginning of August, she received a standing ovation when she was declared Corresponding Secretary, an office which had once been occupied by Madame Blavatsky herself. AE, who conceived a fervent though not a lasting admiration for Mrs. Tingley,[60] and his friend Dick were nominated International Representatives for Ireland.[61]

One of the results of Pryse's instruction was the enrichment of the complex symbolism of AE's poetry. Many of the recurrent images and phrases which seem to be used vaguely and even carelessly have in fact precise Theosophical meanings, though these can be only partly elucidated as some of the teachings involved are not made public. In particular there is an unpublished scheme of forty-nine colours which represent the powers emanating from the Logos – the first Ray divides into seven subsidiary rays and these again each divide seven times. According to Pryse, these powers were symbolised in the classical period by forty-eight constellations together with the solar system, so that the unfallen or redeemed man, who was free from a physical body and possessed them all, is called the Starry King.[62] AE uses this phrase as well as others based on the same symbolism:

Elate for freedom leaps the starry power,
The life which passes mourns its wasted hour.[63]

They saw through the dream-world under
Its heart of rainbow flame
Where the starry people wander;
Like gods they went and came.[64]

The rainbow, embracing the seven colours of the spectrum, represents the powers collectively, as does opal, which usually indicates in AE's poems the appearance or proximity of the gods who dwell in the heaven-world in their radiant solar bodies, the self-luminous beings of his visions:

From the misty mountain under
Shot gleams of an opal star;
Its pathways of rainbow wonder
Rayed to their feet from afar . . .

The lights were coming and going
In many a shining strand,
For the opal fire-kings were blowing
The darkness out of the land.[65]

The manifestation of spiritual powers is also represented by diamond-like brilliance:

I close mine eyes from dream to be
The Diamond-rayed again,
As in the ancient hours ere we
Forgot ourselves to men.[66]

Silver and gold, according to Pryse, symbolise respectively the psychic and spiritual powers, which are awakened in this order:

As his way he upward wings
From all time-encircled things,
Flames the glory round his head
Like a bird with wings outspread
Gold and silver plumes at rest . . .[67]

The image of a gloriously feathered bird is one of AE's favourite symbols for the manifestation of the Light of the Logos. At certain favourable times he was aware of this not only in men and in the earth, but in the atmosphere:

The bird of aether its flaming pinions
Waves over earth the whole night long . . .[68]

AE's poetry is often concerned with the hindrances and temptations which are apt to distract the mystic from his quest. These are likely to centre on the psychic plane with its passionate emotions (as distinct from bodily desires) and its fascinating astral visions. The psychic world is often represented by red, the colour of Dana, in AE's view the Celtic name for the Archaeus or Mighty Mother, who becomes in her infernal aspect a temptress casting a glamour over evil things:

This is the red, red region
Your heart must journey through:
Your pains will here be legion
And joy be death for you.[69]

In spite of the influx of Theosophical and Celtic symbolism, AE's poetry continued to vary greatly in merit; the arcane significance of an image does not necessarily justify its continual recurrence. A case in point is the persistence of descriptions of sunrise and sunset in which AE dwells on the sapphire, amethyst, and other colours which flood the sky. Dawn and twilight are traditionally considered favourable times for concentration and meditation as the tranquillity of the atmosphere tends to still the mind's natural restlessness, and the colours named symbolise the spiritual powers or qualities associated with the turning points of the daily cycle. This technical significance notwithstanding, the verses rarely communicate the power and inward peace of which the poet was undoubtedly conscious.

With the rise of his Celtic interests in 1895, a new note entered into AE's prose writings. Pondering the significance of the Druid initiations in which he believed, he began to urge the readers of the *Irish Theosophist* to recognise and reclaim their forgotten godhood. Abstract philosophy, he insisted, even the philosophy of Madame Blavatsky, will not transform the mortal into the immortal:

> We read too much . . . We follow the trail of the *Monad*, but often it is only in the pages of *The Secret Doctrine*. And we talk much of *Atma, Buddhi* and *Manas* . . . We would compel the Gods to fall in with our philosophy rather than trust in the heavenly guidance. We make diagrams of them . . . We have not comprehended the meaning of the voice which cried, 'Prepare ye the way of the Lord,' or this, 'Lift up your heads, O ye gates.

Be ye lifted up, ye everlasting doors, and the King of Glory shall come in.'[70]

By the beginning of 1896 AE had begun to publish poems which reflected his preoccupation with the ancient Druidic Mysteries. He believed that there was a direct connection between times so ancient that no secular historian had knowledge of them, and a long awaited apocalyptic event that was about to astonish the world. Late in the previous year he and Pryse had collaborated in retelling the story of the seduction of the Gaelic hero Cuchulain by the goddess Fand. According to their version of the tale, which appeared in the *Irish Theosophist,*[71] both the people of Cuchulain and the Tuatha de Danaan had come to Ireland from an unnamed land which is clearly Atlantis, and they had brought with them spiritual powers to enrich their new home, a country destined to be the scene of a great revelation. AE, as his diary shows,[72] connected the story with messianic hopes, and these in turn he must have associated with Madame Blavatsky's claim of 1888 that the first cycle of the present Kali Yuga or Iron Age, comprising five millenia, would come to an end in about nine years, and that a great prophecy involving a squaring of accounts between the races would thereupon be fulfilled.[73] Judge, too, had uttered prophecies. He maintained that the spiritual powers which had made Ireland a holy land in the forgotten past would one day reawaken,[74] and in *The Ocean of Theosophy* he had written of two classes of Avatars, divine incarnations of a Ray of the Logos: some, like Rama and Krishna, were rulers and lawgivers as well as spiritual teachers, while others, like Buddha and Jesus, were teachers and mystics. A new Avatar, he had foretold, would someday appear, and he would combine the characteristics of both. It was probably in the early months of 1896[75] that AE experienced a vision of overwhelming power which convinced him that these prophecies were about to be fulfilled. It burst into the orderly routine of his existence, letting loose forces which worked beneath the surface of his life and only subsided two or three years later after they had transformed its pattern and direction. He was meditating alone in a small room when the vision came upon him without forewarning, and he found himself below a mountain which he was later able to identify as Ben Bulben. Then, in his own words:

> between heaven and earth over the valley was a vast figure aureoled with light, and it descended from that circle of light and assumed human shape, and stood before me and looked at me. The face of this figure was broad and noble in type, beardless and dark-haired. It was in its breadth akin to the face of the young Napoleon, and I would refer both to a common archetype. This being looked at me and vanished, and was instantly replaced by

another vision, and this second vision was of a woman with a blue cloak around her shoulders, who came into a room and lifted a young child upon her lap, and from all Ireland rays of light converged on that child. Then this disappeared and was on the instant followed by another picture in the series; and here I was brought from Ireland to look on the coronation throne at Westminster, and there sat on it a figure of empire which grew weary and let fall the sceptre from its fingers, and itself then drooped and fell and disappeared from the famous seat. And after that in quick succession came another scene, and a gigantic figure, wild and distraught, beating a drum, stalked up and down, and wherever its feet fell there were sparks and the swirling of flame and black smoke upward as from burning cities. It was like the Red Swineherd of legend which beat men into an insane frenzy; and when that distraught figure vanished I saw the whole of Ireland lit up from mountain to sea, spreading its rays to the heavens as in the vision which Brigid the seeress saw and told to Patrick. All I could make of that sequence was that some child of destiny, around whom the future of Ireland was to pivot, was born then or to be born, and that it was to be an avatar was symbolised by the descent of the first figure from the sky, and that before that high destiny was to be accomplished the power of empire was to be weakened, and there was to be one more tragic episode in Irish history.[76]

By May or June, AE and some of his closest associates in the Dublin Lodge saw themselves as a band of disciples waiting to receive the Celtic Avatar. They believed that a wall of spiritual protection like those which guarded India and Tibet had surrounded Ireland for several centuries, and that some of the Masters were even then in the country. In the mountains they continually saw and heard signs of spiritual powers active in preparation for the great event. On Sunday, 10 May, AE had a vision of Dactyli – semi-divine beings who incarnated in the bodies of less degenerate forerunners of modern man – rising over the landscape to be followed by the presence of nearly a score of Atlantean Cyclopes, whose mystical Divine Eyes, the only part of them visible to him, formed a macabre array over the hills.[77] That night Dick felt that the Master K. H. was present, though unseen, at the meeting of the Esoteric Section. Underground chambers where adepts had carried out initiations in ancient times frequently appeared to AE's inner eye and he believed that an old and powerful Irish centre was about to be revived. On 20 May, while meditating, he saw a tall, archaic figure, and thinking that he might be a Master he determined to watch carefully for his appearance at one of the Society's meetings. Sometimes he saw a blazing star in the centre of a sacred mountain, and the colours purple and green signifying the twofold aspect of the power active in the country streaming from it.[78] (Green represents a combination of the two forces of concentration and diffusion necessary for progression, purple the regal dignity of the King Initiate or man reborn in the solar body.) On 21 May, he wrote 'The Dream of the Children,' a poem which describes some of these phenomena.

AE excitedly shared his hopes and fears concerning the coming Avatar with his friend Yeats. About February he had agreed in a general way that the sun's passage from Pisces to Aquarius in a few years' time would mark the transition from a phallic to a more spiritual age.[79] In June, when he was convinced that the new Incarnation was imminent, he confided to Yeats many of the phenomena recorded in his private diary, despite the latter's break with Madame Blavatsky nearly six years before:

> You remember my writing to you about the awakening of the ancient fires which I knew about. Well, it has been confirmed from other sources and we are likely to publish it. The gods have returned to Erin and have centred themselves in the sacred mountains and blow the fires through the country. They have been seen by several in vision, they will awaken the magical instinct everywhere, and the universal heart of the people will turn to the old druidic beliefs. I note through the country the increased faith in faery things. The bells are heard from the mounds and sounding in the hollows of the mountains. A purple sheen in the inner air, perceptible at times in the light of day, spreads itself over the mountains . . . Furthermore, we were told that . . . a branch of the school for the revival of the ancient mysteries to teach real things would be formed here soon. Out of Ireland will arise a light to transform many ages and peoples . . . I believe profoundly that a new Avatar is about to appear . . . It will be one of the kingly Avatars, who is at once ruler of men and magic sage. I had a vision of him some months ago and will know him if he appears.[80]

About the time that he wrote this, AE claimed in print that the sudden inspiration which then vitalised the Dublin disciples was 'not all due to the abrupt descent into our midst of a new messenger,'[81] for it had been ordained that this should coincide with the beginning of a minor cycle, a period when man's potentiality for developing and communicating spirituality was abnormally heightened. On 2 August, he addressed the Convention of the Theosophical Society in Europe, which was attended by Mrs. Tingley, on the stone to be sent from Killarney to the United States to be incorporated in the fabric of the School building for the revival of the lost Mysteries of antiquity,[82] and from July to October he contributed to the *Irish Theosophist,* besides 'The Dream of the Children,' three other poems, which told how the same boy and girl entered the heart of a sacred mountain, witnessed an initiation, conversed with the Tuatha de Danaan, and returned to ancient Egypt that had been their home in long forgotten lives. 'The Childhood of Apollo,' a prose story of an Avatar in preclassical Greece, followed in November.

AE's fervour of expectation was not sustained for long at this pitch. His hopes for a Messiah who would actually be a 'ruler of men' were succeeded for the time being by a gentler faith in a 'Celtic adept' whom he was 'inclined to regard as the genius of the renaissance in its literary and intellectual aspects,' an adept whom he and others had seen in vision by the middle of 1897, and who was living 'in a little whitewashed cottage' in Donegal or Sligo. 'He is middle-aged.' AE wrote to Yeats, 'has a grey golden beard and hair (more golden than grey), face very delicate and absorbed. Eyes have a curious golden fire in them, broad forehead.'[83]

The dramatic intervention in the course of history that AE felt so sure of did not materialize, but the unforgettable Napoleonic figure haunted his memory in later years. For a few months he continued to write on the theme of avatars and thereafter returned to it at times of crisis. In 1912, when Ireland seemed on the brink of civil war, he wondered whether the prophecy of 1896 was about to be belatedly fulfilled. He admitted in *The Candle of Vision,* written mostly in 1917 as the Sinn Fein movement against England was gathering momentum, that only time would show whether it was indeed prophetic or a mere fantasy, but his early belief was still strong and he was not afraid to declare:

> I only know that I look everywhere in the face of youth, in the aspect of every new notability, hoping before I die to recognise the broad-browed avatar of my vision.[84]

Meanwhile, in 1896, as a result of his belief in an imminent revolutionary change, AE began to interest himself in the public work of preparing his fellow countrymen for the great event. On 28 July, a senior Theosophist told him to do more for the Society, to hold outside meetings with the help of Daniel Dunlop and other members,[85] and towards the end of the year they began an expanded programme of functions away from the Lodge.[86] His efforts were not restricted, however, to the field of formal Theosophy. About this time Yeats was beginning to plan a Celtic occult order on the model of the Golden Dawn, and during the next few years AE gave him considerable help. One of Yeats's colleagues in this enterprise was William Sharp, a Scottish journalist whom AE met in

Dublin in 1897,[87] when he had already begun to admire the books this man had published under the name of Fiona Macleod, books about Gaelic mythology, psychic phenomena, and communion with nature. In the spring of 1896, AE persuaded Yeats to co-operate with him in gathering contributions for a volume of literary essays intended to spread the ideas of the Celtic revival among a wide public. They hoped that Sharp, Standish O'Grady, the poet Lionel Johnson, the Gaelic scholar Douglas Hyde, and John Eglinton would be among the contributors, but after some months it became clear that the plan would not materialise. One of AE's aims had been to promote the preservation of Celtic Ireland from the mediocre materialism of British industrial civilisation, a concern that remained with him for the rest of his life.[88] During the next year he tried to spread his ideas without relying on the help of fellow writers. In January he felt an urge to wander through Ireland on foot addressing the people as he had addressed the crowd of idle strollers at Bray,[89] and Yeats feared for his life at the hands of outraged Christians.[90] Fortunately he adopted the safer method of republishing as pamphlets two essays which first appeared in instalments in the *Irish Theosophist* from January to May.

When AE experienced his overwhelming vision of the Avatar, he was still almost wholly unaware of the political life of Ireland, though the influence of O'Grady and Pryse had led him to anchor his deepest emotions in an image of the Gaelic past reflected in the mirror of Theosophy. The following January, Cardinal Logue forbade John Dillon, one of the group of feuding nationalist leaders who succeeded Parnell, to proceed with his intended political campaign in Louth. AE was revolted at the abject cowardice with which Dillon submitted to this fiat, and to his own surprise he discovered that he had at his command the invective to display his indignation.[91] His later social philosophy is foreshadowed in the pamphlet *The Future of Ireland and the Awakening of the Fires,* in which he contrasts Ireland, the most idealistic country in Europe, a country whose people remain close to nature and the powers behind her veil, with the hell that is industrial England. He hails the advent of the new cycle in which his countrymen will no longer bow in terror at the threats of the priest, but resume their ancient glory and proclaim the divinity of man to nations like Britain, where he who loves his fellows 'must feel as if a knife were entering his heart when he looks at those black centres of boasted prosperity, at factory, smoke and mine, the arid life and spiritual death.'

On philosophical and historical grounds Madame Blavatsky was hostile to the Roman Catholic Church, even though her criticism was tempered by occasional compliments on the archaic Christian symbolism which that Church alone had preserved. Her influence affected even Theosophists as kindly in temperament as AE. In his second pamphlet – *Ideals in Ireland: Priest or Hero?* – he confronted what he believed to be the religious bane of Ireland, and asked his countrymen to dethrone the priest and adore instead the Gaelic hero. An instinctive pacifist, he admitted that the gentleness of Christianity was an admirable antidote to the too warlike spirit of the heroic age, but he lambasted the claim of the priests to condemn to eternal punishment the souls of those who disobeyed them:

> I often doubt if the barbarities in eastern lands which we shudder at are in reality half so cruel, if they mean so much anguish as this threat of after-torture means to those who believe in the power of another to inflict it . . . It is a lie which the all-compassionate Father-Spirit never breathed into the ears of his children, a lie which has been told here century after century with such insistence that half the nation has the manhood cowed out of it.

The future of Ireland, AE proclaimed, lay with the young men in the literary societies, who had the opportunity to disinter the long neglected Gaelic heritage and simultaneously to introduce some of 'the aged thought of the world' into Irish literature and life. Henceforth he made this his own aim as a poet, and though he wrote largely to please himself, he published in the hope of helping to create a blend of spirituality, breadth of culture, and national tradition.[92] The patriotic Irish verse of the earlier part of the century he considered intellectually puerile, though he admired the personal nobility of the writers.[93]

On the publication of *Homeward: Songs by the Way,* Edward Dowden had maintained that it was an error for a European poet to employ the alien names and concepts of Hindu tradition. AE wrote to Dowden explaining that he had made his soul on these and it would now be unnatural to him to do otherwise.[94] In his second collection, *The Earth Breath and Other Poems,* published by John Lane in September 1897, he followed the example of Yeats and Katharine Tynan by advancing from a poetry devoid of any mark of nationality to a poetry that was definitely Irish. His own country had become to him as holy as India, and in *Priest or Hero?* he urged that Christianity, in spite of its spirit of love, must always remain an exotic import since it made sacred the distant land of Palestine instead of the earth beneath the worshipper's feet.

In *The Earth Breath,* AE has branched out adventurously in new directions. The book contains several love lyrics, two sonnets, a duologue, a paraphrase of the beginning of St. John's Gospel, and a series of poems much longer and more ambitious than any in *Homeward.* Although he has obviously acquired a serious interest in literature as an art, his general standard of craftsmanship is not as high as in the first volume, and the rhythms, less subtle than before, tend towards monotony. Frank O'Connor blamed the early influence of Nonconformist hymns for this defect of much of AE's verse.[95]

The poet's limitations become clear in the major poems, where he often achieves a striking enough passage only to lapse into triteness shortly after. 'A Vision of Beauty,' for example, is a daring attempt to evoke an impression of the material universe springing from the Archaeus and her efforts to draw human souls back to the spiritual heights through the lure of beauty. The strengths and weaknesses of the poem are oddly mingled. A visual contrast of some power –

On the sapphire coast of night
Fall the ghostly froth and fringes of the ocean of the light

– is closely followed by such phrases as 'the fairy ring of twilight' and 'the pearly glow,' which make the cosmos seem cosy rather than august. Similarly inadequate is the language of 'The Robing of the King,' a poem with distinct possibilities that remain unrealised. After cleverly bringing together a shrivelled ascetic whose spirit is clothed in rainbow beauty and a worldly monarch whose rainbow glory consists only of his train of followers, AE allows the account of the former's mystical ascent to melt away in the literary vagueness of Theosophical colour symbolism. The most interesting of the longer poems, 'The Fountain of Shadowy Beauty,' tells how the soul rises from the deceptive psychic world of tempting images to the Planetary Spirit, thence to the Logos, and finally to the Absolute. Though the narrative moves at times with satisfying speed – the description of the soul's voyage echoes Coleridge's 'Ancient Mariner,' from which AE has clearly learnt something of story-telling – certain favourite words are grossly overworked: 'dream,' 'dreams,' and 'dreamy' recur eight times, and the epithet 'starry' is applied to four different nouns. A more successful though imperfect attempt to reveal the inner grandeur of man is found in the much shorter title poem. This well constructed piece moves from the mineral through the vegetable and animal planes to man, represented by the humble labourer who discovers his own divinity. The feminine endings of the alternate unrhymed lines impart a pleasing subtlety to the rhythm, and the language, without any disastrous lapses, ranges from the commonplace 'purple plumage' of the woods to the vivid 'dark-lipped furrows,' and from the trite 'night in time' to the dignified 'vestiture of pain.'

The last long poem in the collection, 'The Message of St. John,' is largely free from the verbal chiaroscuro which mars so much of the book. Written in a number of verse forms, it encompasses a variety of tones and viewpoints as the poet tries to evoke the awe appropriate to the event of Creation, offers his own meditations on the evangelist and on the spiritual life, and gives an account of St. John the Baptist embellished with appropriate scorn for the Pharisees blinded by logic and learning. Though 'The Message' contains much good writing, the separate parts are not worked into a unified structure.

In passing from *Homeward* to *The Earth Breath,* the reader enters a distinctively Irish world, where Celtic faery lore has displaced the Indian words and names of the earlier collection. The change, however, does not mark a literary advance, for though AE made it clear in his prose that the 'fairies' which appeared to him were beings of awe-inspiring grandeur, in his verse they often dwindle to mawkish creatures touched by the prettiness of the Celtic twilight. This is most readily seen in 'The Dream of the Children,' which tells how a small boy and girl entered a palace of the Tuatha de Danaan. Such phrases as 'the good people' and 'the faery folk,' intended to represent the child's view of the gods, only diminish the latter, as the simile 'Like the bubbles they blew in their play' depreciates the occult rays from the sacred hills. The poem, which recalls Allingham's lyric 'The Fairies,' gives the impression that the author is writing down to children, and some other pieces in the book have a similar effect, as when in 'Weariness' he describes God as 'an elder brother dear.'

Although the volume taken as a whole leaves the reader weary of dawns and twilights, opal radiance and rainbow hues, it does contain a small number of admirable, even haunting poems. In 'Immortality,' a firm, taut rhythm and a sustained metaphor succinctly convey the substance of the intricate thought, as the relationship between fire and smoke is made to illuminate the distinction between the austere demands of the mystic's life and the alluring but fatal temptation of the artist's. A similar clear and intense focus on a single spiritual truth distinguishes the lucid 'Janus'; a different kind of success is found in 'The Man to the Angel,' which has been much quoted by those who have had the good fortune to know it. In this lucid monologue a man addresses in plain, unaffected language a being of another order on that most baffling of all mysteries, the problem of suffering.

> I have wept a million tears:
> Pure and proud one, where are thine,
> What the gain though all thy years
> In unbroken beauty shine?
>
> All your beauty cannot win
> Truth we learn in pain and sighs:
> You can never enter in

To the circle of the wise.

They are but the slaves of light
Who have never known the gloom,
And between the dark and bright
Willed in freedom their own doom.

Think not in your pureness there,
That our pain but follows sin:
There are fires for those who dare
Seek the throne of might to win.

Pure one, from your pride refrain:
Dark and lost amid the strife
I am myriad years of pain
Nearer to the fount of life.

When defiance fierce is thrown
At the God to whom you bow,
Rest the lips of the Unknown
Tenderest upon my brow.

By early April 1897, when the first instalment of *Priest or Hero?* was about to appear in the *Irish Theosophist,* AE was troubled by an attack of melancholy, which prevented him from setting to work on a long poem.[96] He traced this mood back to Pryse's departure, but probably more important was his discovery that he was not as capable as he had thought of dedicating himself wholly to the spiritual life. Gradually, in spite of himself, he had been falling in love with Violet North, to whom, a few months before, he had given a copy of Yeats's selection from Blake's poems inscribed 'To Violet (Alter Ego) from George, Xmas 96.'[97]

Miss North was a talented and unusual young woman, who was able, when Pryse left Dublin, to take over the task of printing the *Irish Theosophist.* Dr. Gibbon has noticed the merits of her prose contributions to the magazine (under the signature 'Laon')[98] and AE considered that she and Paul Gregan were his most promising literary disciples.[99] She had, too, the power of seeing visions and shared the excitement of the inner circle over the expected Avatar, being able to perceive for herself many of the signs.[100] In lesser matters she was inclined to be independent and she had the courage to smoke when this was not common among ladies. Once she and Gregan sat puffing at churchwardens by the fireplace pretending to be Carlyle and Tennyson.[101]

AE was very slow in admitting his new feelings to himself. He was surprised to find that now, when his perception of the invisible world had become deep and sure, his purely human feelings had begun to reassert themselves and they alone were inspiring his verse. At the beginning his love brought instead of happiness bitter regret and inner conflict. Disregarding the vision which had warned him to avoid romance, he would allow his thoughts to dwell on his newly beloved and suddenly images from past lives would pour into his consciousness. If he sought among these for guidance in his bewilderment, he became only further entangled, for sometimes the psyche would hold up before him the ideal of the celibate and ascetic mystic, and sometimes it would tempt him with the glamour of passion and memories of previous existences in which, as he believed, he had known and loved Violet North.[102]

> Who gave thee such a ruby flaming heart
> And such a pure cold spirit?[103]

he asked, seeing his struggle in terms of an inner crucifixion. At first he fought against temptation and tried to persuade himself that he was only superficially drawn or spiritually attracted and that deep down he had 'passed out of love.'[104] According to his belief the effect of physical beauty should be to awaken the memory of the fallen man and impel him to search for the imperishable beauty of the Spirit, which material objects can only dimly reflect:

> O beauty, as thy heart o'erflows
> In tender yielding unto me,
> A vast desire awakes and grows
> Unto forgetfulness of thee.[105]

A number of poems which AE wrote at this time reflect the struggle through which he was passing. In more than one he bids farewell with sorrow and pity to a woman whom he tries to console with the thought that separately they will be free to pursue their journey to the Spirit, and there, in the fulness of time, they will meet again in Its unchanging unity:

> Love and pity are pleading with me this hour.
> What is this voice that stays me forbidding to yield,
> Offering beauty, love, and immortal power,
> Aeons away in some far-off heavenly field?
>
> Though I obey thee, Immortal, my heart is sore.
> Though love be withdrawn for love it bitterly grieves:
> Pity withheld in the breast makes sorrow more.
> Oh that the heart could feel what the mind believes!
>
> Cease, O love, thy fiery and gentle pleading.
> Soft is thy grief, but in tempest through me it rolls.

Dreamst thou not whither the path is leading
Where the Dark Immortal would shepherd our weeping souls?[106]

It is a measure of the intensity of AE's struggle between the rival claims of human love and the spiritual life, that when he began in old age to re-read the story of Heloise and Abelard, which deals with just such a conflict, he felt a momentary terror lest his long buried emotions return to haunt him.[107] Moreover he feared that not only would marriage make it impossible for him to realise his own highest possibilities, but that it would similarly hold back the development of Violet North.[108] Eventually his human feelings were victorious and he began to write such poems as 'The Faces of Memory' and 'The Secret Love,' in which he triumphantly celebrated their romance. In June 1898, they were married.

Before the wedding took place – or, probably, was even planned – AE made the most important decision of his life. Eighteen ninety-seven was a year of change for the Dublin Theosophists. About January they moved the Lodge to 13, Eustace Street, and according to Eglinton the Household came to an end and AE returned to his parents' home, though it is possible that he may have lived for a while at the new premises. In October, when Dunlop emigrated to America to become Mrs. Tingley's secretary. the *Irish Theosophist* was succeeded by the *Internationalist,* edited jointly by AE in Dublin and H. A. W. Coryn in London. By the autumn, AE felt that the time had come to break away from his well established routine; long afterwards he told Dr. Gibbon that the course of initiation had begun to injure his health, and in his fragmentary reminiscences he wrote: 'None of us I think could have maintained for ever the exaltation as Laotze says nobody can remain for ever standing on tiptoe.'[109] He had decided to leave Pim's, where he was now earning £60 a year, and was considering becoming a full-time writer for the Theosophical Society of America, a role which could hardly have provided him with a secure livelihood, when Yeats recommended that he take up employment of a kind wholly outside his previous experience.[110] Horace Plunkett, the founder of the Irish Agricultural Organisation Society for the promotion of co-operation among Ireland's poverty-stricken and technically backward farmers, was looking for a man who could infuse a visionary fervour into what was essentially a business movement. His interest in all aspects of his country's welfare had brought him into touch with Yeats, the foremost poet of the literary renaissance, and the latter suggested AE, who was at once a poet, a patriot, and a practised speaker, and the most efficient cashier Pim's had ever had the good fortune to employ.[111] Mr Denson reports that Patrick Hannon, an employee of the I.A.O.S., also played some part in recommending him to Plunkett. For a short time AE hesitated, wondering how his disciples in the Lodge would fare during his periods of absence, but on being consulted they promised not to abandon the work of the Society.[112] On 3 November he resigned from Pim's and sixteen days later he was interviewed by Plunkett, who noted his versatility, decided that he would make a successful organiser, and arranged for his initial training.[113]

For seven years AE had devoted his life to the study and practice of mysticism. He had become a fiery zealot convinced that Ireland was about to resume her ancient mission as a source of revelation to the world, and he had challenged the priests who were thwarting her fulfilment of this destiny. Despite his bitterness, he believed that the limitless spiritual power he sought for himself and others should be tempered by the gentleness of a universal compassion. He knew that the greatness of a nation depends on the character of its individual citizens, and seeing his fellow-countrymen cowed and stunted by the misery of extreme poverty, he remembered that man was 'a god in exile.'[114] Though he yearned to travel on the lonely journey back to the Spirit and to guide kindred souls on that path, he was constantly mindful of the example of the Buddha's renunciation and he longed to serve all mankind. In November 1897, he found himself confronted with two alternatives: to expound the teaching of Theosophy to fellow disciples, or to show the ignorant and oppressed how to seek prosperity, dignity, and even beauty. He entered Plunkett's movement and though he was often to wonder that he, a poet and mystic, should be instructing farmers, he knew that he had not made the less noble choice.

IV

A Poet among the Farmers (1897–1905)

From youth to old age, AE's outlook was profoundly romantic. Between his spiritual awakening and his meeting with Plunkett, he found what seemed to him the reality underlying the romantic impulse, which he regarded henceforward as an intuition existing to lead man to the discovery of his own forgotten greatness. During the same period, by studying the subtleties of philosophy, he developed his considerable intellect as a powerful counterbalance to his restless imagination. One major element, however, was still wanting to complete his character: in recommending a new departure, Yeats foresaw that his narrowly Theosophical view of Ireland would be enlarged by a first-hand acquaintance with her farms and country towns and a detailed knowledge of the hard lives of her peasants.

At the end of the nineteenth century, the two great evils which racked the country were poverty and faction. The Great Famine of the later 1840's was still a living memory and large scale emigration had continued since that time, so that the population stood at about half the pre-Famine level of eight million. The bulk of the people worked on the land and tried to make a meagre living by farming inefficiently on tiny, uneconomic holdings. Many of them lived in small cottages and some in one-room mud cabins with a single window. A journey to the nearest small town did little to brighten the peasant's life. Devoid of culture, it had nothing to offer but drab, dirty streets, shops meagrely stocked with a jumble of overpriced, shoddy goods, and the solace of a cheerless public house. In such an environment it is not surprising that so many Irishmen turned to drink and that the publican became a powerful figure in his locality.

The poverty was worst in the overpopulated, infertile areas on the west coast known as congested districts. Here the people lived mainly on potatoes, milk, tea, and flour, and sometimes shared their houses with farm animals, even cattle. The land was usually too full of stones for ploughing and they often eked out a livelihood by part-time fishing, or by working for some months of the year as migrant labourers in Ulster or Britain.

Irish poverty was greatly aggravated by the fierce antagonisms between different sections of the people. While the bulk of the land was owned by a Protestant aristocracy, the descendants of British settlers, most of the tenants, except in Ulster, belonged to the Catholic and Celtic majority that had been Gaelic-speaking as recently as the beginning of the nineteenth century. Many landlords contributed to the impoverishment of the country, as had their families for generations, by spending a large part of their incomes abroad or on imported goods. Often the farmer deliberately avoided making the most of his holding, lest his rent be raised.

Irish politics at this time centred on a question which evoked the fiercest loyalties and hatreds. Despite the long line of Protestant nationalists from Wolfe Tone to Parnell, the division between parties largely coincided with the religious cleavage, though more rigorously in the north-east than elsewhere. Catholics, looking back on centuries of oppression and hunger, felt themselves to be under a colonial regime and longed for an Irish government; Protestants, fearful of violence, of losing their property, or of having their personal liberty curtailed at the whim of the Pope, were ferocious in their insistence on maintaining the Union. Every other political consideration paled beside the question of Union or Home Rule, and as a result the Irish seldom made effective use of such powers as they already possessed and neglected to elect members of Parliament who would work for the economic good of the country. From 1869 to 1903, however, one great reform was implemented by the British Government. Through a series of acts they enabled the tenant farmers to buy their holdings. The Treasury advanced the purchase money to the landlords in cash or stock, and the farmers paid in instalments spread over many decades. At the same time a new element of democracy was introduced when Gerald Balfour, Chief Secretary for Ireland, established local self-government in 1898.

The wealthy Anglo-Irish were strangely divided into those who regarded themselves as essentially British and those who felt that despite their descent they were Irishmen. Horace Plunkett, a younger son of the sixteenth Baron Dunsany and from 1892 to 1900 a Unionist M.P., belonged to the latter class. After a conventional education at Eton and Oxford, he sought relief from tuberculosis in the dry climate of Wyoming. Here, in defiance of his sickly constitution, he endured the physical hardship of the life of a cattle rancher while exercising his business capacity in an attempt to establish a personal fortune. Returning to Ireland on the death of his father in 1889, he inherited considerable wealth and the responsibilities of a leading member of the Dunsany family. Henceforward he devoted his life to the service of his fellow countrymen in the best tradition of his class.

A man of medium height, thin, with a slight stoop and a limp handshake, and lacking any aptitude for public speaking, Plunkett gave an impression of weakness which concealed the extraordinary willpower that accompanied his great compassion. His lifelong altruism was proof against the cruellest disappointment and ingratitude, and although he was a sceptic in religion, it is not hard to see why he and AE should have been mutually attracted. By the time he returned to Ireland, Plunkett was well aware that land reform alone would not make the small farmer prosperous. Not only was the farmer technically backward and a child in financial matters, but the country shopkeeper on whom he depended was so ignorant of sound business methods as to be unable to supply him with his needs at reasonable prices. Accordingly, Plunkett warned that the gombeen man – the moneylender who was usually also a shopkeeper – would replace the landlord, and he recommended the establishment of co-operative stores on the English pattern. Within a few years he became more ambitious, and in 1894 he founded the Irish Agricultural Organisation Society to promote the development of several kinds of co-operative institution – especially the creamery, which operated so successfully in Denmark and Sweden, and the credit bank, which flourished in Germany, Italy, and Russia. He laid particular stress on the virtue of self-help and the importance of keeping politics out of the new societies. 'The more business you introduce into politics,' he told his followers, 'and the less politics you introduce into business, the better for both.'[1] Before long he came to feel that valuable as were the material rewards of co-operation, its greatest benefits were moral. Catholics and Protestants, Nationalists and Unionists were already working harmoniously together in the co-operative societies, and the members were becoming more self-reliant and self-confident and taking a new pride in their country. Plunkett was delighted to discover that the most effective way of persuading the very poorest to participate was to appeal to their sense of patriotism. When Yeats advised AE to join the I.A.O.S., he well understood Plunkett's ideal of national character-building and his hope of dispelling the suspicion that divided Irishman from Irishman.[2]

AE accepted a position under Plunkett fully concurring in his aims and ideals, and determined to work for human brotherhood through the co-operative movement without ever mentioning to the farmers the Theosophical beliefs which were his inspiration.[3] In this way, he was convinced, he would help to make Irishmen ready for the great destiny which awaited them, and of which there had been so many visionary signs during the last year. According to Moore, he would accept only a small salary, claiming that no man deserved more for his labour.[4]

AE's first task was to tour the congested districts in the West addressing meetings and persuading the poor to organise co-operative banks. During his preliminary training, which seems to have taken three or four weeks, he studied the principles and working details of these agricultural credit societies, which were designed to provide the farmer with the cheap credit he needed while waiting for his crops or animals to become saleable. According to the Raiffeisen system adopted by Plunkett, a number of men who trust each other band together to borrow money from a commercial bank on the strength of their joint unlimited liability. They then lend portions of this money to themselves individually at a rate of interest one per cent higher than that charged by the bank. The lynchpin of the credit society is the elected committee, which has the responsibility of accepting or rejecting every application for a loan. Their personal share of the liability in the case of default has a wonderfully steadying effect on the judgment of the committee members, and as each society is confined to a small district in which everyone is mutually acquainted, they have ample opportunity to judge the soundness of each request. The applicant must state how he proposes to use the money to make a profit which will enable him to repay the principal with interest. Only if the committee is convinced that his scheme is sound, does he obtain the loan, but he is allowed sufficient time to carry through his plan before he has to make any repayment. The societies are thoroughly democratic, and, although some members increase the loan capital by depositing their savings at a moderate rate, no one has more than one vote.

AE, already well versed in business methods, mastered these principles without difficulty, and set off for Mayo late in December 1897, at a time when only three credit banks existed in Ireland. The forty-mile journey from Ballina to Belmullet took eight hours and ended only at midnight. Travelling in a jaunting-car – a simple horse-drawn vehicle in which the passengers are exposed to the weather – he suffered grievously from the cold and was miserable except for a short time when a little girl recited poetry and talked of the faeries. He spent the Christmas weekend at Belmullet, where the dreariness of the isolated bogland and the poverty of the people struck him with a peculiar horror.[5] In this state of depression, which may have been aggravated by the death of his mother only two months before, he felt that all his inspiration had deserted him, and he began to wonder whether he would ever write another line of verse.[6] His loneliness, however, was somewhat relieved by the company of local priests, which he often found far more congenial than he had expected.

During the days which followed, AE overcame his terror of public speaking and addressed meetings organised for him by the local clergy. Years later, using the editorial 'we,' he wrote an account of his first formal encounter with the peasants of the West:

> ... we prepared our first co-operative speech with great care, and delivered it with fervour, and, as we believed, eloquence, to an audience of Mayo farmers, and sat down flushed and expectant of many converts. Out of a brooding silence rose the parish priest, who put matters straight. 'What he means to say is, that if any of you want a pound to buy young pigs he can get the loan of it by paying one penny.' And he went on to reduce our eloquence to the simplest English. That was a never to be forgotten lesson. It was that boiling down of our remarks created the society in that district. Never again did we strive to be eloquent when organising...[7]

On 30 December, AE spoke to the existing credit society at Belmullet, which had been founded by Father Hegarty. After talking of the duties that members owed to their bank and the need for investing in machines to spray the potatoes, he told them that the basis of the co-operative movement 'was the divine law of brotherhood, and if each lent a hand to each the industrial redemption of Ireland would be a certainty.'[8] He was cheered by the enthusiasm of the co-operators, and the article he wrote in praise of Father Hegarty appeared in a January issue of the *Irish Homestead,* a weekly journal which existed to support the I.A.O.S. The reports of AE's meetings printed in this paper appear to be his own work.[9]

On New Year's Day, 1898, Father Hegarty introduced him to a meeting at Aughoose, Kilcommon, a place of some beauty, where he induced men hitherto ignorant of credit banks to establish one.[10] Eleven days later, with the help of another priest, he again urged the poor to rely on their own efforts:

> We have been in the habit here in Ireland of appealing to the Government to assist us in any difficulty, and no doubt a great deal can be done by a good Government to push forward the interests of the farmers; but I think the time has come for us here in Ireland to help ourselves.

Having explained how the credit bank could be used to win freedom from the gombeen man or usurer, AE concluded:

> Go slowly, choose your members carefully. Recognise that the prosperity of one is the prosperity of all; and there is no reason why you should not succeed.[11]

On the 14th and 16th of the month, he went on to start a bank at Ballyglass with the assistance of yet another priest and of Major Maurice Moore, the novelist's brother; he even found time to take pleasure in the local folklore. This completed his first tour of duty and he returned to Dublin.[12]

Although he had raised the number of credit societies in the country from three to six and believed the work in itself to be valuable, he remained deeply unhappy and was convinced that he had made a wrong decision. The strain of doing this new work competently prevented him from ever relaxing, and he felt that a second month of lonely hotel life amidst such scenes of misery would completely crush his spirit. Rebuking Yeats for persuading him against his better judgment to accept Plunkett's offer, he roundly declared, 'If ever I can get a job in Dublin at the merest living wage I will take it.'[13] Yeats, greatly alarmed, reassured him that the new work was bound to affect him in much this way, but only at first, and wisely told him how much he would gain as poet and mystic from a knowledge of Ireland's tragic side. To his friend Lady Gregory, Yeats expressed the fear that AE might throw the job over without giving it the adequate trial that would, he was sure, enable him to adjust.[14]

He did not, in fact, give up so easily, and at the end of January, after having been elected Vice-President of the Theosophical Lodge at the annual meeting,[15] he returned to Mayo and plunged again into the round of gatherings and the society of country priests who cared as profoundly for the material as for the spiritual welfare of their parishioners. When he had persuaded a group of farmers to start a bank, he would return a day or two later to advise the committee. He continuously pointed to the fields which could be drained, the stones which could be removed, and the livestock which could be bought if a little money were available, and he hammered away relentlessly at the evil of private moneylending:

> The gombeen-man he believed did a flourishing trade at Attymas. He stopped – how much – a shilling out of every pound. (Voices, 'three and four shillings, sir'). Four shillings, that was infamous. The sooner they got out of his clutches the better.[16]

At Lahardane two of these gentlemen had the pleasure of attending a meeting where their business methods were discussed.[17]

AE was entering into his work with a definite zest. Slowly, as had been the case to some extent at Pim's, the new role was beginning to feel less like a straitjacket held in place by force of circumstance. Early in February he wrote to Lady Gregory:

> I notice with amusement that I have the materials for a mob orator somewhere about me, and can now stand up and face a crowd of five hundred people without my heart being somewhere in the toe of my boots.[18]

He was enjoying collecting folklore and meeting unsophisticated peasants who, like himself, could see the faery race. When a handsome old farmer named Caden More told him how in his youth he had spent a night in their palace underneath Mount Nephin, and how he had once seen Queen Maev, whom he called 'the Beauty of all beauty,' AE was inspired to write his lilting poem 'The Gates of Dreamland.'[19] Occasionally he encountered a comic incident: a man asked for a loan from a credit bank to buy a suit and when the committee pointed out that this was not productive, he explained that it would result in his marrying a girl who owned two acres, a pig, and twenty-five pounds.[20]

During February, AE extended his field of operation to Galway, and once, having a single day in Dublin, spent it trying to see his sick father.[21] When a priest at Rossmuck addressed the farmers in Gaelic, he felt that he was not altogether adequate to his task.[22]

Early in March he returned to the city for a longer period, probably for a spell of office work. During these intervals at home he continued to do his share in the editing of the *Internationalist*. He took a special pride in the poems of Violet North and Paul Gregan, and found it difficult to work with his London co-editor and the Lodge Council, who wanted sectarian propaganda and not a free discussion of spiritual ideas.[23] After he had become an organiser in the congested districts, he himself contributed only two articles. One, 'In the Shadow of the Gods,' declared that the faith of the Druids lived on in the peasant mind under a veneer of Christianity; the other, reflecting his new respect for the courage, endurance, and honesty of the very poor, urged Theosophists to search with the eye of compassion for the divine essence in their fellow men – such perception 'in the heart,' he insisted, was better than 'all the story of human thought and its philosophies in the brain,' for the mind 'overweighted with a cumbrous metaphysic grows cold and chill and grey . . .'[24]

More than a decade later, when he was editing the *Homestead,* he described the change that had come over him at this time:

> The editor of this paper in his youth stuffed his soul up with lofty ideals, and read all the sages and dreamed over again all the great dreams. He felt quite happy with his wisdom in the towns among other people who were doing the same thing, but when he went into the country districts and mixed with congested farmers and simple country people, he always felt humiliated, because these country people most often did quite simply without thinking they were doing anything fine at all most of the good deeds and kindnesses to each other which it needed whole eloquent perorations and exhortations to induce people to do in towns.[25]

AE's March visit to Dublin was marked by an event of great importance. After Judge's death, he had joined the large number of his followers who gave their allegiance to Mrs. Tingley, but he lost his admiration for her when they corresponded about one of his articles of which she disapproved.[26] This month he resigned from the association which she headed, the Universal Brotherhood and Theosophical Society. The stumbling block seems to have been her implied insistence on the doctrine of hierarchies, the belief that the spiritual advancement of an individual could be objectively determined and that he should be given the rank and authority appropriate to it.[27] For the members of what had been the Dublin Lodge, AE soon afterwards founded the Hermetic Society (not to be confused with its namesake of 1885), a loosely organised group which met weekly for the study of Madame Blavatsky's teachings and certain mystical classics.

After striking out for spiritual democracy, AE travelled to Donegal and by 21 March was hard at work trying to instil the principles of economic democracy into the victims of the landlords and the gombeen men. About a week later he was summoned from the town of Killybegs to give evidence to a Parliamentary Committee in London on the practice of moneylending in the congested districts. He was rigorously cross-examined by the members, who would have no truck with hearsay:

> Never mind being 'informed.' Can you, from your own knowledge, speak of any case in any part of Ireland where the old gombeen system is carried on?[28]

His answers to this and other questions displayed a thorough knowledge of the wiles of the exploiters and reflected his faith in the Raiffeisen bank. Having taken the opportunity to see Weekes in London,[29] he hurried home to Ireland, and after only four days' absence was back in Killybegs to meet the committee of the society he had started.[30]

AE continued to work in Donegal and was sometimes well rewarded, as when a farmer at Kilmacrennan, learning of the credit bank system, said 'this was the best thing ever heard of in the parish,'[31] and when Father Kelly, the parish priest at Ardara, invited Mr. Lyons, the Methodist minister, to help in the selection of a committee.[32] Ten years later, recalling his first visit to the county, he wrote: 'Everywhere we went along the sea board we heard of truck and gombeen, and we thought "What a lovely country for co-operation!"'[33] Fits of depression, however, still troubled him from time to time, and he began to think that any person of moderate abilities could perform his present task. Usually he felt unable to write, and he gave up editing the *Internationalist*. The parish priests of the West, though admirable in their devotion to their parishioners, were seldom intellectually stimulating, and it was a distinct relief when he had an opportunity to dine with Bishop O'Donnell and try to provoke him into a friendly theological argument. He even thought of leaving the I.A.O.S. and travelling on foot through America, the land of Whitman and Emerson, as he had longed to do ten years before.[34]

In May, he worked in Galway and Mayo, and at the end of the month he enjoyed several days of congenial company. Parliament had adjourned for Whitsuntide and Plunkett used his holiday to tour the congested districts with AE, who was deeply impressed with the tireless way he went from house to house trying to inspire the farmers with hope and self-confidence.[35] Plunkett, for his part, was fascinated by AE's conversation, and listened with delight to a man who shared his own faith in the Irish character and talked in an intriguing way about mysticism.[36] When he had known him for about a year he wrote to Lady Balfour:

> I have never seen such a natural self-effacement – and this for the service of humanity upon no scheme of compensation here or hereafter. And while he outdreams us all, none of us have as shrewd business judgment or as nice a sense of humour . . .[37]

As early as February, Plunkett had realised that AE's extraordinary abilities fitted him for more than the founding of credit banks,[38] and he now appointed him Assistant Secretary to the Organisation. On 8 June, AE wrote to Lady Gregory that he was no longer an organiser but was helping R. A. Anderson in the Dublin office.*[39] Three days later, he took an hour off work to marry Violet North at the Registry Office.[40] John Hughes, the sculptor, and Arthur Dwyer acted as witnesses, and so little publicity was given to the occasion that when Yeats met the couple a few days later AE casually announced, 'By the way, I may as well tell you we are married!'[41]

Mr. and Mrs. Russell lived temporarily at 10, Grove Terrace, then at 6 Castlewood Avenue, both in Rathmines, and moved at the beginning of November to 28, Upper Mount Pleasant Avenue, in the same suburb.[42] During the next few years AE's home began to become one of the intellectual centres of Dublin, a city which was on the threshold of a period so brilliantly creative that it has already become a legend. As Assistant Secretary he still left headquarters at irregular intervals to attend co-operative meetings in all parts of Ireland, but he spent sufficient time in the city to be active in literary, dramatic, and artistic circles, and to run his Hermetic Society. Like many men of wide interests dedicated to the service of their country, AE refused to allow his home and family to dominate his life. He once remarked that he could not endure any woman, however dear to him, attending to his wants all day long.[43] Mrs. Russell brought up their sons, acted as an attentive hostess, and in 1913 published a book of legends entitled *Heroes of the Dawn*. Certain careless habits of her

*The last meeting held by AE as banks organiser reported in the *Irish Homestead* (28 May, 1898) took place on 20 May.

husband caused her unnecessary trouble, and their younger son tells how, having burnt more than one pocket with a lighted pipe, AE 'could do no more than stand before Mother like a penitent apostle, waving his hands gently and helplessly before her reproaches.'[44] She was justifiably irritated, too, when he insisted on cutting the flowers she had painstakingly grown as ornaments for the garden and ruined her plants in the process.[45]

A few weeks after his marriage, AE received an invitation to stay with Lady Gregory, but was unable to take a holiday immediately.[46] He had been a guest at her estate of Coole at Gort in the south of Galway for a few days at the end of July the previous year, and had announced one evening, 'This life bores me, I am waiting for a higher one.'[47] On subsequent visits he met many eminent people and at mealtimes talked in a characteristic way of his past lives, his visions and the ether in which the memory of all things was preserved. One day he and Yeats walked to a nearby blind corner obstructed by a tree, the site, not surprisingly, of many traffic accidents. Though Yeats saw nothing unusual there, AE returned with a pastel drawing of a crouching, long-armed, gnome-like figure, which, he explained, had withdrawn backwards up the tree on their approach.[48] In due course he was admitted to the select band of Irish writers and artists who were permitted to carve their initials on a certain copper-beech tree, but although he soon fell in love with the beauty of the woods and enjoyed painting the scene and sketching the elementals which appeared to him there, he preferred in these early years to spend his holidays at Rosses Point on the coast of Sligo, where he was able to see the Celtic gods whom he was then much preoccupied in drawing.[49] About this time he fell into the habit of rapidly sketching the landscape in coloured chalk when he found himself in the country with a little free time, but on being advised to try pastels instead, he found these the better medium.[50]

In March 1899, Mrs. Russell bore her first child, and AE, who a few years before had intended to remain celibate, wrote to Yeats in a half serious, half ironic vein: 'I think experience is good. Now like a Brahmin after having begotten a son I retire again into a life of ascetic meditation.'[51] Soon the couple were stricken with grief, for their son died not long after birth. AE had the help of his colleague Patrick Hannon when he sought to comfort his wife, and he seems to have expressed his own sorrow in the poem 'In Memoriam.' As he came from the funeral he met Eglinton at the railway station and could hardly hold back his tears as he explained where he had been.[52]

As AE adjusted to his routine at home and at work, he began to find more time for writing and painting, A month after his marriage he started work on a spiritual story, perhaps akin to 'A Strange

Awakening' or 'The Mystic Night's Entertainment,' which he had published serially in the *Irish Theosophist,* and it was probably in the following year that he experienced in meditation a symbolic waking dream that set his poetic ambition soaring. In a cavern like those anciently set aside for the Mysteries, he saw the Irish gods ruled over by Nuada of the Silver Hand and knew that they represented the divine powers in man that had descended to earth by their own will for a noble purpose but had there been overcome by forgetfulness of their high origin. Nuada, the symbol of the will, alone remembered who he was, and Lugh travelled from the Land of Promise to remind him that he bore the responsibility for the redemption of all the gods.[53] By the autumn of 1899,[54] AE had started to work in his spare time on a long poem entitled 'The Feast of Age' retelling this story in epic style, and next year he published an extract from it under the name 'Dana.'[55] At the beginning of 1904, he was still working on 'The Feast of Age' – now renamed 'Nuada' – and was planning to incorporate it in a book of poems on the lives of such avatars as Apollo, Buddha, and Krishna.*[56] Eventually he abandoned the project, but in old age he took up the unfinished 'Nuada' and refashioned it as 'The House of the Titans.'

AE also worked for his ideals by giving public support to the arts, especially when they seemed likely to nourish the reviving Celtic spirit. About July 1898, he agreed to review new poetry for the *Daily Express,* which had just come under Plunkett's control.[57] Between September 1898 and June 1899, he published a series of articles in this newspaper calling for a revival of Celtic spirituality and chivalry in poetry, drama, art, and political life. His first contribution appealed for assistance for a loan exhibition which would give young Irish artists a brief first-hand acquaintance with examples of fine technique. Other Dublin painters rallied to his support, and when the exhibition was held during the winter it paid its expenses. AE was especially enthusiastic about Millet's genius for portraying the concealed regal dignity of humble peasants.[58] The lack of technical competence seemed to him the great deficiency of Irish artists, and in 1900 he himself was attending the Art School irregularly to maintain his standard of draughtsmanship.[59]

Tireless in his work for art and literature, AE found time during December 1898 to make drawings of the characters in Yeats's play *The Countess Cathleen* for Lady Betty Balfour, wife of the Chief Secretary for Ireland, who was staging a series of tableaux or living pictures representing the various episodes.[60] A few months later he painted a poster to advertise the play itself[61] and teased Yeats by

*The manuscript of the unfinished poem on Apollo, is in Colby College Library, Maine.

publishing an amusing parody of it – his first successful attempt at blank verse – in the *Irish Homestead*.[62] Besides an occasional comic sketch, AE contributed serious articles to this paper when the opportunity arose to illustrate some aspect of what he felt to be the deeper meaning of co-operation. He was delighted to find Tolstoy sharing his conviction that economic problems were 'at their root human problems' and that no material largess could permanently benefit the peasants unless their human dignity were recognised and their faith in themselves made firm.[63]

AE was interested in journalism only when it contributed to some facet of the nation's development. In September 1900 he rashly accepted a position as Dublin correspondent for a London newspaper, but resigned after ten days of time-consuming drudgery.[64] The *Daily Express*, on the other hand, provided a valuable outlet for his growing nationalism, and at the end of 1898 he intervened in a dispute which the cosmopolitan Eglinton and the tradition-loving Yeats were conducting in its columns. The former held that art should be simple in subject and universal in appeal, and that it was now impossible to treat the Gaelic themes in the Gaelic spirit, while Yeats argued for a modern Celtic literature rooted in the country and embellished with an aristocratic craftsmanship, though its audience comprise the few and not the many. AE desired to reconcile his friends and show them that their ideals were not incompatible, but he was in reality on the side of Yeats. At this point Eglinton had to face a fourth opponent in the shape of the philosophical William Larminie, another poet who had rehandled Gaelic myths, and the articles came to an end with AE's ringing tribute to the ideal Ireland of the mind, the only impassioned defence of nationality in the whole controversy.[65]

This literary dispute marked the beginning of AE's thirty years of devotion to the ideal which had inspired Irish rebels through the centuries. He soon came to hope that the Ireland of his dreams would be brought nearer to realisation by the severance of the political bond with the country which had all but obliterated the Gaelic past. When his father died in October 1900, he felt a sudden curiosity about an ancestor who was never mentioned in the family, and he hoped that this man might have been the Thomas Russell who was hanged as a follower of Wolfe Tone.[66]

Three months earlier, AE had entered into a fierce public argument with Fiona Macleod, whose Celticism was too timid to cross the boundary into the political field. Reviewing an essay in which she proclaimed that Gaels should be proud to be British, he delivered a sharp attack:

It is perhaps like a woman to advise a cheap peace between race

> and race, but I think there are times when hate is a nobler feeling than friendship, when we feel, with Whitman, confidence in the revolutionary instinct contrary to all bourgeois ideas of what is fit and right . . .[67]

AE was indignant when Fiona, whom he well knew to be William Sharp, protested at a woman being so unchivalrously treated, and he told Lady Gregory privately that if she repeated the offence he would expose her real identity.[68] In public, he hit back with a little masterpiece of invective when she charged him with violating the divine law of love:

> I confess I read this with some scorn. A number of our rapidly dwindling race have their backs to a wall; they are making a last stand for freedom, for the right to choose their own ideals, to make their own laws, to govern their own lives according to the god-implanted [*sic*] law within them; seeing everywhere, too, the wreck of their hopes, the supremacy of an alien will – to such people striving desperately for a principle which is sacred and eternal Miss MacLeod addresses her moral platitudes.

Attacking the British as he had once attacked the Church, he proclaimed that the beauty of the native traditions was being replaced not by the best in English culture but by 'a moral leprosy, a vulgarity of mind,' and pointed to that awful warning, the life of Britain's industrial masses, a life 'further off from beauty, more remote from spirit, more alien from deity than that led by any people hitherto in the memory of the world.'[69] Within a little more than a year, Fiona Macleod admitted to Yeats that 'she' had been in the wrong.[70]

When Lady Gregory asked AE for a contribution to a collection of essays entitled *Ideals in Ireland,* he amalgamated this open letter with the article 'Nationality and Imperialism' he had published a few months earlier.[71] In this paper, he is groping towards an idea he was later to develop fully, the belief that every culture has its origin in a moment of communion between earth and heaven, and is striving throughout its history to embody the spiritual ideal then communicated. He explains how this ideal manifests itself first in a few great aristocrats and gradually gathers the whole of the people into its embrace. Curiously, in view of his later preoccupation with the economic basis of society, he refuses, as a literary man, to touch on the material advantages and drawbacks of a national or an imperial polity.

AE had to fit his intellectual activities into such spare time as the heavy demands of the I.A.O.S. allowed him. He still made frequent journeys into the country and often worked in the Dublin office till seven o'clock at night.[72] When R. A. Anderson, his immediate superior, was out of the city, he was responsible for the running of the office,[73] and occasionally he took over for a short time as editor of the *Irish Homestead*.[74]

Anderson was one of the dedicated and able idealists who alone made the success of Plunkett's Society possible. In 1889, when he first met the co-operative pioneer, the future Secretary of the I.A.O.S. was a young land-agent with little experience and limited prospects. After his initial surprise, he soon caught Plunkett's enthusiasm, and working in the countryside and in the office he acquired a detailed mastery of business management which eventually enabled him to function as the brain of the nationwide organisation. Although he was more easily angered than Plunkett by unjust treatment or personal hostility, he earned AE's admiration as a man of outstanding capability prepared to sacrifice his worldly interests to work for others. In 1900, for the sake of remaining with the I.A.O.S., he gave up his incontestable right to the secretaryship of the new Department of Agriculture, although acceptance would have tripled his salary.

In AE, Plunkett discovered a prophet, and in Anderson an administrator; Father Finlay, an organiser and educator, completed the triumvirate of his principal officers. This plump, bright-eyed Jesuit, a lecturer in economics at University College, Dublin, combined an incisive academic mind with a simple, straightforward manner of speech that enabled him to arouse real enthusiasm even in an apathetic audience. Though he was an enemy of Yeats's mysticism, AE did not resent this, realising that his principles made it inevitable,[75] while Father Finlay, as a co-operator and a Christian, could not but admire the moral idealism on which AE's life was founded.[76]

Another important colleague of AE was T. P. Gill, whom Plunkett appointed editor of the *Daily Express*. Gill was an unusually versatile man and an able journalist, but although he made an entertaining and charming companion a certain deviousness in his character eventually led such men as Plunkett and Anderson to distrust him, especially after he became a thoroughgoing bureaucrat. On one occasion AE tried, perhaps not very seriously, to make him see a vision, so that he might gain some understanding of the new literary movement,[77] and when asked to characterise him he suggested that one of his mottoes ought to be 'The means are more important than the end.'[78]

Lady Gregory approved of AE's new career, and when he first visited Coole after becoming an organiser she thought he seemed happier than before. He, however, disagreed and expressed his regret at having returned into life, which he had renounced as a member of the Household – he even looked back with a certain nostalgia on Pim's, where he had discovered five mystics among his colleagues[79] – but his correspondence shows that such feelings represented only a passing mood. Moreover, at least two Theosophists followed him into the I.O.A.S.: his disciple Paul Gregan succeeded him as banks organiser, and in August 1900, H.F. Norman was appointed editor of the *Irish Homestead*.[80]

When he himself became editor, AE often referred to his personal knowledge of every county in Ireland. Until 1905, he made frequent journeys by bicycle and jaunting-car to address meetings of farmers, and his travels continued to involve considerable hardship. One wet night a small boy led him by the hand over a waterlogged mountain path to attend a meeting in an isolated village.[81] His Theosophical abstention from alcohol – in his younger days he favoured prohibition – made it difficult for him to enjoy the company of other guests at country hotels, and these buildings were in themselves monuments of gloom. A few years later he described one which was obviously built for wealthy gentlemen with retinues of servants:

> The writer certainly felt like a pigmy when, ushered by the light of a very inefficient candle, he was led into an immense and gloomy bedroom. The taper barely showed the distant walls . . . there loomed up in this phantasmal chamber a gigantic bed . . . One approached this monstrous couch with a kind of terror and felt its immense sheets with forebodings of dampness, which were amply justified. One . . . lay there through the long darkness of the night waiting the dawn and rheumatism.[82]

In the poorer districts the meals were extremely monotonous. Describing his diet during five days spent at the best hotel in a western town, he wrote:

> . . . we received no other food except the saltest of salt American bacon with eggs and potatoes . . . We can still see the salt in that bacon through the mist of years shining like frost on the ground, and we can remember the consuming thirst it engendered.[83]

Although AE was notorious for his Yogi-like indifference to good cooking – Mr. Diarmuid Russell remembers his father's habitual unawareness of what he was eating – he did notice an extreme monotony in his diet or, conversely, the deliciousness of such simple country foods as the cockle soup and home-baked bread of Donegal.[84]

During his travels, AE acquired a wide experience of the living conditions, backwardness, and unbusinesslike habits of the Irish poor, as well as their many fine and human qualities. When he visited the Connemara Islands in June 1899, he saw 'houses that were not houses, only some branches leaning against a rock covered with sods,'[85] and he afterwards wrote a vivid description of some of the worst dwellings in the country:

> We knew these unsanitary old cabins. We stood in some of them where we were up to our ankles in animal refuse, where cow and calf and poultry lived with human beings, and an indescribable foetid odour, laden with typhoid germs, pervaded the place, and people made in God's image . . . could lift themselves heavenward no more than the worm.[86]

At the end of 1898, to Yeats's amazement, AE was already drawing up a plan of his own for the congested districts, which roused the enthusiasm of Gerald Balfour, the Chief Secretary for Ireland. A year later he delivered a long lecture on the subject in which he advocated the introduction of co-operative organisations to enable the farmers to borrow cheaply, to buy their raw materials at wholesale prices, to sell their products profitably, and to rent or purchase grazing land jointly. This, he urged, was as essential as land reform, though he was in no way insensitive to the need for larger holdings and security of tenure: in the spring of 1899, he devised a scheme whereby tenants evicted during a recent campaign against the landlords could return to their homes without prejudice to the case of either party, and he himself led the committee which implemented the plan.[87]

AE's greatest strength as an organiser lay in his power to make the poor and uneducated share his dream of a community where each man by working for himself would work for all. In 1908 H. F. Norman, hearing him address a meeting of about forty farmers in County Cavan, observed

> the spare figure bent above a listening audience, to whom listening seems indeed an unwonted activity . . . As he diagnose[s] for them their common economic infirmity, patiently and simply expounding the technique of the remedy, his face is grave and taut. There is more flexibility in the sensitive, mobile hands that clasp and unclasp nervously, and no less eloquently than the lips which deliver their message; eloquent the message but never rhetorical, though now, at the close, as his voice ascends into its treble notes, he is appealing to these rough handed, dark visaged, sombre, realistic, unprosperous men of the spade and hoe to think rather of each other and of their mutual hopes and difficulties than of their own several toils and needs . . . the audience sits tense, rapt, elevated. His dream of brotherhood descends on them. They rise to it. When he ends, there is a relief of emotional tension, an intake of deep breath, such as follows the close of a big symphony.

Such occasions were not forgotten and long afterwards farmers who had been in the audience would ask Norman with deep emotion,

'... and *do* you know George Russell?'[88] Some peasants once missed the church service on a minor festival to hear AE, and one of them made the excuse, 'Shure, an' wasn't we doin' just as good as to be at Mass, listenin' as we was to Jarge's sermon down to Ballymascanlan?' The priest who told the story concluded by admitting, 'And, in the name of God I think they were.'[89]

'When the editor of this paper organised,' AE wrote in the *Homestead,* 'he looked for a fit human being first of all, and when he found him the society was added unto the list.'[90] He would sometimes rouse the cowed spirits of the gombeen man's victims by narrating the Gaelic legends and reminding them of their ancestors of the heroic age.[91] Early in his new career he learned from Father Hegarty the error of demoralising them further by outright gifts of money. The poor clustered round the priest's door and he heard one say, 'The white sun in heaven does not look down on poorer people than this man and myself.'[92] His worst failure as an organiser came in a district in Mayo where the Parish Committee had paid farmers to work their own holdings. After his talk, the audience grumbled, 'Yerra, he's brought no money with him after all,' and when he showed a man how easily he could drain a swamp in his field, he was nonplussed by the question: 'And who's to pay me for working at it?'[93]

Not every priest was as acute as Father Hegarty. AE always insisted that newcomers to co-operation must begin by handling very small sums, and when a clergyman lost interest in a projected credit bank because a large capital was not to be provided, he retorted that to despise the society for that reason was like withholding help from one man because it could not be given to others in need.[94]

Such initial caution was essential, for the farmers whom AE was working with were often men who had no idea that credit should be used to make a profit; in the congested districts they did not understand the meaning of a percentage. The organisers had to supervise the running of the banks very closely, teaching the secretaries how every kind of entry should be made, introducing elderly men to new ideas, and insisting on the importance of punctual repayment of loans and scrupulous observance of the rules. After some experience, the societies were able to borrow and lend on a larger scale, and AE was delighted at the way in which the committee members rapidly acquired businesslike habits and learnt to recognise when money was being wasted.[95]

Many obstacles arose from beliefs and customs long established in remote districts. In some places farmers refused to spray their potatoes because 'It was the will of God to send the blight and so – '[96]

With a similar excess of piety, families who shared their homes with cattle maintained that it was good for the cows to be with the Christians.[97] Even Caden More, who had visited the faery palace under Mount Nephin, disturbed AE in one way: he attributed the deaths of his pigs to their sty being in the way of the fairies[98] – confusing, as the mystic must have believed, life on the physical plane with existence in the mid- or heaven-world. Less exotic was the sheer stupidity which could eventually enrage even the most patient. Several times AE told the story of his encounter with a woman who could not be persuaded to continue selling her eggs to her co-operative society when the local dealer was trying to destroy it by temporarily offering high prices:

> 'The society raised prices when it started, did it not?' 'Yes.' 'Well, why don't you stick to it?' 'The others offer more now.' 'If your society broke up, don't you think the prices would fall back as before?' 'Let it pay more now and I will give the eggs.' . . . After trying in vain to make this woman see the position, for the only time in our life, so far as we can remember, we felt a passionate desire to remove mental obstruction by physical means.[99]

There is little evidence as to how AE's social philosophy was developing while he contended with the day-to-day difficulties of organising, though an article which he published in 1902 reflects his excitement at the way in which participation in a co-operative society enlarged the outlook of the members:

> The I.A.O.S. organiser . . . never leaves the Irish farmer the parochial being he was before. An uneasiness is implanted in the rural mind, and a sense of the vastness of the economic battle of the world in which he is called to take a part for his own sake and for the sake of his country . . . The farmer becomes the 'economic man'; that is, he is determined to oust the Dane or the Canadian or the Siberian, who, greatly daring, have ventured to invade his market while he slept.[100]

During his early years in the I.A.O.S., AE's family had been growing. In 1900 a second child was born to him and was named Brian after the infant who had died. He was once delighted to see beautiful visionary serpents gazing on the boy in his cot,[101] and in his letters to Lady Gregory he made playful comments on his son's antics. Referring to the child's obstinate attempts to penetrate the press containing his paints and papers, he jokingly proposed to set a fearsome-looking elemental to guard it, and drawing a grotesque sketch of the spirit he wondered whether his omnivorous offspring could devour even this. When the baby was a few months old, he wrote:

> The boy continues in a state of hilarity, rolling on his head,

> banging things about – including his parents, eating the indigestible, and pursuing the invisible.[102]

He decided to learn Gaelic to fulfil his duty as a parent[103] and began to take lessons from the writer T. W. Rolleston, but it was not long before the latter left the country and he never found another teacher. Feeling that he could learn a language only by adjusting his ear to the rhythms of its poetry, he had already fixed permanently in his memory some passages of Irish verse.[104]

In April 1900, the family moved to 25 Coulson Avenue, in the suburb of Rathgar, where a daughter was born about the beginning of July 1901, and AE was glad that his son would have a sister. The new baby fell ill but seemed to be recovering when her parents took her to Kilternan, outside Dublin. By the middle of August she had died, and Alice Milligan, the poetess, who had first met AE at the Lodge in Ely Place, helped to console Mrs. Russell.[105] The family's last child was born in November 1902 and was given the Irish name of Diarmuid. One night in December 1906, he woke suddenly in fear of a bright light; his father had just had a remarkable dream in which a golden triangle had formed over a mountain peak and from it an immense hand had reached out towards him.[106]

In Coulson Avenue, the Russells' next door neighbour was Maud Gonne, the fiery and beautiful nationalist who was courted by Yeats for fourteen years but refused to marry him. Another woman patriot – Constance Markievicz – and her Polish husband lived nearby. The actress Maire Nic Shiubhlaigh recalls the Sunday night At Homes in AE's 'little cottage-style house,' occasions 'combining somehow the functions of a learned debate and a pleasant social evening.'

> One discussed [she continues] the work of new writers, analysed the work of established ones. Many a young man, introduced to literature in the Russell drawing-room, has since made his mark as a writer. Distinguished men of letters mingled with the literary-minded clerks and shop assistants near the little fireplace and first manuscripts frequently changed hands for publication.[107]

There were signs, too, of AE's interest in the invisible world: in the corners of the room the brown wallpaper was adorned with his paintings of fairies and gods,[108] and he would talk at times of expanded states of consciousness. His weekly gathering was one of the nuclei of a local renaissance.

As Ireland entered the Edwardian age, Dublin became the focus of a cultural and economic revival, which, drawing deeply on the Celtic past, seemed to promise a renewal of the nation's long lost greatness. In 1893 Douglas Hyde, a Protestant in love with the native tradition, founded the Gaelic League to preserve the Irish language and customs against the advancing English culture which threatened to submerge them. Four years later other patriots started the Feis Ceoil, an Irish music festival. Plunkett regarded his self-help movement as complementary to the Gaelic League, and AE traced the history of co-operation in Ireland back to the economic system of the ancient clans. James Connolly, the political theorist, and James Larkin, the labour leader, combined their socialism with nationalism, and although the Home Rule movement had stagnated since the death of Parnell, a young journalist named Arthur Griffith laid the seed of its revival, tirelessly propounding his theory that the Act of Union was illegal and that the Sovereign was bound by law to rule his Irish kingdom through an Irish parliament. From the rediscovered bardic literature and an acquaintance with peasant life, authors and dramatists drew the inspiration which enabled them to create a great Irish literature in English and to evolve a theatre which captured the attention of the world. George Moore, returning from abroad to take up residence in Dublin, brought a cosmopolitan touch to its culture, while James Joyce, an impoverished youth of genius, was imprinting every detail of the city on his memory. The fine arts flourished in the studios of the painter Nathaniel Hone and the sculptor John Hughes, while Jack Yeats, the poet's brother, devoted brush and pencil to the characters of the unanglicized West. Sarah Purser revived the craft of stained glass, and at the Dun Emer Press the daughters of the Yeats family printed books that were themselves works of art. In a city of eccentrics, Oliver Gogarty, a practical joker with a ribald wit, outshone his contemporaries and reminded his friends of the daredevil bucks of the eighteenth century. Brimming over with energy, the intellectual life of Dublin expressed itself in a revival of the European tradition of the salon. Moore, AE, and other famous men and women held their weekly open house where ideas passed from mind to mind nourishing the embryo of a new Ireland.

AE influenced the young both through his Sunday gatherings and through the Hermetic Society, which many aspiring writers attended. He developed his lifelong habit of searching out and fostering new poets, and when he picked up a provincial newspaper from a remote region of the country, he turned first to the poets' corner to look for signs of an undiscovered genius.[109] His generosity in suggesting ideas, subjects, and plots to other writers was boundless, and he never revealed what he had contributed to their works.[110]

During the first decade of the twentieth century, AE found relaxation and stimulus in the company of George Moore, a man in most respects his opposite. The thin, drooping novelist with a

European culture visited his native land in 1899 and 1900, and a year later moved permanently from London to Dublin not only because he was trying to work up an enthusiasm for the Gaelic League, but also because he detested Britain's part in the Boer War.

Despite his pose as a philanderer and his practical jokes – he insisted on painting his front door green when all the other doors in the street were white – Moore found much congenial company in Dublin. As AE rapidly became his closest literary friend, he marvelled that, 'While we strive after happiness he holds it in his hand . . .'[111] Reluctantly tolerating his ribald side, AE enjoyed Moore's talk of painting, respected the intense willpower with which he struggled to perfect his writing, and laughed at his attempts to be more Irish. He inserted in the *Homestead* an amusing caricature of this enthusiast for a language he did not know. Moore, 'attired as an ancient Gael,' appears to the writer in a vision threatening him with perdition if he fails to learn the sacred speech: 'How can ye ever hope to enter Tir-na-noge unless ye can speak the tongue? Ye will be cast out among the sowlths and thivishes and the Fomors and Phoukas.'[112]

While relishing Moore's anti-clericalism, AE tried to overcome his opacity to mysticism and spiritual belief. 'I think that he wished to be convinced of survival after death,' the poet told Joseph Hone, 'but he asked for evidence that would pass in a police court . . .'[113] Informing Yeats that he intended to 'drive Irish mythology and idealism into him,'[114] he took Moore in the later part of 1900 on a cycling tour round some of the pre-Christian sacred places where he hoped to find material for an article on Celtic mythology.[115] In perfect weather they visited Dowth, Newgrange, and Slievegullion, and AE made several pastel sketches of the landscape and the remains. At Dowth he sat in the inner chamber of the tumulus trying to evoke a vision of the Sidhe, but Moore, enjoying the greenness of the country outside, was unable to prevent the entrance of two most unCeltic clergymen, who put an end to all hopes of psychic experience. They had no better fortune at Newgrange or at Slievegullion. AE interpreted the markings on certain stones to Moore, explaining that the point within three concentric circles represented the earth surrounded by the waters, Tirnanogue, and the infinite Lir. At the inn in Dundalk where they spent the night, the two clergymen who had disturbed them at Dowth were their fellow guests, and over dinner AE retold the Gaelic legends with such ardour that even these unbelievers seemed to be lifted above themselves.

Moore's later account of this episode in *Salve* is misdated and slightly distorted by a delicate undertone of mockery directed at himself more than his friend: he plays around AE like a child bombarding his elder with endless questions. But a letter he wrote to Lady Cunard on his return to Dublin shows that he was in fact seriously impressed by AE's teachings.[116]

The articles on mythology were eventually published in the *United Irishman* in March 1902 and reprinted years later in *The Candle of Vision* under the title 'Celtic Cosmogony.'

The practical side of AE's character astonished Moore and provided him with material for comedy. Early in 1901, when his own attempts at house-hunting proved futile, the mystic not only discovered a perfect home – No. 4, Upper Ely Place, a Georgian residence next to the former Theosophical Lodge – but, while Moore was admiring the marble fireplace and the nearby cottages and garden, he enquired about the condition of the roof and the details of the heating system. Moore settled in comfortably, and for the next ten years AE and other friends came to his Saturday night gatherings where he read from his manuscripts, and acted as a charming and cultured host. In Eglinton's opinion, AE perfected his art as one of the great talkers of Dublin at Moore's salon.

The climax of Moore's public performance in Dublin came in 1903 when, having decided that the Roman Catholic Church was undermining the welfare of the nation, he gave himself the pleasure of publicly converting to Protestantism. A letter to the Archbishop of the Church of Ireland brought the deflating request that he consult his local parish rector. According to Susan Mitchell, Moore (an agnostic) thereupon sought advice from AE, who, dissatisfied with his assumption that Protestant clergymen would not be seriously concerned about his beliefs, protested that he would cause pain to honest ministers. 'But I tell you, Moore,' he expostulated, 'that I know many of these men and they are truly sincere and believe what they preach, and they will ask you to pray, Moore, to go down on your knees, Moore, things you have never done in your life, and you will feel very much out of place.'[117] Moore ignored the warning and after arguing with the rector was able to bring himself to his knees and utter a prayer at the critical moment. Shortly after, when a reviewer referred to him as a Catholic novelist, he wrote to the *Irish Times* protesting that the recent welcome given by the priests to the English King had compelled him to change his religion. Dublin reacted with appropriate laughter.

While AE needed both friendship and opposition from mature writers like Yeats, Moore, and later James Stephens, he also gathered round him a circle of young men and women who were just discovering the pleasure of putting words together. To these poets in the making, he was prophet, schoolmaster, and companion.

In 1897, according to his own not very accurate account, James Cousins, a naive, idealistic young Ulster Protestant for whom the poems in *Homeward: Songs by the Way* were the most important thing in life, moved from Belfast to Dublin. Before long he was taken to AE's salon by the organist in his new church, Thomas Keohler, and he in turn introduced his temperamental Belfast friend George Roberts.[118] A better poet than any of these was the tall, elegant James Starkey, a fanatical book-collector, who published his frail but sometimes exquisite lyrics under the name of Seumas O'Sullivan. Reviewing his verse, AE once paid him the high compliment of inviting readers to study 'a mind that I love.'[119] The most important of his early literary discoveries, however, came in 1902 when he was greatly excited by a poem which appeared in a weekly journal.[120] The writer turned out to be a young railway clerk named Padraic Colum, and AE proceeded to nurture his talent devoutly, for he saw in his work a love of humanity complementary to Yeats's pursuit of beauty and his own preoccupation with ideas.[121] Though eagle-eyed in his search for the slightest sign of merit in a young poet's work, AE was rigorous in pointing out defects and in his insistence that his protégés eliminate carelessness and cliché. 'Work hard, and aim at perfection,' he told them; 'amateurishness is the curse of Ireland.'[122] His love of Seumas O'Sullivan's verse did not prevent him from coming to wish that that poet would sometimes gaze at the solid earth and capture its appearance in words,[123] and he watched almost with bated breath as Colum slowly learned to discipline his imagination.

Quite different was AE's relationship with another young writer, a medical student whom he met one night at Moore's. An argument arose over whether Ireland's round towers predated St. Patrick, and a guest settled it by remarking: 'Of course they were pre-Christian; no parish priest could get through the doorways.' The speaker was Oliver Gogarty – the Buck Mulligan of Joyce's *Ulysses* – in whose wit AE soon encountered unbridled ribaldry and blasphemy inspired, he felt, not by irreverence towards God or life but by the fantasy of a wayward artist. Possessing the daring and genius of a Mercutio, Gogarty became known as an athlete, a surgeon, and the merriest joker in Dublin, and then began to show his astonished friends lyrics at once gay and beautiful. Reading these still underrated poems with their crisp, clear-cut images and Platonic overtones, AE felt that his delight in the author's wild conversation had sprung from a hidden affinity. Gogarty, for his part, conceived a strong affection for AE, who was one of the few illustrious Dubliners to be spared the assaults of his mockery.[124]

One midnight early in August 1902, AE arrived home to find a tall, extraordinarily self-possessed youth waiting on his doorstep and was too kind to turn him away. Their conversation went slowly at first, since the unknown poet, James Joyce, was reluctant to come to the point, but after talking ambiguously about a possible Irish avatar, he loftily explained that he was indifferent to his host's opinion of his poems and proceeded to read them. AE admired their technique but told him, as he was afterwards amused to admit: 'Young man, there is not enough chaos in your mind.'* They discussed Theosophy, which Joyce considered a refuge for renegade Protestants but found intellectually interesting.[125] Writing to Lady Gregory soon after, AE reported of his guest: '. . . he sat with me up to 4 a.m. telling me of the true inwardness of things from his point of view.'[126]

For Joyce, this conversation proved to be the beginning of a valuable acquaintance. AE was somewhat taken aback by his new protégé's arrogance and intellect, but observed acutely that he had an exceptional gift for prose. He tried to smooth his way with Yeats and other potential patrons, and before leaving for Paris at the end of the year Joyce flattered or honoured him by entrusting manuscripts to his safekeeping. James's brother Stanislaus, acting the part of a jealous guardian, took a spiteful dislike to AE, which was doubtless aggravated by James's mistaken assumption that the sage had not troubled to write to Lady Gregory. In 1904, Joyce came back to Dublin and submitted portions of his novel *Stephen Hero* to AE, who admired them and was only briefly annoyed when the author made an obscene effigy with a broom and a pair of ladies' drawers in the deserted rooms of the Hermetic Society. He suggested that Joyce write some simple, inoffensive stories for H. F. Norman's *Irish Homestead,* and this proposal eventually resulted in the masterly collection *Dubliners*. Joyce's return to the Continent with a young woman disturbed AE, but hearing that he had found work as a teacher he felt that regular employment might steady him.[127] Early in their acquaintance, he recognised that this strange youth was different from his contemporaries and was content to help him to find his own way. Joyce's attitude to AE is more difficult to gauge: in *Ulysses* he portrays him superficially as a woolly-minded mystic, but expresses a certain remorse for his ungenerous thoughts since the older man had lent him money when he was in grievous need.

With the less brilliant young people of his immediate circle, AE was on terms of easy intimacy. He played cricket with them,[128] entertained them by drawing caricatures of himself as an agricultural

---

*Ironically, AE's original judgment proved in one sense sound. Joyce produced his works by laborious intellectual synthesis, not by tapping a profound imagination.

organiser,[129] and instructed them in mysticism at his Hermetic Society. In its early days the members of this group met at his home in Upper Mount Pleasant Avenue,[130] but in May 1900 they were able to hire accommodation in Dawson Chambers,[131] a large, decaying building where Charles Weekes had had his publishing office. Here they gathered on Thursday evenings in an austerely furnished, badly lit room, where AE sat behind a table and delivered a lecture on some spiritual theme. Mr. Padraic Colum attended meetings where there were not more than ten people present and AE did most of the talking; he remembers that a copy of *The Secret Doctrine* was kept in the room. Sometimes the poet William Larminie read passages he had translated from the Irish mystical philosopher Johannes Scotus Erigena. The discussions which followed the introductory lecture roamed across the tenuous boundary between literature and mysticism, for AE desired to train poets as well as seers.[132] At times members pinned their verses on the wall, and once AE put up the following comic lines supposed to be spoken by Helen Laird, the Theosophist who became Mrs. Constantine Curran:

I've no exotic deity
Plain God is good enough for me
I wonder, God, if you have heard
Of me. My name is Helen Laird.

I've introduced myself. But you –
I wonder who I'm talking to.
I think of you, and get confused
The Hermits have me so bemused.

My brother Keohler talks to you
As if you were a Keohler too.
With family frankness he will praise
Or damn you up and down your ways.

My brother Starkey is too shy
To live in your society.
He only studies you in rare
Editions of primeval air.

For brother Roberts' view of life
He sees you happy with a wife*
Who minds the house while you're away
Attending business through the day

*Cancelled version: My brother Roberts then will write
Of you as a hermaphrodite

And then again AE my brother,
Croons to you as his mighty mother
While sister Susan's muse declares
You're always stopping love affairs.

My sister Ellie takes of you
A kind of territorial view
An emerald isle I think's her notion
Lying in the Atlantic ocean.

Please, God, this is the only time
I'll ever talk to you in rhyme.**[133]

In the spring of 1904, AE wrote happily to Yeats: 'My hermetists are all beginning to see and hear and I have great hopes of them.'[134] A few months later his group came to an end, and with many of his disciples he joined the Theosophical Society run from Madras. Colonel Olcott issued the charter for the revived Dublin Lodge on 20 October, and the members included Mrs. Russell, Starkey, and Norman.

Protestants and Catholics as well as unattached Theosophists had attended the Hermetic Society. Moore's amusing account of AE cautioning his followers not to be 'too disdainful of the essential worshippers of Iacchus-Iesus, better known in Dublin under the name of Christ . . .'[135] is probably based on fact (the Theosophists did identify Jesus with Dionysus), but the patronising tone was certainly insinuated by the novelist. In view of Madame Blavatsky's hostility to the Christian churches, it is pleasant to be able to record that AE's early fury against the priests was softened by his discovery of the loving care with which the Irish clergy of all denominations ministered to the needs of their poorest parishioners. By nature he was deeply sensitive to the beauty and profundity of the religion which is the basis of European civilisation, and he once admitted that his dislike of Protestantism and Catholicism as he knew them in Ireland had prejudiced him unjustly against the Bible.[136] He admired the Psalms and the Prophets,[137] and his petulant saying that Christianity had a perfect ethic but no psychology or cosmogony[138] is contradicted by his veneration for St. John the Evangelist, St Paul, and Origen.[139] More reasonably, he insisted that Irish Christians had failed to create the works of art or philosophy which would have borne witness to inwardly experienced religion as opposed to dogmatic belief. In fifteen centuries the faith had produced only two spiritual thinkers whom he could respect: the

**Apart from Helen Laird and AE himself, the members referred to are Thomas Keohler, James Starkey, George Roberts, Susan Mitchell, and Ella Young.

mediaeval Catholic Neoplatonist Johannes Scotus Erigena and the Anglo-Irish Protestant Bishop Berkeley.[140] He was convinced that the mantle of prophecy had long ago passed from ecclesiastic to poet, and at the end of his life he proclaimed: 'No Church today can convince me that it is inspired until the words arising from it even in anger break in a storm of beauty on the ear.'[141]

To AE, the national religion of Ireland was the version of Druidism he had reconstructed along Theosophical lines. Explaining his position to his fellow countrymen, he wrote:

> It is true there is One God, whom alone we may worship; but is the nature He has made nobler in men's eyes because they have denied the divinity of His children and their invisible presence on the earth?[142]

To those who knew him, it was obvious that AE was no decadent explorer of spiritual evil, but he, like Yeats, was opposed throughout his life by Catholics lay and clerical who regarded him as the enemy of their faith, and an Irish reviewer of his early essays could find it necessary to observe that his interest was in the heavenly and not the infernal realm.[143]

The revival of Gaelic myth and legend led to an attempt to present the antique heroes on the stage. In January 1899, Yeats, Lady Gregory, and Edward Martyn founded the Irish Literary Theatre to produce drama by Irish writers, and they were soon joined by Moore. Although AE was not a member, he acted as a guarantor[144] and found time to paint a poster for Martyn's play *Maeve*.[145] In July 1901, he published in the *All-Ireland Review* a dramatised version of part of the story of Deirdre as a protest against the degradation of the Gaelic heroes in Moore's and Yeats's play *Diarmuid and Grania;* according to Alice Milligan,[146] it was inspired by some recent tableaux centred on the Irish heroine. The following month he was impressed by a performance of Miss Milligan's *Deliverance of Red Hugh*[147] staged by Frank and William Fay, two well known amateur actors and producers with rising ambitions. The brothers mentioned their desire to produce specifically Irish plays to James Cousins, who showed them the scenes in the *All-Ireland Review* and introduced them to the author.[148] AE readily gave them permission to perform his work and set about writing two more acts. On 2 and 3 January, before the last part was available, a private dress rehearsal of the completed portion was held in George Coffey's garden to celebrate his son's twelfth birthday; AE, taking the part of the hero Naisi, became completely absorbed in his role and once terrified the rest of the cast by crashing his wooden spear on the stage to reinforce his words.[149] For the public production in the spring, the actors obtained the use of St.

Teresa's Temperance Hall, a small and rather uncomfortable room where audiences were distracted by the noise of nearby singing and billiards. Here AE sat and smoked at rehearsals and won the affection of the performers by his friendly interest and wide ranging conversation. Walking back to Rathgar Avenue late at night with William Fay, he talked of Plato and the Indian scriptures, introducing the astonished actor to a world of wonders. In an effort to control the total effect of his play, he spent many evenings designing the costumes and the colour scheme, and together with William Fay he painted the scenery.[150] One Sunday afternoon he was mildly dismayed when they were interrupted at their work by a priest from the attached church who objected to this piece of sabbath-breaking.[151] Pleased by the enthusiastic rehearsals, he asked Yeats to allow his one-act *Cathleen Ni Houlihan* to be staged with *Deirdre*. After much hesitation, and a consultation with Lady Gregory, who had wanted it for the Irish Literary Theatre, Yeats agreed.[152]

AE's *Deirdre* was written in a prose that now seems over literary, but it appealed to contemporary taste as rhythmical and poetic. Deirdre herself was made into a seeress, and the traditionally treacherous nature of King Conor was somewhat softened; but AE portrayed passions rather than characters and, influenced by the Greek tragedies he revered, was chiefly concerned to show men and women of heroic stature trapped in a fate ordained by the gods.

The plays were performed to a packed hall on 2 April, 1902, and the two succeeding nights, and were received with great enthusiasm. Even on the first evening people had to be turned away.[153] *Deirdre* was presented first, and a gauze curtain suspended in front of the stage lent an air of remote grandeur to the scenes conjured up out of ancient legend, while the actors, carefully trained by William Fay – an almost fanatical elocutionist – adopted statue-like poses to pronounce their lines. A thrill of national self-discovery passed through the audience as the name 'Cuchulain' was spoken for the first time in an Irish theatre, and at the end of the play AE himself took the part of the Druid Cathvah and chanted in a way that many never forgot the spell which brought about the catastrophe destined to divide the brotherhood of the Red Branch. A woman in the audience afterwards accused him of sorcery, insisting that he had sent three waves of blackness rolling over the spectators, an effect which, though innocent, seems to have been intentional. When *Cathleen Ni Houlihan* followed, the audience at first took the dialect speech as an indication of humour, but Maude Gonne made an overwhelming impression as the personification of Ireland's soul. Finally, there was a call for the authors, and AE delivered a characteristic speech in which he praised the magnanimity of the ancient heroes declaring: 'Better to perish through an excess of noble trust than to live through the vigilance of suspicion.'[154]

The success of *Deirdre* increased AE's enthusiasm for the theatre and encouraged him to devote his literary and business talents to its development. Alluding to the mystic powers of the human voice, he zealously defended himself against O'Grady's charge that he had degraded the heroes by parading them on the stage.[155] For a while he imagined that he had in him the makings of a dramatist, and he immediately began a play on the Children of Lir[156] and a comedy designed to present Philip Francis Little in an atmosphere of spiritual gaiety as a counter-balance to the crude dramatic portrait on which Moore was then engaged.[157] By May he was planning a tragedy on Cuchulain,[158] and a few months later he decided to treat his favourite subject of Cuchulain and Ferdia in a sequel to *Deirdre*.[159] None of these projects was ever completed and AE's further contribution to the stage took quite a different form.

On the opening night Yeats disliked *Deirdre*, but on seeing it again he changed his mind and on 5 April he wrote to Lady Gregory praising its quiet, dreamlike beauty, much like that of a mural frieze. In the work of the Fays he saw the possibility of a national drama, and a few months later he gave them a rather slight comedy. Early next year, authors and actors came together to establish formally a theatrical association. The actors wanted their favourite – AE – for President, but the latter told them gravely, 'No, Yeats is your man,'[160] and with some difficulty persuaded them to accept his brilliant and unapproachable friend. On 1 February, 1903, the Irish National Theatre Society was formed with Yeats as President, AE, Maud Gonne, and Douglas Hyde as Vice-Presidents, and William Fay as Stage Manager.

While AE had been working for Plunkett, his friendship with Yeats had remained close, and their strong affection had been at the root of such disagreements as arose between them. AE's letters to Yeats's protectress, Lady Gregory, reflect his distress at everything that seemed to distract Yeats from working at the poetry he had been born to write – his pleasure in the foolish quarrels over the centenary celebrations of the rebellion of 1798, his idleness, even his infatuation with the drama. When his friend was staying at Coole, he advised Lady Gregory to make him pay for his meals with a fixed quantity of verse: 'Treat him as the Balearic slingers did their children. No work, no breakfast.'[161] Once he burst out in indignation that Yeats should spend so much time on the Order of the Golden Dawn while leaving his sisters to support his father, but he retracted a week later, as his conscience invariably troubled him when he pronounced judgment on another's duty.[162] In 1902 both men became interested in finding a notation for recording the chant of a speaking voice reciting verse, and AE soon regretted suggesting that an accompaniment on the psaltery might be possible, as Yeats left an instrument with him and expected him to spend time exploring the idea.[163] He found a musician who was able to record his chants using semi- and quarter-tones, and it turned out that, while Yeats had a wide range, he composed all his poems to only two tunes.[164]

AE's interest in drama, as in all the arts, was primarily spiritual; he believed that to produce even an indifferent poem or play was good for the writer's soul. Yeats, who put the art before the artist, despised most of the poets whom AE fostered, and Moore records how, when the wealthy Lord Dunsany proposed to found a literary journal for their benefit, he sneered: 'I hear, Lord Dunsany, that you are going to supply groundsel for AE's canaries.'[165] While AE wanted a small, intimate, democratic theatre where his friends could express themselves – Cousins, Roberts, Colum, and Seumas O'Sullivan were members – Yeats planned to create a great national institution autocratically controlled. The two men became leaders of rival factions in the Theatre Society, and their disagreements gradually led them into a long period of estrangement.

In the autumn of 1902, AE and Maud Gonne ignored Yeats's warning that serious disputes would arise if definite rules were not laid down for the theatre, and the following February AE wrote to him in some trepidation explaining that he had had to draw up a constitution in his absence to prevent the secession of members who were indignant at plays being selected for performance without their being consulted. Yeats accepted the situation with good grace, but was seriously annoyed in the summer when AE defended Cousins' comedy *Sold,* which he considered a worthless play by an untalented writer who should not be encouraged. Another disagreement broke out early in 1904 when the Society, preferring to work in Ireland, refused an invitation to perform at the International Exposition in St. Louis, but several members resigned and went privately having obtained AE's consent to produce his *Deirdre*. Yeats, firmly withholding his own plays from the renegades, accused AE of disloyalty to the Society and urged him to withdraw his permission. The latter, angry at this intrusion into his private affairs, but recognising that his friend and not himself was the dramatist with whom the Society's future lay, resigned his Vice-Presidency to avoid undermining the unity of the theatre. In his formal letter to George Roberts, the Secretary, he explained:

> . . . regarding my literary work, small as it is, as the vehicle of ideas which I believe have a certain human value I am not disposed to restrict their circulation in any way for I feel that if

I did I would be acting contrary to my intuitions of what was right.[166]

About this time Yeats's English admirer Miss Horniman, a fellow member of the Golden Dawn, and devoted to the stage, arranged to hire a building in Dublin at her own expense for the Irish National Theatre Society. They were now able to leave their little hall in Camden Street, which was not sealed off from outside noise, and they opened the famous Abbey Theatre on 27 December, 1904. There was still dissension within the Society: Yeats, Lady Gregory, and their new ally John Synge (an old acquaintance whose genius AE appreciated though he never came to know him well), were arrayed against a crowd of smaller personalities. In August 1905, when the company seemed likely to lapse into chaos, AE again came to the rescue, but this time he was on Yeats's side since he believed that Miss Horniman had intended the new theatre for him. With painstaking efficiency he drew up a new constitution under which the actors would resign their membership to become paid employees and decisions would be made by a reading and a business committee, each consisting of people competent in the appropriate field. He explained that he had only stayed in the Society at the urging of William Fay and that he would resign once the new rules were implemented. The task of persuading the actors to give up their membership in the organisation they had done so much to build also fell to him, and Yeats, confessing to his own tactless and bullying manner, was grateful for AE's help in a situation he could not have handled alone. The scheme was accepted and the Society became a limited company. Most of the actors withdrew from it entirely at the same time as AE, and it became a thoroughly professional organisation. 'In 1905,' wrote Maire Nic Shiubhlaigh, the leading lady, 'when AE left the National Theatre Society, I think it was then, for me, that the Society died.'[167] For some years after these events, Yeats and AE preferred to remain within their separate circles: their differences had come to seem more significant to them than their common aspirations.

Throughout his involvement with the theatre, AE had deplored Yeats's diversion from poetry to drama, and well before his own withdrawal he began to regret having encouraged his protégés to wander into the same barren bypath. Four months after the first production of *Deirdre,* he realised that he himself was no dramatist, and he rejoiced to find that he was writing lyrics again after a lapse of two years.[168] In December 1903 he issued a selection of old and new poems in a limited edition under the title *The Nuts of Knowledge,* and next month he brought out his third regularly published collection, *The Divine Vision and Other Poems.*

While *The Earth Breath* marks no advance on *Homeward: Songs by the Way, The Divine Vision* is a more accomplished volume than *The Earth Breath*. The unsatisfying visual imagery of the earlier volumes, with its over abundance of colour and absence of form, has become much less intrusive as the mystic's austere raptures have ceased to exclude more human emotions. Though still speaking of arcane illuminations, AE now writes also of the pathos and challenge of youth's departure, the sorrow engraved in an Irishwoman's face, and the joy and anguish of romantic love. The trickle of Irishness in *The Earth Breath* has become a flood, and the landscape over which the poet has travelled and his Theosophical interpretation of Celtic mythology contribute major elements to the new collection.

Most of the poems in *The Divine Vision* are short, the only successor to the ambitious pieces in *The Earth Breath* being 'The Feast of Age,' a finer achievement than its forerunners. This re-creation of the experience of candidates in the druidic mysteries is invested with a dignity deriving from the slow, solemn rhythm of its alternate pentameters and dimeters. Through this device, AE conveys a sense of the cosmic calm which enters into the very ecstasy overtaking the initiates as they ascend, together with non-human spirits, to the first emanations from the Deity:

Now while our hearts the ancient quietness
Floods with its tide,
The things of air and fire and height no less
In it abide;
And from their wanderings over sea and shore
They rise as one
Unto the vastness, and with us adore
The midnight sun,
And enter the innumerable All
And shine like gold,
And starlike gleam in the immortal's hall,
The heavenly fold . . .

A similar verse form lends majesty to the title poem, which is in effect an ode to compassion, the crowning virtue that reveals to the mystic the divine nature concealed in his fellow men. With the mastery of rhythm, even the too familiar imagery of vacated heavenly thrones and kings who have forsaken their ancient royalty takes on a new gravity.

More typical of the volume are the shorter lyrics intimately connected with the land. The most beautiful of these is probably the prefatory chant 'When twilight flutters the mountains over,' later renamed 'Breaghy.' The simplicity of the style and structure redeems this treatment of an overworked theme – the awakening of spiritual powers in nature and man at the onset of evening. Mysterious lights appear and the bird of aether waves its plumes, but the visual images are neither overcrowded nor blurred. The language is unpretentious and harmonious; in particular the lightly touched alliteration on the letter 'f' gives an appropriate impression of softness – the softness of hovering flight, not of weakness:

> When twilight flutters the mountains over,
> The faery lights from the earth unfold:
> And over the caves enchanted hover
> The giant heroes and gods of old.
> The bird of aether its flaming pinions
> Waves over earth the whole night long:
> The stars drop down in their blue dominions
> To hymn together their choral song . . .

Unlike this piece, most of the book's lyrics are tinged with melancholy. A notable example is 'The Gates of Dreamland,' which tells of the gods tempting a mortal to enter their palace within a sacred mountain, and which, despite its debt to Yeats's 'Lake Isle of Innisfree,' contrasts most favourably with 'The Dream of the Children' in *The Earth Breath*. Instead of attempting – and failing – to describe the deities directly, AE is content to evoke their presence by dimly glimpsed but distinct images – the silver hand of Nuada, 'glimmering feet of sunshine,' and 'half-open lips of faery.' The chant he puts into their mouths, with its insistence that 'the very sunlight's weary,' is as haunting as the lilt of the whole poem, which depends largely on the anapaest with which each of the long iambic lines begins.

The verbal and sound patterns of many of the other poems are contrived with equal skill, but the language is not always as adequate as that of 'The Gates of Dreamland' and 'The Feast of Age.' The woman of 'In Connemara' is described at first with some exactness, only to be degraded by association with the clichés of 'pearl-dew' and the night's 'purple gloom,' while the fine evocation of desolate bogland early in 'The Voice of the Waters' is succeeded by 'Flame and flood and stars and mountains' tumbling in undistinguished confusion from 'the primal waters.'

Visual imagery is frequently less important in the love poems, which range in quality from the heart-breaking 'Ordeal' already quoted in full,* to the uninspired 'Rest.' 'Remembrance,' one of the most impressive of the series, offers an example of verbal craftsmanship employed to express a complex of personal passions. There

*p. 83 above.

is a calculated repetition of key thoughts, words, and sounds through three stanzas as they move from 'the heart-sweet tide' to 'the heart' that 'was riven' and the 'heart-ache we left behind.' A surging intensity of emotion builds up as remorse is added to love, and faith in the soul's destiny to remorse.

The Divine Vision is the work of a mystic, a lover, and a patriot who is also a conscious literary artist. Although its quality is very uneven, the range of feeling and the pleasing variety of melody and verse form give the book a cumulative charm not to be found in its two forerunners.

In January 1905, AE issued *The Mask of Apollo and Other Stories,* comprising a selection of the tales he had contributed to the *Irish Theosophist* during years of spiritual exaltation that seemed, as the Preface makes clear, far removed indeed from the life he was now living. Perhaps more important to him at this time than his own writings was a little book named *New Songs,* of which he was the editor. Published in March 1904, this anthology consisted of lyrics by eight young poets of his circle – Padraic Colum, Eva Gore-Booth, Thomas Keohler, Alice Milligan, Susan Mitchell, Seumas O'Sullivan, George Roberts, and Ella Young. In his introductory note he explained that the volume was intended as a foretaste of the new poetry now being created in Ireland.

During this period AE began to treat his painting with a new seriousness. In 1902 he was still concentrating on portraits of the Irish gods he saw at Rosses Point, though his project for an exhibition of these in the autumn came to nothing.[169] About the same time he decorated with a pastel mural the room where Yeats's sisters set up their Dun Emer Press, and he drew the symbolic Irish sword with which they adorned *The Nuts of Knowledge,* their second publication. In 1903 he designed two of the tapestries which Lily Yeats wove for Loughrea Cathedral in Galway and mischievously thought of disguising the Celtic gods as angels and archangels so that Christians 'would become worshippers of the Sidhe without knowing it.'[170]

AE seems to have given up oil-painting from the time he left the Art School about 1890 until the turn of the century. In 1904 the flamboyant, pleasure-loving Count Markievicz persuaded him to join himself and his wife in their plans for a public exhibition to be held during the summer.[171] AE was eager to advance the cause of a genuinely Celtic art, but he became very nervous at the thought of exposing his work to the public gaze and would have withdrawn had he felt free to do so. During the spring and summer he painted furiously to be ready for the ordeal, and when the exhibition opened late in August he was pleasantly surprised at the enthusiasm with which complete strangers bought his paintings. He made more than forty sales and as a family man found that his profit of about £160 compensated very adequately for the temporary bareness of his walls.[172] From this time his painting became an important additional source of income. Each summer from 1905 to 1915 he joined other artists to exhibit the unsold portion of his year's work in Dublin, and probably broke off the habit in the end only because full-time painters objected that his desire to bring art to the comparatively poor was interfering with their livelihood.[173] For some years the Markievicz's continued to exhibit with him, and in 1905 he joined with the Count and Countess, Yeats, and other citizens to found the United Arts Club as a social centre for intellectually lively Dubliners.[174]

Having started out as a portrayer of Ireland's invisible inhabitants, AE was gradually turning more and more to landscapes. Painting, the passion of his early youth, was always the activity that gave him the greatest delight: he liked to contrast the beauty of the finished product with the ugly scrawl of his literary manuscripts – 'pure colours and lovely form' with 'blurred and blotted pages, crossed out, interlined, changed and obliterated'[175] – and he devoted his annual holiday to this avocation. For a time he hesitated between Rosses Point in Sligo and Sheep Haven in Donegal as the site of his summer pilgrimage, but by 1904 he had settled for the latter, which already seemed to him 'the spiritual centre of Ireland, and the loveliest place on the face of the earth . . .'[176] Here the roads wind enticingly among the hills and hollows of mountainous, infertile country bordering the Atlantic, and in the sheltered bay overlooked by a steep slope the broad sands of the Haven stretch out in an enormous semi-circle. At the nearby village of Dunfanaghy the local people, unused to the notion of holidays, at first thought of him as an idle young man,[177] but in the troubled times that were later to follow he won the regard of many who were not able to understand him. Once he intervened with the Government to prevent an injustice to a state employee;[178] on another occasion he tried without success to explain a bewilderingly complex notice about national insurance to his unsophisticated host.[179] Occasionally he brought Mrs. Russell, who, to the surprise of the Donegal people, wore short skirts and smoked. When she encountered a visionary woman singing a mournful song, it was put down to the effects of tobacco until a drunken man was drowned at the spot shortly after.[180] Sometimes the children, too, accompanied their parents, and when the opportunity arose AE liked to bring at least one friend with whom to enjoy the solitude, since he could talk freely as he smoked and painted. He tried to persuade his American friend and patron, the sometimes irascible and imperious but also cultured and generous lawyer John Quinn, to join him, and he temptingly mentioned that he had found among the hills two farmers who relished his own verse and a third who admired Browning.[181]

While staying in Donegal, AE lived in a hillside cottage at Breaghy, just outside Dunfanaghy, and one of his letters to Yeats shows that he had already adopted this custom in 1905.[182] He often left Breaghy to stay for a while in a tiny building known as 'the fairy house,' which stood in the woods on Marble Hill overlooking the bay. It belonged to the Laws, who had built it near their home for their children to play in, and it consisted of one large room, simply furnished for AE to use as a studio, together with a sort of attic in which he slept. On the stone above the fireplace he painted the Irish Sword of Light. Part of AE's delight in Donegal came from his friendship with the Laws, which may have begun as early as his first visit to Dunfanaghy. In 1904 Hugh Law, the Nationalist M.P. for West Donegal, and AE served together on the provisional committee of the newly founded Rural Library Association, and six years later, in a letter which he sent to the *Homestead*, Law wrote: 'You have long honoured me with one of the most delightful friendships of my life . . .'[183]

The beauty of the Donegal scenery was entrancing whatever the weather. When it was fine, AE wandered over the hills making sketches and enjoying the wind or set up his easel and painted; when it rained he retired to continue his work under shelter.[184] Each year he brought a large supply of sketches and unfinished canvases back to Dublin as the starting point of the pictures he would complete during the next eleven months.[185]

When Moore first began to live in Dublin, he was disappointed to find AE wholly insensitive to the genius of the French impressionists, but in 1905 Hugh Lane, Lady Gregory's nephew, showed some of their masterpieces in the city and he began to recognise his error. The exhibits that most influenced him, however, were the Corots and Monticellis, and he once had a dream in which a Corot swelled to enormous proportions revealing the technique that the artist had employed to paint the sky.[186] The blurred forms, small vague figures, and dim or shimmering light of Monticelli's landscapes had an unfortunate influence on his own; his short-sightedness in any case prevented him from painting detail accurately.[187] Many of his paintings have badly deteriorated owing to his inadequate technique: Thomas Bodkin has described his ill-cared-for palette and brushes and dirty paint-box, and the excessive use of turpentine which caused his pigments to crack. To make matters worse, he would suddenly change his plan in the midst of working and carelessly paint the new conception over the old.[188] George Roberts amusingly describes Moore's silent astonishment as AE dared to display to him, an art critic, the fruits of an early Donegal holiday.[189] Many of his contemporaries, however, seeing his characteristic landscapes decorated with figures while the colours were still clean and bright, sensed something of the spirit that had inspired them. In 1907, he told an interviewer:

> When I am painting a little scene in Connemara or a bogland stretch, the people of the bog are part of my landscape. They grow up with it and form themselves. The bog is not the picture, nor the people, but all seem to me part of one being.[190]

More explicitly he wrote to John Quinn:

> What I want to do is to paint landscape as if it had no other existence than as an imagination of the Divine Mind, to paint man as if his life overflowed into that imagination, and to paint the Sidhe as mingling with his life; indeed, the unity of God and man and nature in one single being – an almost impossible idea to convey in paint.[191]

The County Museum in Armagh is fortunate to possess a collection of AE's visionary pastels, portraits, and landscapes of unusual beauty and in a remarkably fine state of preservation.

AE's discovery of Dunfanaghy may be connected with his first visit to Dungloe, about twenty miles to the south-west. Between the two towns lies the watery bogland of the Rosses where some of the poorest farmers in Ireland then eked out the meagrest of livings under the shadow of the gombeen man. Here, in 1903, AE addressed a mixed gathering of haves and have-nots on the advantages of starting a co-operative bank and promised that the Congested Districts Board would lend them £50 if local subscribers also came forward. A number of shopkeepers pledged deposits and proposed each other as committee members, but AE noticed that a young farmer who had also subscribed had not been nominated and his name was added to the list. This man, Patrick Gallagher, had been brought up in a one-room cottage and had left school at the age of ten; shortly before the Bank was started, after reading some leaflets published by the Department of Agriculture and Technical Instruction, he had introduced the first plough ever used in the district; in the coming years he was to lead his neighbours, who were as poor as himself, in the establishment of the most remarkable co-operative society in Ireland. Fighting the meanest tricks of the local traders, who stooped so low as to accuse him falsely of being a Unionist, he proved himself the equal in courage and public spirit of Plunkett, AE and Anderson. As he embarked on enterprise after enterprise, creating a garment industry for the women, constructing a pier at

Dungloe, quarrying granite, and building a powerhouse, it became clear that he had a kind of genius; AE felt that had he emigrated to America and worked for himself he would have become a millionaire, and in the *Irish Homestead* he constantly praised the Co-operative Society of Templecrone parish as an example to the entire country.[192]

While learning to pack eggs in County Londonderry, Patrick Gallagher found to his surprise that his instructor, though an Orangeman, was not malevolent. This simple incident illustrates the way in which the organisers of the I.A.O.S. – both Nationalist and Unionist – envisaged that their work would help to break down the sharp divisions that split the nation. On rare occasions, however, Plunkett himself ignored his own wise counsel on the error of arousing partisan feelings. One of these lapses occurred in 1904, when Plunkett – now Sir Horace – published *Ireland in the New Century,* an admirably lucid study of his co-operative policy. Ignoring the frank account of Protestant bigotry, the Catholic press not unnaturally protested loudly at the few pages in which he claimed that their faith was in some ways otherworldly and anti-economic. AE felt it necessary to come to his leader's defence by appealing for a more magnanimous and rational spirit in Irish journalism. Within the month he was able to issue a pamphlet named *Controversy in Ireland,* a reprint of his essay together with an attack on it which served as a prime example of the vulgar abuse it lamented.

Plunkett had long before summarised his aims in the slogan 'Better farming, better business, better living.' His conception of the third of these was somewhat vague, and over a period of years AE expanded it into a definite and colourful programme capable of inspiring hope and enthusiasm. In June 1904, he deplored in a partly metaphysical, partly sociological article, the contempt for romantic love common in Ireland, and pointed to the absence of any widespread desire to create beauty for the beloved as the cause of Irish homes being 'probably more squalid than with any other people equally prosperous in Europe.'[193] As his influence grew, he was to concern himself more and more with the indispensable part played by women in the development of civilisation.

Employment with the I.A.O.S. did not provide a secure position. The income of the organisation was irregular, and early in 1904 AE anticipated that it would collapse in a few months compelling him to find another means of livelihood.[194] The emergency passed over, but he had other reasons for desiring a change. In January 1905 he expressed the hope that he would be able to retire from his present position, which still involved constant lecturing to audiences of farmers,[195] and Moore relates that he fell ill early in the summer and could not have resumed his travels without serious danger to his health or even his life.[196] Shortly after returning from his summer holiday in Donegal, he succeeded his friend H. F. Norman as editor of the *Irish Homestead,* and this position gave such scope to his talents that he became in time the most distinguished journalist in Ireland.

By nature AE was happiest when he could organise his life according to a fixed routine, and he now had the opportunity to serve his country in more congenial circumstances. For eight years he had been making constant and irregular journeys from his Dublin home and office to every part of Ireland. The timid, ardent youth who had withdrawn from the competitive modern world to educate himself in eastern philosophy had emerged to become the centre of a bewildering whirlpool of activities. Giving second place to his own creative impulses, he had tried to serve as one of the focal points around which the civilisation he dreamed of could begin to crystallise: artists and mystics were to create the soul of Ireland, while farmers united in a cohesive social order were to constitute the body through which that soul could find expression. For twenty-five years AE continued to centre his existence on these two aspects of the national being.

V

At the Editorial Desk (1905–1914)

Although AE's greatest pleasure was to withdraw to Donegal with at least one congenial companion, he thoroughly appreciated the amenities which a city offers when it is fulfilling its function as a centre of civilisation. Even in London, which as early as 1897 he regarded as spiritually desiccating,[1] he always relished a visit to the National Gallery. In 1905 he rejoiced to become a settled inhabitant of Dublin, whose theatre, literature, art exhibitions, and intellectual society he did so much to foster. Yet he never forgot the gloomy underside of urban life, and from the time he pitied the overworked draymen at Pim's he always remained acutely sensitive to the misery of the very poor. In November 1904, he published in the London *Theosophical Review* a lyric entitled 'The Heroes,' which tells how, as he was passing sad at heart through the Dublin slum, a spirit-messenger appeared to quicken his vision so that he saw the beauty of souls untarnished by the degradation of the bodies in which they dwelt, and he remembered how each of these was a hero who had descended to earth to

> . . . wrestle with the chaos till the anarch to the light be bowed.[2]

In this faith AE continued to labour for the unborn civilisation in which all Irishmen would share.

The *Irish Homestead,* which served to disseminate co-operative news and technical information, was issued weekly from the central office of the I.A.O.S. at 22, Lincoln Place. The environment was hardly congenial as the employees were disturbed by the screams of patients in a neighbouring dental hospital, and laboratories where human dissection was practised were visible from the windows. Within a year or two the journal ceased to be a part of the Organisation Society and began to be independently supported,[3] whereupon it became free to advocate such forms of competition with private trade as co-operative stores, which the former, being state-aided, was barred from promoting.

H. F. Norman had proved a vigorous and enterprising editor. Two months after his appointment in August 1900, he introduced the leading article, a feature which, in AE's hands, was to give the paper unique distinction and bring it readers far removed from the field of professional agriculture. Besides drawing attention to co-operative developments abroad and engaging in polemics against the enemies of the movement, Norman campaigned for improved technical education, greater business honesty, more tillage and less grazing, and an insistence by farmers that both Unionist and Nationalist politicians pledge their support to co-operation. Especially prominent were his articles on the need to stem the emigration from the land by brightening rural life. Under his guidance the *Homestead* showed an obvious sympathy with the Gaelic League, which was reviving traditional arts and crafts in the countryside, and in November 1901 he promised that the paper would keep abreast of the literary movement. New short stories by Irish writers and Gaelic poems with English translations were thenceforth a regular feature. There was no change in policy when Norman was succeeded by AE: the latter prosecuted with at least equal vigour every one of the campaigns that has been mentioned.

The editor of the *Irish Homestead* undertook an exacting task. Each week AE wrote a long leading article and several columns of informational, admonitory, and cultural notes,* besides assembling agricultural news items and technical articles by other contributors. He wrote rapidly (one of his letters refers to a two-page editorial completed in an hour and a half),[4] but he often spent much time collecting facts beforehand. In one issue he remarked that he had to scan about sixty agricultural publications weekly,[5] and on another occasion he wrote of his editorial procedure: 'We generally manage to keep the paper fresh by delaying comment for a fortnight, until we can dig beneath the surface of our mind for new ideas.'[6] An important part of his duty consisted of arousing a spirit of enterprise and loyalty in obstinate, uneducated men who put short-term profit above long-term advantage, and who preferred striking a bargain over a glass of whisky to work of any kind. The sturdy people of north-west Donegal were the exception, not the rule, in the Irish countryside. Continually, for years on end, AE had to belabour the same points in his columns, trying to awaken conscience and

*Other writers may have made minor contributions to the anonymous 'Notes of the Week,' but familiar quotations and allusions and references to himself as editor testify to AE's authorship of by far the greater portion. Long passages in his books *Co-operation and Nationality* (1912) and *The National Being* (1916) consist of extracts from his leading articles and these 'Notes.' Before going on his summer holiday, he seems to have written a supply of editorials to tide over his absence (confirmed in a letter from Mr. Gerald Heard to the author, 11 January, 1966). In the case of 'Notes and Comments' in the *Irish Statesman*, which he edited from 1923 to 1930, authorship has to be assessed from internal evidence as there were many contributors. AE himself did, however, explicitly take responsibility as editor for all opinions there expressed (issue of 14 January, 1928, p. 438).

ambition where the growth of these qualities had been stifled by short-sighted shrewdness induced by generations of oppression. Irish home life, he claimed, was appalling in its ugliness and filth. The manure heap often stood by the cabin door and the rural diet was debilitating and monotonous: the farmer sold his tastiest, most nutritious produce and fed his family on tea, potatoes, and imported American bacon. The countryman was not only lazy and lethargic – AE referred frequently to 'Meath of the idle pastures'[7] – but he lived in a timeless world, had no sense of the sanctity of a contract, and lacked the foresight to insure his livestock. Even if he joined a co-operative organisation, he sold his produce elsewhere if the price were temporarily a fraction higher. When his society flourished he was reluctant to let it pay a small annual fee to the I.A.O.S., to which it owed its prosperity, nor could he see the advantages of his local institution joining one of the three large federations – agencies for the purchase and marketing of dairy products, eggs, and agricultural goods on a national scale. When he elected a representative on his County Council – who in turn voted for a member of the body which indirectly controlled the purse-strings of the Department of Agriculture – he never troubled to insist that the candidate support co-operation; the trader and the usurer being more energetic, the *Homestead* had often to report that democratic bodies were denouncing the co-operative organisations of the men who elected them. Having constantly to labour the same themes, AE often repeated his allusions, illustrations and phrasing, and it was probably this that eventually led to his habit of frequently drawing on a fixed though vast repertoire of set speeches in his conversation.

Less prosaic than these continuous admonitions, were the campaigns he conducted against the enemies of the movement. Nationalist politicians tended to discourage all schemes other than land reform for the improvement of Irish life as red-herrings distracting attention from the Home Rule struggle; AE liked to illustrate the enervating effect of this doctrine by quoting a drunken Belfast workman who joyously proclaimed, 'A won't do a han's turn till Ireland's free!'[8] and he quipped that the main arguments for and against Home Rule were 'the intolerable stupidity of politicians on the one side and the stupid intolerance of politicians on the other side.'[9] He had, too, to fend off the unscrupulous attacks of the threatened middlemen and the eccentric suspicions of private individuals. It has been seen that as early as 1893 he possessed two prose styles – one plain and vigorous, the other literary and mannered; in the *Homestead* he naturally employed the former and in his role as knight-crusader defending the co-operative foothold in the land of the gombeen man, he rapidly developed a mastery of polemic prose, which has never been fully appreciated. In one of his editorials he explained:

> . . . we try from week to week to steer the movement past sunken rocks, sand banks, and pirates, using ridicule as our main weapon in battle, as we find it is the most effective. Ireland has grown so solemn and pompous from standing so long on its hind legs on platforms that it dreads nothing more than a jest; and, indeed, it would hardly be an exaggeration to say that most Irishmen dread being laughed at by their neighbours while alive more than they fear being damned after they die.[10]

It is a little surprising to find the author of poetic prose (influenced, Yeats suggested, by Fiona Macleod) and the fierce rhetorician of *Priest or Hero?* in full command of a delectable, mocking irony. A somewhat conservative gentleman, feeling it his duty to warn his neighbours against the dangers of a credit society, fell victim to AE's pen:

> We should have thought that a Captain out of the Royal Navy would not get easily scared. Men whose profession it is to get torpedoed or to torpedo other people should have no nerves. But Captain Crofton, R. N., has got a bad attack of them, arising out of a visit he paid to the annual general meeting of the Farnaught Agricultural Bank; so he writes to the *Leitrim Advertiser* giving his views . . . 'Is there not,' he asks, 'something else in this question of co-operation more than appears on the surface to be considered? . . . If carried to its logical conclusion, does it not lead to something like socialism or collectivism – to the nationalisation of the railways, so dear to the socialist, and then, I suppose, of all steamship companies?' By the last words we know the Captain sees the British Navy is in peril . . . The British Empire may be ruled from Farnaught, and Irish revolutionaries, trained by Rev. J. G. Digges, may be put in control of the Dreadnoughts, Terribles, and other monster men of war . . .'[11]

In a different vein, AE cast a lurid light upon the callous exactions of the country usurer:

> We referred a couple of months ago to Dungloe, in the far north-west of Donegal, where the gombeen man and higgler, the only surviving contemporaries of the cave tiger, the plesiosaurus, and other primaeval monsters, still roved about picking the bones of their victims. The creature will soon be exinct, as the co-operative hunter has found his way into this remote region, and is shooting his swift arrows. Anyone who wants to see these survivors of the ferocious man-devouring creatures which once wallowed in the primordial slime, had better make haste, and take the train to

> Dungloe, where they can still be stalked and their habits observed.[12]

AE could be equally severe when exposing the deficiencies of co-operators. Commenting on the inspection of a creamery 'which seemed like a nursery for young plagues and pestilences to play in before they went out into the world,' he suggested that its manager

> was trying to create some new luxury like Gorgonzola cheese or ripe old Stilton or *pâté de foie gras,* which is made from diseased livers of geese . . . We are afraid the temperament of art or genius is incompatible with business, and while the manager was evolving his *pâté de foie gras* of diseased butter he forgot to enter up his books. The visit was made at the end of July, but there were no entries in the cash book for five weeks previously, the milk book, butter sales, impersonal ledger, stock book, retail sales book, and estimate book were some of them faint, yet pursuing weeks or months behind date, while some had dropped out completely . . . There are all the symptoms of genius in the management which the unsympathetic investigator, good enough for ordinary creameries, was unable to comprehend. So what was the use of his suggesting limewashing the walls, or scrubbing the floors, or getting a Geber tester, or cleaning pipes, or refusing milk as 'absolutely unfit even for feeding pigs?' Cleaning walls and pipes and separators, forsooth, when these were the masterpieces of months of studied negligence, fitted to impart the choicest flavours to *pâté de beurre malade*.[13]

The production of the *Irish Homestead* was a task for more than one person, and AE's principal helper was his Assistant Editor, Susan Mitchell. This handsome, cheerful woman with a wicked wit was a member of the Hermetic Society and a contributor to *New Songs,* and she had a gift for light verse and graceful prose as well as for serious, often devotional lyrics. AE developed a strong affection for her, and Eglinton observes that their friendship was not without some adverse effect on his home life. When she pounced on his unread copy of Ernest Boyd's newly published reminiscences, he noted with some amusement that she was 'because of her sex insatiably curious about all forms of opinions about people,'[14] and during an Anglo-Irish crisis he admitted that she was more easily swept away by political passion than he, but added: ' . . . her kind heart always modifies her extreme head and I do not believe she would harm a Unionist fly.'[15]

Early in 1906, less than a year after he had taken over the editorship of the *Homestead,* AE and his family moved to 17, Rathgar Avenue, and in November 1908 the headquarters of the I.A.O.S. were shifted from Lincoln Place to 84, Merrion Square, which was named

Plunkett House. Both these addresses became places of pilgrimage for the innumerable travellers, Irish and foreign, who wished to meet the formidably accomplished but invariably approachable sage. The enquiring visitor usually went first to the majestic Georgian terrace house which Plunkett's admirers had presented to him. Ascending four elegantly railed flights of stairs, he passed Plunkett's office on the first floor and came to a spacious room on the second. Here AE, a large man with a heavy russet beard, thick brown hair, and steel-rimmed spectacles, sat comfortably ensconsed behind an enormous desk piled high with a mountainous wilderness of books and papers. (When Lady Cynthia Asquith was astonished by this editorial anarchy, he explained 'that one must have either physical or mental disorder and he had chosen the former.'[16]) If the pilgrim were observant, he would notice AE's long grey-blue eyes and his small, finely moulded hands. By this time, having ceased to travel, the poet had begun to grow fat.[17] His affection for old clothes (he once boasted of having worn the same hat for ten years),[18] his crumpled tweed suit, and his shaggy beard contributed to his casual untidiness: James Stephens suggested that his overcoat might have been put on with a shovel.[19] On the brown wallpaper of the office were distinctively Celtic murals, which he painted and repainted. These were mostly heroic and supernatural figures, and among other images there survive a woman with a flaming torch standing by a stately stone column, and a sinister, painted wolf creeping over the lintel of a real doorway.

Whatever the subject of the visitor's enquiry, he would receive a courteous and if possible a helpful response, for AE took a personal interest in the most humble individual. If he were fortunate he would be invited to the editor's weekly At Home, and next Sunday evening he would find himself on board a tramcar bound for the middle class suburb of Rathgar where this most unbourgeois man now lived. Soon he would arrive at a small terrace house, and mounting the steps which led up to the unlatched front door, he would be met almost immediately by his host, emerging with outstretched hands as though alerted by a sixth sense. Inside the house, folding doors separated the two main rooms – the studio in front and the living room behind. The visitor might be invited into the former to look at AE's paintings, which were hung round the walls and propped against the skirting board. The other guests would be crowded into the living room, where there were more pictures – some visionary – and the books which AE loved to lend and pressed eagerly on his friends though many were not returned.[20] His library was laid out on three sets of low shelves, one devoted to Irish subjects, another containing spiritual and occult volumes (these alone were out of bounds to borrowers), and the third holding a miscellaneous collection.[21] If the supply of chairs ran out, some of the guests followed their host's example and sat on the floor. At times they separated into small groups, but often AE conducted a general conversation holding forth intermittently in monologues yet taking the trouble to encourage the less articulate to offer their opinions. Ideas of all kinds – economic, political, mystical and literary – were freely discussed by the famous and the obscure, and there were reminiscences of the past; AE, for example, would talk delightedly of his early friendship with Yeats. As the evening wore on Mrs. Russell would bring in tea and cakes, and the uninterrupted talk would continue into the early hours of the morning.

AE remained at 17, Rathgar Avenue, until he left Dublin in 1933. Here his sons grew up under their mother's care knowing their father only as a somewhat remote figure with settled habits. He used to read large numbers of detective stories for relaxation and sometimes wandered forlornly about the house when he had exhausted his supply.[22] By 1912 he was enjoying pictures of far-away places and 'moving visions of wild beasts, birds, fishes, and reptiles'[23] on the cinema screen, though he deplored the misuse of the new invention as a mental drug by those who went night after night and allowed the constant stream of sense impressions to blot out thought;[24] in time a weekly visit to a silent film became part of his routine.[25] After he became editor of the *Homestead*, he spent every Sunday[26] and every Christmas Day[27] painting, feeling that he was honouring the latter more in this way than he would by the conventional over-indulgence in food and drink.

AE strongly disliked formal occasions and preferred to meet his friends in a relaxed atmosphere at his home or office or at the Hermetic Society. He continued to be surrounded by young writers and to make important friendships, though after the publication of *New Songs* he never again discovered a whole generation of poets.

During the summer of 1905, he was delighted to receive a letter from a young Englishman praising his poetry for its spiritual content rather than its style. The writer, Clifford Bax, a youthful devotee of the arts and of Theosophical thought, called on AE at his home in the August of the following year. The latter remarked as he welcomed his visitor: 'My wife is a better visionary than I am, only she does not ponder over what she sees.'[28] Bax was as impressed by the author as he had been by his works; he seemed to see ages of experience in his eyes and was to think of him forty-five years later as one of the two noblest men he had known.

A much more important friendship began about 1907 when AE, as he afterwards claimed, read a short letter and perceived that an astonishing talent lay behind it.[29] Searching out the writer at the solicitor's office where he was a clerk, he found a little gnome of a man with a huge head almost hidden behind his typewriter. Soon the poverty-stricken and often undernourished James Stephens was a prominent guest at the Sunday evening gatherings, where all were called on to admire his verses. The gift of fantastic humour which bubbled over in his gay, whimsical talk and writings seemed to match the jerking and twisting of his diminutive body and the shifting expression on his face. AE delighted in the fanciful, richly human world of his poetry, and praised him for speaking, unlike most Irish writers, for the whole man, body and soul. The relationship between the two writers grew very close and Stephens soon found himself drawn deeply into the study of Indian mysticism. AE felt that this helped to deepen his character[30] and he came to acknowledge him as the best friend he had discovered since early youth.[31] Finding him irreplaceable during the long periods when he lived abroad, he tended to blame Mrs. Stephens for keeping her husband out of Ireland.

The intimacy between them did not preclude occasional moments of friction. Stephens, according to his later recollection, once challenged AE's truthfulness when the latter recited a long quotation and attributed it to O'Grady. AE indignantly left the room but returned about fifteen minutes later with the book and readily accepted the other's apology.[32] One Sunday evening Stephens was irritated by a group of AE's admirers who sat crosslegged on cushions reverently adoring their idol. He called to a friend on the other side of the room: 'Have you seen Mutt and Jeff, today, John?' and began to talk about the influence of American comic strips on art. AE's curiosity was provoked and on being shown some samples he exclaimed in astonished indignation: 'The artist who did them ought to be boiled in oil.' Supposedly he afterwards succumbed to the fascination of the picture stories and even had American papers sent on to him when he was in Donegal.[33]

In spite of their intense mutual affection, AE and Stephens preserved a certain objectivity when assessing each other's work. AE was not pleased by the literary result of Stephens' mystical studies and wrote in a review: 'I hope he will not be angry with me when I say I prefer his tinker drunken to his Deity sober.'[34] Stephens' tendency to address God as though he were a boon companion began to offend AE, who wrote a parody of his verses in this vein to discourage him:

> Hi, God, get off that throne! Get down
> You've had your turn, and turn about

'S fair play you know. Give me that crown
That cushion too. Be off! S'cat! Get out! . . .[35]

While he recognised quite soon that the fantasy-spinner would do his best work in prose, he regretted that he allowed facile, mechanical verses to slip into print and illustrated his criticism with another parody:

That is this and this is that,
Up is down and clown is king.
Why the eyesight of a bat
When one need not see a thing?
Let your words trip as they ought
Carelessly without a thought.

Words themselves will multiply
With no guidance of the mind
High and sky and I and my
Easily beget their kind,
All that rhymes with high and dry
Flows with ceaseless fluency . . .[36]

Stephens, for his part, complained of AE's poetry: 'He would not observe that fairly early in life he had evolved his own mannerisms, formulas, clichés, and would not cease from over-using them.'[37]

Compared to his intimacy with Stephens, AE's friendship with Bernard Shaw was superficial, though it gave great pleasure to both men. They first met in the Dublin National Gallery on 29 September, 1908, and each claimed afterwards that he had had a long, absorbing conversation with a complete stranger. After they were formally introduced at the Abbey Theatre on the evening of the same day they continued to find each other congenial.[38] AE grew to admire Shaw's courage and consistency and felt from the beginning that his arrogance was nothing but a pose to hide an essential humility and sensitiveness. 'I have a little clairvoyance,' he wrote, 'and I knew when I met him that he was one of the kindest of human beings.'[39] He recognised, however, the dramatist's limitations as well as his brilliance. 'Shaw,' he protested in 1912, 'has made a pure culture of his own cleverness and inoculated himself with it, and his mind is utterly incapable of taking in anything which has half tones or quarter tones and which cannot be translated into terms of pure reason.'[40] Yet he felt that he differed from such merely external writers as H. G. Wells and Arnold Bennett in that he was 'tormented by suppressed spirituality,'[41] and on reading *Back to Methuselah* he advised him to study Indian philosophy.[42] Shaw, on the other hand, admired AE without any such reservations, and even classed the *Irish Homestead* with the *Tatler* and the *Spectator*.[43]

Shaw was not a promising subject for Theosophical propaganda, but James Stephens sometimes attended the Hermetic Society, which AE refounded in 1909, sickened by the state of the official Theosophical movement under the leadership of Annie Besant, who had been elected President two years earlier. He believed that Mrs. Besant was 'silly mystically if eloquent and golden tongued otherwise,'[44] and that having no spiritual insight of her own she had come under the evil influence of Leadbeater, who hypnotised her till she saw whatever he wished.[45] Leadbeater became involved in a sexual scandal and Mr. Diarmuid Russell remembers his father's blunt denunciation: 'Leadbeater is a bad man.'[46] Writing to Clifford Bax, AE lamented that the Society was drained of spiritual life:

> . . . all things heavenly are judged by reason and morality, and the flagging horses of emotion are whipped up to duty after every moral pronouncement. It's dreadful, after old H.P.B.[47]

As James Cousins walked down the front steps at 17, Rathgar Avenue, at night on the eve of his departure for India in 1915, 'AE stood like a great angry deity against the light inside, and said with fervour, his hands brought down clenched by his sides: "Cousins, beware of that charlatan, Annie Besant." '[48]

The re-established Hermetic Society met on Thursday evenings in the Harcourt Street building which housed the Leinster School of Music. Mr. Arthur Power describes how the men and women who attended had to make their way down a dark passage and give the prearranged signal, a triple knock, as there were certain persons whom it was desired to exclude. The room where the meetings were held was bare and unadorned, except for a photograph of Madame Blavatsky and one of AE's visionary paintings. The instruction was based on *The Secret Doctrine,* a copy of which lay on the desk. After reading an extract, AE would comment on it, and launch into a digression on Gaelic mythology or the idea of a Celtic state; quotations from his favourite sacred books illustrated his discourse. Mr. Power declares that AE 'was the best, wisest, and wittiest talker I ever listened to in Paris, London, or elsewhere'; his mind seemed to be 'a fountain of fire casting beauty up everlastingly into the air.'[49]

H. T. Hunt Grubb, a member of the Hermetic Society some years later, wrote nine articles[50] in which he described many of AE's teachings, apparently without realising that they were identical in substance with those of Madame Blavatsky. AE discussed most of the subjects touched upon in the second and third chapters of this book, often illustrating his points with stories and images. Following *The Secret Doctrine,* for example, he explained the two intertwining serpents of the classical Caduceus of Mercury as symbols of spirit and matter, while their juncture at the base represented the manifested universe. In elucidating the occult significance of sound, he would sometimes chant the syllable 'Om' in what was almost a chromatic scale. He talked of ancient civilisations unknown to history, some on continents now submerged and some having only wooden buildings which had perished without trace. At times he sorrowed over the destruction of ancient manuscripts, such as those of the Druids and of the great library at Alexandria, holding that many contained invaluable knowledge about initiations in the ancient world. Often he reminisced describing experiences he later recorded in *The Candle of Vision* and *Song and Its Fountains,* and on occasion he would tell amusing stories. One of these concerned a Victorian missionary who tried to convert some American Indians to a belief in a fatherly God like a huge old man in the sky, and when the 'savages' would only speak of the Great Spirit present everywhere, he lamented to a friend, 'O, those poor, benighted heathen, I can get no good of them.'[51]

After the issue of *The Divine Vision* in 1904, AE made less effort to spread spiritual awareness through his poetry. Except for a brief selection produced by the Dun Emer Press, he published no more verse in volume form for the next nine years. A long poem on which he was working in the summer of 1911 seems to have come to nothing,[52] though he occasionally contributed verse to periodicals, sometimes in connection with current events. On 26 January, 1907, he was present at the opening night of Synge's comedy *The Playboy of the Western World* and heard the hissing which greeted a supposed allusion to Parnell's adultery. On subsequent nights the police had to be called in to control the uproar against a play alleged to defame the character of 'the finest peasantry in the world.' Protesting against this narrow-minded attitude to a masterly and in part fantastic comedy, AE lamented in a rather unimpressive sonnet that the spirit of Aristophanes and of Aeschylus was silenced in Ireland.[53] Three years later, in January 1910, a band of Russian Anarchists fought a losing gun battle with the London police in Sidney Street, having killed several members of the Force a few days earlier. In some 'doggerel,' as he called it, which he wrote for a revolutionary paper, AE pointed the contrast between the concentrated willpower of the rebels, a distorted reflection of the divinity in man, and the soullessness of the power they assailed:

Here's a wreath upon their coffins, since no one else is found

To say a kindly word for my poor brothers in the ground.
They had no Christian burial when dropped into the sod,
And they hinted at 'No mercy' who sent them up to God.
They may have been low rascals, but they showed before they died
That many-millioned Nation which had no soul inside,
The fire of the primeval man, a flash of the Promethean will,
Before Life's candle guttered down and Sidney Street was still.[54]

The most important of AE's occasional poems appeared in the *Sinn Fein* of 14 November, 1908. His co-operative programme was sometimes attacked by wholehearted nationalists who objected to the adoption of non-Irish ideas; in the powerful lyric 'On Behalf of Some Irishmen Not Followers of Tradition,' he appealed to his countrymen to shun the defeatism of the persecuted race that survives on sickly dreams of the past, glimmering for a while with the feeble light of decay as it slowly expires from lack of contact with the vital outside world:

The sum of all the past is theirs,
The creeds, the deeds, the fame, the name,
Whose death-created glory flares
And dims the spark of living flame.
They weave the necromancer's spell,
And burst the graves where martyrs slept,
Their ancient story to retell,
Renewing tears the dead have wept.

The next lines hint at an argument he often propounded in the *Homestead,* where he prophesied that if the Irish did not create a new civilisation they would by the law of nature disappear to be succeeded by a more vigorous race:

And they would have us join their dirge,
This worship of an extinct fire
In which they drift beyond the verge
Where races all outworn expire.

Affirming nevertheless his loyalty to the concept of a distinctly Irish identity, he concluded with words which recall the motto of the Theosophical Society, 'There is no Religion higher than Truth':

We would no Irish sign efface,
But yet our lips would gladlier hail
The firstborn of the Coming Race

Than the last splendour of the Gael.
No blazoned banner we unfold –
One charge alone we give to youth,
Against the sceptred myth to hold
The golden heresy of truth.[55]

In the course of advocating in the *Homestead* a co-operative future for Ireland, AE became embroiled in a series of bitter controversies. The first of these he inherited from his predecessor, H. F. Norman. The British Co-operative Wholesale Society had started a number of creameries in Ireland on proprietary lines to buy and process the milk of the local dairy farmers, and in 1902 Norman reproached them for the breach of co-operative principles involved in acting as a profit-seeking middleman between producer and consumer. AE continued the fight, gladly acknowledging the achievements of the C.W.S. in its own country, but ferociously branding it as a giant gombeen man abroad, treating the Irish as an inferior race while hypocritically pretending to promote their dairying industry. Not until 1909 was an agreement reached for the purchase of the creameries by Irish co-operators.

While the outcome of the contest with the C.W.S. was still undecided, a more dramatic and a more personal feud started to absorb much of AE's attention. A Department of Agriculture and Technical Instruction, created through Plunkett's initiative, had begun to operate in Ireland in 1900, and this official body was intended to supplement the voluntary work of the I.A.O.S. with the small amount of state aid necessary to promote scientific agriculture: while the private organisation attended to the 'better business' of Plunkett's slogan, the civil servants concerned themselves with 'better farming.' The Vice-President of the new Department, though responsible to the nominal President – the Chief Secretary for Ireland – was in effect the country's Minister for Agriculture. Plunkett held this post for seven years, ensuring that his two creations, the I.A.O.S. and the Department, worked together as he had envisaged, but in 1907 he was forced to resign owing to the pressure of the Irish Nationalist M.P.'s on whose support the ruling Liberal Party depended. The Government appointed as his successor T. W. Russell, a Scotsman long resident in Ireland and a veteran of the land struggle. AE scanned the horizon anxiously for signs of any coming storm, but at first it seemed that the new Vice-President was well disposed to agricultural co-operation. He was, however, the grandson of an evicted tenant, and it became clear that he nourished a personal hatred for the aristocratic Plunkett; in addition, he was to be goaded constantly by a group of Nationalist M.P.'s headed by

John Dillon, men who drew their main financial support from small country traders. Russell and Dillon set out with fanatical determination to wreck the I.A.O.S.

The enemies of Plunkett's movement attacked it primarily with slander: they charged that the I.A.O.S. was a trading body and secretly a Unionist organisation set up to undermine the campaign for Home Rule. About the beginning of 1908, an unfortunate accident gave them an opening. The *Freeman's Journal*, a Nationalist newspaper, published the text of a private letter written by the poet T. W. Rolleston, who was not a member of the I.A.O.S., to an Irish-American in St. Louis. The letter expressed satisfaction at the way in which the movement was liberating the farmers from the tyranny of the middlemen who had hitherto dominated the Nationalist Party, and T. W. Russell seized upon the opportunity to have the modest subsidy which the Department allowed the I.A.O.S. stopped at the end of the year: AE bravely encouraged his readers to welcome the complete freedom of the movement from state control.

In 1910, T. W. Russell struck a second and a meaner blow. Deciding that the small sums which the Department had lent to co-operative credit banks were not in safe hands, he set out to recover the money, and, contrary to a promise he had made, without allowing the I.A.O.S. to investigate, he started proceedings against two societies. Certain that there was no reason to believe the banks unsound, AE brought all his powers of ridicule and denunciation to bear upon this enemy, who had taken command of an institution created by Plunkett. He announced that 'The right honourable gentleman could not keep for one month a promise made . . .'[56] and printed a description of T. W. Russell thumping the table before a committee of the House of Lords and expressing amazement at being charged with political bias.[57] Somewhat unfairly, he put his own interpretation upon a not immodest reference by Russell to a compliment paid him by an American journalist, who had said that the Department and its Head, rather than Dublin Castle, were now at the centre of Irish life:[58]

> The Vice-President having been informed by Mr. W. T. Stead that he was the real King of Ireland, felt it was high time to have a triumphal procession after the fashion of the ancient Romans, and he brought bound to the chariot wheels their Excellencies, whom he put in their proper place by telling them Mr. Stead's views were his own also.[59]

Referring to his methods of manipulating evidence, AE declared:

> When Mr. T. W. Russell goes before his Maker he will not talk so glibly, when the eternal eyes are fixed on him, about other

people's actions, and his arithmetic will be more accurate.

When the time came for the Vice-President to resign his post, AE added, he would leave it 'with the reputation of a man who was courageous but whose word is not worth the breath it is uttered with.'[60] Time eventually vindicated AE's stand on the credit banks, for all of the money was recovered except for three shillings and one penny.[61]

In the meantime T. W. Russell had returned to the charge by setting the Department to organise what he called 'non-controversial co-operation.' After so often having had to deny that the I.A.O.S. was a trading body, AE gleefully reported that the Department was now peddling tradesmen's goods to farmers and warned the poor against relying on the state and not on themselves. The I.A.O.S., having survived for some time on private subscriptions, applied to the official Development Commission for a share of the money which the Government had earmarked for the promotion of agricultural co-operation. The Agricultural Organisation Society in England and its Scottish counterpart, institutions modelled on the I.A.O.S., had already received grants, but T. W. Russell claimed that in Ireland it was the Department of Agriculture and not a private organisation that should be subsidised. In the *Homestead,* AE asked the affiliated societies for testimonials that the I.A.O.S. was free from party politics and received an overwhelming affirmative response, while the Development Commissioners rejected T. W. Russell's application for funds on the grounds that his scheme was not co-operation at all. AE continued to attack the Vice-President, but, practising the chivalry he so much admired, he periodically admitted that his namesake was not without good qualities:

> He has been a courageous opponent who has always come out to the edge of the platform when he has had anything to say. We have not had to fight in the dark . . . A less courageous man than Mr. T. W. Russell would have fought altogether behind official entrenchments, where it would have been very difficult to see what he was about.[62]

In 1913, after a delay of a year and a half, Dillon's and Russell's efforts to deprive the I.A.O.S. of the grant were finally frustrated; only a donation of £1,800 from Plunkett had saved it from collapse.[63]

In order to defend the movement more effectively against the false charge that it was anti-national, as well as to present in a more formal way his concept of a rural civilisation, AE published early in 1912 a short book entitled *Co-operation and Nationality: a Guide for Rural Reformers from This to the Next Generation.* More than a third of this work consisted of passages from his leading articles and 'Notes of the Week' incorporated with only the slightest variations;

these extracts were probably reproduced from memory.[64] Much of the book is written in the vigorous, natural and often witty language of AE's *Homestead* articles, sliding easily, without any obtrusive transition, into a more impassioned style. Only occasionally do poetic phrases like 'fabled gardens' and 'how and in what manner,'[65] all too common in most of his prose books, jar upon the reader. The exposition of economic and social idealism does, however, lose some of its impact through being largely detached from the concrete details of Irish daily life so vividly presented in the weekly journal, and as a result reviewers tended to find it impressionistic rather than precise.

The lack of integrity that AE complained of in T. W. Russell seemed to him a vice that pervaded Irish life. He attacked farmers who watered their milk, traders who adulterated their butter, and co-operative societies that practised corruption in making appointments or giving contracts. Gombeen men usually made a great show of piety, but one was detected selling candles of adulterated wax to his church.[66] In 1911, AE began a campaign to make the Department reveal the names of the numerous merchants whom it had discovered to be selling impure seeds, but not till 1915, when war-time circumstances made an increase in production essential, was a blacklist issued. Such experiences gave him a new reason to dislike Irish Christianity. Though he campaigned against the illegal practice of Sunday work in co-operative dairies as an infringement on "the only day of the week when a man can call his soul his own"[67] he was later to protest loudly that Irish clergyman paid far too much attention to sectarian theology and not nearly enough to ethics.[68] Even the sayings in the Gospels, he complained, though in themselves sublime and profound, were not applied explicitly to economic matters, and in 1916 he wrote to Shaw:

> The reason Christianity had no hold in the state was that it itself was a reaction against a state religion, what Moses laid down as laws of the state were also laws of the Judaean God. Jesus broke up the ethical law by the ethical spirit and made men individualists. The next Avatar, let us hope, will be a social reformer, a state messiah laying down the laws of God as the laws of the state . . .[69]

In conducting his sometimes fierce campaigns against men and customs which he felt were corroding the life of the country, AE was often made uneasy by the thought of spiritual teachings that forbade anger. In May 1908, he described in 'Notes of the Week' his awe on learning some months earlier that Standish O'Grady, whose innate nobility he so idealised, was among his readers:

> We felt uncomfortable whenever we thought of it, like a man who feels that a recording angel is watching his conduct closely . . .

> The gentlemen with whom we so often have controversies . . . do not know how much they owe to the memory which came upon us sometimes that Mr. O'Grady might read and condemn an extra savage sentence as hitting below the belt.[70]

AE was careful, nevertheless, to draw a clear distinction between the exercise of compulsion in a just cause and the anger which often did but never should accompany it. Believing that without the acquisition of willpower man could not recover his ancient divinity, he condemned those who mistook apathy for peace, and hoped the successes of the unscrupulous would 'finally force the good, kind people who hate fighting to round out their natures by adding power to goodness . . .'[71] When O'Grady wanted to start utopian communes where the most indolent and reckless would be forgiven until seventy times seven, he warned that to take the Gospel sayings in isolation from one another, as Tolstoy and others had done, was to distort the Christian message. Pointing to the command that the Apostles shake the dust of recalcitrant cities off their feet, to the scourging of the moneychangers, and to the saying 'I came not to send peace, but a sword,' he urged:

> . . . it seems to us that it is quite possible, in accordance with the spirit of the Gospels, and absolutely without anger or malice, to get rid of an incorrigible idler or drunkard and to put such a person under discipline which will force him to come to some kind of self-restraint . . .[72]

Besides fighting the battles of the movement, AE made practical suggestions on his own account. When, for example, it became clear that Parliament would never find time to pass a Bill giving credit banks the trading powers they enjoyed on the Continent, he suggested they re-register, using the Industrial and Provident Societies Act instead of the Friendly Societies Act.[73] Similarly, he opposed a suggested minimum wage for landless agricultural labourers, as he calculated that if the total profits from the nation's farms were divided equally among all workers on the land, they would be paid only eleven shillings and tenpence a week, hardly more than the present customary wage:[74] scientific farming, the cultivation of their cottage gardens, and membership in credit banks and co-operative stores offered them more hope.

A campaign for tariff reform, which roused strong feelings in England both for and against protection, led AE to discuss the problem frequently in the *Homestead.* He did not omit to point out that should the present policy of free trade be abandoned, the English would decide what was good for Ireland, and they would decide it 'to please themselves and not to please us.'[75] The Irish farmer, he insisted, should rely on his own efficiency as a producer rather than on a handicap artificially imposed on his rivals. In order to reach a wider audience and to encourage dispassionate thought on the subject, he published six closely reasoned articles in the *Irish Times* during February and March 1909. Rejecting any blanket policy of doctrinaire protection or free trade, he analysed specific cases on their merits, arguing, for example, that tariffs could benefit the Irish linen, market gardening, and dairy industries, but would seriously hamper meat production. He made a special point of warning the public that any duties paid would eventually come out of the consumer's pocket and that urban workers would fiercely resist an increase in the price of food. Finally, in connection with the demands of trade unions, he referred to an analysis of the collapse of Rome as a result of the provision of free bread and circuses, an analysis which, strangely, he often cited in the *Homestead,* though it was worked out from an extreme capitalist viewpoint by the Egyptologist Flinders Petrie in his book *Janus in Modern Life*. To his surprise, AE was hailed as the only expert in Ireland on the subject of protection. 'I have chilled the blood of Tariff Reformers over here,' he wrote to Weekes, noting the absence of any attempt 'to upset my facts or views.'[76]

After AE had edited the *Irish Homestead* for about two years, he was no longer content to restrict himself to the almost routine duty of advising and admonishing the members and managers of co-operative societies. He was beginning to consider more and more the wider possibilities of co-operation and its relation to the problems of the modern world. As he published his thoughts week by week and evolved new ideas in response to current events and to letters from his readers, he gradually came to find that he was one of a number of European and American intellectuals, including Sir Horace Plunkett, President Theodore Roosevelt, and the Russian Kropotkin, who were seeking an alternative to the grim, machine-like society based on urban industry. He was a synthesiser more than an original thinker, and he acquired only a cursory knowledge of economics, as his friend Henry Wallace testified[77] and as he himself admitted:

> I had begun after I was thirty or thereabouts to evolve a quick superficial intelligence, interests in art, economics and politics and the ideas which excited my own generation. It was that quickness of mind which enabled me a little later to live as a critic of politics, economics and literature.[78]

The constant migration from the countryside to the cities may be taken as the starting point of AE's thought. This problem, which is still worldwide, was especially serious for Ireland because, having few cities and little industry, she lost many of her most ambitious and energetic young people to the United States. He recognised, as his predecessor, Norman, had done, that the drabness of rural life was driving the young from the land, and late in 1907 he put forward the argument that throughout history the benefits of civilisation, its intellectual adventures and material magnificence, had been the possession of the townsman, and that the time had come for the creation of a rural civilisation based on the fully organised co-operative parish.[79] Soon he was contending that human stock swiftly degenerated in an urban environment and that the cities depended for their survival on an influx of healthier immigrants from the countryside – a theory that today has a somewhat romantic air. Pointing out that certain historians attributed the fall of Rome to the decay of Italian agriculture, he prophesied that mankind would find itself compelled to return in anguish to the land it was deserting:

> Nature or the powers that be, the guardians of humanity, never allow life to stray permanently or hopelessly from the natural order, and, if men will not willingly live a natural life, then, with pestilence and famine in the cities, they are scourged back . . .[80]

AE maintained that rural life was intrinsically capable of holding the countryman's lifelong interest; there was nowhere a greater mystery than the annual wonder of nature's cycle, and to add to its fascination there was the rapidly advancing science which was about to 'transform and intellectualize the nature of the farmer's operations.'[81] Co-operatives, moreover, should use their profits to build village halls, which would serve as social centres, and to bring books, plays, and music into the country. Above all, the quality of life depended on the work of women, whose duty it was to create beauty and comfort. 'Men,' wrote AE, 'would have remained in cave dwellings if women had not insisted on proper apartments.'[82] The arts of the goldsmith, the weaver, and the architect – even civilisation itself – arose to satisfy her demands. But women in Ireland had a slave mentality and submitted unprotestingly to marriages 'for cows and fortunes';[83] against these AE conducted a vigorous campaign, lamenting the loveless and uninspiring homes which resulted. He insisted that 'women are equals of men, not in this thing or in that, but in the complete worth of being, weighed in a divine balance, there would not be a hair's breadth of difference between them';[84] according to Norman, during his youth he had refused for a time to salute a woman by removing his hat for it would have implied she was spiritually inferior.[85] In April 1910, AE suggested in his 'Notes of the Week' the founding of a women's guild to create the beauty and comfort of which he had written, and a month later, after some discussion in the correspondence columns of the paper, an association was started under the name of the

United Irishwomen.[86] The following year he expressed his great satisfaction at his part in bringing about this permanent enrichment of the Irish scene:

> The editor of this paper takes more pride in the fact that he helped in some measure in the formation of United Irishwomen than in any other thing he has done since he began to write about the building up of a rural civilisation in Ireland, and the over-generous acknowledgement of the little aid he has been able to give these Irishwomen has been one of the great pleasures of his life.[87]

From 1908[88] he also supported the campaign for female suffrage. He even wrote a lighthearted comedy on women in Parliament, though it was never performed or published. 'The Honourable Enid Majoribanks M.P.' is full of surprisingly lively dialogue, and the characters are distinct if rather simple.

To encourage both sexes to beautify Ireland, AE often described the achievements of other countries. Somewhat inconsistently in view of his belief that civilisation had always by-passed the farmer, he claimed the prosperous society of mediaeval Ireland newly rediscovered by the historian Mrs. Stopford Green as an example of the rural civilisation he dreamed of. Its basis, he said, was the clan, a communal or co-operative organisation, and such clans had existed all over Europe until the great national states had shattered them.[89] He had already studied the description of these organisations in Kropotkin's *Mutual Aid,* a book he frequently mentioned in the *Homestead;* here they are termed village communities and described as almost ubiquitous in Europe, Asia, and Africa. Thus AE asserted: '. . . the ideal of the co-operative community is the most natural of any, the most universal and the oldest of all social ideals in the world . . .'[90] While he admitted that the Irish clans had been basically military institutions, he stressed his belief that they had held their land in common; in the co-operative movement he saw an opportunity to revive in a more peaceful form this social expression of the national genius, just as he saw in the literary movement a resumption of the spiritual quest of the ancient Gaels. The modern equivalent of the mediaeval clan was to be the co-operative parish, a closely knit self-governing community producing most of its own food, manufacturing many of its own goods, buying and selling collectively, organising its own social and artistic life, and bringing the amenities of civilisation to its own district. Individual ownership of land would continue, for the peasant proprietors had laboured for decades to pay for their farms, but in such a society a man's interests would exactly coincide with those of his neighbours and he would take a creative pride in his locality and feel that he was a part of a larger whole. In these small regions there would develop an intensity of life such as had existed in the city states of ancient Greece and mediaeval Italy: even Denmark's example might be far surpassed. AE contrasted his ideal of the small, organic community with the socialist aim of a single giant organisation, which was too vast to create a sense of identity in the individual, and with the competitive capitalist society whose irreligious doctrine of every man for himself fostered callousness and greed. It was the social environment, he proclaimed, that moulded the moral character of the average citizen: 'One man in every hundred is a freak, a person lit up by a lamp from within . . . As for the other ninety-nine, they are just what the social order makes them.'[91] The co-operative parish would combine the brotherhood of Christianity and of socialism with the self-reliance of individualism.

AE's experience confirmed the opinion of the theorists of co-operation that the unit of the system must be an association small enough for the members to be personally acquainted, but he looked to the development of a network of societies covering the country, sharing the same aims, and working together, to expand the peasant's local patriotism and sense of identity until it embraced all Ireland. The nationhood that now existed largely in the minds of political orators would become a reality, and the government would no longer be able to create separate Departments of Agriculture for the East and West without arousing a public outcry.[92]

The enemies of agricultural co-operation often believed that it was the farmers' declaration of war on the towns. AE argued that agriculture was the primary industry, and a redress of the lopsided balance of power between town and country was the only way to prevent the disintegration of society. At the end of 1908, he welcomed a meeting organised in Belfast by Harold Barbour, one of the most prominent workers in the I.A.O.S., as a pioneer attempt to establish the contact between the urban and rural co-operators that could lead to eventual unification.[93] Soon he came to visualise more precisely a countrywide organisation of co-operatives with associations of urban consumers buying directly from societies of rural producers. In this way would be born the Co-operative Commonwealth, the state of the future, which, neither capitalist nor socialist, would combine liberty with fraternity. There would be room, too, for appropriate government enterprises and for the gifted capitalist, who might sometimes need the complete control of his own undertaking. In this connection AE declared: 'There will always be, we believe, and we also hope, a place for the energetic individualist in society . . .'[94] A new role would be found, too, for the middleman who was displaced because he fulfilled no essential function in the community; when a country grocer wrote to the *Homestead* of his difficulties, he was advised to combine with other grocers and buy in bulk to by-pass the inferior goods of the wholesaler,[95] and the paper recorded the case of a shopkeeper who sold out to a co-operative society, served as its manager, and multiplied the turnover several times.[96] In his book *The Re-Conquest of Ireland,* James Connolly, the socialist thinker who was executed as a leader of the 1916 Easter Rising, acclaimed AE's genius in expounding the ideal of the Co-operative Commonwealth in his journal.

In May 1907, the Parliament of the United Kingdom was considering a Bill which would bring the Irish Department of Agriculture under the control of a Council directly elected by the people. AE urged that the existing indirectly elected Agricultural Board was greatly preferable. If the proposed change were accepted, voters would support candidates for their party allegiance instead of their expert knowledge.[97] In the coming years he developed this idea into a political theory complementary to his economic programme, and his thought on the subject was greatly stimulated early in 1910 when Charles Weekes sent him F. S. Oliver's biography of Alexander Hamilton, who had drawn up a polity for the United States. The book arrived when he was thinking of publishing his sketch of a possible system of government for Ireland, since this was being entirely neglected by the Nationalists who were struggling for Home Rule.[98]

A democratic electorate, AE complained, tended to choose the clever talker, 'the least common denominator of its opinions,'[99] whereas a vocational association recognised men who were competent in its own field. If each occupation were governed by its elected council, a central parliament of the conventional kind would arbitrate when separate interests clashed, would rule in other fields, and would maintain the personal liberty of the subject. The greatest need of a democracy was for a respected elite of upstanding and able individuals, for an 'aristocracy of intellect and character.'[100]

AE clearly saw that the emergence of a rural civilisation, a Co-operative Commonwealth, or even a prosperous Ireland, depended on the spread and improvement of education, which was then divorced from practical affairs and from any feeling of national identity. He pleaded for a syllabus including elementary science and economics and the history and legends of the country. An acquaintance with the noble characters of Gaelic literature would lead the young to absorb some of their qualities – even the heroes of penny dreadfuls gave examples of courage and honesty.[101] England could best make amends for her commercial crimes against Ireland in the eighteenth century by heavily subsidising education – 'For the greatest thing we lost in the destruction of our industries was the human qualities which were destroyed along with them – experience, business habits, and commercial wisdom.'[102] Worst of all was the intolerable dullness of the textbooks, which stifled the natural curiosity and intelligence of children and smothered their sense of wonder, leading AE to curse 'the black art of education as it is practised in Ireland.'[103]

In September 1911, an authoritarian-minded correspondent advocated that striking railwaymen be put under martial law. His letter gave AE the idea – he afterwards heard that William James had thought of it before[104] – of conscripting every youth to work for two years on such projects as the reclamation of wasteland, the planting of trees, and the construction of buildings. Not only would young citizens receive valuable training and discipline, but the government would be able to undertake great public works that the country could not otherwise afford. Again, AE's imagination flew to the legendary cities of the ancient world, when he sought a model for the civilisation that Ireland might create.[105]

The number of co-operative societies sponsored by the I.A.O.S. grew rapidly from year to year, and by 1909 a hundred thousand Irish farmers out of a total of about half a million had become members. AE, who continually lauded the optimism of Whitman and denounced the pessimism which stifled initiative, confidently began an argument in his 'Notes of the Week': 'If we can organise the whole of Ireland, and we will have it organised thoroughly in fifteen years . . .'[106] But ominous events were clouding the international scene and even an optimist could not close his eyes to the possibility of a European war.

Though AE's principal interest was in his own country, he did not omit to take account of political and economic conditions outside Ireland. His first ten years as editor of the *Homestead* coincided with a decade of Liberal rule in the United Kingdom. During this period, organised labour was asserting itself with increasing force against the power of capital, and the Government, which remained in power through the support of the Irish Nationalists and of numerous working class voters, passed a series of acts providing old age pensions, workmen's compensation, health and unemployment insurance, and other compulsory benefits. At home, the Socialist Party was gathering support; abroad, Britain was faced by an industrialised Germany, which, having harnessed science to production and established cartels to fix prices and output, now sought to rival England as a colonial and naval power. In the 1880's Bismarck, ruling through an elected but submissive legislature, had secured internal stability despite a rural exodus and a swelling urban proletariat. While suppressing Socialists, he had given the working class the paternal protection of compulsory health, accident, and old age insurance about twenty years before the British Government followed his example. Shortly after the turn of the century, Britain began to watch with apprehension as Germany constructed a fleet of Dreadnoughts to challenge her hundred year's command of the seas.

AE surveyed the modern world from the standpoint of a co-operator, an Irish nationalist, and a Theosophist. Desiring above all things that conflict between nations, classes, and individuals should be superseded by brotherhood, he watched with growing alarm the clash between capital and labour. The former, it seemed to him, wielded as yet the real power, subtly manipulating public opinion so as not to be overborne by democracy. When Lloyd George proposed his National Insurance scheme in 1911, he at first welcomed it on moral grounds but felt that Ireland, as distinct from England, could not afford it. Before the Bill was passed, however, he formed the opinion that it was in reality a device to make the public subsidise inadequate wages, and that the employers would recover the cost of their own contribution by raising prices, thus causing inflation while undermining the dignity and self-reliance of the workers. Such schemes, he believed, could be no more than a stop-gap postponing a life-and-death struggle between the two sides likely to issue, perhaps after violent revolution, in socialist states with armies of official bullies and spies – states not very different from capitalist autocracies. He dreaded the prospect of a regimented society and saw it foreshadowed in the rigid organisation already perfected in Germany. Borrowing Hilaire Belloc's vivid phrase 'the servile state,' he passionately advocated the Co-operative Commonwealth as a more human alternative. In November 1911, he supplemented his numerous warnings in the columns of the *Homestead* with a long letter to the *Freeman's Journal*. Looking back to the horrors of the industrial revolution left to run its course by a government committed to *laissez-faire*, he wrote:

> The ruling classes had adopted as their own the first of the three watchwords of the French Revolution. They found it paid, and were disposed to go further . . . Statecraft, hoary with the experience of a thousand years, stroked its venerable beard reflectively. Fraternity it felt, as a skilfully worked principle [,] might return as good dividends as Liberty did. Labour was dissatisfied with its low wage and the neglected ending of its miserable day. In the name of Fraternity, the State attacked the discontent. It brought relief to the ruling classes by contributing

> indirectly, but surely, to the wages bill of their employe[e]s. It provided their workmen with cheap dwellings at the expense of the public . . . The worker was often sick and out of employment. Fraternity could conquer this also. National Insurance was prepared for these evils, and is just about to efface them . . . The end of all this will be the servile State whose swift coming Mr. Hilaire Belloc deplores, or, when the hunger induced by wages being compulsorily lowered by the State has made the worker savage enough, we may have some form of State Socialism where the third watchword of the French Revolution will be held sacred, and we will have Equality, without either Liberty or Fraternity.[107]

By 1909, AE was making frequent reference to the much feared possibility of a European war and a German invasion. In December 1910, having consulted military experts,[108] he began a campaign to persuade his countrymen to grow all that they required to feed themselves, and export only the surplus, for if a conflict broke out imports might be cut off and Ireland's own produce already pledged, as happened in the Great Famine, to English buyers; he did not believe that international arbitration or any other panacea – though he was not always consistent on the point – would transform the behaviour of nations: 'The war mania is a disease which it will take many centuries to eradicate, perhaps many thousands of years.'[109]

The Theosophy which underlay AE's view of Ireland and of the future of the world occasionally becomes apparent to the prepared reader in the pages of the *Homestead.* When a correspondent objected to the collection of money for an art gallery in a city where so many were hungry, AE replied:

> We remember many years ago seeing a painting by a great artist in which the human form seemed half divine in its beauty, and it set us crying out in our heart for a world where all would be beautiful, and we could hardly say how much of that old passion has gone into our desire for the making of a rural civilisation where people might live naturally in sweet air and sunlight and grow again into that likeness to Deity which they had on them in the beginning of the world.

Goodness, truth, and beauty, he continued, must be sought together:

> Goodness without truth and beauty leads to pure materialism. Truth unaccompanied leads to cruelty, and beauty without the others is the flesh and the devil.[110]

In warning the world that nature or the powers guarding humanity would drive men back to the country,* AE was referring obliquely

*See p. 143 above.

to the Theosophical Masters, while it was his fundamental conviction that the Planetary Spirit, expressing itself though diverse civilisations, was now inspiring humanity to create a worldwide co-operative social order:

> As we read volume after volume showing these stupendous developments in three continents . . . this simultaneous motion of farmers towards co-operative action seems almost as if it were guided by the secret Ruler of the World. All of it practically was done in half a century . . . The yellow man and the brown man and the black man have also heard the summons to co-operate in their souls, and the coloured races can show as good results as the uncoloured . . . Is the world spirit laying down the foundations of a co-operative commonwealth, the federation of the world, to issue in a new era for humanity?[111]

The labour of continuous writing began to tell on AE's spirits after only a few years of editorial experience; often, he had no idea what he would find to discuss in the next issue.[112] In November 1909, when Clifford Bax asked him to contribute an article to his magazine *Orpheus*, he undertook instead to paint an initiation scene: '. . . if you knew,' he protested, 'what it meant to write about fifteen columns of journalism every week you would understand after four or five years of it how one loathes the sight of a pen and how the thought of writing a line one is not forced to write makes one sick.'[113] He went on to explain that he had to eke out the meagre salary which the *Homestead* could afford to pay him by selling his paintings. (To live by selling poetry seemed to him like committing simony.)[114] The position was still the same seven years later, and even such payments as the *Homestead* did make were then irregular.[115] The deep satisfaction that impelled him to continue his work in these circumstances is sometimes expressed in his correspondence and on occasion in the paper itself. Pointing out to the managers of co-operative creameries the great moral influence they could exert in their districts by reason of their superior education, he compared his own privileged position:

> The present writer has always regarded himself as fortunate above other literary men in this country, because he was not flinging his words to the wind or to people who, however they agreed with what was written, were unorganised and unable to influence the course of events.[116]

Sir Horace Plunkett, as his diary shows, was deeply impressed by AE's editorial brilliance. Early in January 1911, the former returned from the United States to his home at Foxrock, Kilteragh, and was pleased to find that R. A. Anderson had just brought AE there to convalesce after an operation on an abscess in his throat.[117] AE was a frequent guest at Foxrock, which he undertook about this time to decorate with a wall painting.[118] The resultant landscape frieze, it was generally agreed, was his artistic masterpiece, but it was destroyed in the Irish Civil War. Plunkett, formerly a moderate Unionist, had now become a moderate Home Ruler, and in November 1912 two of the most prominent Ulster employers, Thomas Andrews and Thomas Sinclair, visited Foxrock to attempt his reconversion to Unionism. Their diligence, however, went unrewarded as AE demolished their arguments to Plunkett's entire satisfaction.[119]

At the beginning of 1911, Moore's departure from Dublin made an unpleasant break in AE's weekly routine. He had threatened to no avail to spread the story that the novelist was really leaving to marry his cook in order to avoid losing her services. For the first time in seven years AE was faced with the prospect of Mooreless Saturday evenings, and for a while he wandered round unhappily on this night of the week unable to fill the vacuum.[120] *Ave* and *Salve,* the fanciful autobiographical first fruits of Moore's stay in Dublin, were published in 1911 and 1912. Although these literary masterpieces have lost little of their savour, much cruelty went to their making: the feathered elegance and unerring flight of the satirical arrows can have given small consolation to the victims of Moore's unscrupulous, and often unjust attacks. As a foil to these unfortunates, AE was presented as a spotless saint and sage, but his escape did not please him and he declared that he would have preferred to have been the villain.[121] With characteristic malice, Moore decided to make his friend's displeasure an excuse for charging him in the last volume of the trilogy with neglecting his wife for another lady. When AE threatened him with a lawsuit,[122] he dropped the plan and contented himself with several pages of spiteful observations suggesting that the mystic's carelessness about money and lack of interest in his food must irritate his wife, that his mind was too restless for meditation, that his education was seriously incomplete, and that he was not as happy as he seemed. As a parting shot he claimed that Eglinton had warned him to take great care in speaking of AE's domestic life. In March 1914, many Dubliners were awaiting in justified trepidation the publication of *Vale*. When it finally appeared, AE, relieved at the comparative mildness of Moore's treatment,[123] had mixed feelings. He disliked the erotic undertone and must have been horrified by the hateful attack on the altruistic Plunkett, but he admired Moore's freedom from the slavery to religious, political, and social convention which paralysed so much of Irish life. 'I can't help liking Moore in spite of his bad taste,' he wrote to John Quinn. 'He is no hypocrite and is never afraid to say what he thinks.'[124] In the *Homestead* he referred to Moore's 'malicious phantasy' even while acknowledging its genius.[125]

The friendship between the two authors was not to last much longer. When *The Brook Kerith,* a novel on the origins of Christianity, appeared in August 1916, AE objected that whereas Jesus and Paul were at the very least intellectuals who changed the course of history, the author had portrayed them as fools.[126] Moore felt some distress at this, but the real break came after Susan Mitchell, two months later, published a study in which the novelist was subjected to a little of the ridicule he had showered on others. AE reviewed her book in his 'Notes of the Week,' praising the elegant sentences daintily by-passing 'the more unpleasant things in [her] subject,' but commending also her attention to 'the good qualities in her hero, which, to tell the truth, have been overlooked by most people in Ireland most unjustly, but he has himself to blame for that.'[127] The persecutor-turned-victim believed that AE's was the real brain behind the satire; for many years he broke off all intercourse and he took to calling his former companion 'the Donegal dauber.'

In due course James Stephens replaced Moore in AE's affections, becoming a more intimate friend than the other had ever been. The ensuing years seem to have been particularly happy for him: after the Troubles he was to look back on the period preceding the Great War as the most creative era of modern Ireland. Clifford Bax's brother Arnold, a distinguished composer who came to live in Rathgar in the winter of 1911, records that AE later referred to the period from 1912 to 1914 as Dublin's Golden Age.

Having been introduced to the mystic by his brother, Arnold used to attend the Sunday salon. An English Celtic enthusiast who was then part of the circle always wore an Irish kilt and insisted on speaking Gaelic until AE, 'for once irritated out of his Olympian calm, frankly told him that it was damned bad manners to talk to other people in a language of which they knew nothing.'[128] In 1912 Arnold Bax joined AE in Donegal where, despite his uneasiness at talk of otherworldly visions, he too heard faery music.

AE had now become one of the greatest talkers of Dublin, a city famous for the quality of its conversation. He had only two rivals, James Stephens, the master of comic fantasy, and the scholar MacKenna. 'Who is there,' wrote AE, 'who had heard Stephen MacKenna speak for an hour, running the scale from wildest humour to an eloquence lofty as Burke, or to the white light of Plotinus, would have changed that entertainment to watch even an Abbey Masterpiece?'[129] AE's own talk ranged over the whole field of his interests; he was as ready to launch forth on dairy farming as on the Bhagavadgita or the origins of the Abbey Theatre. Images, quotations, and epigrammatic phrases flowed in a melodious stream that drew the listener into the speaker's own intellectual realm. While talking, he usually held his pipe, and from time to time he gestured with his hands. If he read a passage from a book, he would hold it close to his eyes on account of his shortsightedness. He spoke with a mellow Ulster accent and the rhythms of his speech seemed to some inclined to become too pronounced: Yeats was once heard to protest, 'For God's sake get Russell a harp.'[130] As he became older, the habit of the monologue grew on him. One of his friends noticed that his talk on Sunday was often repeated in his next leading article in the *Homestead,* and Mr. Colum remarks that to read *The Living Torch,* Dr. Gibbon's brilliant selection from his articles in the *Irish Statesman,* is to hear again his familiar voice.[131]

James Stephens wrote: 'AE as a bulk was gay; he inclined to sit on the top of the morning all day.'[132] When the conversation ran spontaneously, the lighter side of his personality was given free rein. His humour, which delighted his friends, appears only occasionally in his writing. Teasing a visiting English lady, he warned her 'that she would never resist the Celtic atmosphere, struggle how she might, but would soon be wandering in the mountain mists with a fillet round her head.'[133] When Yeats's sisters were at their wits' end trying to persuade their father to return from America, he suggested they cable: 'Family all dying. Come to receive last messages.'[134] Dr. Gibbon recalls the gusto with which he parodied his own poetry,[135] and he caricatured the style of Yeats's lyrics for Susan Mitchell's anthology *Secret Springs of Dublin Song*. Surprisingly, he could even laugh on the surface of his mind at ideas that he held profoundly sacred, and there are many instances of this in the *Homestead:*

> The person who can see no difference in [*sic*] a young chicken and an old cock or hen will have no success in life. Certainly, his society won't. He should have been born in India, and been a Brahmin, trying to realise that there is only one substance in the universe, and that cocks, hens, humanity, and time itself, are only illusions.[136]

AE warned an admirer that she would find his poems very different from himself: 'The AE . . . who writes poetry is a very solemn person not at all like the vagrant and jesting person he is incarnated in.'[137] To Katharine Tynan he lamented that he could only write melancholy verse,[138] and this was certainly one of the disappointments of his life, for in the prefatory note to his *Collected Poems* he recalled: 'When I first discovered for myself how near was the King in His beauty I thought I would be the singer of the happiest songs.' The merriment that was squeezed out of his books was left over to brighten his life.

By this period the greatness of AE had become evident to his contemporaries; for many of them it lay in the rare perfection of his character rather than in the sum of his varied achievements. The mystic, the poet, the artist, the practical man, and the editor had coalesced in a radiant personality that communicated a zest for living, limitless compassion, an ardent love of beauty, and an unquenchable optimism in the future of the universe, to a wide circle of friends, acquaintances and readers. In articles and memoirs they recorded their wonder at finding a man who seemed to have re-created in himself the harmony that he had discovered in the universe and to have opened up in some secret recess of his being a wellspring of the spiritual qualities that all religions praise. They felt intuitively that he had annihilated in himself every trace of hatred, greed, and malice, and had almost succeeded in renouncing in his heart personal ambition and pride. He seemed to have transcended the egotism from which sprang the emotions that dominated normal life. Entering into his presence, the worldly glimpsed his serenity and briefly escaped from their own self-centred emotional shells. In a country seething with many hatreds, men who were irreconcilable political enemies met peacefully in his home. Katharine Tynan wrote of him:

> He is of the world, unworldly – the world's stain has never touched him; without religion, yet profoundly religious; the peace of God which passeth understanding lies all about him . . . There is no room in him for any of the small meannesses of humanity. There is something strangely benign about him. He keeps his image of God undistorted, undefaced, as few of us have kept it. When I am struck cold, remembering that such and such a one, something uniquely precious of God's making, is no longer of this world, I turn to think upon George Russell, that untroublesome genius. I am glad that in all probability he will survive me, for of him more than anyone else I have ever known I would say: 'We shall never look on his like again.'[139]

Mr. Diarmuid Russell, who only came to know his father intimately in adult life, writes of the atmosphere that surrounded him:

> . . . he possessed, more than any other person I have met, an air of spiritual power, an emanation of sweetness and tenderness that was almost as perceptible as the light from a lamp – and as hard to describe.[140]

Wishing to evoke his presence, many resorted to the word 'goodness' – and felt its inadequacy. His friend Dr. Constantine Curran found a Franciscan quality in his life and tried to define his effect on the authors he helped:

> . . . during his life he was to these writers, and now in memory remains part of their conscience, a tribunal before which the ignoble dwindles.[141]

Stephen MacKenna almost wept when AE, in a passing mood of despondency, wrote of his service in the co-operative movement as a desertion of his spiritual duty: 'I say to myself "It was done for the beloved Motherland, this errantry of mine," but I know in my heart that the service I gave was an easier and lower service than doing the best and highest it was in me to do.' In his reply MacKenna declared: 'I have always thought of you, always in all these long years, as one of the noble expressions of the divine mind . . .'[142] To Clifford Bax, AE was

> one of those rare spirits who bring to men the realisation of their own divinity, who make the spiritual life seem adventurous, attractive, and vivid, so that we go forth into the world with a new interest and a new joy at heart.[143]

Carrie Rea, another friend to whom he was a spiritual guide, said after his death:

> . . . I have always thought of him as one who came out of the Great Unknown, and who after a short period partially withdrew again. He might have had neither father, mother nor brother.[144]

Mr. Padraic Colum, too, sensed that there was a kind of homelessness about him, which yet was in no way melancholy.[145] Many descriptions of AE recall the young George Richmond's feeling that talking with the elderly Blake was like conversing with the prophet Isaiah. Maurice Joy, at one time secretary to Plunkett, wrote:

> He could be the simplest and warmest of companions, and when one walked with him, all human as he was, along an Irish country road in the moonlight, one at least could understand why it was that on the road to Emmaus the hearts of certain fishermen burned within them.[146]

Many who knew him felt that only a few endearing foibles detracted from AE's perfection. He was somewhat vain about his memory and when requested to recite some of his poems would ask which were preferred, as if to show that he knew them all by heart. Mr. Diarmuid Russell recounts with amusement how 'he used to argue with me, occasionally with some asperity, about the merits of billiard and cricket players, although neither of us knew anything about either subject.'[147]

When other writers described him, AE was always astonished at the portrait that emerged, and on reading St. John Ervine's fine appreciation of him in *Some Impressions of My Elders,* he admitted:

'The subject never knows himself as the object and is not a good judge of the drawing . . .'[148] His correspondence shows that despite his appearance of serenity he was often troubled in mind at the course of events in Ireland, which sometimes brought him near to despair. Yet such feelings seem rarely to have touched the depths of his consciousness; except briefly, during the worst crises and perhaps near the end of his life, he almost always enjoyed at some level an inner peace. In 1925, alluding to his continued practice of meditation, he explained to Pryse that he was content to live among people who had little insight into the divine nature of man:

> So long as you can travel back and peer inside the heavenly house or listen at its doors you must have a happiness. I sometimes wish I had given up everything else for mysticism but I had to do something here, not much, but still I have left among the people in this country some utterances which came out of the spirit, and though I feel there is a dark sorcery over everything I shall go back to myself in due time . . .[149]

Though he fell short of the sanctity of a St. Francis of Assisi or a Mahatma Gandhi, AE attained a degree of spirituality utterly beyond most men.

By 1912 Ireland was entering on a troubled decade. The Liberal Government at Westminster at last introduced the Home Rule Bill in the hope of which the Irish Nationalist Members had long supported them. The powers to be conferred on a Dublin parliament were very limited: defence, foreign relations, and even finance were to be excluded. With the encouragement of the Leader of the Opposition, Bonar Law, the Ulster Protestants, led by Sir Edward Carson, prepared to resist by any means that proved to be necessary, and 200,000 of them signed a Solemn Covenant to this effect. Early in the year, AE had long talks in Dublin with the English politician Leopold Amery, who was doing his best to justify Nationalist suspicions that any economic improvements brought about by the I.A.O.S. would be used to show how the country was prospering under the Union.[150] In April, Kipling issued as a broadside his poem 'Ulster' in which he sought to support the Unionist stand by inflaming racial and religious passions. AE, speaking as an Ulsterman from a Protestant family, replied with an open letter to the London *Daily News;* in a rhetorical style but with irrefutable arguments, he exposed the fallacies in Kipling's position and grieved that a writer with true gifts of imagination and tenderness should have disgraced the name of poet by exploiting his country for gain in prominently copyrighted verses.

By January 1913, when the Home Rule Bill was passed by the Commons, Ulster had recruited a large private army. AE spent several days of this month in London, where he called on Moore, met the young poet Mr. Ralph Hodgson, whose lyrics he very justly admired, and rejected the claims of post-Impressionist art* as he had once rejected those of Impressionism. More important, he lunched on his last day with Asquith, the Prime Minister, and Birrell, the Chief Secretary for Ireland. During the evening he was introduced by F. S. Oliver to Arthur Balfour, and in the course of a long conversation he agreed with the latter's belief that there were only two feasible solutions to the Irish Question – complete Union or complete self-government without, in either case, any distinction between North and South. On the same day he met A. R. Orage, the former Theosophist whose brilliant propaganda for Guild Socialism he often mentioned in the *Homestead,* believing that the study of Indian philosophy had made his judgment extraordinarily searching and profound. On his return to Dublin he still had hopes that the House of Lords would not exercise its power to delay Home Rule for two years.[151]

During the spring, AE was much preoccupied with the preparation of a collected edition of his poems. He had had this project in mind for at least four years, and in May he set to work in earnest to get the copyright for his three existing volumes into his own hands. Charles Weekes, who was acting as his London agent, was shrill in his insistence that the contract for the new edition should be given to George Roberts, the excitable, red-haired little man who had contributed to *New Songs* and who was now running Maunsel's, the premier publishers of the new Anglo-Irish literature. AE persisted in explaining that Roberts had turned into a cantankerous and unscrupulous businessman, who was imposing unreasonable conditions on young poets struggling to make a living; he had even quarrelled with the amiable Katharine Tynan and the easygoing James Stephens, though AE had impressed on him his belief that the latter was going to be a most important writer. Eventually Weekes had to accept the position, and the contract was given to Macmillan's of London, who had published *The Divine Vision.*[152] In June, during his Donegal holiday, AE arranged the contents of the edition, excluding those verses he thought inferior and grouping the others so that adjacent poems illuminated a common theme or, occasionally, contrasted with one another.[153] The book appeared in September and was enthusiastically received by reviewers and private individuals. James Stephens wrote that he had understood

*Two years before, in the *Irish Times* of 26 January, 1911, he had already published an attack on this school entitled 'The Post Impressionists: Art and Barbarism,' in which he pilloried its enervated, visionless incompetence and the folly of its 'easily-hypnotised' admirers, the victims of a 'few picture dealers in France.'

AE's verse for the first time.[154]

Scattered through the volume are twenty-one previously uncollected poems, several being of unusual interest or quality. Two of these record visions of the infinite and immortal that came upon the poet as he walked in Dublin – according to an American acquaintance he sometimes had such experiences when he left his office at sunset.[155] In 'The City,' the sudden wonder of the vision is expressed through short, stabbing sentences that break up the onrush of the sweeping hexameters, and the familiar celestial imagery takes on a new power as it is brought alongside the grim realities of the urban streets. 'Transformations,' a protest against the debased modern Christianity holding souls enslaved in 'dark churches where the blind mislead the blind,' is less firmly anchored in the metropolis which is its starting point. AE's editorial battles are reflected in the clear, rhetorical stanzas of 'The Iron Age,' which denounces the choice of mean-souled hucksters as political leaders. It ends with a plea for the consolation of one last Avatar before the world enters the longest, darkest portion of the Kali Yuga or Iron Age:

Send forth, who promised long ago,
'I will not leave thee or forsake,'
Someone to whom our hearts may flow
With adoration, though we make
The crucifixion be the sign,
The meed of all the kingly line.

The morning stars were heard to sing
When man towered golden in the prime.
One equal memory let us bring
Before we face our night in time.
Grant us one only evening star,
The iron age's avatar.

Two notable poems are remote from the contemporary scene. In 'Krishna,' AE rapturously hymns the god as an Incarnation of the Logos. Neatly employing initial capitals to denote his divine aspect and the lower case to indicate his human nature, the poet turns the whimsies of the latter touched on in the scriptural fragment he is imitating[156] into gross vices; covertly, it seems, he is challenging in paradoxes the worshippers of the all-virtuous Christ. While the swift octameter couplets embody a devotional ardour, there is a degree of monotony in the placing of the caesura, and the contrast between the concrete scenes of earthly life and the infinite abstract perfection of the deity never comes sharply enough into focus. No such blurring mars the perfection of 'The Virgin Mother,' a song of praise to the earth seen as a form of the Archaeus, the source of all beauty. The diction is simple and free from clichés, and a distinctive rhythmic and syntactical pattern gives each stanza its own vitality.

Who is that goddess to whom men should pray,
But her from whom their hearts have turned away,
Out of whose virgin being they were born,
Whose mother nature they have named with scorn
Calling its holy substance common clay.

Yet from this so despised earth was made
The milky whiteness of those queens who swayed
Their generations with a light caress,
And from some image of whose loveliness
The heart built up high heaven when it prayed.

Lover, your heart, the heart on which it lies,
Your eyes that gaze and those alluring eyes,
Your lips, the lips they kiss, alike had birth
Within that dark divinity of earth,
Within that mother being you despise.

Ah, when I think this earth on which I tread
Hath borne these blossoms of the lovely dead,
And makes the living heart I love to beat,
I look with sudden awe beneath my feet
As you with erring reverence overhead.

Shortly after AE's return from Donegal, the American Commission of Rural Enquiry, sent by the United States Government to study agricultural co-operation in Europe, spent a week in Ireland. On 15 July, the members assembled at Plunkett House and AE opened the meeting by lecturing on 'The Rural Community.'[157] The visitors were profoundly impressed by his vision of a rural civilisation[158] – some of them were even moved to tears[159] – but he noticed, too, their deep-seated fear of socialism and their national 'mania for independence.'[160]

It was probably about this time that AE met Charles McCarthy, who had dedicated his life to others as effectively as Plunkett, H. F. Norman and Patrick Gallagher: to become acquainted with such men is one of the rewards of studying AE. McCarthy, an unpolished but deeply compassionate Irish-American friend of

Plunkett, had risen from poverty and obscurity to champion the cause of co-operation and democracy among the farmers of the dairy state of Wisconsin. Using his prowess as a footballer to finance his education, he became an expert in politics, economics, and law, and served both the State University and the State Legislature. By building up the extension service of the former and founding a Reference Library for the latter, he took education to the countryside and made specialised knowledge available to the politician. Although he served as Librarian to the Legislature and lectured at the University, he, like AE, avoided acquiring personal wealth. During his visits to Ireland to study the work of the I.A.O.S., he used to call on AE at Plunkett House, and by late 1913 the latter was drawing attention in the *Homestead* to developments in Wisconsin, calling on Irish universities to follow the example of the great academy where McCarthy taught by bringing their activities into a closer relationship with modern life.

At the beginning of August, Dublin was on the threshold of an historical showdown between labour and capital. James Stephens had just left for Paris, and AE, temporarily depressed, wrote scathingly in the *Homestead* of the swarms of would-be intellectuals left behind:

> . . . Dublin is a dreadful place, where the man who loves truth as a passion is surrounded by people who form intimacies with ideas as a fashion and he feels an outcast, and most of all he hates the person who as a relief from idleness has learned to chatter about the very ideas the truth seeker has made his own out of reverence for truth.[161]

He was bitter, too, at the Dublin Corporation's refusal to build an art gallery which would have secured for the city a valuable collection of paintings as a gift from Sir Hugh Lane. The businessmen responsible revealed themselves, in AE's words, 'as the meanest, the most uncultured, the most materialistic and canting crowd which ever made a citizen ashamed of his fellow-countrymen.'[162]

Two years before, during a bout of strikes, he had pleaded for friendly contacts between organised capital and organised labour, and especially for a general recognition of the needs of the workers, as the only alternative to an impending industrial Armageddon.[163] At the beginning of 1912, when the National Insurance Act was about to come into force, he prophesied: 'We anticipate labour troubles during the next two years which will make the labour troubles of the past seem a mere murmur of gnats.'[164] It was widely recognised that conditions in the Dublin slums were the worst in Western Europe: more than 100,000 people were packed in filthy, decaying tenement buildings with five, six, or even more often living in a single room.

The leaders of the workers and the employers in the great strike and lockout were James Larkin, a big, dark, passionate man, and William Martin Murphy, a handsome, imperturbable capitalist. Both men were born fighters. It was probably some years before that AE had suddenly become psychically aware of the presence of a powerful personality while he was sitting on the top of a Dublin tramcar; looking up he saw a large man at the opposite end of the vehicle, and on being introduced to him a few days later he learnt that it was Larkin who had thus affected him.[165] Surprisingly the leader of the workers, though raised in poverty, appreciated art and beauty, and declared that Murphy, for his meanness in the matter of Sir Hugh Lane's offer, would be condemned to keep an art gallery in Hell. Larkin, the leader of the Irish Transport and General Workers' Union, was ably assisted by James Connolly, a fellow Catholic, socialist, and Nationalist, whose approach to labour problems was more intellectual. AE preferred Larkin's personality to Connolly's,[166] but regretted that unlike the latter he had no constructive policy.[167]

The strike began on the morning of 26 August, 1913, when, at Larkin's bidding, the drivers and conductors of Murphy's trams abandoned their vehicles and walked home. Strikers' meetings and large scale police violence followed, and Larkin and Connolly were briefly imprisoned. On 3 September, four hundred employers solemnly pledged themselves at Murphy's instigation not to employ workers who refused to forswear permanently any connection with Larkin's Union. In a leading article, AE blamed the capitalists for the police brutality, which had been directed at onlookers as well as strikers, and asserted that neither capital nor labour had a positive programme. He cited the fine examples of productive and distributive co-operation in Belfast and referred to the achievements of the Italian glassworkers, who had endured extraordinary hardships to escape from their masters and erect their own co-operative factories.[168]

The four hundred employers retaliated by staging a giant lock-out and triumphantly proclaimed that they themselves would continue to eat three good meals a day. AE was among the writers who gathered at Liberty Hall to try to help the hungry men and women who queued there for food tickets,[169] and he joined the Industrial Peace Committee, which after some weeks became the Civic League. Out of the latter developed the Irish Citizen Army, led by the mercurial Ulster Protestant Captain James White – 'that marvellous gentleman,'[170] as AE, who designed the flag for the force,[171] called him. The Army, founded in October to provide protection against the violence of police and strike-breakers, was issued with boots and staves for drilling and soon became a nationalist force like the Irish Volunteers started in Dublin about the same time as a reaction to the warlike preparations in Ulster. Seeing the city almost divided into a number of armed camps, AE charged his countrymen in the *Homestead* with having neglected intellect and imagination so that they now had to resort to physical force to fill the mental vacuum.[172] Privately he wrote to Stephen MacKenna, 'one goes about these days with a burden on the heart all the time,' and went on to speculate whether the Avatar he had seen in vision in 1896 was about to appear at last.[173]

On 7 October, the *Irish Times* carried an open letter from AE denouncing the masters of industry as bad citizens, bad employers, and bad businessmen. Having decided, not necessarily without just cause, on a lockout, they should have made tireless efforts to reach agreement knowing that the fate of twenty thousand families hung in the balance. Instead of this, they 'determined deliberately, in cold anger, to starve out one-third of the population of this city, to break the manhood of the men by the sight of the suffering of their wives and hunger of their children.' Holding up to them an image of their own cruelty and arrogance, AE charged:

> If you had between you collectively a portion of human soul as large as a threepenny bit, you would have sat night and day with the representatives of labour, trying this or that solution of the trouble, mindful of the women and children, who at least were innocent of wrong against you.

Finally, he warned them that the hatred they were arousing would persist for generations to destroy them: they were 'blind Samsons pulling down the pillars of the social order.'[174] A few days after the appearance of this attack, H. M. Tomlinson and George Leach, two English journalists who were braving the violence of the Dublin streets, visited AE at Plunkett House. Tomlinson, awed and uplifted by his remote, Buddha-like orations to the young intellectuals crowding his office, wondered how he could ever have come down to earth to achieve the noble rationality of his open letter, while Leach whispered as they descended the stairs, 'Don't you think we ought to have taken our boots off when we came in?'[174a]

British trade unions and co-operative societies sent huge shiploads of food to relieve the hunger in the Dublin slums. Opinion within Ireland itself was strangely divided. In *Sinn Fein,* Arthur Griffith, though in favour of unions in principle, attacked the strikers for practising 'English Trade Unionism in Ireland.' About the middle of October, hungry children from the Dublin slums began to be evacuated to temporary foster homes in Britain. Griffith again protested at this link with the land of the enemy, and Archbishop Walsh announced that the children's Catholic faith was in danger. Larkin himself would have preferred them to have been moved to other parts of Dublin. A mob gathered on the quayside to prevent further embarkation, and members of the Ancient Order of Hibernians, a sinister nationalist organisation which excluded non-Catholics and supported the employers, assaulted the parents. Mrs. Dora Montefiore, who had come from London, was arrested and charged with kidnapping.

On 28 October, Larkin, convicted of sedition, was sentenced to seven months' imprisonment. Two days later AE decided to join the speakers at a protest meeting scheduled for 1 November in the Albert Hall in London; meanwhile, he pointed out in an article in the *Irish Worker* that sedition was now no crime in Ireland – Unionists and Nationalists were openly preparing for civil strife. In his best vein of irony he explained why Larkin deserved his sentence:

> He was preventing a sociological experiment of great importance to Ireland from being carried out. We have never accurately determined how little human beings can live on, and how little air space is necessary for families . . . It is quite possible that after exhaustive experiments had been carried out . . . we might have found out that human beings could be packed comfortably in rooms like bees in a hive, and could generate heat to warm themselves by their very number without the necessity for coal . . . Nothing is more annoying to scientific investigators than the unscientific, humanitarian-like James Larkin, who comes along and upsets all calculations and destroys the labour of generations in the evolution of the underman, which was going along so well.[175]

At the Albert Hall, where James Connolly, Bernard Shaw, Mrs. Montefiore, and Larkin's sister Delia were among his companions on the platform, AE enlarged nobly on these themes, but unfortunately pitched his voice too low so that only a small portion of the audience caught his words.[176] Describing the crisis in Dublin, he bitterly categorised his fellow citizens:

> People are to us either human or sub-human. They are either on the side of those who are fighting for human conditions in labour or they are with those who are trying to degrade it and thrust it into the abyss.
>
> Ah! but I forgot; there has sprung up a third party, who are super-human beings, they have so little concern for the body at all, that they assert it is better for children to be starved than to be moved from the Christian atmosphere of the Dublin slums . . .

> If any poor parents think otherwise, and would send their children for a little from that earthly paradise, they will find the docks and railway stations barred by these super-human beings and by the police, and they are pitched headlong out of the station, set upon and beaten, and their children snatched from them.

After referring ironically to the Archbishop as 'a very holy man,' he went on to speak of the slums, and echoed words he had first used sixteen years before in *The Future of Ireland and the Awakening of the Fires*:

> It maddens one to think that man the immortal, man the divine, should exist in such degradation, that his heirship of the ages should be the life of a brute.

Sketching the actions taken by both sides, he led up to his view of the politicians:

> The men have been deserted by those who were their natural leaders. For ten weeks the miserable creatures who misrepresent them in Parliament kept silent. When they were up for the first time in their lives against anything real they scurried back like rats to their hole. These cacklers about self-government had no word to say on the politics of their own city, but after ten weeks of silence they came out with six lines of a letter signed by all the six poltroons. They disclaimed all responsibility for what is happening in the city and county they represent. It was no concern of theirs; but they would agree to anything the Archbishop might say!

These men had proven cowards, but the workers, fired by Larkin, had shown themselves to be of heroic mould:

> . . . a man has arisen who has lifted the curtain which veiled from us the real manhood in the city of Dublin. Nearly all the manhood is found among obscure myriads who are paid from five to twenty-five shillings per week . . . when the masters issued that humiliating document, asking men – on penalty of dismissal – to swear never to join a trades union, thousands of men . . . refused to obey. They would not sign away their freedom, their right to choose their own heroes and their own ideas. Most of these men had no strike funds to fall back on. They had wives and children depending on them. Quietly and grimly they took through hunger the path to the Heavenly City.

AE well knew that he was jeopardizing his future in the co-operative movement – three days later he wrote to Weekes that he might soon be looking for new employment – but he declared in the Albert Hall:

> I am a literary man and not a manual worker. I am but a voice, while they are the deed and the being, but I would be ashamed ever in my life again to speak of an ideal if I did not stand by these men

and say of them what I hold to be true.[177]

Not only were the Church authorities angered by his remarks on the Archbishop, but they understandably took the phrase 'super-human beings' to refer to themselves. Even the committee of the I.A.O.S. which met to consider AE's action made the same error, though, as he complained in the *Homestead,* they 'might have consulted the daily papers where they would have found in police reports who the real culprits were.'[178] Meanwhile, the Ancient Order of Hibernians, who knew that they were meant, had taken secret though unsuccessful measures to have the journal suppressed.[179]

The deadlock between the employers and the workers continued, the Dublin press being overwhelmingly on the side of capital. On 11 November, AE composed his final warning, an open letter suppressed in Dublin but printed in the London *Times,* prophesying that if the Dublin authorities, newspapers, and capitalists persisted in their course they would provoke an inherently gentle people to rise in violent revolt:

> Dublin seems to be stumbling darkly and blindly to a tragedy, and the silence of those who foresee and do not speak is a crime. It is time for the Chorus to cry out to warn the antagonists in the drama.[180]

The hunger of the workers and the dislocation of industry dragged on into 1914 through further months of suffering, while the strikes and lock-out collapsed by stages without any agreement being reached. Neither side achieved its aims, as the demands of labour were not met and the Irish Transport and General Workers' Union was not suppressed. Larkin attempted to set up a producers' co-operative, but he ignored AE's warnings in the *Homestead* that co-operators should proceed from distribution to production in order to be sure of a market, and his venture failed.[181]

A by-product of AE's support of the workers was the revival of one of his oldest friendships. On the day that he spoke at the Albert Hall, an article by Yeats denouncing the employers appeared in the *Irish Worker*. AE wrote to him:

> Please let me congratulate you on your speech at the Peace Meeting and above all on your article in *The Irish Worker*. I have differed from you in many things but I felt all my old friendship and affection surging up as I read what you said.[182]

The two poets resumed their friendship, but AE regretted the way in which Yeats had changed, deliberately adopting a majestic pose in the belief that his inner life would be transmuted to match it. To Moore he exclaimed a year or two later: 'Why can't he be natural? Such a delightful creature he was when young! And at rare moments when he forgets himself he is still interesting as ever almost.'[183] Reminiscing in old age, AE took a more sympathetic view of Yeats's arrogance, explaining it as a necessary protective mask to cut him off from intimacy with all but those few people who, like Lady Gregory, possessed imaginations which harmonized with his own. Similarly, AE realized that to accomplish an independent life work he had had to escape from the magnetic field of his friend's more powerful personality.[184] Many members of their social circle noticed that on Yeats's entry AE would relapse from volubility into silence, as though he were overawed, and Douglas Goldring reports that Yeats, too, was inhibited in the other's presence.[185]

The drift towards civil war continued during the winter, spring, and summer of 1914. By March, AE felt that the *Homestead,* like most things in Ireland, was merely marking time until Ulster decided whether her loyalty to the King was strong enough to make her rebel against his Government's decree.[186] Meanwhile he was preoccupied with the labour problem and was using his 'Notes of the Week' to advocate various forms of co-operation among city workers, though a few weeks later he admitted that the problem of turning an urban agglomeration into an organic community baffled him.[187] By March, too, he was also working on a sequel to *Co-operation and Nationality*.[188] Feeling unjustly that the latter was no more than a hurried piece of journalism,[189] he had begun a systematic synthesis of his ideas on urban and rural co-operation and his concept of nationhood; the new book, *The National Being,* was to be the belated fulfilment of his project of 1910 for a programme which would give Ireland a chance of gaining something more by Home Rule than a mere duplicate of the British polity. The threat of internecine conflict only subsided when the United Kingdom declared war on Germany on 4 August and the implementation of Home Rule was suspended until the restoration of peace. The whole of Europe was entering an era of violence, and the working out of the details of the Co-operative Commonwealth ceased to constitute the centre of AE's professional life.

VI

A Pacifist Faces Violence

(i) Warfare at a Distance (1914–1918)

One of AE's great certainties was that war, even if purely defensive, was unethical, and though his faith in non-violence was later partially shaken, the articles he published in the *Homestead* shortly before the outbreak of the Great War reflect an attitude to physical force very close to that of Mahatma Gandhi. His pacifism was associated with a belief that a resort to violence was always a sign of intellectual failure. The fourteen months following the start of Larkin's strike were marked by a considerable change in his contributions to the paper. The long passages in which he continued to work out the ideas adumbrated in *Co-operation and Nationality* – many of them later incorporated in *The National Being* – almost disappeared, while he concentrated instead on the analysis of current circumstances. In his New Year message for 1914, he spoke of the coming crisis when men would be swept up in a universal 'mood of dilated consciousness' and stripped of their social masks. Referring Theosophically to the power of thought, he wrote:

> The noises one makes with one's lips have really no effect, and we might go on expressing wishes for this or that until the last fiery twilight of Time had faded into the divine darkness without the words we utter accomplishing any more than setting up some transitory vibrations in the air. But thoughts are different things. A thought is a real force. The universe was born out of the Divine thought, and man when he really thinks or truly imagines an ideal is setting real forces to work which will finally bring about events and happenings in his life and the life of his country . . .

Thought was vital now, he explained, because the nation was in a molten state:

> . . . if the co-operators who have real ideals and a real policy for Ireland keep to their ideals and preach their policy, all that is best in Ireland will turn to them with longing, and when the human metal cools it will have received a co-operative character which will not easily be effaced.[1]

In February, regretting that so many more were prepared to die for their beliefs than were ready to live by them, AE expounded his view of violence:

> It is much easier to allow yourself to be killed than to be killing self out all your life to win the heaven of the selfless. There is an absolute morality, and below that there are relative moralities. The purely spiritual man who has a superb reliance on divine law to justify and sustain him will return good for evil, will endure all things without anger, and will not take to the sword because he believes he is throwing into the scales something which will outweigh all physical powers. But if he has not this illumination, then if a man is oppressed it is relatively better morals for him to fight than to be a slave, because that is the choice for him.[2]

Similarly, Mahatma Gandhi insisted that while the highest path was that of non-violent non-co-operation, it was better to fight than to flee out of cowardice or to collaborate with evildoers; true pacifism incorporated and transcended the courage necessary for self-defence.

AE watched in horror as arms were smuggled into the North in April and into the South in July, but he rejoiced that despite all temptations the co-operators continued to exclude politics from their meetings; in one Ulster society men drilling on opposite sides worked in friendship on the committee.[3] When Plunkett, at the height of the crisis, made the grave error of speaking in favour of Home Rule at a co-operative conference, AE wrote to him bluntly:

> If you refer again to this matter, I shall either have to make a public protest in *The Homestead* or resign my editorship of the paper.[4]

In the journal, he asserted that the movement had now such a hold on Ireland that only civil war could destroy it, and that if it continued for ten more years no one would desire partition.[5]

Three years earlier, AE had acclaimed as irrefutable the argument in Norman Angell's book *The Great Illusion* that peoples and governments must be taught to recognise that war under modern conditions would ruin the victors as well as the vanquished by destroying international credit,[6] and in April 1914 he suggested to his countrymen that this theory applied equally to civil war.[7] In the same article he stated that a war correspondent (H. W. Nevinson, though he did not name him)[8] had told him that no newspaper would dare to print a true description of what he had witnessed. Three months later, however, after his return from his holiday at Dunfanaghy, where he had seen Ulster and Nationalist volunteers active on the other side of the bay,[9] he was trying to resign himself to the inevitable:

> Reason has abdicated its seat, never very safe, in the Irish character, and the two parties are now like trains without drivers but with steam up gathering force and swiftness as they rush to meet each other along the same track. What is there to be done but to

keep as cheerful as one can until it is all over. After all, the soul is immortal, and if a number of people want to tear its overcoat, the mortal body, off from each other, there is still the Heavenworld: the universe is sweet at heart; and if the great eternities are not threatened with destruction, we ought to be able to go about our business stoically.[10]

Two weeks afterwards Europe found itself on the brink of its first general war for a hundred years. The fate of a continent, AE declared, depended on a handful of mediocrities, political middlemen who perhaps wielded the power of life and death over civilisation itself. He reflected:

. . . when people have no clear conception of a social order or a peculiar civilisation to be built up, and are manoeuvred into a conflict which may result in the destruction of such forms of civilisation as they possess, it seems to us that the struggle is like 'a tale told by an idiot, full of sound and fury signifying nothing.'[11]

Forty-eight hours after these words were published, Germany invaded Belgium, and a day later, on 4 August, the United Kingdom declared war on Germany. Like Plunkett, AE admired German efficiency and organising ability, but dreaded the Prussian militarism which had come to dominate it at the cost of freedom, brotherhood, and human kindness. 'The Germans used to have real culture,' he wrote to his American publisher, 'now they have only wide spread mechanical and scientific education a very different thing.'[12] He sympathised with the British revulsion against the German invasion of small, neutral Belgium, and unlike some of his fellow Nationalists was firmly on the side of the Allies. When the Vice-Provost of Trinity College tried in November to suppress a meeting in honour of Thomas Davis because Padraic Pearse, who opposed recruitment, was to be one of the speakers, AE protested at this Prussian infringement on the British tradition of free speech.[13] A few days later he received a letter from Bernard Shaw, who was anxious to point out that if Irishmen sided with the Germans they were betraying France, their traditional ally.[14] Shaw asked AE whether he and Plunkett advised him to speak out publicly, and AE replied by telegram on 26 November:

Advise letter simultaneously three papers Irish Times Freemans Journal Irish Daily Independent You best man Plunkett agrees Russell.

A few weeks after the beginning of the War, Lloyd Morris, an American on his way home from Europe, passed through Dublin and one afternoon called on AE. The latter seems to have been outwardly unchanged, and his visitor afterwards recalled:

The man who welcomed [me] was tall, broad-shouldered, heavy-

> set, and dressed in a baggy suit of brown homespun. His massive head was crowned with a thick crop of rumpled, graying brown hair, and he wore a long, full beard. Behind spectacles, his remarkable eyes twinkled humorously. Knowledge of the ineffable met you in those eyes.

As AE talked in a matter-of-fact tone of the artist's inability to convey more than a hint of the mystic's vision and of his own illuminations, Morris felt that his usual opacity to mystical influence and belief was evaporating. AE spoke, too, of co-operation and the closely knit, organic society, the members of which had taken the first step towards transcending (not abdicating) the personal self. Morris remained until it was dark, and just before leaving referred to the War:

> The war, said AE., showed the baseness into which modern civilisation had finally been betrayed, because of its cult of individuality. To cherish and value individuality is to seem to take the part of life in the conflict of life and death; but it is to enlist on the side of death, and wilfully to seek annihilation. It is, he remarked, opening the door of his house on the night, to ally oneself with the powers of darkness and cruelty. It is, he concluded, to renounce the soul's implicit destiny.[15]

In spite of Stephens' departure, AE continued to enjoy a busy social life; he still received a constant stream of Irish and foreign visitors at his home and office, including many young soldiers who came for his blessing before leaving for the front.[16] All his life he went on making new friends, and about this period[17] he met a short, bearded, pipe-smoking bachelor named Osborn Bergin, who had taken refuge from life in the study of the Gaelic language and literature, and made himself the world's foremost authority on the subject. Shy, lonely, and touchy, he had developed a crusty exterior, which began to thaw before the warmth of AE's personality, and despite their differing mental habits – one was devoted to minute scholarly accuracy, the other to broad, general ideas – they became constant companions. AE used to give Bergin detective stories to bring him back to humanity,[18] and he in return lent AE Raleigh's study of Shakespeare and persuaded him to read the dramatist attentively for the first time.[19]

In September, AE managed to escape for two days to enjoy the countryside at Virginia, Co. Cavan, with James Stephens and Thomas Bodkin. They rowed on the lake, where Stephens composed a poem, and AE painted in Lord Headfort's woods until they were all expelled by a gamekeeper. Bodkin taught the poets to play poker, and AE proved by far the most efficient at the game. He had a brief infatuation with it, even insisting on locking the compartment door in the train and playing on top of the suitcases on the journey back to Dublin. Afterwards he seemed rather uncomfortable when Bodkin related the incident in front of his more serious-minded friends.[20]

The interlude must have been very welcome, for with the outbreak of war, AE took on new tasks. As a practical man with a wide knowledge of economic conditions in Ireland, he received a time-consuming Government appointment as adviser to a number of committees.[21] Three less business-like fellow artists even left to him the arrangements for their joint exhibition, which opened at the end of October[22] and turned out to be the last but one in Dublin to which he made a significant contribution. At the same time he was continuing to work on *The National Being*.

The universal indignation in Britain at the German treatment of Belgium was accompanied by a less admirable outburst of fanatical militarism. In September, the London *Times* published AE's poem 'Gods of War,' an expression of disgust at the complaints of clergymen that their bishops would not allow them to join in the slaughter.[23]

> Choose ye your rightful gods, nor pay
> Lip reverence that the heart denies.
> O Nations, is not Zeus to-day,
> The thunderer from the epic skies,
> More than the Prince of Peace? Is Thor
> Not nobler for a world at war?[24]

Ireland was free from the threat of immediate but not of eventual civil conflict, and AE had a profound feeling, which he could not quite account for, that the country was destined to endure 'one more heart-searching trial, baring our lives to the very spirit, and that within the next few years.'[25]

As soon as war had been declared, he started a series of campaigns in the *Homestead* to urge farmers to do their duty by their country. He refused to give an opinion as to whether they should enlist, since he himself was too old to do so,[26] but concentrated on marshalling every possible argument which might persuade them to produce the maximum quantity of food for the Irish people. In his editorial for 8 August, he referred to the prophetic articles of December 1910 and January 1911 in which he had pleaded that the country learn to feed itself, and during the following months he combined threats with enticements, pointing out that the War offered farmers the greatest financial opportunity they had ever had, but, should they neglect their duty, the Government would be compelled to place them under rigorous State control. His wrath was now directed against the incongruous official tenderness to middlemen in a time of national emergency and against the spineless consumers who preferred being fleeced to forming co-operatives. Of food profiteers he wrote: 'Such people ought to be whipped, if physical punishment is justifiable in any circumstances.'[27] After some time he was able to point out that statistics showed it was more dangerous to be born in disease-ridden, poverty stricken Dublin than to spend a year in the trenches.

In September 1914 the Home Rule Act received Royal Assent, and at the same time a Suspensory Act was passed to delay its implementation until after the War. For the next three months, while conducting his practical campaigns, AE used the columns of the *Homestead* to work out the conception of national identity that he was incorporating in his book. He held that every distinctive culture was the embodiment of an aspiration implanted in a race by a higher power (he once said that India pursued wisdom, Greece beauty, Rome justice, and Christendom love),[28] and he searched for the secret of Ireland's peculiar genius. It was to be found, he decided, in the constitution of the ancient clans, whose members held their land in common and chose men of outstanding character for their leaders; they were therefore democratic in their economic life and aristocratic in their politics, and the modern Irish found it natural to follow in this tradition, with which the co-operative system was in perfect accord. AE was thus able to ascribe a specifically Celtic quality to the aristocracy of character and intellect he had advocated in *Co-operation and Nationality*.

The phenomenon of the War itself had an impact on his theorising. Seeing great numbers of citizens giving up their comfort and safety to become part of a military machine, he came to believe that the co-operative organisation of the community would be capable of creating a comparable spirit of fearlessness, self-sacrifice, and service in civil life.[29] He omitted, however, to consider the element of compulsion brought to bear in wartime through the force of public opinion and through all that is implied in Blake's phrase 'fearing our officers more than the enemy.'

The prophet and the moralist in AE made their pronouncements on the War. Three months after it began he interpreted the conflict in terms of cosmic justice or *Karma,* maintaining that war could not be ended by war or hatred, but only by their opposites. By the law of the universe human societies, whether noble or base, duplicated themselves, and as Egypt had been reproduced in Chaldea and Carthage in Rome, so the British Empire had evoked the German and had to face a trial of strength with its own mirror image.[30] During the coming years he continued to prophesy that this would not be the last giant war and permanent peace was only to be won by the spiritual evolution of humanity:

> They tell us that they war on war. Why do they treat
> our wit with scorn?
> The Dragon from the Dragon Seed, the breed was true
> since life was born.[31]

In April 1915, seeking a wider audience, he published an article in the London *Times* warning Britain that as war with foreign powers and dictatorship at home had failed to crush the democratic idea at the root of the French Revolution, so the present war would fail to prevent the spread of the reaction to that idea, the German concept of the ruthlessly efficient, rigidly organised autocratic state.[32] About this time his poems on similar themes were appearing in the same newspaper: in 'Ares' he expounded his favourite belief that until men developed all their faculties, adding power, the attribute of the Holy Spirit, to the more easily cultivated imagination and intellect, there would be outbreaks of barbarous violence to shatter the peace they had not rightly earned.

By the spring of 1915, the horror of the conflict had begun to tell on AE's spirits. 'Words,' he wrote to Weekes, 'are a poor and cracked mirror of one's feelings. One lives with a strained heart all the time.'[33] Many of his friends were on the battlefield, and R. A. Anderson had already lost two of his three sons – the younger had intended to devote his life to the co-operative movement. In this year AE began to complain in his letters of the onset of old age: he was nearing fifty and felt that he would compose no more lyrics of value. 'I am damned tired of the world and want to go back to the stars,' he declared to James Stephens, and hearing that the latter aspired to become the Balzac of his countrymen he commented:

> If you could be the torpedo to explode them I would be enchanted. They are all dead in their bodies and the whimsies which delight you in them are posthumous vibrations.[34]

He recoiled equally from the mindless violence which prevailed in Ireland and the unprecedented holocaust on the Continent. In another letter he rebuked Stephens for listening to glib talk of post-War reconciliation:

> I do not think the French will ever forgive the Germans their ill-treatment of the civil population, the raping of women in France and the cruelties mentioned in the official French, Belgian and English reports . . . How any people could imagine that those actually on the spot who have witnessed with their own eyes the destruction of homes and towns could so easily turn I cannot understand.[35]

Writing later to John Quinn, however, he denied that any people could be innately or irredeemably evil, and blamed the ideals and conduct of the Germans on their education.[36] With his deep sympathy for the sufferings of those engaged in combat, he was overwhelmed to receive a compliment from Captain Sir John Keane, who read his paper in the trenches: 'A letter from the front to the HOMESTEAD is the greatest compliment it has ever received, and . . . our modesty broke down under the strain.'[37]

About September 1915, AE collected his poems on the European conflict in a little volume entitled *Gods of War,* which was privately printed and given away to friends. Though stereotyped phrases occasionally weaken the challenge to the prevailing war fever, the rhetorical clarity of these denunciations of bloodshed lends them a distinction denied to much of AE's verse. While the title poem echoes too closely the last chorus of Shelley's *Hellas,* 'A European Litany' is more successful in drawing aside the veil of piety from those whose true god is power. With daring irony AE addresses the familiar words of Christian prayer to the human rulers whom the nations have taken for their gods:

You, who now wield by earthly right
The sceptres God-conferred of old,
Who know no law above your might,
No sceptre higher than you hold:
We pray you in the ancient words,
Have pity on the people, lords!

. . . .

Whom shall we pray to now to give
The daily bread for us and ours,
For by ourselves we cannot live?
Hear, we beseech you, awful powers,
For blood of kin in payment shed
Give us this day our daily bread!

You take the father and the son,
The brother and the kin away.
We can but cry 'Thy will be done,'
As to the gods of yesterday.
When childhood is bereft of all,
Will you be Father at its call?

Despite the puritan ferocity of his moralising, AE would hardly have been true to himself had he held out no hope to his reader. In 'Apocalyptic' the comfort is double-edged as he wildly calls on the victim of priest and dictator to exult in the struggle, which must end in escape or death. But in 'Continuity,' one of his best lyrics, he sings of his faith, as gentle as it is strong, in the perpetual guardianship of the Creator:

> Life in an instant will be rent
> Where death is glittering blind and wild –
> The Heavenly Brooding is intent
> To that last instant on Its child.
> . . . .
> Though the crushed jewels droop and fade
> The Artist's labours will not cease,
> And of the ruins shall be made
> Some yet more lovely masterpiece.

The longest poem in the book, 'Shadows and Lights,' also approaches a spirit of conventional piety. Developing throughout his simple, basic image of earthly events seen as the shadows of heavenly counterparts, he demands in anguish through four long stanzas whether wars among the gods are not the cause of human strife:

> Are ye not guilty, answer, ye above?

Then, like his favourite George Herbert, turning again to God, he admits that man gazes on the shadows and wilfully averts his eyes from the lights. The long, eloquent sentences of his confession begin with lines solemnly weighed down with internal pauses and supernumerary syllables:

> Ah, no, the circle of the heavenly ones,
> That ring of burning, grave, inflexible powers . . .
> That through their day from dawn to twilight keep
> The peace of heaven, and have no feuds like ours.

Most of these moving, impressively varied lyrics were added to the 1919 edition of his *Collected Poems*.

Art and prose as well as poetry continued to offer AE a refuge from the grief around him. When he took his usual holiday in Donegal, he received the first artist's permit (complete with photograph) to be issued in the British Isles:[38] three of his friends had earlier been arrested as spies when they had dared to paint out of doors.[39] While he was still working on *The National Being,* he began another book, *The Candle of Vision,* an account of his mystical experiences, as well as a long blank verse legend, which was apparently never finished.[40] In December 1915 he published *Imaginations and Reveries,* a selection of his prose contributions to periodicals which reflected the enormous range of his interests. It included not only essays, but the stories from the *Irish Theosophist* earlier reprinted in *The Mask of Apollo* and his play *Deirdre*. His wealthy American friend John Quinn was delighted that the book was dedicated to him, for he counted AE among the very few Irishmen he knew who had never begged him for favours.[41]

After November 1914, little that was later to be incorporated in *The National Being* appeared in the *Homestead*. AE devoted his editorial contributions to advising and admonishing, and tried to guide the farmers and the nation during the period of emergency. He realised with delight that in one of his contributors, Thomas Wibberley, he had discovered an agricultural genius,[42] and announced that the latter's systems of ensilage and continuous cropping overcame the difficulties which had hitherto inhibited winter dairying in Ireland.

In spring 1915 Lloyd George, the Chancellor of the Exchequer, decided to introduce higher taxes and other measures to reduce the consumption of alcohol during the War. AE, with his Theosophist's abhorrence of alcohol, was revolted when the Irish M.P.'s protested that these restrictions would wreck a crucial sector of their country's economy and were able to provoke nationwide demonstrations in support of the liquor industry. He flayed this attempt to identify patriotism with the interests of the drink trade, as he often belaboured the Irish readiness to choose publicans for their representatives. In October he commented on Dublin's election of a Member who immediately declared that he would not have been a candidate if only he had been able to make his little pub pay: democracy, AE argued, is on trial in this War and if it 'is going to get gombeenmen and publicans to represent it, then it will crumble . . . and it will deserve to disappear.'[43] He desired, in fact, total prohibition, and so strong were his feelings that he declared: 'We would willingly throw in the pipe, which is so dear to us personally, if the other and worse poison were prohibited also.'[44] Strangely, he regarded cider as healthy and beneficial 'when it is not manufactured as a rival to fresh poteen just out of the still,'[45] and despite all his campaigns against whisky he did not change this opinion.

AE's most interesting contributions to the paper at this period are the many articles in which he prophesied the future reactions to present events. He was pleased to find that he had anticipated by several months a statement by the President of the British Board of Agriculture that the new submarine warfare would in future force the Government to give strong support to the farmers,[46] though in Britain the official promise was not in fact kept when the War was over. More remarkably, he foresaw the urgent need to prepare for peace, since demobilisation would cause large-scale unemployment and economic depression. There was a serious danger, he warned, of famine among the urban proletariat and of internal revolution all over Europe, but with good management the farmers would be able to feed themselves and perhaps save their fellow countrymen from hunger. In the month that war was declared he had realised that the United States would become the world's leading nation,[47] a point that he repeated intermittently.

On 20 April, 1916, AE travelled to Raheen, County Clare, to spend Easter weekend with his friend Edward MacLysaght, a poet, historian, farmer, and Nationalist. Five days later they set out together on the return journey, but at Ballybrophy they heard rumours that Sinn Fein had risen and seized Dublin. The train went no further and they had to return to Raheen to talk over the situation in agonizing ignorance of the facts. Next morning MacLysaght accompanied his guest as far as Limerick, and continuing alone AE reached Ballybrophy without difficulty, but had to make his way back to Dublin as best as he could, covering fourteen miles of the distance on foot.[48] He arrived to find smoke and fire rising from ruined buildings in the city centre and gunfire resounding in the streets, as British troops closed in on the strongpoints held by the hopelessly outnumbered soldiers of a stillborn Irish Republic. On Easter Monday, the Irish Volunteers and the Citizen Army, led by Padraic Pearse and James Connolly, had risen in rebellion at a previously appointed time although they knew that the simultaneous outbreaks planned in the provinces would not occur and victory was impossible. On Thursday, 27 April, the leaders of the Rising surrendered, ready to face execution but anxious to avoid further loss of life among their followers. That night three bullets flew past AE as he stood on his doorstep half a mile from the nearest fighting.[49]

During the next few days most normal activities were suspended in Dublin. The office of the *Homestead* had been set ablaze and its records destroyed,[50] and the next issue of the paper did not appear till 13 May, by which time the British Government had made a blunder that was to sever Ireland from the United Kingdom. At first, stunned by the suddenness of events and shocked by the idea of undermining the war effort, the public and the Nationalist M.P.'s had sided with the authorities, but when the Government followed up its initial panic by shooting the rebel leaders in cold blood, it forfeited the sympathy of the Irish people.

AE felt that the mood he had prophesied at the beginning of 1914 had arrived. 'People got a kind of dilated consciousness from the sound of guns, bombs, shells, and the burning of the city,' he wrote to John Quinn, ' . . . [and] did the most amazing things . . .' A normally sane businessman threatened to shoot anyone who disobeyed him, and a British officer could slaughter a completely innocent Irishman like the gentle pacifist Sheehy Skeffington, whose sole offence was an attempt to stop looting in the streets. 'I found out through talking to my excited friends,' AE continued, 'what wild, elemental passions lay below their quiet, everyday demeanour.'[51] He was delighted to encounter an English soldier, Sir Francis Fletcher Vane, who performed his duty without losing his calmness or humanity, and who insisted on just treatment of the Irish despite the objections of his fellow officers.[52]

Three of the executed leaders had been well known to AE, and though he was unable to approve of their resort to violence[53] and did not wholly share their ideals, he could only look with admiration, even awe, on men who had been ready to die for their beliefs. He had long respected the chivalrous and idealistic Padraic Pearse and his school at Rathfarnham, where boys were educated in the Gaelic tradition, and remembering Pearse's admiration for Standish O'Grady felt certain that he had seen himself in imagination standing like Cuchulain alone before a host.[54] It has been claimed by an anonymous writer that the Catholic-Nationalist mysticism of Pearse was influenced by AE,[55] though intellectually the latter was more in sympathy with Connolly's socialism than with Pearse's dream of a purely Gaelic society. Before his death Connolly told his wife to discuss the future of the family with AE, who thereupon organised a subscription and tried to obtain permission from the military authorities for the widow to emigrate to America.[56] For the poet and lecturer Thomas MacDonagh he had had less respect, never thinking that his highflown words about Ireland would be matched by deeds of equal valour. He remembered now that years before they had been walking together in the country when MacDonagh spoke of a boyhood vision of a star and a cup, which he had come to interpret as symbols of liberty and death.[57]

Publicly, AE refused to comment on the Easter Rising, apart from claiming that it was the poverty in the Dublin slums, unchanged since the great strike three years before, that had caused the uncultured rank and file to follow their idealistic leaders.[58] Indeed he regarded the revolt as the fulfilment of the prophecy in his open letter of November 1913. He expressed his admiration for the men who had been shot and their ally, his friend Countess Markievicz, who had been imprisoned, in the poem 'Salutation,' which he circulated only privately for fear of antagonising Ulster co-operators. His old acquaintance the Nationalist Sir Roger Casement, arrested just before the Rising for seeking German help, was also sentenced to death. Eighteen months earlier AE had dismissed him lightly:

He is a romantic person of the picturesque kind, with no heavy

AE's parents: Thomas Elias Russell and Marianne Russell. A photograph taken c.1870. Courtesy Alan Denson.

Above left: A photograph of AE, c.1890, from John Eglinton's *Memoir of AE,* 1937. Above right: AE in 1904, by John Butler Yeats, the elder. Courtesy of Senator M.B. Yeats and Miss Anne Yeats (to whom acknowledgement is made to include those paintings by J.B. Yeats in this book) and to the Abbey Theatre. Below left: Mrs. G.W. Russell, with Sara Allgood in 1911, taken by Lady Glenavy. Below right: Susan Mitchell, by John B. Yeats, the elder, courtesy of National Gallery of Ireland.

Above left: Standish O'Grady, by John B. Yeats, courtesy National Gallery of Ireland. Above right: W.Q. Judge. Below left: James Pryse, courtesy Alan Denson. Below right: Charles A. Weekes, courtesy Alan Denson.

Above: Lurgan, Co. Armagh, c.1870. From the Lawrence Collection, courtesy National Library of Ireland. Below: Pim's, South Great George's Street, Dublin, c.1967, where AE worked in the 1890s.

Above left: 3 Upper Ely Place, Dublin, home of the Household and Dublin Lodge. Above right: AE's house at 17 Rathgar Avenue, Dublin. Below: the only extant photograph of AE's office in Plunkett House, 84 Merrion Square, Dublin.

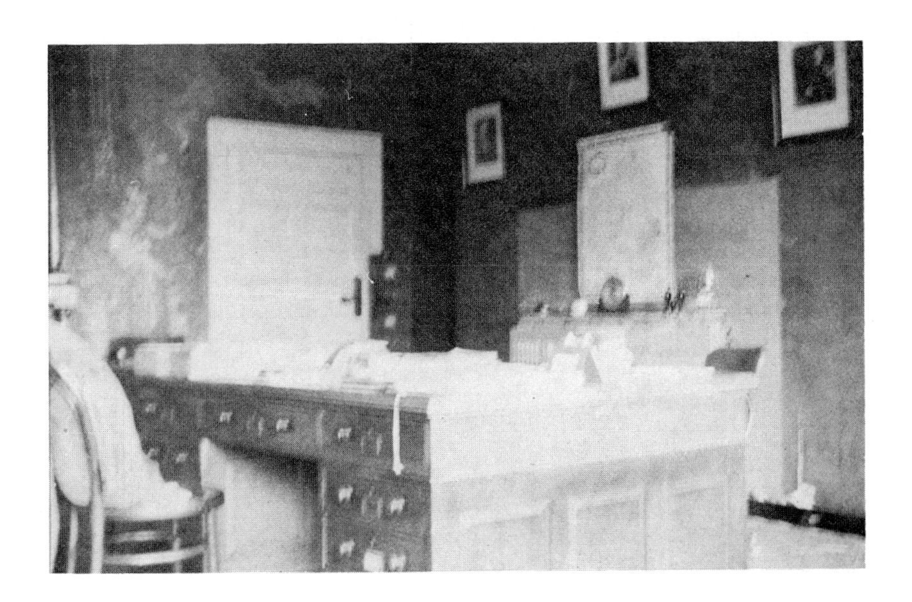

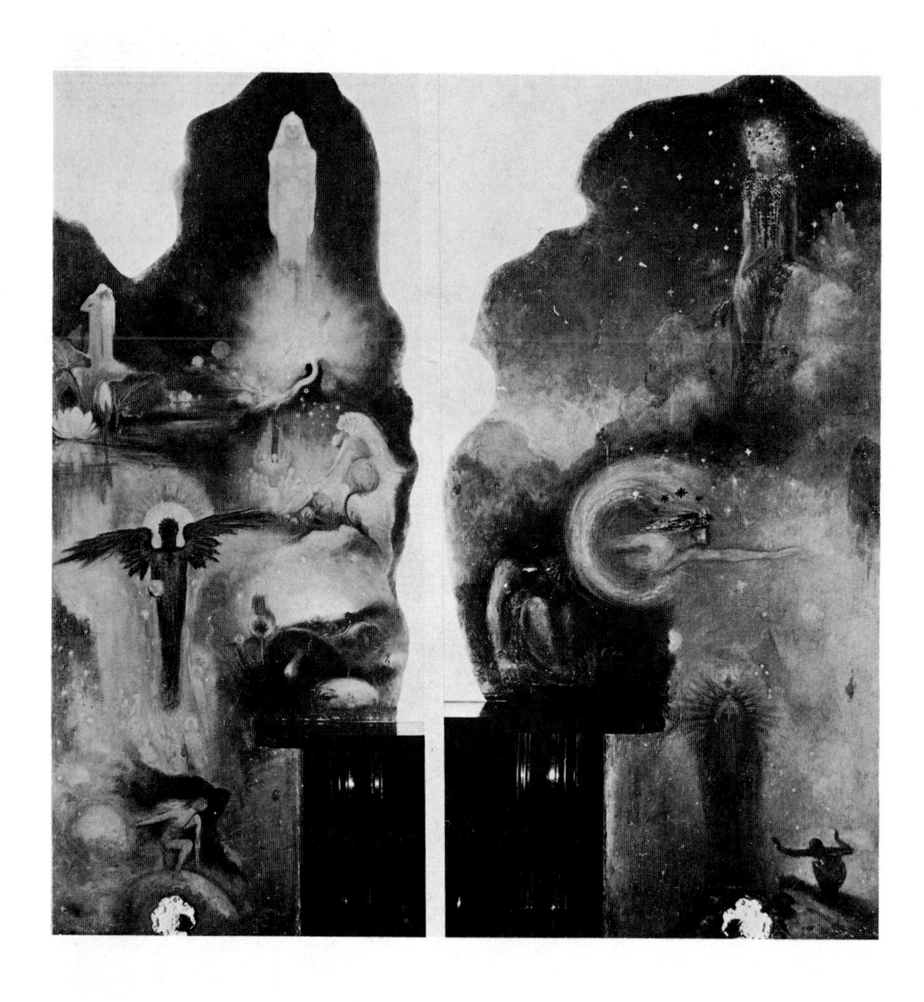

Some of AE's murals in 3 Upper Ely Place. 'Brother Russell has begun to illuminate the walls of the place with wonderful paintings symbolising the journey of the pilgrim soul', from *The Path* (New York), vol. 7, September 1892, p. 202. One of the wall paintings is signed 'G.W.R., W.B.Y.'. Photos. Green Studio.

Some of AE's murals in his office in Plunkett House, reproduced by courtesy of the National Gallery of Ireland in whose possession the murals (on wallpaper) now are.

The Earth Breath and
Other Poems by A. E.

Published by John Lane, Sign of the
Bodley Head, New York and London

SONG AND ITS FOUNTAINS

BY

A. E.

"Explore the River of the Soul, whence or in what order you have come; so that although you have become a servant to the body, you may again rise to the Order from which you descended, joining works to sacred reason."
The Chaldæan Oracles.

MACMILLAN AND CO., LIMITED
ST. MARTIN'S STREET, LONDON
1932

Title pages of four of AE's books. The sketches were all drawn for the late Constance Sitwell. Publisher's collection.

THE AVATARS
A FUTURIST FANTASY

BY

A. E.

The Light is the real person in the picture.
CLAUD MONET

MACMILLAN AND CO., LIMITED
ST. MARTIN'S STREET, LONDON
1933

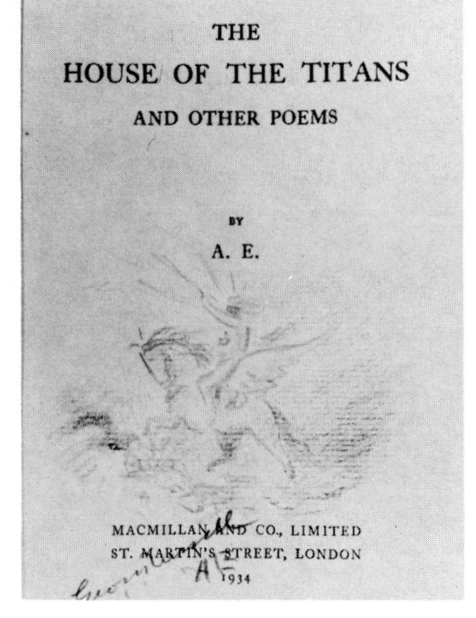
THE
HOUSE OF THE TITANS
AND OTHER POEMS

BY

A. E.

MACMILLAN AND CO., LIMITED
ST. MARTIN'S STREET, LONDON
1934

Above left: Sir Horace Plunkett, by J.B. Yeats, the elder, courtesy National Gallery of Ireland. Above right: AE – a photograph taken by E.C. Purdy, in Washington D.C., for the U.S. Department of Agriculture, 21 February 1935. Below: 'Chin-angles' or 'How the Poets Passed', a caricature by Isa MacNie. The story is told that W.B. Yeats who was then living at 82 Merrion Square set out to visit AE at 84, at the same time as AE had gone to visit him. They missed each other, and the cartoon shows how it happened.

THE
IRISH HOMESTEAD

The Organ of Irish Agricultural and Industrial Development.

Vol. XII.—No. 32 SATURDAY, August 11, 1906. Price 1d. By Post 1½d

CONTENTS.

Above: specimen headline of *The Irish Homestead.* Below: headline of the first issue of *The Irish Statesman,* 15 September 1922.

The Irish Statesman

With which is incorporated THE IRISH HOMESTEAD

Vol. I. No. 1.] SATURDAY, SEPTEMBER 15, 1923. [Threepence

CONTENTS

Medallion portraits by
Theodore Spicer-Simson.

Oil paintings by AE. Above: a mystical subject, courtesy of Municipal Gallery of Modern Art, Dublin, photo: Barry Mason. Below: a landscape; North of Muckish, publisher's collection.

Two illustrations from John Eglinton's *Memoir of AE,* 1937. Above: the 'cottage studio' at Marble Hill. Below: AE sketching on the sands below Marble Hill.

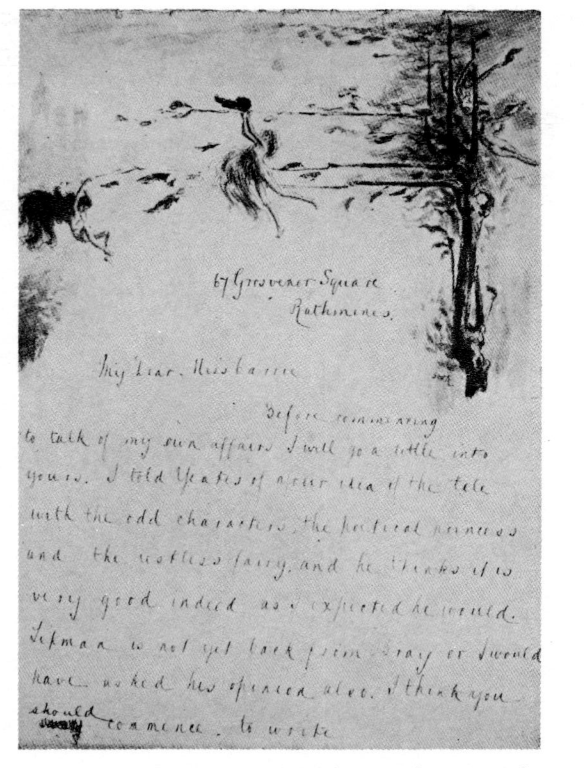
67 Grosvenor Square
Rathmines.

My dear Miss Carrie

Before commencing to talk of my own affairs I will go a little into yours. I told Yeates of your idea of the tale with the odd characters, the poetical princess and the restless fairy, and he thinks it is very good indeed as I expected he would. Lipman is not yet back from Bray or I would have asked his opinion also. I think you should commence to write

14 Tavistock Place
Russell Square
London W1

17/6/35.

Dear Constance Please call me AE. I am unfamiliar with the name I was born with. I am sorry indeed I will not be in Donegal when you are there. I am going at the latter end of this week to Bournemouth for a fortnight a friend told me of a nice house beside pine woods & with a garden where I can sit or soak in sun if there is one & I will be able to renew my friendship with John Eglinton whom I have not seen for fifteen years, a charming writer and a boyhood friend of mine. I am glad indeed if you found anything I said spiritually exciting. I only wish I had not been so dumb in soul & body after six months of my trouble. I was once a creature with some electrical intensity but now seem to myself to be in a state of pralaya or decay. Wentz after his stay in Ireland went to India travelled in Thibet, found many wonderful mss, "The Thibetan Book of the Dead" "The Tale of Milarepa" which he edited & which were published by Oxford Press. He went on pilgrimages, lived with

Examples of AE's handwriting. Left a page from a letter to Carrie Rea, c. June 1886, courtesy County Museum, Armagh. Right: a page from a letter to Constance Sitwell, 17 June 1935, nearly fifty years later, publisher's collection.

> mentality to embarrass him in his actions. A thousand years ago he would have been a knight errant doing wild things, hunting for the Holy Grail or spitting dragons on his spear.[59]

He now wrote to the Prime Minister Asquith on Casement's behalf,[60] but like other Irishmen was unsuccessful in his pleading.

In the *Homestead*, AE made several anguished pleas for national unity, and for the creation of an economic system which would render town and country interdependent and abolish the misery of the urban workers. On 1 June, while British leaders were working on an abortive scheme for immediate partition and Home Rule, he wrote to Arthur Balfour, whom he had met three and a half years before, pointing out that John Redmond, the Parliamentary leader of the Nationalists, was unaware of the growing support for the fiercely anti-British Sinn Fein. He proposed that Home Rule be given to all Ireland, but that the Irish peers, who were mostly Protestant, should constitute a House of Lords with a power of veto over legislation; others, he believed, would, like himself, be prepared to sacrifice some of their democratic convictions for the sake of the nation.[61] By May he was participating in a private attempt to work out a practical constitution acceptable to all Irishmen.[62]

Depressed by the political prospect, AE was glad to leave Dublin in mid-June. Describing himself as 'a wandering artist with a heap of paints and canvases and an interminable power to talk,'[63] he accepted an invitation to spend his month's holiday at MacLysaght's home in Clare instead of in Donegal, which may have been inaccessible due to the emergency. With some reluctance he consumed the large meals which Mrs. MacLysaght insisted on providing, and when he received a copy of Shaw's *Androcles and the Lion,* he enjoyed discussing with his Roman Catholic host the author's irreverent treatment of Christian doctrine, which was incongruously combined with a demand for the application of Christ's teaching to economics.[64]

The attempt to hammer out a constitution continued during the following months. In September, AE wrote to Quinn: 'I have been trying to get a small group together to form an Irish constitution association, to form subcommittees of 3 each to go seriously into all the problems of government in Ireland . . .'[65] He felt that he and his associates were following in the footsteps of Alexander Hamilton and the Federalists. Three or four weeks later, *The National Being* appeared and by the end of the year he could see no chance of a political solution and could only hope that the ideas expounded in his book would gradually be adopted.[66] In the meantime, the manuscript of *The Candle of Vision* was growing.[67]

To AE's amusement the publishers sent him a copy of *The National Being* for review, but he declined the opportunity to 'call attention to profundities the casual reviewer overlooked.'[68] The work expounds the synthesis of ideas which he had been developing in the columns of the *Homestead* for eight years, and extracts from the paper make up at least a third of it. Stylistically the best of his books, being vigorously written and fairly free from over literary phrasing, it was also the most popular, and to AE's pleasure it was translated into a number of languages.[69] Tagore admired it intensely.

When the leaders of the Easter Rising staged their insurrection despite the failure of the plan for a countrywide revolt, they probably foresaw that their martyrdom would inspire the Irish people to launch out on a final struggle for independence. After their execution sympathy for the war aims of the Allies rapidly declined, and the policies of the Parliamentary Nationalists elected in 1910 ceased to reflect public opinion. Sinn Fein attracted mass support and the British Government was forced to hold Ireland down by military force. AE continued his efforts to promote a peaceful solution, though he was as profoundly moved as more violent men by the self-sacrifice of Pearse and Connolly and their associates. Walking down Sackville Street at Easter 1917, he was reminded by the ruins of how, at the season of Christ's Resurrection, the spirit of Ireland, too, had been reborn, and he embodied his emotion in moving verse:

Last year at Easter there were faces pale and bright,
    For the Lord had arisen from the grave which was fear.
Hearts were airy, eyes filled with inner light.
    It was wrought this miracle among the ruins here.

Among the ruins here last Easter year awoke
    The timeless immortal, and for a sheaf of hours
It was fearless, wilful and laughing, though on it broke
    The wrath of the Iron Age, the weight of the iron powers.

They were not vanquished. The stars were on their side,
    The host of stars that glitter about their heavenly goal:
They see, as torch from torch is kindled, the fires flash wide,
    A host of kindling spirits in the dark of Ireland's soul.[70]

It may have been some months later that AE, in writing *The Candle of Vision,* interpreted the turmoil in Ireland as signifying a resumption of the spiritual explorations of the ancient Gaelic poets, which had been disrupted by foreign invasions before they could culminate in the creation of a sacred book. As in 1896, he felt that there were clear signs that higher powers were working through the nation:

> To some there come startling flashes of vision, and others feel a hand of power touching them thrust out from a hidden world. Whether they know it or not they are the servants of gods who speak or act through them . . .[71]

This belief was perhaps the principal cause of his writing *The Candle of Vision.* His continued discovery of new poets gave him confidence that the cultural and spiritual revival of earlier decades was persisting and he was especially excited to encounter the brilliant talent of Austin Clarke in 1917.[72] Mr. Clarke had written a long poem on Dermot and Grania, and was to benefit greatly from AE's suggestion that Irish poets should follow William Larminie's precept and example by imitating in English the patterns of Gaelic assonance. At an early stage in their acquaintance, he had a disturbing encounter with his patron's occult power. The latter was talking in his living room about the effects of concentrating on certain images, when Clarke looked out of the window and saw against the background of the Dublin Hills a giant spirit like those in his host's paintings; a second glance showed that it was still there, and this was enough to make him shun that window for ever after.[73]

A second event which brought AE great spiritual satisfaction in this year was the publication during August of the first instalment of Stephen MacKenna's graceful and lucid translation of Plotinus, a philosopher he had not previously studied in detail.[74] Monk Gibbon, another young poet he had recently met, heard him read slowly and with great feeling from the newly issued volume.[75] At the same period he was much impressed by James Stephens' growing enthusiasm for Blake, to whom he had originally introduced him, and felt that he would himself try to penetrate the difficult Prophetic Books, which even Yeats's enthusiasm had not persuaded him to tackle extensively in youth.[76]

In March 1917, AE joined James Douglas, a Quaker businessman, and Colonel Maurice Moore, the novelist's brother, in circulating privately constitutional proposals which he believed to reflect the majority opinion.[77] A number of people co-operated to develop the programme and on 26 May, five days after the Government had announced that it would summon a representative Convention to consider the problem, AE published in the *Irish Times* the first of three instalments of an essay in which he had distilled the views that had been arrived at. This essay, 'Thoughts for a Convention,' which he had written hurriedly in two afternoons snatched from other activities,[78] was reprinted as a pamphlet early in June together with a statement of endorsement in general terms signed by well known people of all parties. AE had busied himself to obtain signatures which would carry real weight, such as that of the Sinn Feiner

Gavan Duffy and he had been agreeably surprised when Archbishop Walsh, whom he had treated with scorn during Larkin's strike, appended his name.[79]

Thoughts for a Convention called on all Irishmen to approach the problem in a spirit of realism and reasonableness, and to make a genuine and chivalrous attempt to understand the sincerely held viewpoints of their opponents. After a lucid introduction, in which he tried to give an undistorted picture of the fears and aspirations of Unionists and Nationalists, he warned Britain and Ulster that partition, destroying the balance between the industrial North and the agricultural South, or incomplete Home Rule would not assuage but would perpetuate hatred, and confronted Sinn Fein with the fact that Ulster would never consent to leave the Empire. Ireland could prosper as a united dominion, for its parliament would never penalise its only centre of industry, and Ulster, if she feared religious bias in the administration, could have autonomy on the Swiss or Canadian pattern. Joint defence should be maintained with Britain, and Ireland would contribute her share of the cost to the imperial treasury on condition that the money was spent on military equipment and training in Ireland.

AE was pleased with the wide circulation of his pamphlet and wrote to Weekes that the editor of the *Irish Times* had told him he 'had shaken the unionist faith to its innermost tabernacle.'[80] It seems to have made an appreciable impact on the Unionists of the South but AE was realistic enough to doubt its effect on the North.[81] About the time of its publication he left for his month's holiday in Donegal.[82]

The Prime Minister, Lloyd George, intended that the Convention should represent all areas of public opinion and formulate a scheme of Home Rule which would be entirely the work of Irishmen. A large number of elected representatives from city and county councils were convened, together with churchmen, industrial magnates, and spokesmen for the labour unions and political parties. From the outset, however, the assembly laboured under great and partly invisible handicaps: the Ulster Unionists were secretly commissioned to act as delegates of their party, the north-east counties were determined never to form part of a united, autonomous Ireland, and Sinn Fein entirely boycotted the Convention. To compensate for this last, the British Government nominated AE and MacLysaght to speak for the strongly Nationalist viewpoint. AE had mixed feelings about attending but his conscience prompted him to leave no possibility untried[83] and he decided to yield to Plunkett's urgent persuasion on condition that MacLysaght also took part.[84] He brought with him his characteristic blend of moral idealism and hard-headed command of facts, and tried to arrange for friendly, informal contacts between the representatives of North and South.[85]

The Convention first met on 25 July, 1917, in the antique elegance of Trinity College, Dublin, in a hall redecorated for the occasion. As a member of the committee convened to recommend a chairman for the Convention, AE proposed Plunkett,[86] an unwise move in view of the latter's limitations as a speaker. Plunkett was, however, elected, and the real business of the assembly began on 21 August. Pollock, Chairman of the Belfast Chamber of Commerce, and AE joined issue on the crucial matter of finance. It was AE's view that only when a nation controlled its own finance was it free to develop a civilisation appropriate to its peculiar genius. As he wrote later:

> . . . whoever controls the taxation and trade policy of a country controls its destiny and the entire character of its civilization. The body with control over customs, excise, income-tax, supertax, excess profits duty and external trade has it in its power to make that country predominantly industrial or agricultural or to make a balance between urban and rural interests.[87]

AE answered Pollock in detail, claiming that a self-governing Ireland would not erect trade barriers against her best customer and that Ulster's prosperity, of which the whole country was proud, depended not on the Union but on the geographical proximity of Britain. He earnestly warned the assembly that though the Sinn Feiners, many of whom he knew, would accept any reasonable settlement, grievous violence would follow should they fail to reach agreement: he could 'hear the whistle of flying bullets in the street; see the gutter filled with blood while the souls of young men sent prematurely into the presence of their God protested against the Convention and its want of wisdom.'[88]

In September, sittings were held in Belfast, where the members visited thriving industrial establishments, and later in Cork, where threatened Sinn Fein demonstrations failed to materialise. Little progress was made. For seven months the sullen Ulster representatives were hardly more communicative than the absent Sinn Feiners, though the Northern labour leaders did not altogether share the industrialists' implacable hostility to Home Rule. The one faint hope of compromise appeared in a proposal by Lord Midleton to establish an all-Ireland Parliament but leave customs and all imperial services under the jurisdiction of Westminster. On this the Southern Unionists and moderate Nationalists were able to agree. AE would have been prepared for the nation to make this sacrifice only if Ulster had consented to remain a part of it. Ironically he found himself aligned not only with MacLysaght and the Catholic bishops, but with his old enemy the Dublin industrialist William

Martin Murphy. In the debate of 22 to 24 January, he explained the urgency of his appeal for a settlement which would allow the energy of the nation to be withdrawn from political agitation and race hatred and applied to the building of an Irish civilisation in friendship with the English people. It was essential that they should enjoy self-government before they were caught up in the inevitable spread of socialistic and revolutionary ideas from Russia to the West. 'There is going,' he proclaimed, 'to be wild weather through the world, and we want an Irish captain and an Irish crew in command of the Irish ship.'[89]

From the beginning of the Convention, AE was very much aware how severely it was limited by the absence of the fervent Nationalists. When in December the Government revealed that they did not intend to submit its proposals to an Irish referendum, he felt strongly inclined to resign, for he realised that the Sinn Feiners would in no way feel bound by them, but so long as there was the faintest hope he held it his duty to remain.[90] MacLysaght, to whom he had confided his feelings, withdrew with effect from 22 January on the ground that Ulster's agreement, which it was impossible to secure, seemed to be a prerequisite of Government action on the Convention's recommendations. About this time, in an attempt to resolve the deadlock, a representative delegation from the Convention was arranging to meet some Cabinet ministers in London to seek clarification of the Government's position on the problems of Ulster's agreement to a settlement and Irish control of Irish customs. Plunkett was relying on AE, with his deep conviction and intellectual insight, to make the British ministers understand how, in the light of the current worldwide demands for self-determination, Nationalist Ireland regarded the Government's pledges to Ulster as binding only on the individuals who made them.[91] On 1 February, 1918, AE sent his letter of resignation to Plunkett.

> . . . I have come to believe that the Convention, constituted as it is, and hampered by the pledge of Ministers to the people of Belfast, cannot be the instrument by means of which an Irish settlement can be attained . . . I view with the greatest foreboding the future of Ireland and I do not think I have any part to play politically in a country ravaged by such passions, and I intend to devote such energy and thought to other movements with which I have more affinities.[92]

To Plunkett's plea that he reconsider his decision and expound his objections in person to the Cabinet, he replied in more passionate terms expressing his firm conviction that the British Government could not be brought to see reason and his determination to continue serving the I.A.O.S.:

> It is a lamentable thing but the entire responsibility for the state of Ireland is on the shoulders of the English politicians. Asquith, Law and George gave Belfast pledges and, after having inflamed them to the last degree possible against their fellow countrymen, the English arm them with promises and send them in to humbug us and tell the world they are allowing Ireland to settle its own destiny . . . A man must be either an Irishman or an Englishman in this matter. I am Irish.[93]

In a letter to Lloyd George, AE explained that he still adhered to the views expressed in *Thoughts for a Convention,* that he believed Ulster's interests could be fully safeguarded by representation in an all-Ireland parliament, by local autonomy in education and other matters connected with religion, and by a provision in an Anglo-Irish treaty for free trade in all goods originating in either country. The Government had not confined itself to safeguarding Ulster's legitimate interests by a legitimate guarantee, but had given 'an unconditional pledge that it would be supported against the wishes of the vast majority of the Irish people.' In the light of his personal knowledge – not possessed by any other member of the Convention – of Pearse, Connolly, MacDonagh, and living Sinn Fein leaders, he warned the Prime Minister of impending violence not to be averted by any unworkable half-measure of self-government such as Lord Midleton's scheme:

> . . . we have for the first time in Ireland a disinterested nationalism not deriving its power from grievances connected with land or even oppressive Government but solely from the growing self-consciousness of nationality, and this has with the younger generation all the force of a religion, with the carelessness about death, suffering or material loss which we find among the devotees of a religion. Any Government established which does not allow this national impulse free play, will be wrecked by it.[94]

To Plunkett's intense disappointment the Convention failed to reach agreement, and in April he had to take majority and minority reports to London. In his confidential account compiled for the King, he referred to the brilliant part AE had played, but the latter's was a lone voice warning an obstinate Prime Minister that he was being advised by men altogether out of touch with the dominant emotion of the people. Lloyd George promised legislation on the basis of the majority report.

What most appalled AE at this time was the blind, all-engulfing hatred that was taking possession of so many Irish minds. As one of the very few in whose presence and home men passionately committed to opposite sides could meet in social harmony, he attempted to counter the all but universal failure – inside and outside the Convention – to understand clearly one's opponent's views. In the first of two letters published in the *Irish Times* during December 1917, he cited Flinders Petrie's argument in *The Revolutions of Civilisation* that only the blood and culture of an invader revived a decaying society, and pleaded that the modern Irish nation was not Celtic or Norman or Saxon but an inextricable mixture with a new racial identity. Moreover the increasing bitterness between those who risked their lives fighting for independence at home and those whose equal sense of duty impelled them to fight for Ireland and the Empire in the Great War was wholly without justification: both were faithful servants of their country and where the sacrifice was equal, equal honour was due. The letter ends with one of AE's noblest poems, an expanded version of 'Salutation' in which he pays tribute to the martyrs of two causes which in eternity will be seen as facets of the same ideal. As critics have observed, these stanzas, without distinction of diction or imagery, attain through their total pattern a most moving eloquence.

To the Memory of Some I Knew Who are Dead and Who Loved Ireland

Their dream had left me numb and cold,
But yet my spirit rose in pride,
Refashioning in burnished gold
The images of those who died,
Or were shut in the penal cell.
Here's to you, Pearse, your dream not mine,
But yet the thought, for this you fell,
Has turned life's water into wine.

You who have died on Eastern hills
Or fields of France as undismayed,
Who lit with interlinkéd wills
The long heroic barricade,
You, too, in all the dreams you had,
Thought of some thing for Ireland done.
Was it not so, Oh, shining lad,
What lured you, Alan Anderson?

I listened to high talk from you,
Thomas McDonagh, and it seemed
The words were idle, but they grew
To nobleness by death redeemed.
Life cannot utter words more great

Than life may meet by sacrifice,
High words were equalled by high fate,
You paid the price. You paid the price.

You who have fought on fields afar,
That other Ireland did you wrong
Who said you shadowed Ireland's star,
Nor gave you laurel wreath nor song.
You proved by death as true as they,
In mightier conflicts played your part,
Equal your sacrifice may weigh,
Dear Kettle, of the generous heart.

The hope lives on age after age,
Earth with its beauty might be won
For labour as a heritage,
For this has Ireland lost a son.
This hope unto a flame to fan
Men have put life by with a smile,
Here's to you Connolly, my man,
Who cast the last torch on the pile.

You too, had Ireland in your care,
Who watched o'er pits of blood and mire,
From iron roots leap up in air
Wild forests, magical, of fire;
Yet while the Nuts of Death were shed
Your memory would ever stray
To your own isle. Oh, gallant dead –
This wreath, Will Redmond, on your clay.

Here's to you, men I never met,
Yet hope to meet behind the veil,
Thronged on some starry parapet,
That looks down upon Innisfail,
And sees the confluence of dreams
That clashed together in our night,
One river, born from many streams,
Roll in one blaze of blinding light.[95]*

*Alan Anderson, son of R. A. Anderson, Secretary of the I.A.O.S., had determined to devote his life to the co-operative movement; Thomas M. Kettle, M.P., brilliant young economist and litterateur, had worked with AE during the 1913 strike; William Redmond was the brother of John Redmond, leader of the Parliamentary Nationalists.

In his second letter, AE pointed to the need for a combination of the North's efficiency with the South's love of beauty, and appealed to the Christianity and Celtic chivalry of his readers. Defending the injunction 'Love your enemies,' he proclaimed that if hatred, an evil greater even than violence, were once put aside, the immortal essence, the Self, in a man recognised Itself in the heart of another when both overcame fear for the body in the exultation of heroic combat:

> It is natural to love our enemies. In so far as fear of the body is cast aside, in so far as for the moment man is fire and spirit, he can discern only what is akin to his immortality, and he thrills in recognition of those, who like himself, have overcome mortality and its fears.

After propounding this somewhat eccentric development of mystical philosophy, he replied to Archbishop Crozier, who had explained that Christians are not commanded to love other people's enemies:

> It is not those who fight who violate most that high law of human nature, but the interpreters of Scripture who remain at home trying to effect some economy of meaning in difficult texts.[96]

On resigning from the Convention, AE returned with relief to *The Candle of Vision*[97] and the vigorous prosecution of his campaign to persuade farmers to produce to their maximum capacity. Month by month he watched the fulfilment of his prophecy that if the farmers failed in their duty they would be bound hand and foot in a network of official regulations. He blamed both the cultivators and the authorities, and the Excess Profits Tax of sixty, then eighty per cent drew his especial wrath as an encouragement to profiteers, who merely shared their gains with the Government, as statistics confirmed: the tax should have been a hundred per cent. Later he was able to claim that he had been the first to expose this and other methods of secretly exploiting the public.[98] Most of all, he deplored the continuing obsession of the Irish people with the Home Rule Question while famine and the problems of the peace stared them in the face.

As early as the outbreak of the War, AE had realised that when peace was restored men would look back astonished 'as those who have left one world for another.'[99] He now pinpointed as the principal foci of change the discharge of thousands of fearless soldiers trained to kill, and the worldwide reorganisation of industry into huge syndicates, a process specially successful in Germany. To present a united front in a world overrun by economic gigantism, Irish farmers would have to give their loyalty to the ill supported co-operative federations, the keystone of their co-operative movement, which conducted business operations on a national scale. For farmers and even for small businessmen, the penalty for failure to organise would be rigorous control, either by the bureaucrats of a socialist state or by capitalists and shareholders. In Ireland, he admitted, there would be no social upheaval, because the revolutionaries wanted only political change, but this danger was real in England. In 1917 he prophesied, with only slight inaccuracy, that the Conservatives and Liberals would combine against a growing Labour Party, and that there would be a Labour Government in Britain within five or six years, even if the threat of revolution passed over.[100]

In the spring of 1918 there was another political crisis. On 9 April, Lloyd George announced that conscription would be enforced in Britain, and the British, having already sacrificed an unprecedented number of young lives, were not prepared to tolerate the exemption of the Irish. Like many of the leading men of the nation, AE forecast civil war, and he warned that if the workers were taken from the land and the small industries, famine would follow by the winter and the country's economy would be crushed. In his dejection he exclaimed in the *Homestead:*

> If the Government's intentions are carried out, we see Ireland after the war slowly, since people must live however broken-spirited, beginning anew its co-operative enterprises and trying to recreate some kind of prosperity out of the ruin of things . . . We have no doubt God is in His Heaven, but it seems more remote from earth than usual, and the people about to die may well be, if it is a good cause they die for, more cheerful than those who will have to live in the poor age, and see their children and their children's children trapped by these mighty devils of State and Empire . . .[101]

In a long letter published in the *Manchester Guardian* of 10 May, he spoke out on the political side of the question and tried to explain to the British that the Irish felt themselves to be a subject people: if conscription were applied, Ireland would resist by force and the English, blinded by grief at their own losses, might find that the ultimate cost of reconquest was the disruption of the Empire.[102]

This attempt to ward off the seemingly inevitable constituted a brief return to the world of the politicians, from which AE had tried to extricate himself on resigning from the Convention; it seemed to him a negation of all that was creative in the human soul. He would continue, he told his friends, to serve the I.A.O.S., and after the announcement of conscription he wrote to St. John Ervine dissociating himself from the optimism of Plunkett's renewed attempt to secure a compromise settlement and adding exultantly:

> Macmillan and Co are bringing out a book of mine this year I think which will finally make it impossible for me to take part in politics in Ireland as it is full of religious heresies and will give me a bad name.[103]

Before the book appeared, he found time to take his usual holiday in Donegal, where he enjoyed for a time the company of James Stephens,[104] and to make one more attempt to influence the political situation. On 11 October he joined James Douglas and the Irish labour leader Thomas Johnson in pleading Ireland's cause before the British Labour Party Executive and the Parliamentary Committee of the Trades Union Congress. He stayed with Sidney and Beatrice Webb, and the latter was fascinated by his conversation, though her outlook was too far removed from his for real understanding. She noticed his ambivalent attitude to science, which he valued for its practical utility and as a form of intellectual training, but feared as a threat to faith in the unseen.[105] 'Personally,' he had written in the *Homestead*, 'we believe that there are no natural explanations of anything in nature, and that is the reason why science is so continually wrong.'[106]

The application of conscription to Ireland was postponed till the autumn, by which time the Armistice rendered it needless.

On 22 October, *The Candle of Vision* was published and AE was pleasantly surprised by its success – it was reprinted five times within two years – though he attributed its popularity to the style:[107] he had rewritten the individual chapters seven or eight times to make them as readable as possible despite their difficult content.[108] It gave him great pleasure to correspond with an elderly clergyman who was interested in a possible relationship between his book and St. John's Revelation.[109]

In *The Candle of Vision* AE surveyed the mystical experiences of half a lifetime seeking to convey the wonder and awe which his encounter with realities so far transcending those of bodily existence aroused in him. He felt that in using his skill as a professional writer in this way he was fulfilling a duty which other mystics, like his master Pryse, who knew more than he, were unable to perform. Unfortunately, despite his recognition of the need to establish 'the geography of the spirit,'[110] he omitted to give an explanation of his terms and frame of reference, with the result that the treatise is confusing in much the same way as a complicated travel book without a map. Moreover the conscious effort to find a style to match his vision resulted in a poetic prose which has lost the charm it had for many of his contemporaries: the inversions and archaisms of his books seem artificial and florid beside the unselfconscious vigour of his journalism. Luckily the overlay of mannerism is no more than a thin veneer and his unwavering certainty of man's forgotten godhood shines through to make *The Candle of Vision* a profoundly moving book.

When the ceasefire came into force on 11 November, AE shared in the general rejoicing. 'It is impossible,' he wrote in his editorial Notes, 'not to feel the wildest gaiety of spirits knowing that the world war is over, though the signing of an armistice is not the signing of a peace treaty.'[111] With characteristic prescience, he spoke of the danger of imposing on the defeated countries terms which would lead to another war. Between the Armistice and the Peace Conference, however, Lloyd George was confirmed in power by an understandably vindictive electorate, while Clemenceau, the Prime Minister of France, represented a nation that was equally bent on revenge.

As a result of the Great War there were profound political changes in Europe: the Austro-Hungarian Empire crumbled, several of its constituent parts becoming republics and Hungary falling briefly under Communist rule; Germany exchanged its Kaiser for democratic socialist politicians, and in 1924 Britain elected its first Labour government. But the outstanding example of the social revolution that AE had been prophesying since 1915 occurred in Russia, where in March 1917 the war-weary people overthrew the Czarist autocracy and set up a liberal regime. In July he observed with delight that their flourishing co-operative societies had at last been allowed to form a central union, which would act as a wholesale federation for the entire country.[112] Four months later the Bolsheviks, by a mixture of cunning, fanatical propaganda, and violence, succeeded in destroying the well meaning but ineffective Provisional Government, and in March 1918 they made peace with Germany at the cost of ceding huge portions of the Czarist Empire. Ten days after they had seized power, AE reported that the Russian people, having thrown off the chains of the old bureaucracy, were expanding their co-operative societies at an astonishing rate and seemed to be well on the way to creating the Co-operative Commonwealth.[113] He took little notice of a letter he published in his correspondence column a fortnight later warning that the new Soviets were likely to destroy the co-operative organisations. For the next three years he continued to report optimistically on the growth of the movement in Russia and claimed that in Ireland too it could provide an element of stability in times of anarchy. Just after the Armistice he wrote to the Dublin *Voice of Labour* citing the testimony of a Canadian eyewitness and other evidence to show that the Western accounts of large-scale bloodshed were politically motivated and false.[114] In June 1919 he was able to quote at length the *Economic Supple-*

ment to the War Office *Review of the Foreign Press* in support of his opinion that the official state socialism had been unable to make headway against the co-operative movement,[115] and he ignored an urgent message from Yeats, who, more perceptive about Communism than about Fascism, denounced Marxist values as 'in this age the spear-head of materialism and leading to inevitable murder.'[116] Only in October 1920 did AE realise how determined the Bolsheviks were to impose their ideas on the people and that by nationalising the co-operative movement and making membership compulsory, they had destroyed its spirit. Foreign invasions by Britain and other capitalist countries may, he suggested, have strengthened their hand, and he concluded:

> For Russia itself, that country of lovable people, we can only hope a resurrection in some social order which will be a human mean between the autocracy of the Czardom and the autocracy of the Soviet administration.[117]

(ii) Gunfire in the Streets (1918–1923)

In December 1918 a General Election was held in the British Isles and Lloyd George's coalition was returned to power. AE observed wryly that the English workers 'obviously mistrust men of their own class and put their trust in trusts';[118] less flippantly, he wrote a year later of the disastrous strength of a social tradition which bamboozled wage earners into choosing between Tory and Liberal 'gentlemen' for their rulers, when the ideal of the gentleman had long ceased to be realised in practice.[119]

In Ireland, apart from north-east Ulster, an overwhelming majority of Sinn Feiners were returned and the old Parliamentary Nationalist Party was virtually swept out of existence. The Sinn Fein members refused to sit at Westminster and set up their own Dail or Parliament in Dublin. Electing Mr. de Valera, a veteran of the Easter Rising, as President of the Republic, they established their own administration and for a time the country had two governments. The Sinn Fein courts of justice, many of which were served by professional lawyers, have been much praised, and in September 1919 AE found it worthwhile to cite a warning about winter scarcity by Mr. Robert Barton, the Director of Agriculture in Dail Eireann.[120] In this month the British authorities proscribed the Dail, and the previous sporadic violence rapidly developed into a full-scale guerilla war between Sinn Fein, led by the formidable and brilliant Michael Collins, and the Royal Irish Constabulary reinforced by ex-officers known as the Auxiliaries and by the notoriously savage Black-and-Tans.

During 1919 and the first half of 1920, despite the obvious threat of anarchy, AE's *Homestead* articles expressed his confidence that the co-operative movement had overcome its greatest difficulties and could not ultimately fail to dominate the Irish economy. The farmers seemed to have cast off their long standing dependence on state aid, and ideas for new co-operative enterprises were springing up in the individual societies.

Although AE especially emphasised at this period the crucial importance of excluding politics from all co-operative affairs, his own nationalist sympathies were often imperfectly disguised in the *Homestead*. He pointed out that the British Government not only maintained many of their wartime regulations but operated them in a manner prejudicial to Ireland. By fixing a lower price for Irish than for English cheese, the London authorities were imposing a tariff; by restricting in Ireland but not in England the quantity of bacon which might be cured, and by insisting that Irish cattle exported to the Continent must pass through an English port, they were in effect exacting a tribute. AE claimed, indeed, that in many of its programmes the Government was acting in concert with the representatives of great industrial combines, whose gains it neatly skimmed through the continued Excess Profits Tax:

> It was seen that the system of control set up during the war for military reasons might be made to serve a grandiose economic policy in time of peace. That policy was to guide by regulation into Great Britain all the raw materials which formerly came there simply because it was a good market . . . By export duties, import duties, regulations, permits, licences, monopolist purchase and manufacture the raw materials of half the world were to flow into the factories of the trusts and out again to a world which must buy because of necessity, and nations outside the empire must pay with their raw materials for articles of which there was a practical monopoly within the empire.[121]

Shortly after writing this denunciation, AE cited as evidence the Government's profitable purchase and resale of all the wool within the Empire, the facts of which they had tried unsuccessfully to conceal.[122] He protested, too, at the absurd war indemnities demanded by the Allies, and at the inhuman continuation of the blockade against starving Germany and Austria, a policy that was as foolish as it was wicked since it perpetuated hatred while depriving a struggling Britain of invaluable markets: privately he proposed that the objections to it could be divided into 'Arguments for Human Beings' and 'Arguments for Capitalists.'[123]

In September 1919, AE suffered a considerable intellectual disappointment, but he did not allow it to ruffle his good humour or outweigh his sense of fairness. Professor Eoin McNeill showed that there was no foundation for the assertion of earlier historians that the Gaelic clans held their land in common. Darrell Figgis rushed to the defence of the old theory, but was quite unable to make out a convincing case, and AE admitted that Irish economic democracy began not, as he had supposed, in ancient times, but with the short-lived co-operative community founded on the Vandeleur estate at Ralahine, County Clare, in 1830.[124]

Another curious episode occurred after AE heard in May 1920 that Stamboliski, the peasant's son who had become Prime Minister of Bulgaria, was introducing civil conscription, and he wondered whether any Bulgarian had read his article on the subject incorporated in *The National Being*.[125] Later a lady told him that she had given a copy of the book to Stamboliski himself, and he had taken the idea from there.[126]

Notwithstanding the disturbed condition of the country and the economy, AE still found a certain amount of time for literary work, even apart from his *Homestead* reviews of poetry, drama, and fiction, which had of recent years become much more numerous. In the penultimate chapter of *The National Being,* he had expounded his belief that the evolution of nations round certain ideals was part of the cosmic plan. By February 1919,[127] he had begun another book, which he later called *The Interpreters,* exploring in more detail the origin of these ideals. At the end of the year, he published one of his best poems, a long narrative related to this theme and centred on the Easter Rising. 'Michael,' the culmination of all his brooding over the insurrection, was composed, he believed, beyond the threshold of the waking consciousness. The opening passage and an isolated, apparently unconnected line came spontaneously into his mind after a night's sleep, and he allowed the rest of the poem to emerge from his dream consciousness while he walked over the hills, perhaps on his summer holiday.[128] As the hero, a youth brought up in a Donegal fishing village, stands on the shore at twilight on the eve of his departure for the city, he is granted a vision of the secret life within nature. In the spiritual crystal boat that had appeared long before in 'The Fountain of Shadowy Beauty,' he is carried momentarily into the Heaven-world. After a realistic impression of the village life and a surprisingly fresh and clear description of the region's beauty, the scene shifts to Dublin. Here Michael is kept from slowly forgetting his home by the influence of Gaelic enthusiasts, who eventually lead him to sacrifice his life in the Easter Rising. As he dies on the barricade, the crystal boat and the vision of the Heaven-world reappear, and AE proclaims that the Divine Mind is working through man and drawing him Godwards by every political ideal.

Like other Dubliners, AE found that his personal life was restricted and disrupted by the violence that plagued the capital in common with the rest of the country. Writing in January 1920 of the daily reports of raids on police barracks, imprisonment without trial, and the occasional wrecking of towns, he confessed: 'Still I would rather live in Ireland than anywhere else and one comes to accept all these excitements as the thorns in a little Dark Rose which one loves very much and which are part of its personality.'[129] In February, a midnight curfew was imposed in Dublin, and the following month AE complained that the city was virtually under martial law. While greatly respecting the non-violent majority of Sinn Feiners, he felt that none of the leaders had the personality required to guide the country to a great creative future. He had met Mr. de Valera more than once and found him 'personally pleasant and attractive' but could not forgive 'some nonsense he talked about "blasting Ulster out of the way." '[130] AE's Unionist, Sinn Fein, and British friends continued to visit him and one night the police arrested Maud Gonne and Joseph King, an English M.P., as they left his home. Throughout the period of the Troubles, while gunmen stalked the streets, he was courageous enough to leave his front door open as usual on Sunday evenings.[131] It may have been at this period that he broke off for a time his habit of daily meditation. He wrote to Weekes in 1926:

> You ask how I escaped the Ancient Darkness. By renewing every day my old habit of meditation on the spirit[,] every day setting aside time for it, and rarely allowing it to be encroached on. There were some years in which I was so absorbed in external activities that my meditations were intermittent. I have with some effort of will brought myself round to a state where, when I begin meditation, I find myself in some relation to a spiritual nature.[132]

In December 1919, Lloyd George introduced a new Home Rule Bill in the House of Commons in the hope of persuading Sinn Fein that further violence was needless. According to this Bill, north-east Ulster and the remainder of the country were to have separate parliaments, matters of joint concern were to be considered by a Council of Ireland, and important powers were to be reserved to Westminster. Four months later Sir Auckland Geddes, on the eve of his departure for the United States to serve as British Ambassador, spoke publicly in praise of this scheme, and AE wrote an article for the New York *Freeman* exposing the hollowness of his arguments. This eloquently lucid rejoinder was quickly reprinted as a pamphlet under the title *The Economics of Ireland and the Policy of the British*

Government. It explained how, by keeping control over direct and indirect taxation and customs, the Westminster Parliament would continue to prevent the growth of Irish industry and to decide the nature of the economy and therefore of the society and civilisation. Expounding the classic arguments of subject peoples, AE pointed out that in return for an annual tribute of £18,000,000, which was impoverishing the people, three quarters of the country was at present being subjected to military occupation, while its leaders were imprisoned, a commission studying its economic potential was suppressed, and its producers were prohibited from exporting. 'It is not self-government,' AE concluded, 'the British are bestowing on us; they are digging for us a dungeon even deeper than Pitt digged for us in the Act of Union.' In a letter published in the London *Times* a year later on 28 March, 1921, he tried to make the English public, too, understand the effect on Ireland of the annual depletion of its income.

Writing to an Irish American on 17 April, 1920, AE expressed his confidence that the agricultural co-operative movement was flourishing in Ireland and was about to move on to bigger things.[133] In the same month five co-operative creameries in County Tipperary were attacked by police and soldiers; machinery was smashed, goods were destroyed and stolen, and in two cases the buildings were burned.[134] Early in June, AE reported these attacks in the *Homestead,* and during the coming months, with growing melancholy, he recorded many similar outrages. Abandoning the British tradition of justice and fair play which still restrained the regular troops, the Auxiliaries and Black-and-Tans were making a desperate attempt to cope with the elusive Sinn Feiners who sought to obtain by force the republican status which the electorate had asked for in vain. Coming from a wealthy to a poverty stricken country, they picked on the most prosperous branch of the national industry; when any of their number were ambushed or a barracks was attacked, they destroyed the local co-operative creamery, wreaking vengeance on the unarmed and hoping by such means to terrify non-combatants into giving information. Sir Hamar Greenwood, Chief Secretary for Ireland, at first attempted to deny that there was evidence associating Crown forces with the wreckings, and when this pretence could no longer be kept up he refused an enquiry. In the *Homestead,* AE denounced him as a liar and called for his resignation.[135] The destruction continued; sometimes a reconstructed creamery was wrecked a second time. Compensation was refused by the Government and left to be paid by the County Councils out of funds to which the ratepaying farmers themselves contributed. In 1921 British troops blockaded north-west Donegal in an attempt to starve the population into surrender. Patrick Gallagher of Dungloe, whom AE and Plunkett regarded as a model co-operator, chartered a steamer and sailed with a cargo of eggs to Glasgow, where the Scottish Co-operative Society gave him all the food he asked for on credit enabling him to break the blockade. Seeing England attempting to establish a dictatorship in southern Ireland, the United States dominated by trusts, and Germany governed by democratic socialists, AE claimed that the state of these countries was due to the exchange of characteristics natural in war, where each side grows to resemble what it hates. Similarly, he maintained, the Russian revolutionaries, who were fighting for the sake of freedom, ended by returning to the autocracy of their predecessors. In retrospect the transformation, except in Russia, can be seen as limited and brief, but AE was more acute when he foretold in 1921 that the United States would become the centre of world power, perhaps closely followed by Russia, and that Germany, absorbing Austria, might recover her pre-war greatness.[136]

Physical violence was far from being the only source of Ireland's economic troubles at this time. By 1921 England was suffering from the post-war depression that AE had forecast since 1915, and serious strikes and large-scale unemployment greatly reduced her value as a customer. The economies of several European countries seemed likely to disintegrate and there was substantial unemployment in the U.S.A. AE began to ponder over the dilemma of a world in which the power to produce goods exceeded the buyer's capacity to purchase them (a danger he had noticed as early as 1913) and the consequent peril of leading industrial countries indulging in wars for the limited supply of markets.[137] He laid the immediate responsibility for creating booms and slumps on a handful of bank directors who stimulated and depressed the economy by granting or withholding credit. In connection with these problems he recommended to his readers *Credit-Power and Democracy* by A. R. Orage and Major C. H. Douglas with the warning: 'The latter is tough reading, but unless there is tough thinking in Ireland we will not make very much out of it, Free State, Dominion or Republic.'[138] Douglas and Orage's analysis of the world's economic quandary impressed him as extraordinarily acute, but from the first he doubted the feasibility of their scheme for the issue of communal credit or purchasing power, and years later he described a book by Douglas as 'the fairiest tale of economic science I have ever read.'[139]

On the day to day level, AE urged continuously that since international trade was so precarious, Irish farmers should continue the wartime policy of aiming at national self-sufficiency. During the

Anglo-Irish War, railway services were badly dislocated and he advocated the installation of cold storage and the adoption of motor transport. It was a time for improvisation, faith in the ideals of the movement, and extraordinary courage.

The condition of the country did not prevent AE from taking his usual holiday in Donegal in the summer of 1920.[140] Soon after his return it became clear that the wrecking of creameries had been made part of a deliberate though unofficial policy and the pleadings of the I.A.O.S. proved of no avail. Plunkett, Anderson, AE, and other pioneers of the Irish co-operative movement were almost helpless in the face of this wanton attempt to destroy their life's work. The coming of the Co-operative Commonwealth, AE declared, would be delayed for at least a generation,[141] though from time to time he tried to console himself and his readers with the thought that persecution would eventually refine and strengthen the spirit of the societies. He advised creameries to extend the range of their business by engaging in less vulnerable activities, to put all the evidence about an attack into the hands of solicitors, and to insure their premises even at the present extraordinary rates. What most alarmed him was the fear that the newly emerging spirit of enterprise and hard-won technical competence would be lost.

In August, writing to E. H. W. Meyerstein, the eccentric Anglo-Jewish novelist and poet, AE lamented the havoc being wrought on the one movement in Ireland free from sectarian and party passions. He would not, he said, blame the individual Englishman unless he approved of his Government's conduct, and went on to detail British actions:

> It is not only policemen are shot here but civilians in far greater number are killed or imprisoned. Half a dozen trains have been wrecked by the military, dozens of factories burned and there have been over thirty thousand raids by military on private houses in many cases involving looting and destruction of property as well as brutal treatment of civilians. This has been going on so long I have lost the power of being angry.[142]

During this month Terence MacSwiney, the imprisoned Lord Mayor of Cork, embarked on an heroic hunger-strike, and AE, his admiration kindled as the prisoner held out week after week, wrote a powerful sonnet lauding this manifestation of an inflexible Promethean will:

> See, though the oil be low, more purely still and higher
> The flame burns in the body's lamp. The watchers still
> Gaze with unseeing eyes while the Promethean will,
> The Uncreated Light, the Everlasting Fire,
> Sustain themselves against the torturer's desire,

Even as the fabled Titan chained upon the hill.
Burn on, shine here, thou immortality, until
We too can light our lamps at the funereal pyre;
Till we too can be noble, unshakeable, undismayed;
Till we too can burn with the holy flame, and know
There is that within us can conquer the dragon pain,
And go to death alone, slowly and unafraid.
The candles of God already are burning row on row:
Farewell, light-bringer; fly to thy fountain again.[143]

Reading this tribute on its appearance in the London *Times*, MacSwiney was deeply touched and sent a message to AE through a mutual friend.[144] His fast ended in death on 25 October, and the Lord Mayor's martyrdom not only strengthened the fervour of the Irish who were fighting for their freedom, but helped many Englishmen to understand the intensity of their neighbours' convictions. Reading his posthumous book *Principles of Freedom*, AE came to feel that MacSwiney had been a man of philosophical depth akin to Emerson and Epictetus.[145]

On 21 November, Lloyd George summoned AE to London,[146] and three days later, over breakfast at 10 Downing Street, they discussed possibilities for a settlement. AE had a low opinion of the Prime Minister, regarding him as a glib talker without ideas other than those he picked up from the conversation of people less shallow than himself,[147] and during the interview he observed 'cunning in every wrinkle' of his face.[148] As he left the official residence, he remembered a point that had slipped his memory and turned back to mention it, but was told that the Prime Minister already had another visitor. At the time, he thought that he had made a truce possible[149] (apparently by recommending that Sinn Fein be induced to accept Commonwealth membership in return for the inclusion of Ulster),[150] but events in Ireland moved so swiftly that his plan came to nothing. It may have been on this trip that he called on Lord Northcliffe, the newspaper magnate, who, being Irish, asked what he could do for the cause. AE requested that he publicise it in the United States, and he did this to such effect that substantial pressure was brought to bear on Great Britain by her most important ally.[151]

On the night of 11 December there occurred the greatest crime of the Anglo-Irish War, when the Auxiliaries and Black-and-Tans burned a large part of the city of Cork. Exactly a week later, AE published in the *Homestead* a carefully argued, factual article addressed to the British people and demanding a judicial inquiry into the attacks on creameries and the payment of compensation by the Crown. He insisted that the I.A.O.S. had nothing to fear from an impartial investigation of the Chief Secretary's charge that the societies were centres of revolutionary activities: should this prove to be the case, the movement would have destroyed itself from within. Copies of this article, entitled 'A Plea for Justice,' together with the appended list of attacks, were circulated in the form of a pamphlet. In his editorial of 25 December, AE approached the national crisis from a spiritual viewpoint, asserting that there was no such thing as justified hatred or righteous anger, that these emotions inevitably brought not peace but further antagonism, as Christ indicated in his saying 'For with the same measure that ye mete withal it shall be measured to you again.' Making a personal confession, he wrote: 'We have tried to fight for justice without anger, and we have torn up many pages of angry manuscript lest we might add to the passions which were laying waste our country.' Covertly he alluded to the Theosophical doctrine of recurrent cycles:

> In that season of mid-winter while everything external is lifeless and cold, in the soul of the world the forces are moving which shall make spring and summer come again, and bring life and sap into the fields and trees, and it is even true in the psychic nature of man that at this season if he forms desires they have an added power . . .

As in his New Year editorial of 1914, he referred to the creative power of thought, and urged his readers to conceive clear images of an Irish civilisation:

> Now, if at any time of the year, we can think such thoughts and have the secret fountains of vitality in nature flooding our thoughts with power: if even a small number of people brood on such things in such a way their thought will have a greater power than the passions of crowds who live on a lower plane of being, for the most potent forces are the spiritual forces. It was these which built up the universe . . .[152]

It was probably this year that AE spent Christmas Eve with Joseph O'Neill while war was raging in the country. He had recently developed a friendship with this shy inspector of schools and his poet wife, Mary Devenport, and the three of them sat up nearly till dawn pretending that Ireland was free and in need of a monarch of her own. In a spirit of fantasy AE considered his friends one after another, discovering in each some incredible royal virtue and then dismissing him for a vice equally absurd.[153]

On 23 December, the King signed Lloyd George's Home Rule Act partitioning Ireland and granting partial self-government separately to North and South. North-east Ulster, which in 1914 had been prepared to fight to prevent any part of the country from receiving autonomy, reluctantly accepted the new law; it was allotted two counties known to have Sinn Fein majorities since a four-county area would not be viable. The South contemptuously rejected the half-measure, and the fighting continued with undiminished savagery on both sides.

Early in December, AE had admitted to a friend that he was too downcast to be able to write.[154] By mid-January 1921 he was seeking some relief from the troubles around him by working on *The Interpreters*,[155] though he had little time to spare for it. In February, Yeats asked him to write an essay expounding his old idea that a true national culture overshadowed and gave a common character to the creative work of individuals; he wanted him to relate this conception to his economic theories to make a suitable contribution to a book designed to influence the new Ireland. AE had not time to write the essay, and an alternative plan to have a section of *The Interpreters* published in advance by the Cuala Press also collapsed.[156]

By March the original midnight curfew in Dublin had been brought forward by four hours. AE cared little about the danger of bullets in the streets – when asked by the O'Neills whether he was afraid of death he replied: 'Why should I fear to go to Tir-na-n'Og?'[157] – but he resented the curb on his social life and complained to Frank Harris: 'It is rather a nuisance to be compelled to be indoors by 8.00 as I do most of my thinking while walking about.'[158] The threatened destruction of the co-operative movement was for him the real calamity of the time, and only by a great effort of will did he retain his hope for the future. 'To those,' he wrote in his journal, 'who have spent their lives in the effort to build up a non-political movement, uniting men of all parties and creeds in Ireland in work for the common good, these reports come with peculiar poignancy, more perhaps than is created by the death of individuals.'[159] His English friend H. W. Nevinson observed how: 'he was almost in despair at the overthrow of his life's work. Yet he did not despair.'[160] Desmond MacCarthy, at this time Dublin correspondent of the *Manchester Guardian*, found AE's office in Plunkett House a happy refuge from the raging passions that engulfed the country.[161] The wrath that he usually managed to restrain in his journalism was sometimes let loose in his private life: asked what punishment should be meted out to a lying reporter of the Conservative *Morning Post*, he answered, his eyes flashing with anger: 'Lead him to the frontier and pitch him over.' 'But,' it was objected, 'we have no frontier, AE; we have only the sea.' 'So much the better; pitch him into the sea.'[162] Dr. Gibbon records that for a time he refused to set foot in England, yet ultimately 'nothing could overthrow that central serenity and stability of soul.'[163] A lighter moment came when, in common with the rest of Dublin, he was amused at Sir Hamar Greenwood's reference to him in the House of Commons as 'an extreme Sinn Feiner.'[164]

AE did not suppose that all the wrongs were on one side. While holding that in the conflict between the two countries Ireland was in the right, he was well aware that inexcusable crimes and murders were committed by Sinn Feiners as certainly as by Crown agents. Referring in 1924 to General Macready's confessing in his memoirs to the crimes of the Auxiliaries and Greenwood's lies, he called for a similar honesty about Sinn Fein.[165] With his pacifist convictions he was reluctant to accept the conventional distinction between war and murder, and this led to a strange misunderstanding with the Unionist John Eglinton. As the two men were travelling together on the top of a Dublin tram, AE denied that there was any difference between killing in war and in peace, and Eglinton accused him of defending murder.[166] AE, taking this to mean that he was himself a murderer because his sympathies were with the Irish side, indignantly alighted at the next stop. Within a few weeks he forgot the incident, but in 1926 Eglinton still imagined that he had a grudge against him.[167]

During the early months of 1921, American aid flowed into Ireland through the White Cross organisation established by Plunkett. After more than a million dollars had been subscribed, Judge Richard Campbell was sent to Ireland to arrange for its disbursement. The first person he interviewed was AE, whose calmness and businesslike detachment impressed him deeply, and their meeting proved to be the beginning of a long friendship marked by intellectual sympathy.[168]

AE persisted in his patriotic efforts on both the political and economic fronts. When General Crozier, who had just resigned his command of the Auxiliaries as a protest against his Government's policy, drew up plans for a truce, AE sent them to his friend Erskine Childers, one of the most fanatical nationalists, but they proved unacceptable to Lloyd George.[169] On April 30, he published in the *Homestead* 'Thoughts for British Co-operators,' a sequel to the fruitless 'Plea for Justice' of the previous year. This appeal that the attacks on co-operative societies might be investigated by three British judges, men in whom the virtue of impartiality was engrained by reason of their profession, was, like its predecessor, reissued as a pamphlet. It was about this time that the attacks came to an end.

During March or April, writing for an American audience, AE defended the Irish people's struggle as their attempt to escape from the domination of an alien race, but simultaneously admitted to a grave doubt as to whether physical force was ever justifiable since other means of fighting for right existed; one of his letters shows that he had in mind Mahatma Gandhi's non-violent non-co-operation.[170] His essay, 'The Inner and the Outer Ireland,' was published in the May issue of the New York *Pearson's Magazine* together with Frank Harris' comment: 'This is the best, the truest, and most original article I have ever received in my forty years as Editor.' Reading this opinion, Shaw endorsed it with the remark: 'A.E.'s article always is the best.'[171] Sinn Fein was sufficiently impressed by the essay to have it reprinted as a pamphlet in Dublin, and it was separately published in London and translated into French and Spanish.

Apparently at the request of Harris, AE set to work on a second article, but found it more difficult as he wished to do justice to the Ulster and British viewpoints.[172] In 'Conditions of an Irish Settlement,' finished by the beginning of June[173] but not published till September, he proposed an immediate armistice and an assembly of the M.P.'s of North and South to design an all-Ireland constitution with certain safeguards for Ulster and the legitimate interests of Britain. He desired also that Ireland should accept responsibility for part of the national debt, not only for her neighbour's sake but for her own: Alexander Hamilton's theory that a new state should secure the loyalty of the wealthy by becoming their debtor had greatly impressed him, and he was to refer to it continually during the next few years.

While the Anglo-Irish War continued to rage, AE publicly expounded a theory of verbal melody which he had persuaded Yeats to accept as valid.[174] In a long letter published in the *Times Literary Supplement* for 19 May, 1921, and intended to provoke further research, he suggested that just as colours in painting made patterns through contrast as well as harmony, vowels and consonants might contribute to the cadence of verse as much by opposition as by coincidence.

At the beginning of June AE, unable to reach Donegal,[175] left Dublin to spend his summer holiday with a friend at Roundwood, County Wicklow.[176] By this time, the decline in the Irish economy gave cause for great anxiety, but a change for the better was near at hand. In May, the Government had held General Elections in North and South to implement their new Home Rule Act, and though the Sinn Feiners returned unopposed in nearly all the Southern constituencies refused to co-operate, a Northern parliament was opened on 22 June. King George V, on his own initiative, had had an appeal for reconciliation inserted in his inaugural speech, and two days later Lloyd George seized on the opportunity to invite de Valera and the Ulster leader Sir James Craig to London for negotiations. In his editorial for 2 July AE, newly returned from his holiday, combined an expression of confidence that an imminent settlement would release a great burst of creative energy with a warning against over sanguine hopes. To the great relief of the war-weary majority a truce went into effect nine days later. Pointing out that Ireland had not been at peace since 1914, AE wrote:

> In the city of Dublin . . . the truce has been reflected on smiling faces . . . and it is quite possible to renew at night the long-lost art of conversation which was rapidly decaying because in the evening a man had hardly warmed to a discussion with his friends when they looked at their watches and fled hastily before the Curfew left them to the peril of the streets with lorries and machine guns.[177]

The negotiations proceeded in London, and after some weeks Lloyd George made in private a firm offer of conditions for a settlement. On the evening of Sunday, 14 August, Constance Markievicz, with some other ferociously Republican women, burst into AE's house and announced joyfully that the terms had been rejected and the war would be resumed. AE, who was sitting alone with his friend Nevinson, was thrown into gloom.[178] A few days later, calling for a plebiscite, he announced in his paper that if the fighting recommenced it would be even more savage than before and the co-operative movement would be ruined.[179] With his usual courage he recovered his spirits, and when, on the 23rd, the Dail endorsed the Cabinet's defiance of the British, he refused to despair.

The British Government, reeling under the pressure of a divided public opinion, economic troubles, and American sympathy for Ireland, did not treat their offer as final, and the two sides tried to agree on conditions for a formal conference. In the *Homestead*, AE emphasised the need for constructive thought on the details of an Irish civilisation and the urgency of establishing a sound educational system without which independence would be profitless. During September, he published in the *Manchester Guardian* another political article, which once again was reprinted as a pamphlet. 'Ireland and the Empire at the Court of Conscience' was intended as a warning to Irishmen to give the most solemn thought to Britain's proposals before deciding for peace or war. It offered no programme and came to no conclusion, but expounded in somewhat rhetorical terms both the Republican and Unionist positions, showing that there were indeed formidable arguments on either side.

It appears to have been in December that AE fulfilled a long-standing ambition when he succeeded in meeting Michael Collins. They discussed economics and AE was extraordinarily impressed by his intellectual power as well as his personal charm.[180] The terms in which AE spoke of Collins, both before and after his assassination, suggest that he came nearer than any other man he ever met to fulfilling the dream of a great Irish leader that had haunted him ever since his vision of an avatar in 1896. He saw him not only as a brave and successful soldier but as potentially a great statesman, and reviewing his posthumous book *The Path to Freedom* he wrote:

> We feel Collins, consciously or unconsciously, was judging political and economic systems by his own lavish humanity. His was no starved human nature and it resented the starvation of either mind or body. We have not had such a big human personality in Irish politics for generations.[181]

AE's opinion of the other leading Republicans was very different. Though he had a strong personal affection for the small, tense Erskine Childers, whom he once spoke of as 'brilliant of mind, generous and beautiful of spirit,'[182] he felt that both he and the austere Mr. de Valera[183] had precise, mathematical minds unsuited to politics; they treated the latter as an exact science and were unwilling to compromise, putting abstract principles above the creation of a noble and humane society.

A Conference was agreed upon, and on 11 October five plenipotentiaries, authorised by the Dail to negotiate, travelled to London. The team consisted of Arthur Griffith and Michael Collins together with three less famous men – Robert Barton, a Republican though a Protestant aristocrat, and Eamonn Duggan and Gavan Duffy, who both had legal knowledge. Their principal secretary, Erskine Childers, who is sometimes accused of having acted as de Valera's private spy on the plenipotentiaries, had a long interview with AE just before he left, and passed on to his colleagues the latter's opinion that an Irish government should strive if possible to accept only debts owed to its own citizens.[184]

On 21 October, while the London Conference was in progress, AE had an informal discussion with Pollock, who had represented the Belfast industrial interest at the Convention, and two of his associates. In his report of their conversation, probably drawn up for the Dail, he observed that he found the Ulstermen friendly but reluctant to talk freely. They explained that they could not at present trust Sinn Fein's leaders, who were completely unknown to them, but seemed impressed at AE's account of the serious economic studies which the organisation's committees had already completed. Realising that if North and South did not adopt a common fiscal policy at the outset, the latter would have to develop its own industries fostered by tariffs, they undertook to pass on the suggestion of a customs union to their Government.[185]

In the summer, AE had not been able to spend a full month at Roundwood and he returned in November to finish his holiday.

Afterwards, on the 25th, he paid a brief visit to London for discussions with Arthur Henderson, the Labour politician, and Lloyd George.[186] While the Conference was sitting, his hopes seem to have soared. In the *Homestead* he spoke exultantly of an imminent outburst of energy in the co-operative movement which would lead to a second wave of development carrying forward the work of the pioneers. It must have been about this time that he persuaded Constance Markievicz, the Sinn Fein Minister of Labour, to give contracts to a road-building union,[187] and writing for an American magazine, he prophesied that within a generation Ireland would be covered with co-operative rural communities and that the productive guilds of urban workers which had already sprung up would have many successors; certain that Ireland's greatest period lay before it, he declared:

> I cannot believe that the legend of the Gael, which began among the gods, will die out in some petty peasant republic . . . What began greatly I think will end greatly, and there will be some flare-up of genius before the torch of the Gael is extinguished . . .[188]

On the evening of Monday, 5 December, Lloyd George presented an ultimatum to the five plenipotentiaries: Britain had made all the concessions that were possible – if they did not immediately accept the terms now offered there would be war. In the early hours of Tuesday morning, in great anguish of spirit, they signed. Ireland was to remain within the Empire, partition was to be maintained if Ulster wished, and the Royal Navy was to have the right to use Irish harbours; in all other respects the South, henceforward to be known as the Free State, was to be independent. These terms had to be ratified by the Dail and the Westminster Parliament.

On Tuesday evening, AE travelled to Plunkett's home with Robert Bratton, an I.A.O.S. organiser. He was in high spirits at the prospect of peace and independence and asked his companion what course he thought Ulster would take. When Bratton replied she would remain separate, he became momentarily angry and called out loudly: 'What are your political views anyway?' Bratton admitted to some confusion in his own mind, but was sure he was not a Republican.

'Anyway, Mr. Russell,' he concluded, 'I don't think your question is quite a fair one.'

'Oh, don't you indeed!' AE shouted. 'Well, I don't give a damn who knows my political views.'[189]

Constance Markievicz remained tenaciously Republican and scorned the new terms. When AE gladly opted for the Free State, she exclaimed: 'George – you're an idiot!'[190]

At this point the non-political stance of the *Homestead* was to some extent abandoned. Southern Unionism belonged to the past and a fierce contest raged between those who wished to ratify the Treaty and those who were enraged by Lloyd George's blackmail. Collins and Griffith headed the former party; de Valera, willing to concede only 'External Association' with the British Commonwealth, led the latter. Now that Ireland's fate hung in the balance, AE used the columns of his paper to propagate his view that to reject the Treaty was to destroy the nation. It was not the name – Free State or Republic – that mattered, but the quality of life in the country; the settlement gave Ireland all the power she needed to create her own distinctive society and it was a grave error to treat politics as a rigid and exact science. In the strained atmosphere, there was intense anger against Ulster for seceding, and to AE's distress the South declared a trade boycott against her. For the first time some co-operative societies divided on a political issue. AE believed that eighty-five per cent of the people wished to accept the Treaty, but so many members of the Dail had suffered in the Anglo-Irish War that he felt uncertain how the House would vote.[191] He publicly denounced those deputies who threatened to continue the struggle regardless of the majority opinion, pointing out that 'they make foolish their past declarations about government by consent of the governed.'[192]

The decision was taken on 7 January, 1922, in a packed chamber. Sitting beside a coloured student from Trinity College, AE listened to the debate. To Griffith, the difference between External Association, which involved substantial concessions to Britain, and Commonwealth membership was only a quibble, but some were prepared to give their lives for it. To AE's surprise and pleasure, Griffith delivered a far finer speech than he had thought him capable of, making, as he said, 'that dear, woolly-minded De Valera' appear 'a sheep beside an exceedingly intelligent and yet not too wicked goat.'[193] When he sat down the question was put and the Treaty was ratified by sixty-four votes to fifty-seven.

Although the British Parliament was to endorse the Treaty in March, Ireland's troubles were not yet over. De Valera, insisting that the Republic must continue until the people dissolved it, resigned from his position as President of the Dail, and Griffith formed a Provisional Government with Collins as his Minister of Finance. AE foresaw a more honest administration than the country had ever known, for the new rulers were men who had faced death for a principle.[194] Anticipating the rapid growth of economic democracy, he wrote: 'the ideal of Ireland a co-operative commonwealth is continually discussed by the amazing young men who have been running Ireland for the past four or five years.'[195] There was much talk of a tariff policy and AE persistently warned against a hasty decision for or against protection: he still hoped that Ulster might accept a customs union, and to his delight the trade boycott was lifted within three weeks of the Dail's acceptance of the Treaty.[196]

In January, Yeats wrote to him expressing great surprise that Lloyd George had conceded so much, and repeating his suggestion for the advance publication of an extract from *The Interpreters*.[197] AE replied that he had not been able to touch the book for months and mentioned some of the numerous committees he had to attend when he was not working on the *Homestead;* he had also undertaken to address the Sociological Society in London and was desperately seeking time to complete his lecture. His letter ardently expressed a new-found hope and excitement:

> Ireland is intensely interesting, more so than I have found it since I was a boy. The young men are full of possibilities, and I watch them and study their minds . . .[198]

On 21 February, AE delivered the talk that he had taken such pains to prepare. After building castles in the air round the ideas of economic democracy and a bilingual Ireland, he spoke with some dread of the threat of immediate civil war. While many enemies of the Treaty were fearless idealists fighting for a cause which was in theory right, rebels of another kind followed in their track:

> In the shadows in Ireland, North and South, lurks reptilian human life, bigots who in the name of Christ spit on his precepts and who have put on the whole armoury of hate, and men, and women too, who have known the dark intoxication of blood, and who seek half unconsciously for the renewal of that sinister ecstasy.[199]

In March, AE corresponded with Yeats on the possibility of forming a literary Academy, but was lukewarm about the idea and came to the conclusion, with which Yeats agreed, that it would be better to reform the existing Royal Irish Academy.[200] He was amused to learn that a St. Patrick's Day service held in an American church this month had been based on his writings. The choir had sung some of his poems as hymns, while the rector had recited others as prayers and had preached his sermon on *The National Being*.[201]

During March and April, AE referred in the *Homestead* to the continuing violence in the country. Though it had subsided sufficiently for him to recommend the re-opening of major co-operative enterprises like the meat-packing factory at Waterford, wandering bands of armed men were still living off the country. The army that had fought the Black-and-Tans and Auxiliaries was now divided into pro-Treaty and anti-Treaty sections, which intermittently clashed. On 13 April, a detachment of anti-Treaty soldiers took possession of the Four Courts in Dublin, and their leader, Rory O'Connor, gave the impression that he would attempt to establish a military dictatorship. By the end of the month, AE was very downcast and he suggested as Lennox Robinson recorded, that someone should write a play 'about how the generations for 700 years fought for the liberation of beautiful Cathleen ni Houlihan, and when they set her free she walked out, a fierce vituperative old hag.'[202] About ten days later his spirits had rallied and he wrote to Lady Gregory:

> The country is with the Free State and the Republicans are finding themselves more and more isolated. There is a danger in that as having taken up a resolute attitude based on physical force they must either fade out or be laughed out or else exercise the physical force . . . However I think things will come right slowly perhaps.[203]

The British Government had prescribed that a General Election should be held in the Free State before the end of July. AE had hoped that economic issues would at last be made the subject of a political campaign and was sharply disappointed when it became clear that the parties would be fighting on the question of the Treaty.[204] Suddenly, on 20 May, to the alarm of Lloyd George's colleague Churchill, de Valera and Collins agreed that pro- and anti-Treaty politicians would not stand against each other, but Sinn Fein as a whole would field a panel of candidates in which the two groups would be represented in the same proportions as in the present Dail; after the election they intended to establish a coalition government to restore order. AE referred in his editorial columns to the puzzling agreement between the politicals, and noting that the factions were to co-operate in suppressing lawlessness he observed ominously that the greater the number of armed men in any place, the worse the disorder.[205]

In June, apparently still unable to reach Donegal, he took his holiday at Glengariff at the head of Bantry Bay in County Cork, where he stayed on an island in a romantic Grecian building. His spacious room, from which the sea and a formal garden were visible, impressed a later visitor with 'its fluted marble columns, its chaste, classical decorations, and its stone floors covered by the skins of tiger and bear and deer.' Here he cleaned his palette so heedlessly that the pigments left permanent marks on the stone.[206] From this tranquil corner of Ireland he returned to Dublin to find that the pact between Collins and de Valera had been abandoned, the election had been held on 16 June, and fifty-eight pro-Treaty, thirty-six anti-Treaty, and thirty-four other deputies (who incidentally favoured the settlement) had been returned. The Free State Constitution agreed upon by Britain and Ireland had been published in the newspapers only on the morning of Election Day. AE was delighted that it permitted the Government to set up elected vocational councils for the various industries, each with the power to nominate the Minister for the appropriate Department. He had advocated this scheme in *The National Being* and during the coming years he was frequently to plead that it should be implemented. Meanwhile, before the merits of the Constitution could be put to the test, Ireland had another ordeal to face, for the Republicans had not yet abandoned armed struggle.

In view of Rory O'Connor's continued occupation of the Four Courts, Churchill, speaking in the House of Commons on 26 June, issued a virtual ultimatum implying that the Free State Government must choose between war with the Republicans and war with Britain. Two days later, after O'Connor had refused to surrender, the pro-Treaty soldiers began to bombard the Courts with cannon borrowed from the British army. At this signal, the Republicans mobilised their followers and seized scattered buildings in various parts of Dublin: for eight days fighting disrupted the life of the capital. After the Four Courts were reduced to rubble, the Free State Government turned their artillery against a group of hotels in O'Connell Street, where Pearse had faced British guns in 1916. These hotels were now the Republican headquarters in Dublin, and before the Government could consolidate their victory, de Valera and other leaders contrived to escape and pass unrecognised through the city to rally their forces elsewhere in Ireland. Thus began a ferocious civil war in which armed bands moved over the countryside killing, looting, and destroying. The republicans assassinated Free State members of the Dail, and the Government – its members confined day and night within the walls of the College of Science – responded by executing Republican prisoners. When Erskine Childers was captured in November, AE, who kept up his friendships with people on both sides, appealed to President Cosgrave for clemency but was unable to save him from the firing squad.[207]

The ten months of civil war were a time of fear and economic decay. No man who had been involved in the struggle for national freedom knew when former friends would ambush him or even break into his home and carry him off to summary execution. AE valued his social life too highly to take precautions for his personal safety. His door remained open on Sunday nights, and every Friday evening he visited Gogarty. According to the latter, he once became so absorbed in expounding his ideas that he ignored the occasional bullet flying through the bay window to crash into the plaster, and the ottoman on which he was sitting had to be moved to a safer part of the room.[208]

The Civil War coincided with a period of economic depression in much of Europe. While its beginnings interfered with AE's professional routine – because of the battle in O'Connell Street, no

Homestead was published on 1 July – he thought chiefly of its effect on the life of the country. Sorrowfully he noted how the Republican gunmen had remade themselves in the image of the Black-and-Tans they hated, and he published many bitter and some witty observations on men who preferred fighting to thinking, and who were passing on their tastes to the rising generation. He expressed the pious hope that in future 'men who believe in physical force will apply it in digging or paving, or ploughing, forms of application of physical force of which they fight very shy at present.'[209] In such circumstances he could only emphasise the importance of persisting in the prosaic tasks of scientific farming and co-operative business, and in a long article in which he again echoed his New Year editorial of 1914, he reaffirmed his belief in the potency of thought and urged his readers to react to the sound of gunfire by filling their minds with constructive images of a new civilisation.[210] For a time he was uncertain whether the Free State Government would support agricultural co-operation, but in mid-July it was announced that the subsidy to the I.A.O.S. would be continued. He still feared that the persisting violence might cause the collapse of the organisation forcing him to seek a living abroad,[211] but though the Republicans adopted the barbaric policy of burning country houses belonging to supporters of the Treaty, they did not attack the farmers' societies.

In the first half of August, Lady Gregory visited AE in Dublin and noted in her journal that he 'is more cheerful, thinks a better time must come and that we should be ready to take up our work; thinks there may be a great intellectual awakening.'[212] On the 12th, Ireland was stunned to learn of the death of Arthur Griffith from a heart attack; ten days later a worse calamity befell when Griffith's successor, the young Michael Collins, was killed in a Republican ambush. Watching the hundreds of thousands who walked in the funeral processions to honour the dead leaders, AE took the opportunity to moralise on the Irish weakness for hero-worship, and he pointed to the need for a thoughtful allegiance to policies in place of a blind devotion to individuals:

> If the nation knew its own mind and had trust in itself no matter how great the man who died, while there would be sorrow equal to the greatness, there would be small sense of national disaster because a nation conscious of its own firm purpose would never let that purpose be defeated by the passing of any individual.[213]

William Cosgrave, who succeeded Collins, invited AE to become a member of the Senate, a Second Chamber to be composed of eminent citizens as opposed to the professional politicians of the Dail. Unlike Yeats, he turned down this opportunity. 'If I was more independent financially,' he explained to Lady Gregory, 'I would consider it a duty to go on and it would be a relief from writing as it is with Willie. But I would lose my soul if I went on writing about politics and economics in the paper I edit and then considered the same things as a Senator.'[214] A legend grew up that he had consulted his ancestral gods before refusing.

During August, AE was able to detach his mind from external events sufficiently to complete the manuscript of *The Interpreters*. 'I[t] was difficult to write,' he observed, 'with the country upset and I do not know now whether it is good or bad. I thought it would be a good book but at last I felt as if I was marching through subtleties to the dismemberment of my mind.'[215] It was published on 7 November, and he came to feel that, though it was his least popular prose work, it was also his best.[216]

In *The Interpreters*, AE explores more fully many of the ideas adumbrated in his political pamphlets. One of the keys to its understanding is to be found in his belief that the teachings in Madame Blavatsky's *Secret Doctrine* would be confirmed by the discoveries of natural science and archaeology.[217] The book is set in a future age when the materialistic investigation of nature has been exhausted and scientists have traced all phenomena back to the three primal manifestations of Deity – mind, substance, and energy, or the Logos, the Archaeus, and the Light of the Logos. It is of great interest as showing the common root to which AE traced his sometimes contradictory aspirations, which are represented by the speakers whose dialogue comprises the major part of the text. Though they are in one sense facets of the author's personality, they are also modelled on his friends and acquaintances. Rebels against a world state, as they await execution they spend their last night arguing over the spiritual origins of their ideals. The poet Lavelle, who is most nearly identified with AE himself, is a devotee of the Planetary Spirit, that ray of the Logos which reveals itself through its body, the earth, a manifestation of the Archaeus. He regards each true civilisation as an expression of that Spirit, which speaks with one voice in Ireland and another in the Arabian desert, and does not speak at all through such mongrel cultures as the British, which have no mythology authentically their own. The architect Rian, who recalls the young Yeats and perhaps John Hughes, lives for beauty, while Culain, endowed with the stature and magnetism of Larkin, makes his ideal universal brotherhood. There may be touches of Gogarty and Stephens in Leroy, a fantastic humourist with the latter's large head and small body, who distrusts all organised society. The prisoner Heyt, modelled on Murphy, the employers' leader in 1913, is an eminent imperialist arrested by mistake. He at first appears as an arrogant and unlovely character, but it is gradually shown that he, too, has grandeur in his soul, for he seeks to bring all humanity into harmony with the power of Deity which governs the universe. Brehon, an old historian first introduced as a portrait of Standish O'Grady, draws the threads of the argument together. He shows that Culain is inspired by the Logos, the unity in which all souls are contained, Heyt by the Light of the Logos, and Lavelle, questing for beauty, by the Archaeus, while in Leroy there is a balance of the forces emanating from these three aspects of the Godhead. It is Brehon's task, too, to be the mouthpiece for AE's Gandhian doctrine of non-violence.

Though well constructed and intellectually coherent, *The Interpreters* is not a literary success. While the speakers have some individuality, AE's prose still bears the marks of an art that does not conceal art, and is unredeemed by the impassioned conviction that inspires *The Candle of Vision*. In one of Rian's speeches, for example, the colloquial 'old grumbler that you are' sits uneasily beside the simile in the sentence 'That divine architecture must have coloured their thought as a sunset makes everything in harmony with its own light.'[218] Both the narrative and the dialogue are too self-consciously melodious, and literary idioms, over polished images, and rhetorical parallelisms come between the reader and the clear line of the argument.

The partition which had followed the violent struggle for independence weighed heavily on almost every Irish mind. It was now made worse by the anti-Catholic pogroms and Sinn Fein terrorism raging in Ulster, and AE, like many of his countrymen, felt that economic bonds between North and South would help to bring nearer the day of reunification. In the *Homestead* for 7 October, he expressed his hope that the paper would help to link the severed sections of the I.A.O.S., which were henceforward to receive subsidies from different governments. A week later there was a sudden crisis: in a long article he announced that the decline in advertising revenue had made the continued existence of the journal impossible unless farmers and co-operators subscribed within ten days share capital for £1,000; he frankly admitted that if the Civil War lasted another year their money would be lost. Should this sum not be forthcoming, he added:

> the present editor . . . must find some other occupation, perhaps in another country . . . He believed it was possible to build up in Ireland on democratic and co-operative lines a real civilisation which would be a model to the world. The madness of a section of the Irish people has wrecked these and many other hopes, or if they survive in any [form] their fruition is postponed for years. There are hardly any who held such high hopes based on what they believed was the character of their countrymen who do not feel at

> the present time a shiver of humiliation when they think of the wreckage of their dreams, the hatreds which are festering, the ruin of the culture and social order which has taken place.[219]

AE was surprised and touched by the response to his appeal. The sum he had asked for was subscribed within a week, and with another burst of optimism he expressed his faith in the future effectiveness of the paper. 'We are convinced,' he wrote, 'that the policy it has advocated will triumph in Ireland in spite of the shocks to the economic system . . . during these last two years.'[220]

Notwithstanding his Whitmanesque mood, AE knew that he could no longer hope for the birth of the Co-operative Commonwealth in his own lifetime, and he sought consolation in visualising the future fulfilment of a far greater dream, the descent of the Incarnation who had failed to appear a quarter of a century before. On December 19, he wrote the first page of *The Avatars*,[221] a romance which he sought to imbue with the gaiety he held to be a part of the spiritual quest. Eight days later he sent to the *Irish Times* a long open letter in which he pleaded with the Republicans: in a series of lucid paragraphs, he exposed the fallacies in the arguments with which they tried to justify their warfare against the majority, but his hope that this appeal would help to establish an atmosphere conducive to settlement[222] remained unrealised.

During the early months of 1923, the irregulars continued to attack barracks, ambush Government troops, and wreck railway property. In January, a band of gunmen fired the house that Sir Horace Plunkett had built at Foxrock to entertain his friends, and along with all his treasures, the murals which AE regarded as his finest paintings[223] were completely destroyed. While the dairy societies seemed likely to pull through, the economy of the country as a whole remained in a perilous state. In the Dublin quarterly, *Studies*, AE published his most sombre warning.[224]

> I cannot understand the faith of those who act on the belief that a nation is immortal and can survive any strain. Nations are no more immortal than individuals. The dust of the desert is over great cities whose inhabitants loved their country with no less a passion than Irish nationalists have loved theirs . . . If a nation is like a dissolute youth who impairs his vitality by excesses, it will perish as surely and by as inexorable a law of life as the debauchee.

In his own paper, he denounced the cowardice and apathy of a people who were allowing a handful of fanatics to destroy their country, and castigated the men whose relentless allegiance to a political abstraction threatened to obliterate the many-sided achievements of the Irish Renaissance; mercilessly he flayed 'the nauseating cant of militarists that war purifies the moral air and brings humanity back to primitive truth and honesty,'[225] and the spurious idealism of gunmen who 'rely entirely on physical force, which is the last resort of materialism and the declared bankruptcy of the moral, intellectual and spiritual nature.'[226] Simultaneously he redoubled his efforts to persuade the Government and people that the only hope for the future lay in an intensive programme of national education:

> if education is starved it is a sacrifice of the next generation to this which is the most ignoble and unnatural of all sacrifices, the parents battening on the children, which is contrary to all human instinct.[227]

At this period Plunkett, too, rallying after the cruel loss of his home, was turning his attention to the importance of guiding public opinion. For some months he had been recruiting Irish-American capital to restart the shortlived *Irish Statesman* as a non-party but pro-Treaty weekly disseminating expert advice for the guidance of the Free State. By October 1922, he had already begun to look for an editor and had thought of AE, but Bernard Shaw advised him that the latter did not have the necessary editorial technique and recommended Robert Lynd. Fortunately Plunkett was unconvinced by Shaw's argument and early in May 1923 he offered the position to AE, who refused it, but proposed instead to enlarge the scope of the *Homestead* greatly. In a letter to Yeats he explained his motives:

> As I am situated at present I have some spare time I can devote to writing books like 'The National Being', 'The Candle of Vision' and 'The Interpreters' . . . I would prefer the few hundreds I receive for editing the Homestead to three times the amount for editing a paper which would take all my thought, prevent my doing any literary work for myself and which would not leave me the consolation of thinking I was creating a tradition of decent life among the mass of the people . . . The sole idea I have had in working in Ireland was by my poetry and prose books to bring some of the aged thought of the world into Ireland and by my work on the Homestead to win acceptance for some fundamental ideas about a social order among the common people.[228]

Plunkett, however, was now thoroughly convinced that he had picked on the right man, and by the beginning of June[229] he had filled AE with enthusiasm for an *Irish Statesman* in which room was to be found for the main features of the *Homestead,* allowing the latter's crusade for a more humane social order to continue.

The arrangements for the starting of the new paper occupied four months, and long before the first number appeared the Civil War had drawn gradually to a close. As insurgents had flowed into the Government prison camps, the Republican supplies and morale had been eroded. On 30 April, the rebels announced a unilateral ceasefire, but no Government threats or promises could induce them to surrender their weapons. As the negotiations continued, AE wrote indignantly to Padraic Colum, now resident in the U.S.A.: 'I don't think I ever remember in Ireland a more poisonous and ignoble and lying propaganda than the Republicans have set on foot.'[230] On 24 May, de Valera ordered his followers to conceal all arms in secret dumps: the advent of peace was marred by the implied threat that fighting would be resumed if he and his party so desired. Those opponents of the Treaty who had been elected to the Dail still refused to take their seats and form the kernel of the Opposition, as this would have involved swearing allegiance to the Crown.

The country remained too unsettled to allow AE to visit Donegal in June, and he again took his holiday at Glengariff.[231] About this time he personally investigated several Republican charges that the Government had mistreated prisoners and found them all false. Mentioning this in a letter to Frank Harris, an opponent of the Free State, he concluded: 'I think the Republic is a good cause in the worst hands.'[232]

When he agreed to edit the *Irish Statesman,* AE was already the finest journalist in Ireland. Apart from producing purely literary articles which were far from negligible, he had for eighteen years preached his social philosophy to the farmers and to all who would listen, and had gradually acquired a mastery of persuasive prose in all its moods. While assembling the technical advice of the best agriculturalists, he had himself provided a weekly survey of the background of current events against which business was conducted. Year by year, he had shown that an understanding of human nature was much more important for accurate prophecy than the theoretical knowledge of the professional economists, who neglected the psychological factor.

Occasionally AE was led astray in his hopes and predictions by his ingrained optimism. Early in 1921 he foretold that Partition would not last more than a decade,[233] and although the Co-operative Commonwealth offered a more humane ideal than the socialist or capitalist systems, it may be doubted whether it was ever likely to have become a reality in early twentieth-century Ireland. Membership in the agricultural co-operative societies never extended to more than a quarter of the farmers, and many of these were men who could not keep accounts, who did not know why machinery should be oiled, and who had no idea of the difference between the I.A.O.S. and the Department of Agriculture.[234] While AE recognised that the creation of a genuinely national movement depended on the success of the federations linking the local bodies, his repeated assertions that these were flourishing are contradicted by R. A. Anderson, who chronicled the troubles of the Agency Society in his book *With Horace Plunkett in Ireland.*

During the later years of the *Homestead,* the Dublin Strike and the continuous warfare at home and abroad had tested AE's faith in humanity and in pacifism, and in 1924 he admitted that while his intuition still assured him that all violence was wrong, his intellect refused to confirm this conviction.[235] A few years later he told an American professor:

> I am and always have been a pacifist; but what am I to believe now? Although I have always condemned violence, we got nothing in Ireland by peaceful means. Yes, all the freedom the Irish have attained has been won by fighting, violence and bloodshed.[236]

Though AE was no longer certain that the non-violence he had advocated in *The Interpreters* could have prevailed against Britain's effort to hold Ireland by force, in all other respects his faith was unshaken, and when he took up the burden of the *Irish Statesman* he was as steadfast a Theosophist and a co-operator as he had ever been.

VII

The Conscience of a Nation (1923–1930)

During the summer of 1923, Edgar DeWitt Jones, an American journalist studying conditions in Ireland, called on AE at his home and engaged him in a discussion that ranged from American poetry to the antiquities of Dublin. The Irishman's humanity and intellectual enthusiasms left a lasting impression on Jones, who later published his recollections:

> AE's longish brown pointed beard was showing a little gray; his head crowned with Tennysonian locks was massive and noble. I see him now – the flowing windsor tie, gray tweed lounge suit, loose and comfortable, mark the ease and fluency of the man, feel the warmth of his radiant personality, calm, poised, yet buoyant, the whole man very much alive.[1]

AE was about to enter on a period when his vast reserves of energy would be used to the full, a period that was probably among the most satisfying in his life. When he became editor of the *Irish Statesman* in September, he was a national figure at the height of his fame and influence, and he knew that his editorial columns would be studied by the nation's intellectuals, and even by the ruling politicians. The new paper was incomparably more demanding than the *Homestead* – a colleague remarks: 'There were times when he had to write at the speed at which other men fly.'[2] In October he explained to Pryse, 'It is very heavy work as it necessitates my studying up things I had never thought about very carefully,' and he complained that 'at present I feel "caught on the wheel" and the spirit at remote distances.'[3] Pinned down in his office – correcting proofs, reading manuscripts, and writing[4] – he felt the burden of the daily grind, and each spring, as June drew nearer, was filled with longing for the lonely hills of Donegal. Though he painted less than formerly during the year,[5]* his holiday remained sacrosanct and he somehow managed to enjoy a rich private life. His poetic inspiration returned by fits and starts, and he still presided over the Thursday meetings of his cherished Hermetic Society. Here he sometimes

*Visiting an early exhibition of the Dublin artist Mr. Cecil Salkeld in 1925, he walked round the room twice in silent admiration. On the way out he stopped before Salkeld with hat on head and arms folded, and said with a profound sigh, 'Young man, I used to be a painter once.'[5a]

launched into long digressions which would appear almost verbatim in the next issue of the *Statesman*.[6] He continued to denounce official Theosophy as spiritually barren and was specially scandalised to find Charles Johnston editing a review which was pro-capital and anti-labour.[7]

In the autumn of 1923, AE embarked on a curious experiment. James Pryse, who was translating *Prometheus Bound,* attempted to imprint an image of Aeschylus on one of the letters he sent him from Los Angeles, hoping that his former disciple would be able to paint the vision to furnish an illustration for his book. 'I have tried to get your astral image breathed in the leaf,' AE replied, 'but I am afraid it is so long since I was working with you that my faculties have been blunted by agricultural organisation, writing[,] editing and what not that I feel insecure in this work where you are the adept.' He saw, however, 'a powerful head, eagle and beaked features, with a great back to the head as well as a noble and capacious forehead,'[8] and despite some damage in the preparation for publication,[9] AE's oil painting eventually appeared in black and white as the frontispiece of Pryse's volume.

At this time the famous Sunday evening salon at 17, Rathgar Avenue, was one of the most inviting features in the social landscape of the Free State capital. Here, crowded in small rooms and braving the billows of smoke surging from the sage's pipe, guests with diverse interests and social backgrounds, many of them foreign visitors, enjoyed the comfort of informality and talked without constraint. Sitting sometimes in the centre, less often in a corner, AE took pains to draw the shy and the humble into the conversation, and he himself embarked on long disquisitions. 'As the evening progressed,' writes Dr. Gibbon, 'and he talked more and more, a gentle dew of perspiration would break out on his face, one would notice the light shining on his gold spectacles, his blue tie, his loosely-laced boots, the ruffled brown hair and the golden beard turning grey; while all the time the caressing, soothing voice focused attention on the thought...'[10]

With the tea and cakes, the leisurely probing of ideas, and the lighthearted reminiscences of AE's early days, these gatherings had, as Monk Gibbon noticed, a bourgeois atmosphere very different from the aristocratic stateliness of the select Monday gatherings at Yeats's Georgian house in Merrion Square.[11] But if some witnesses give the impression of a mental cosiness at AE's salon, most speak of the tangible presence of his limitless goodwill and a profoundly spiritual beneficence extended to all comers. One of the younger friends who first knew him when he was middle-aged, Mlle. Simone Téry, has written a memorable account,[12] the accuracy of which Dr.

Gibbon confirms. In 1924 or early the following year, this gay, sensitive, and acute young Frenchwoman was astonished to discover a man who was able to cater with equal ease to the spiritual and material needs of his fellows – to find a house for George Moore, to analyse the nation's economy, or to bring peace to a troubled soul. While unobtrusively holding (rather to her irritation)[13] to the moral standards of a Puritan, he was wholly free from the Puritan's self-righteousness. At peace within himself, he regarded the world with unbounded compassion, allowed a mischievous humour to play on the surface of his mind, and offered everyone he met his concentrated attention. Yet when he spoke in his drawing-room of the Gaelic gods, he seemed as though possessed and unconscious of his listeners as he set off in pursuit of a far-off vision of beauty. 'All life,' she wrote, 'is concentrated in his tenderly blue-grey eyes, luminous, tranquil, with the blue of the sky after rain. One would say that his clear eyes laugh behind his spectacles and a gentle mischief lights them up.'[14] Above all, she felt the mysterious quality by which his very presence could radiate peace and happiness without his conscious effort.

Although his most intimate friend, James Stephens, was living in Paris, AE did not want for congenial companions during the early twenties. Characteristically he formed a regular routine of evening visits, allotting Monday night to Yeats, Wednesday to Constantine Curran, Friday to Gogarty, and Saturday to Joseph O'Neill, though from time to time there were changes in this programme. Gogarty was now a respected surgeon, an accomplished poet, and a flamboyant senator – he almost hoodwinked the Upper Chamber into adding the phoenix to the list of protected birds – and O'Neill had emerged from the world of education to become a Civil Service Commissioner.* AE's most ambiguous friendship was with Yeats, newly returned to Ireland to share in the shaping of the Free State. An active member of the Senate, he made his Dublin home at 82, Merrion Square, almost next door to Plunkett House, and a famous cartoon shows the two poets passing each other unawares, AE staring earthwards on his way to visit Yeats, and Yeats intent on the sky as he goes to call on AE. Their relationship had long been guarded, for neither dared give free rein to his affection for the other. On the eve of Yeats's return, AE had written: 'For years he talks when he meets me as if he were lecturing a public meeting about art or

*In his *Memoir of AE*, Eglinton prints Mrs. O'Neill's account of how AE (who was competent at simple cookery) found her husband alone one night clumsily attempting to prepare himself a meal. "But, man," the poet exclaimed, "you don't need all that grease in the pan. Get me a bowl. I must pour off three-fourths of it. Slice those potatoes while I cook the cutlets."

literature, and I am bored.'[15] Yeats's pleasure in the ritual of such formal occasions as the Tailteann Games amused AE: 'I,' he exclaimed in August 1924, 'would walk miles to avoid them.'[16] In a small gathering at Yeats's salon, both men would orate freely, cutting in on each other's monologue when opportunity offered, but AE avoided discussing the fundamentals of metaphysics and belief on which they had long differed. Once, after sitting silently while two of Yeats's guests attacked Madame Blavatsky, he walked home with Monk Gibbon and advised him to read *The Secret Doctrine,* insisting: 'It is the only one of her books that really matters. There you will find it all.'[17]

In spite of its limitations, post-Treaty Dublin offered AE a most congenial environment. The scene of cherished memories and the centre of future hopes, it could still blossom in his imagination as a city of mythical stature. In his paper he expanded lovingly on the comic saga outshining Moore's that could be written about it if only the laws of libel permitted:

> There are later adventures of Irish literary men, both in soul and body, since he left Ireland which surpass anything true or imagined in *Ave, Salve, Vale* . . . what a tale might be written in which Yeats would evoke spirits by his magic, and Padraic Pearse would fight almost alone like Cuculain at the Ford, and Stephen MacKenna would fight for the independence of Greece, and James Stephens live things more wild and fantastic than anything in *The Crock of Gold* or *The Demigods* . . . But I, who could never tell what I know here, when I go back to Tirnanoge will tell to Finn, Oscar and the other ancients of our race tales of adventure as astonishing as their own.[18]

On a more prosaic level, AE was confident that the setback of the Civil War would be overcome despite a temporary relapse into materialism – a relapse that had the advantage of promoting national efficiency. From the time he began to edit the new journal, he spoke intermittently of a brilliant future to be attained within fifteen or twenty-five years.

Editing the *Irish Statesman* involved AE in continuous writing, all of it done by hand as he disliked the mechanical click of the typewriter too much to gain any facility with it.[19] In a typical week he contributed book reviews, two articles on current affairs, and a major portion of the extensive 'Notes and Comments.' Some of these last were written by his colleague James Good, a cheerful, shrewd journalist who had spent most of his life in Ulster,[20] though AE was prepared as editor to defend any of them;[21] elsewhere in the paper he would publish views with which he disagreed. Often he added a criticism of an art exhibition to his other work.

Besides the writing and editing, and a never-ending stream of visitors, there were business matters to be attended to. On Friday afternoons AE acted as host at a directors' meeting, which was also a pleasant social occasion to which he could look forward.[22] When Susan Mitchell, who was still his assistant, was absent, he himself made the tea and prepared the cake.[23]

Owing to the demands of his new position, AE had to put on one side the seven completed chapters of *The Avatars*,[24] but he found much to compensate him for this sacrifice. The scope of the *Irish Statesman* was enormous, and he was free to publish his thoughts on national and international affairs, art and literature, and even, from time to time, on his own conception of the universe. To get the paper off to a good start, he printed articles and poems by such renowned authors as Bernard Shaw, Oliver Gogarty, Padraic Colum, Lennox Robinson, and James Stephens. The last named, under his pseudonym James Esse, mischievously interviewed himself! Correspondents in London and, more important, the alienated North, supplied weekly letters, and AE made a point of inviting experts on education, agriculture, and finance to expound their opinions, while his friend H. F. Norman wrote regularly on music. As soon as the paper was firmly established, its columns were to be opened to the newest generation of Irish authors.[25]

When the *Homestead* was succeeded by the *Statesman*, Ireland still had to raise herself from the economic and political chaos of the Civil War. A quarter of the country had seceded, the mass of unemployed were contributing to the sporadic violence, local government was disintegrating, and foreign markets were depressed. The authorities, preoccupied with these emergencies, had not yet drawn up a distinctive policy to justify the dream of independence for which so many had died.

AE, Plunkett, and the American backers insisted that the *Irish Statesman* was a non-party paper, founded to support the Free State. In fact, while AE never concealed his soft spot for the small Labour Party, this was tantamount to siding with Cosgrave's Cumann na n Gaedheal against de Valera's Republicans, who later took the name Fianna Fail. In article after article he urged the Government to construct a clear policy on the basis of exact statistical knowledge and ridiculed de Valera ('a Puritan romantic' and devotee of 'amateur politics')[26] and his followers for their total lack of a creative programme. 'Young Ireland,' he wrote.

> took only too kindly to the job of pulling down. It scorned delights and lived laborious days filling petrol tins and detonating land-mines. It crouched behind chimney-pots through bleak winter nights pumping a stream of lead upon the housetops without a

> single demand for overtime or the enforcement of trade union conditions.[27]

Despite such passages as this, the *Statesman,* while richer in ideas, was poorer in feuds than the *Homestead,* even though AE gave Republicans the freedom of his correspondence columns. When the redoubtable Maud Gonne took advantage of this, he found himself in the unusual position of being attacked as one who 'set a lower standard of morality to the nation than he practised as an individual.'[28] His fiercest antagonist, Mary MacSwiney, sister of the martyr Terence MacSwiney, eventually drew from him the formidable rebuke: 'One thing he [the Editor] never has done. He has never in his life encouraged Irishmen to kill each other. We wonder if Miss MacSwiney's conscience is as clear.'[29]

While AE's goal – a rural, democratic, and uniquely Irish civilisation – was essentially romantic, the means he advocated to that end were sufficiently down-to-earth to suit the most hard-headed realist. His editorial columns reflect a Roman practicality rather than a Greek sublimity. The expansion of schools and colleges, he insisted, must be the lynchpin of Ireland's new policy, and he wrote continuously of the need for less expensive administration. The efficiency of commissioners appointed to take over local government, the decentralisation of the courts, and the promising Shannon hydro-electric scheme were among his favourite topics. Compulsory Gaelic in schools he accepted as a worthwhile experiment, but pointed to the need for modern literature and journalism in the language if it were not to be abandoned by the diminishing core of native speakers in the West, who would soon be clamouring for access to all the benefits of modern civilisation. Above all, he demanded honesty and efficiency in agriculture, business, and government, and strict adherence to the Treaty, as the hallmarks of the new Ireland.

Following the dictates of reason and experience, AE softened his earlier stand on alcohol. With occasional backward glances, he abandoned his old call for total prohibition, and admitted, while welcoming the Government's attempt to control rather than suppress drinking,

> we have never been convinced that virtue can be imposed by legislation. All that can be done is to obstruct the worst manifestations of devilry.[30]

He confessed that prohibition had so far failed in America.

One of AE's editorial aims was to draw his countrymen's attention to the importance of international affairs. As he surveyed events in all parts of the world in the weekly 'Notes and Comments,' he speculated on the many-faceted causes of war – economic, political, and psychological – and placed his rather faint hopes in the League of Nations.

During the post-War period, the inheritors of nineteenth-century liberalism watched in amazement as economics tottered, Communists fomented revolutions, and European nations sank back into the pit of dictatorship. AE and Yeats reacted in opposite ways to the two most effective of the new despotisms, the Soviet and the Fascist. It has already been explained how, while Yeats detested the egalitarian ideal of the Bolsheviks, AE began by mistaking them for friends of co-operation, though he came to recognise in their regime 'an autocracy more rigid and ruthless than that of the Romanoffs.'[31] The heroic posturing of Mussolini won some respect from Yeats, but AE denounced the Fascists who attacked the brilliant Italian co-operatives as 'lawless hirelings of the reactionaries.'[32] The dictator, however, followed his destructive phase with plans for a parliament representing thirteen great occupational confederations, part of a grandiose scheme for moulding the entire nation into a single economic and social machine responsive to his will. Reminded of his own design for a parliamentary chamber elected by vocational councils, AE felt something very like awe at the daring of Mussolini's attempt to create a nationwide 'solidarity and harmony of consciousness,'[33] which yet seemed almost contrary to human nature. Admitting that he himself would find Fascist rule intolerable – 'I doubt whether I would willingly submit to be dictated to by the wisest of mortals' – he confessed: 'I find in myself the utmost curiosity about these dictatorships, their psychological or philosophic basis . . . I read eagerly any intellectual account of the Fascist mentality.'[34] In the last analysis, he blamed the English-language press for ignoring the positive achievements of the Russian and Italian regimes, while publicising their very real horrors.[35]

Like the *Irish Homestead,* the *Irish Statesman* has a Theosophical inspiration, which occasionally becomes visible in AE's digressions. References to the Logos – beauty is defined as 'the reflection of the Divine Mind in humanity or nature'[36] – and to the Pauline trinity of body, soul, and spirit are not infrequent. While he does not hesitate to ridicule an obviously bogus account of past lives, AE will not allow archaeologists to deduce from such few skulls as have chanced to survive that prehistoric man, contrary to Madame Blavatsky's doctrine, had a lower mentality than his modern descendants.[37] Similarly, he scorns the shallow gossip which A.P. Sinnett publishes as the teaching of the Masters,[38] but covertly alludes to the work of the latter when numbering Lawrence of Arabia among the avatars: 'We surmise this,' he writes, 'of the Caesars, Tamurlanes, Napoleons, Alexanders, that the spiritual rulers of the world have used them to bring about new destinies . . .'[39]

A careful study of the *Irish Statesman* shows that AE, despite his essentially pre-scientific outlook, made a considerable effort to come to terms with the intellectual life of the modern world. Calling for the re-opening of the Dublin College of Science, temporarily occupied by the Government, he argued: 'The teaching in the College, with its insistence on precision of method, on careful experiment, and proof by investigation, is the best antidote which could be provided against the sloppy idealism which passes for thought in Ireland.'[40] At a deeper level, he tried to persuade himself that science was an ally, not an enemy of spirituality, and cautiously welcomed Einstein's theory of relativity as a conception making 'for an undogmatic state of consciousness.'[41] Once he even proclaimed: 'It is the unscientific who are the materialists, whose intellect is not quickened, and the divinity which is everywhere eludes their stupid gaze.'[42] His misgivings, nevertheless, can be read between the lines of 'Beauty and Science,' a piece of blank verse composed 'After reading A. S. Eddington's "Science and the Physical World." '[43] Much in the manner of D. H. Lawrence denying the reality of the evolution he could not feel in his own body, AE declared:

But, heart, we can prove their mathematic to have erred . . .

Yet, a few lines further on he retracted far enough to claim that should the atoms indeed move according to the physicists' formulae:

. . . they are mind-governed
And yield to beauty which may be the power
Our science seeks that can break up the atom.

In the field of psychology AE, though unreservedly hostile to 'the materialism of Freud and his school,'[44] was intellectually excited by the theories of Jung. While he disliked a report of the latter's emphasis on suppressed desires gaining strength in the subconscious,[45] he later praised (if the anonymous passage in question is indeed his) the 'level of subtlety and understanding' informing the essay 'Women in Europe':[46] had he lived to study Jung's later works on the transcendence of the ego through individuation, he would undoubtedly have withdrawn some at least of his reservations. He perceived as clearly as the great psychologist that the 'evil' in human nature has somehow to be integrated into the whole man: speaking of Joyce's exploration of the soul's underworld in *Ulysses,* he announced: ' . . . the great deeps in us all must be dredged so before our natures can truly be purified and porous to the sea of light.'[47]

In economics he was still preoccupied with the problem of world-wide over-production, but could find no solution that seemed satisfactory. The work of the famous economist Keynes greatly impressed him, and in 1925 he was among the few who endorsed Keynes's opposition to Britain's return to the Gold Standard since it would enrich the rentiers at the cost of penalising the manufacturers and increasing unemployment.[48] In the same year the research of the Statistical and Social Inquiry Society of Ireland confirmed AE's recent conjecture that the country's supposed adverse balance of trade was illusory.[49]

A considerable portion of every issue of the *Statesman* was devoted to literature. In the course of writing occasional reviews for the *Homestead,* AE had already adumbrated the critical principles which now guided him, especially in the judgement of poetry. Before the Great War, he had speculated in his 'Notes of the Week' on the possibility that the modern poets, who had created no epic heroes to inspire their contemporaries, could be blamed for Ireland's acceptance of sordid nobodies as political leaders.[50] In the controversy that followed, he had drawn a careful distinction between the craft of the word-smith and the inspiration of the poet: the writer and the artisan, he had argued, 'must not expect us to call them great men because there is a delicate evocation of a sunset in the words, or a gay remodelling of a butterfly's wings in the jewellery.' There is no excuse for the modern author who 'claims for skill in the craft the praise long ago given to the greatness of soul expressed through the craft by the artist in words'; if his work is hollow, 'it is his duty by fervent brooding to create a spirit and an ideal worth giving to the world.'[51] Some fashionable writers, AE came to feel, shared an obsession with technique with the Cubist painters, whom he fiercely assailed as he had long ago assailed the Impressionists.[52] In his *Statesman* reviews, he classified poetic inspiration according to its origin in one of the various levels of consciousness described in Indian philosophy. Thus Gogarty's lyrics came from the waking mind,[53] and the poetry of Spenser, Keats, the early Tennyson, and the young Yeats from the dream-consciousness, but there was a still higher kind of art:

> I feel somehow that with Shakespeare and some others consciousness has transcended the dream state, and has come to a magical awakening beyond, perhaps corresponding to that stage which in India is called spirit waking . . . and I think in this state, higher than dream, the supreme works of art are created.[54]

The theory was capable of fairly subtle application, as when AE claimed that the haunting quality of Leonardo's painting came from the intrusion of the waking mind into the dream world.[55] There was a place in it, too, for reason as well as craftsmanship, for thought was one of the powers which sped the poet's mind on its way towards the

Logos: on the intellectual plane spiritual experience was expressed as philosophy. Of De Quincey's poetic prose, AE complained: '. . . for the most part I find the entry into the dream consciousness has been attained at the expense of the rational which the best poetry never relinquishes.'[56] He habitually advised poets to master at least one of the world's great philosophies.

The books pouring into the *Statesman* office for review virtually gave AE's mind free play over the whole field of literature, and reading his criticism one can easily see why James Stephens and Frank O'Connor, who were alive to the weaknesses of his verse, praised the acuteness of his judgment. Understandably, he was least at home in the Augustan age, though it is surprising to find him relishing Congreve's wit and Dryden's energy.[57] In the area of fiction, his early delight in the storyteller's art persisted, but he had long distrusted the tradition of the English novel, with its concentration on recording the material minutiae of daily existence and on creating character for its own sake:

> But we think every work of art should contribute in all its details to the evocation of an idea, as in the Oedipus of Sophocles, from the movement and speeches of all the characters arises in the onlooker the idea of Nemesis, an invisible being pervading life, and we are awed as if we suddenly found ourselves in the presence of the mysteries.[58]

In making this reasonable distinction between a lesser and a greater kind of literature, AE traced the parting of the ways to Shakespeare, asserting that his genius for creating character had overshadowed his occasional expression of profound intuitions and misled the novelists into following an earthbound trail.[59] His appreciation of the dramatist was strangely limited (what, one wonders, did he make of the fate-ridden *Macbeth* or the philosophical *Tempest?*), but he could have enriched his argument with a contrast between the 'European' Chaucer of *Troilus and Criseyde* and the 'English' Chaucer of *The Canterbury Tales*.

While the timing of AE's literary essays was determined by the chances of book publication, the subjects of his political articles depended on the course of events. During the autumn of 1923, the most important problem facing the Free State Government was still the elimination of political violence. Late in October, some thousands of Republican prisoners held without trial attempted to blackmail the authorities into releasing them by undertaking a fast to death: AE denounced 'the inexorable cruelty of the sentimentalist, feeding on emotions, on strained hearts, on public prayers, and martyrdoms, to whose sinister and depraved moral appetite common-sense is as distasteful as cold water to the habitual drinker of rum.'[60] Torn between his loyalty to the Free State and his belief that both sides had committed murder, he consulted with Yeats and Lady Gregory. In the *Statesman* he was pleading, as Lady Gregory wished, that the Government should act magnanimously by freeing the majority, but he admitted to her he had little hope his advice would be followed.[61] In the event, the prisoners admitted defeat before the end of November, and the crisis passed over.

Nineteen twenty-four proved to be a year of new controversies. In June, AE was distressed to find himself forced to oppose James Larkin, the hero of the Great Strike of 1913, who had returned from America the year before and now forsook his own principle of working-class solidarity to start a feud that split the Irish labour movement. AE's early rebukes were delivered as gently as possible, but he ended by comparing Larkin to his bugbear, de Valera.

A more prolonged controversy was the verbal wrestling match with the British Government for possession of the French pictures which Sir Hugh Lane, drowned when the *Lusitania* was torpedoed, had left to Dublin Corporation in an unwitnessed codicil. Encouraged by Lady Gregory, AE had already made public appeals on Dublin's behalf, and from 1924 to 1929 his intermittent protests enlivened the pages of the *Statesman*. The London authorities were not impressed by the precedents of various unwitnessed wills and codicils which had been legalized when it was to England's advantage, and AE was goaded to fury by their irrelevant self-justifications and petty concessions. A week after he had acknowledged (with reservations) Baldwin's 'emotional sincerity' and 'fine conscience,'[62] he declared:

> The British Premier possesses the typical British conscience in a state of acute inflammation. He sentimentalises over loving kindness to labour and lengthens its hours of work in its more perilous occupation. He accepts the pictures and the Gallery which was built on the promise of the pictures being kept, and tries to salve his conscience by the promise to lend some of them to the city which has been robbed of them . . . We will have a limelight cast on these incidents, and not in this country only. We will make it known in two Continents until it becomes the typical story to symbolise the wormings of [the] British soul after something that does not belong to it.[63]

The most important of the new disputes concerned the adjustment of the partition between Northern Ireland and the Free State. On this issue AE made an extraordinary but not irrational *volte-face*. Under the terms of the Treaty, a Commission was to arrange the transfer of territory according to the wishes of the inhabitants, and many southerners expected the Free State to acquire the counties of

Fermanagh and Tyrone, which had Catholic Nationalist majorities. From May to August, 1924, AE insisted that the British Government was in honour bound to arrange a plebiscite, but about the beginning of September the fiery American Fenian John Devoy declared that the question of a border adjustment was trivial compared with the need to work for a future reunion of North and South by mutual agreement. Applauding such reasonableness from a lifelong revolutionary, AE began to vacillate, and when the British wriggled out of what were probably their Treaty obligations in exchange for writing off the Free State's share of the National Debt, he realised that there were genuinely compelling reasons for accepting the situation: a significant change in the boundary would have roused fresh hatred against the large Catholic population remaining in Ulster, as well as dealing a blow to such hopes of reunion as remained. Whatever the North chose to do, he pointed out, it was the duty of southerners to show them goodwill: 'If we do not sincerely wish them success and prosperity we are not good Irishmen, we are not good human beings.'[64]

Although the Government went out of its way to accord fair treatment to Free State Protestants, non-Catholics often found themselves attacked by members of the dominant Church for promoting innocent-seeming policies. A nun, the headmistress of a girl's school, was said to have named AE, Yeats, Liam O'Flaherty, and Lennox Robinson as four of the five bad men who were destroying Dublin.[65] This sectarian fervour was often accompanied by racial passion leading to the claim that Catholic Gaels alone were true Irishmen. Only a persecution-complex created by centuries of oppression can account for Yeats's and AE's support of free education being construed as a conspiracy against the faith, or for Aodh de Blacam's assertion that contributions to the *Irish Statesman* by anti-Christians 'gave almost unpardonable offence.'[66] Doubtless de Blacam was referring to such articles as Yeats's attack on a move to ensure that divorce be permanently barred in the Free State. Though AE published his friend's article – and two weeks later a reply – he himself was austere enough to support the prohibition, which he held should be enforced on non-sectarian, social grounds that Protestants as well as Catholics could and would endorse.

De Blacam may also have resented AE's valiant but losing battle against the Censorship Bill which has done much to make independent Ireland look intellectually ridiculous to the rest of the Free World. Ill-educated country people were stampeded into demanding a ban on books they would never read. Rural libraries were stormed and it was reported that two lives of Christ by foreign Catholics were withdrawn at Tralee; elsewhere the works of Tolstoy and Maeterlinck were burnt. AE entirely favoured the suppression of pornography – he himself complained that the film censorship was too lax[67] – but, from the spring of 1925 till the *Statesman* ceased publication, he opposed with all his might the wild and irrational clamour for the exclusion of modern thought from Ireland. His only success was to have a few of the worst clauses excised from the Bill, though he seems eventually to have found some consolation in the 'fierce anticlerical spirit' arising among educated Catholics.[68] In 1928, he even had to defend the handsome Free State coins decorated with animal images (he believed he had been the first to suggest an Irish currency)[69] from the charge that they were pagan. 'We are afraid,' he wrote, 'St. Francis's name is much better known in Ireland than his teaching.'[70]

During the early twenties, the *Irish Statesman's* main enemy was the anti-Treaty party. By 1925, Plunkett was overjoyed at the success of his plans, and he wrote to Judge Campbell on 25 February: 'I knew that AE would be a great editor, but I do think he has excelled himself in the guidance he has given to the Government of the Free State and in the way he has protected them from the Republicans.'[71] Plunkett went on to claim that without the support of the *Statesman,* Cosgrave's Government would have fallen, and in subsequent letters to Campbell he spoke of AE, unrivalled in his understanding of the country's economic situation, having made an indispensable contribution to the restoration of normal conditions. The paper, however, did not stand on secure financial foundations, and there was considerable anxiety during 1925 as to whether the American guarantors, who disagreed about the implications of their pledges, would contribute sufficient extra funds to ensure its survival.

About the beginning of June, in an interview published in the London *New Leader,* AE claimed that the Treaty was justifying itself in terms of the Free State's economic and administrative progress.[72] Speaking as a citizen he approved of the reaction from the traditional inefficiency to an effective, centralised bureaucracy, but as a co-operator he berated the public for their relapse into the old attitude of reliance on the state. 'A kind of disgust about self-help,' he lamented in the *Statesman,* 'seems to have arisen. To mention the name of Denmark causes a vomiting sensation among many farmers . . .'[73] Yet he continuously applauded the work of Patrick Hogan, Minister of Agriculture, who in promoting technical efficiency and uniform standards seemed to be completing 'the structure of which Sir Horace [Plunkett] laid the foundations a generation earlier.'[74] In a private letter written less than a month after his *New Leader* interview, he discussed the current trend from a third viewpoint, relating it to his ultimate hopes for Ireland:

> We . . . are reacting against the idealism which led us to war and civil war and I fear we are in for an era of materialism. Our new government is however honest and energetic and from a romantic conception of Ireland is being evolved the idea of the highly efficient modern state. I would like to live for fifteen years more because I think we will react again to the imaginative and spiritual and we shall probably begin a fight for spiritual freedom. Our religions are outworn and we must find cultural substitutes.[75]

While AE's intellect laboured over editorials, his psyche was spinning airy lyrics which contrasted strangely with his down-to-earth prose. In June 1925, Macmillan published a volume of his more recent poems, mostly gathered from the pages of the *Statesman*, under the title *Voices of the Stones*. The inclusion of 'Michael' and the noble sonnet honouring MacSwiney gave the collection a distinction which would hardly have been earned by the other verses. While the flickering colour imagery of the early books has happily vanished and the diction is often relatively unliterary, favourite epithets ('golden,' 'starry') are grossly over-used and most of the images leave no resonance in the imagination. Too often a promising beginning leads to a lame conclusion: the subtle winding rhythm in the first stanza of 'Exiles' is soon followed by the familiar diadem and sceptre symbolism of previous volumes, and the contrasting solar galleon and human coracle of 'Mutiny' give way to the trite 'green fields of home.' There is a certain monotony in the choice of themes – the immortal within the mortal, the preservation of what seems to be devoured by time – and, more important, the visionary experience behind the poem is usually unrealised, so that the reader is left with nothing more than a generalised sentiment about the universe: in what sense, for example, are the boys of 'Old Wine' nourished by the infinite? In the grotesque animal imagery of 'Watchers,' however, the presence of evil is for once really felt despite a melodramatic touch and the hackneyed 'black as night,' and the switch from the poet's viewpoint to that of the celestial guardian gives this sonnet on a soul sunk in vice an unusual vigour. A surprising success is the brief lyric 'Ancient,' a seeming trifle which yet conveys, through its play upon a few key words, an acute sense of the human soul trapped in but able to rise above a phantom creation.

Much of *Voices of the Stones* shows the influence of other poets. 'Time' clearly echoes 'Time, You Old Gipsy Man' by Ralph Hodgson, whose fine poetry AE greatly admired,[76] and the title and content of 'Michael' are not the only signs of Wordsworth's overshadowing presence. 'Transience' could well be a meditation on the 'Thoughts that do often lie too deep for tears' of the 'Immortality

Ode,' and the labourer in 'Survival' – significantly AE had watched the man at work[77] – is described with a Wordsworthian simplicity:

> The spade along the ridges runs
> As if it had a race with death.

In making the humble flower of 'A Murmur in the Grass' articulate, AE is trying to follow in Blake's footsteps, but though the verses have a pleasant tinkle, the vegetable seems to express its cosmic longings in a very feeble voice. The most derivative poem in the book is probably the ambitious 'Natural Magic,' a Keatsian attempt to recreate in elaborate ten-line stanzas each phase of a brief, intense experience. ('Distant!' at the start of the third stanza even echoes 'Forlorn!' in the 'Ode to a Nightingale.') The would-be concrete picture of a forest scene is marred by such poeticisms as 'o'er' and 'myriad,' and the 'Living and lustrous and ethereal shapes' of the vision are virtually formless. All these influences lie too near the surface, worked into the form and texture of the poems but not transmuted.

The approach towards a less artificial diction in AE's later verse, a trend which was to have more interesting results in his next collection, may be associated with his own feeling that his conscious mind, rich with a lifetime's experience, had a greater share in its composition. 'Promise,' included in *Voices of the Stones,* seemed to him almost the last poem which was 'given' in the old manner.[78] Another lyric in the volume – 'A Lost Dream' – was a conscious experiment with a Gaelic pattern of assonance.

Despite the constant demands of his journal, AE occasionally considered other literary projects. Three months after *Voices of the Stones* was issued, he was thinking of compiling an anthology of passages from the world's sacred books and mystical philosophers arranged to illuminate such themes as creation, avatars, ethics, psychology and meditation.[79] The idea of producing an autobiography also struck him: on 14 July, 1926, he told the comic story of Moore's conversion to the company at Constantine Curran's, and remarked, 'I'd like to write my Reminiscences!' 'Why don't you?' asked Joseph Holloway. 'I'm sure they'd make great reading!'[80]

AE's intention of printing the work of new writers as soon as the *Statesman* was established was amply fulfilled. 'I like literary controversies,' he wrote to Herbert Palmer in December 1925; 'I am trying to nurse them up here among the younger men.'[81] Friendships with a number of promising authors greatly enriched his life at this period, although it sometimes involved him in painful incidents. Drawn in October 1924 into a dispute over Lennox Robinson, the lanky, shrill-voiced young dramatist, who was accused of publishing a blasphemous story, AE had divided feelings.

Hating the piece of literature in question, he was distressed to find himself at odds with Yeats, and showed much confusion at a committee meeting where the form of censure on Robinson was to be decided. Unwilling to defend the culprit, yet reluctant to injure him, he declared after long hesitation, 'I am for the milder form.'[82] About the same time, when another of the rising Irish authors eloped with a married woman, AE admired the courage shown by the couple in living together publicly, but greatly pitied the grief-stricken husband.[83]

No such episodes marred AE's friendship with the amiable young novelist L. A. G. Strong, whom he met in August 1924 and who responded with quiet intensity to the unique personality of the mystic. While the latter besought him to cultivate his talent with care, he was storing up the impressions which led him to write: 'Of all the men and women I have met, AE met life with the greatest serenity . . . The effect he made was like that of certain rare experiences of the spirit wherein one is given a glimpse of beauty or of harmony on a very deep level . . .'[84] When he asked for a saying to guide his life, AE told him: 'Seek on earth what you have found in heaven.'[85] A more rumbustious character, the huge, black-haired poet F. R. Higgins, a man of Chestertonian girth addicted to alcohol and malicious gossip, was equally sensitive to the beauty of AE's character. Describing a visit to his office, he wrote: '. . . from the first sound of his voice, with its wooing gentleness, the visitor was made at home . . . And for the first time in your life you felt that you had truly met with a wonderful man. You were only one of many minds who questioned AE and left his presence in peace. You differed from him but you were drawn towards him. Indeed his immense humanism attracted opposites.'[86]

AE first met Strong at Yeats's salon. During the course of the evening, James Stephens arrived and poured out his admiration for a play he had just seen at the Abbey Theatre – *The Shadow of a Gunman* by the former bricklayer Sean O'Casey.[87] Touched by the dramatist's passionate pity for the slum-dwellers, AE had already acclaimed him in the *Statesman* as an ally in the twin causes of art and humanity, and a few months later he wrote nobly of *Juno and the Paycock*, forgiving its absurd Theosophist-seducer:

> Dublin laughs at this revelation now. It sees people can laugh in Hell, and it laughs along with them. It is not so bad after all. It need not tear down its slums, they can be endured a little longer.[88]

O'Casey, for his part, was later to show bitter contempt for AE, perhaps because in 1928 AE, while opposing the Abbey's rejection of his *Silver Tassie*, held that he should have been invited to rehearsals and persuaded to revise the experimental second act.[89]

AE published O'Casey's fierce ridicule of his article on the play, but when the dramatist started another feud at the end of 1929, his letters soon grew so abusive that AE had to suppress them. With typical courtesy he informed his readers:

> Mr. Sean O'Casey wishes it to be known that he did not drop the controversy he had initiated with the Editor of this paper, but that a third letter which he sent was denied publication.[90]

About the beginning of 1925, two young men called at Plunkett House to protest against AE's treatment of a manifesto they had issued against Yeats. One of the youths, a librarian named Michael O'Donovan who had recently been interned in a camp for Republican prisoners, was to become deservedly famous for his incisive short stories published under the pseudonym Frank O'Connor; his companion, Geoffrey Phibbs, was a poet. When they arrived, O'Connor was ready to despise AE, but he was disarmed when they both burst out laughing at Phibbs's claim that the new generation had had no youth. Before leaving, he was asked to contribute to the *Statesman,* and it was not long before AE propelled him into Dublin literary circles.

A strong mutual attachment developed between AE and O'Connor, despite a certain clash of personality. While AE sought for general truths, O'Connor focused on whatever was most individual in a character or object. On asking what tree was represented in one of AE's paintings, he was disappointed by the vague reply: 'Oh, no particular tree. Just a tree!' Occasionally he was surprised by glimpses of the brilliant mind usually veiled by set speeches, but he was most drawn to AE by an emotional need for a comforting father-figure. Once, when he complained of feeling written out, the older man filled the part admirably, asking: 'Did you ever hear a hen that has laid an egg? She says, "Oh, God! God! God! God! There are going to be no more eggs"!'[91] In O'Connor's powerful imagination, characters took on sharper edges and conflicts became more dramatic: his portrait of AE in *My Father's Son* is distorted by a distinct touch of caricature, strengthened by his imperfect verbal memory.

AE observed that O'Casey's plays, like Joyce's *Ulysses,* the grim novels of O'Flaherty, and, a little later, O'Connor's stories, marked a swing to realism among recent Anglo-Irish authors reacting against the idealism and romance of their predecessors. In his private correspondence he often referred to this, trying to explain it by a strangely un-Indian application of the Hindu doctrine of the seven *lokas* and seven *talas,* the celestial, terrestrial, and infernal planes into which the whole natural and supernatural creation is divided. Interpreting these psychologically as representing subjective and objective states respectively, he claimed that the literary development was a descent from a *loka* into its corresponding *tala*. Despite his enjoyment of much of the new writing, he looked eagerly for signs of a re-ascent, anticipating an intellectual rather than an imaginative phase.[92]

During the 1920s there was a great upsurge of new literary forms embodying the experience of the post-Victorian world, and it is not surprising that AE, with his roots in the Celtic revival, often found his judgment and his feelings at odds when he was confronted with the masterpieces of an alien era. Ezra Pound he at first pigeon-holed as 'the keeper of a literary museum'[93] but later wrote of his *Selected Poems:* 'This book almost convinces me that the man of talent, if he be serious enough about his art[,] may approach the work of genius.'[94] While he recognised the high quality of T. S. Eliot's verse, he could not sympathise with his study of modern man's imprisonment in introspective despair. In such poems as *The Waste Land,* he complained, 'the personal ego looks at its own peculiarities in a mirror.'[95] Eliot's criticism, however, full of nostalgia for tradition and a unified philosophical world-view, proved far more congenial, and he fell on the essay on Dante as a welcome oasis in a spiritual desert.[96] He delivered no public verdict on D. H. Lawrence, but a slighting reference in one of his letters[97] suggests that he did not admire the novelist's attempt to construct a private spiritual philosophy. For the gifted Scots poet Hugh MacDiarmid, he had, in contrast, the greatest respect, and he was filled with wonder to find that Lallans, unlike Irish peasant speech, could be made to convey the subtleties of thought and feeling of a man steeped in world culture.[98]

None of these writers touched AE's emotions or national pride as did Yeats and, less intimately, Joyce. In 1918, when instalments of *Ulysses* began to appear in the *Little Review,* John Quinn had copies sent to AE, who admired the author's literary skill but found the tone unpleasant.[99] Later the entire novel came into his hands, but he could not read it through,[100] though he noted that America, for all her gifted poets, had 'no sky-touching genius, no one even who burrows so deeply as our James Joyce.'[101] When extracts from the incomplete *Finnegans Wake* began to be published under the title *Work in Progress,* he understandably dismissed the new punning language as 'unutterably boring.' 'I am sorry,' he added, 'for there was a powerful though unlovable intelligence in the earlier books . . .'[102] In 1928, however, he received the section entitled *Anna Livia Plurabelle,* and a gasp of delighted astonishment is almost audible behind his words of praise:

. . . this strange slithery slipping, dreamy nightmarish prose is

> more astonishing than anything Joyce has yet written, and whatever else he may be, he is a virtuoso in the use of words . . . As a technical feat it is unique. A chapter excites us. The whole volume may prove a labour too great for any to peruse to its end. But this passage is certainly worth study, and perhaps if one could understand it the whole book could be understood.[103]

Three months later, AE prophesied: '. . . we think his heroic effort to create a new vocabulary will have effects on literature in the future.'[104]

While Joyce was composing one of the world's great novels, Yeats was performing the astounding feat of transforming himself in middle age from a minor into a major poet. Encouraged by Ezra Pound, he hammered a modern heroic idiom out of the speech of his contemporaries, and put his mature skill to work to improve his early verse. AE, who cherished Yeats's youthful lyrics as though with a lover's jealousy, found it hard to endure these revisions however much he objectively recognised them as improvements.[105] But while he could not bestow his literary devotion twice with the same ardour, he came to perceive the full glory of the later masterpieces and to praise 'that beauty made out of bare words to which Mr. Yeats came at last.'[106]

On the evening of 10 July, 1919, AE was amused to hear from Yeats that much of the material for his current project, a major philosophical work, was derived from Mrs. Yeats's automatic writings: the source of the revelations did not impress him.[107] Five years later *A Vision* had still not appeared, and AE, reviewing Yeats's *Essays,* warned him against substituting thought for inspiration:

> The poet accepts, consciously or unconsciously, *Anima Mundi* as his subconscious self, and if he philosophises too much he is in danger of substituting a bare theory for that rich depth.[108]

One evening in 1925, a few hours after he had completed the book, Yeats entertained AE and other guests. He chuckled to think how his *magnum opus* would bewilder the critics, while AE forecast that they would handle it as gingerly as possible.[109] In the event, AE himself was the first to tackle it. Admiring the consistency of the intricate analysis of cycles and phases, he yet admitted, 'Here I fall away from a mind I have followed, I think with understanding, since I was a boy': he was disturbed at Yeats's apparent teaching that all was predetermined so that the individual 'is only free to accept or rebel, but not to alter what is fated.'[110] It was not until the appearance of *The Winding Stair* in 1929, that AE could feel certain that Yeats had not been following a sterile bypath. 'It is one of the rarest things in literature,' he wrote, to find a poet of whom it might be said that his wine was like that in the feast in the Scriptures, where the best was kept until the last. Here in this later poetry is the justification of the poet's intellectual adventures into philosophy, mysticism and symbolism, into magic and spiritualism . . . The prose record of these adventures made some lovers of his work think of him as a lost poet, and then he came back from these discarded regions of thought with poetry which was fresh and strange and beautiful . . .[111]

The example of Yeats's inexhaustible patience in perfecting every line of his work taught lesser Irish poets to take the technical side of their art seriously. AE was especially delighted that two of them – Austin Clarke and F. R. Higgins – successfully followed William Larminie's suggestion of substituting Gaelic assonance for English rhyme.[112] He recognised not only Mr. Clarke's early promise, but the peculiar quality of his later and finer verse – 'the curious remote legendary manner of the lyrics,' intimate and decorative and like 'tapestry glimmering with rich subdued colour.'[113]

In the later 1920's, a series of changes began to overcast AE's life. With the growing demand for puritanical laws, a wholly Gaelic culture, and a self-sufficient economy, a new feeling of intellectual claustrophobia oppressed many of the Anglo-Irish, and as the political pendulum started to swing towards the Republicans, those who rejoiced in the material progress of the Free State foresaw that this would fall victim to the lust for another conflict with England. For old men whose contemporaries were dying, the threat of personal solitude was added to the fear of finding themselves aliens in their own land.

On 4 March, 1926, Susan Mitchell died from cancer. AE was grievously distressed, for this was the first time, as he explained to Padraic Colum, that he had lost a close companion with whom he had been in daily contact for many years,[114] and he lamented to Lady Gregory that all the other friends who meant as much to him now lived abroad;[115] in a letter to an American acquaintance, he implied that only James Stephens had the same inexhaustible gaiety.[116] For a brief time he even felt as though there were no immortality to redeem his loss, and when he sat down at his office table he had to force his pen to move over the paper.[117]

As the decade wore on, AE's drawing room was less and less frequented on Sunday evenings, until a visitor was as likely as not to find him alone and any noise at the door was sufficient to make him leap up with pathetic eagerness.[118] Even the austere Mahatma Gandhi loved companions to join him in his experiments in puritan living, and AE needed an abundance of friends to receive and return affection. In reaction to the burden of age, he became preoccupied with youth – the young politicians fashioning the future Ireland, the young writers adding another tier to her literature, the young friends newly entering his life. There is an especial poignance in his acute sense of a child-nature buried within his aging soul, a counterpart to his adolescent discovery of an ancient psyche overshadowing his conscious mind. 'I have always believed,' he wrote in the *Statesman*, 'that if we turned within ourselves we would find somewhere in the heart of age a child laughing or weeping or puzzled, quite unchanged by the forest growth of humanity which has overshadowed its tiny beginning.'[119] Such feelings helped him to look on death as a release, for, as he said, 'I expect when this old body opens its doors an aery child will go out in the wind and run to the wonder worlds and to meet its friends made young again.'[120]

As early as 1925 James Cousins, back on a holiday from India, found AE alone with Padraic Colum on Sunday night, but such was not always the case and L. A. G. Strong gives an amusing account of an occasion in 1926 when both Colum and Stephens were present:

> Stephens coruscated: nothing could stop him. A monologue cascaded from him of the wildest, happiest, most fantastic nonsense. He started with an extravaganza on the love life of spiders, which he claimed to have observed on his garden fence at Wembley, and he went on – for the benefit of two American guests – with a demented elaboration of his alleged experiences on a lecture tour in the States. The Americans at first were worried – 'Mr. Stephens, I can't help feeling there must be some mistake' – but they soon saw that he was romancing, and laughed as happily as everyone else. And to all this AE listened beaming, with occasional retirements to brew more tea at a sort of wizard's cauldron which murmured in the adjoining room.[121]

At this period of his life AE's friends noticed that his monologues were becoming more insistent and sometimes left other people no opportunity to speak. 'Margaret Cunningham, a friend of long standing,' writes Dr. Gibbon, 'remembers at least one such occasion, when a traveller from some foreign country was silenced for a whole evening by AE's pertinacious irrelevancy.'[122] He was still, however, a good listener when experts were talking.[123] In the *Statesman*, he often enunciated his beliefs in the form of rhetorical questions – 'But who can say that that primitive myth was not the shrivelled residue of what was once mighty religion?' – and Dr. Gibbon observes that he did the same thing when talking among his friends: 'Often in conversation he would throw out an idea as airy speculation which he hoped might presently be accepted as truth.'[124] Despite his feelings of age and loneliness, he kept his sense of humour and still enjoyed making fun of people and situations. He even took delight in a young author's claim that he was a has-been. 'No young man,' he declared, 'should really respect his elders. In other countries people respect a name. In Ireland, if you stick your head up, someone will throw a stone at it, and it stops you from getting a swelled head.'[125]

In April 1926, Mr. Diarmuid Russell joined the staff of the *Irish Statesman* and for the first time really got to know his father. Long afterwards he set down a vivid record of his impressions:

> In this room was a desk so covered with piles of old letters and other documents that, in order to see AE, visitors had to circle around to the side. I myself was quietly obscured by an ancient roll-top desk, and from this niche was able to listen to conversations and to become acquainted with the innumerable sides of Father's character as represented by the varied people who came to see him – farmers, clergymen, economists, artists, writers, Hindu mystics, young poets with their first verses. It was surprising that he managed to do any work, and it was only his remarkable powers of concentration that allowed him to bear the many interruptions patiently. Often an editorial might be interrupted half a dozen times, and after each interruption he would turn to writing again without hesitation . . .[126]

AE found the experience of being able to treat his son almost as an equal decidedly refreshing. 'I remember how pleased I was,' he wrote to Van Wyck Brooks in 1934, 'meeting my son after five years' absence and seeing how he had grown up, had lost all unnatural awe and began to poke fun at me and to tell me that a lyric I had written "was quite good for you." I felt that "filial duty" was at an end and we could be natural as with other unrelated people.'[127]

Two months after his son's appointment, AE took his annual holiday in Donegal. He had only been back in the office about six weeks when he was lured away by Mr. and Mrs. Constantine Curran, who had persuaded him to join them while they were in Paris, if only so that he could see James Stephens, Simone Téry, and the art galleries. He travelled by himself having warned Curran that 'if he does not meet me here I will loudly commit suicide leaving a note that it was due to him that I arrived alone in Paris not knowing a word of the language but relying on false and fickle friends.'[128] Though AE loved to imagine the soaring grandeur of Babylon and Nineveh, he had no more interest in the graces of Continental architecture than in French wines or cookery or the cosmopolitan crowds parading in the streets: it took a small courtyard associated with his favourite hero, Dumas' D'Artagnan, to stir his emotions. The party visited the theatre only once – to see Prosper Mérimée's comedy *Le Carrosse du Saint Sacrement*, at which it was the visual spectacle that appealed to him – but he immersed himself happily in conversations with James Stephens and Simone Téry that lasted into the early hours of the morning. Mr. Curran has described the scenes that most delighted him:

> He liked the wide skies, spaces and vistas that Paris so prodigally affords. Each morning before the *corvée* of sight-seeing began, before the *bouquinistes* had opened their boxes, he would be out on the quai with the sketching-book and chalks he always carried, revelling in the morning light along the river: and Paris never was so captivating as in that haze of grey and silver. He liked the great basin in the Luxembourg gardens where the children sail their boats; the stained glass in the Sainte Chapelle[;] a long day on the water at Versailles, leaving the Palais carefully unvisited; the view during dinner with Mrs. Cornelius Sullivan* from the Butte Montmartre, when the darkening valley between the two hills grew starred with the lights of Paris; another evening in the Bois with the same charming hostess when the lights in the trees and the dancers turned the Pré-Catalan into a Monticelli . . .

Mr. Curran accompanied AE to the art galleries where he pored over Fra Angelico's 'Coronation of the Blessed Virgin,' Watteau (whom he called a few months later 'the true poet of [an] artificial world'),[129] Henri Rousseau, and, most of all, Monet.

> His judgments were swift and decisive, always coherent and – given his viewpoint – wholly intelligible. He went through rooms looking for his property, with the rapidity of a globe-trotter, discarding all else but quick to recognise even in the discards a few inches of beauty or an accomplished passage of painting . . . he looked first for the dream, the record of some visionary beauty, then he was concerned with the technical rendering of light.[130]

Although AE's tastes in art, literature, and philosophy were firmly established, he continued to find new intellectual excitements in his later years. During this period he was much concerned with the thought that sound might radiate as universally as the light which enabled the eye to perceive even distant stars. The whole universe, he believed, could be apprehended 'as sound, as a song perhaps, the Logos made audible!'[131] He was excited, too, by the speculations of new thinkers. In 1926 Mrs. Fiske Warren, the intellectual wife of a wealthy American idealist, sent him a copy of Keyserling's *Travel Diary of a Philosopher*. AE was particularly enraptured by this author's analysis of the Indian and Chinese civilisations, and writing to thank Mrs. Warren he told her: 'I find myself led out of moulds in which my mind had been congesting and set free to think

---

*The wife of an American guarantor of the *Irish Statesman*.

in a wider aether than before.'[132] Shortly afterwards, he came upon *The Decline of the West,* and though he felt from the first that Spengler had oversimplified history to fit his scheme, he expressed his delight and astonishment at the subtlety of his thought: 'It has been the most exciting literary adventure of recent years for me . . . It is much richer than Keyserling's "Travel Diary of a Philosopher" which still had good things in it . . . [Spengler] made history live to me for the first time.'[133] Recommending the book to James Cousins, he suggested that the cultures enumerated by the German scholar paralleled the sub-races of Theosophy.[134]

Meanwhile a series of alarms disturbed the political scene, and AE rose to the defence of the ruling party. Frightened by the approaching General Election of June 1927, he lauded the achievements of the Free State Government and insisted that the Opposition programme would throw the country back 'to the heart-breaking uncertainty of the period before the Treaty.'[135] The proponents of this perilous scheme of renouncing the agreement with Britain had still refused to take the Oath of Allegiance and enter the Dail, but they campaigned under the ambiguous slogan 'Fianna Fail is going in,' and won forty-four seats, only three fewer than their main opponents. On 10 July Kevin O'Higgins, Vice-President of the Executive Council, was assassinated, and he became, in AE's words, 'the first martyr for law.'[136] Cosgrave, attempting to force a return to political normality, prepared a Bill to bar candidates for election who refused to promise they would subscribe to the Oath. AE regretted this measure and repeated his earlier counsel that Republicans resign and stand for re-election after announcing their readiness to swear allegiance, but on 10 August de Valera led his followers to Leinster House, where each in turn stated that he was not taking an oath but merely signing a document to gain admission to the Dail. AE confessed with wry satisfaction that 'the devisers of the Electoral Amendment Bill knew the psychology of Fianna Fail in and out far better than we did,'[137] but when the minority Government announced a second General Election for September, he began to berate the Republicans' immoral sophistry and self-deception. Alluding to their excuse that the Bible was some distance from the text of the oath, he complained, 'These kind of explanations will give encouragement and hints to all the perjurers and moral degenerates in the country.'[138] When the election was over, the Government had improved its position and was able to form a stable coalition.

The *Irish Statesman* was still not free from financial problems, and in January 1928 AE left James Good in charge of the paper and crossed the Atlantic to supplement its resources through a lecture tour organised by a committee which Judge Campbell headed. His passion for Emerson and Whitman had long given him a serious interest in American civilisation, though reports of the formidable pace of life in the U.S.A. had always made him glad that he lived in the Old World. As early as 1915, he had observed that the 'highest minds in our modern civilisations' were tending 'to have something cosmic in their character and to become true citizens of the planet,'[139] and a year before his tour he named Emerson, Whitman, and Thoreau as harbingers 'of something which might be spoken of as cosmic or planetary consciousness'; referring to America's material achievements, he affirmed, 'I feel certain that so great a people will not be content with externalities, that the poets of whom Whitman was the prophet, the thinkers of whom Emerson was but an anticipation must be born there.'[140]

On 14 January, 1928, AE sailed from Liverpool on the *Albertic* full of trepidation at the prospect of delivering endless public lectures. 'I believe the Americans,' he confided to Eglinton, 'are very kind, indeed kill you with kindness, with many dinners, receptions, speeches and what not.'[141] Eleven days later the ship bore him within sight of the alien geometrical skyline of New York. 'I see,' he wrote later, 'as the boat comes into New York harbour a gigantic mass of heaven-assailing architecture . . . One's heart beats quicker, such is the sensation of immense power in the builders of those monstrous cliffs of concrete and steel that blaze in the evening light.'[142] Soon a group of reporters arrived on board to question him about the Free State, and he refused to discuss politics but defended the teaching of Gaelic, claiming that the language would fertilise the growth of a modern Irish civilisation.[143] Before long he was surrounded by the skyscrapers of the city, and his romantic imagination exulted:

> There is no end of this giant architecture. Forever new comrades rise up beside the elder giants; they tower up in new beautiful and wonderful lines. At Manhattan, where they are thickest, in the depths below the streets are darkened, and the eye grows dizzy looking up searching for a sky. It finds high in air great blocks of shadow and light outsoaring Doré or Martin, who piled up a fabulous architecture, temple beyond temple, in their imagination of Babylon or Nineveh . . . One would imagine at night, where a remote light on a topmost storey catches the eye, that some Chaldean wizard was there calculating horoscopes for Nebuchadnezzar.[144]

AE felt that could he have sat down in the streets and meditated a revelation might have come to him.[145]

Besides awe-inspiring architecture, New York provided a packed programme of social engagements and much congenial company. By a lucky chance AE encountered Simone Téry on her way home from a trip to China, and in their delight they hired a taxi and drove round the park for four hours.[146] This must have been something of a relief from the less personal engagements that occupied most of his time. On the evening of the 27th he dined at the home of Plunkett's friend James Byrne, where his talk held spellbound a group of Americans, including editors, lawyers, industrialists, and even a general. Ernest Boyd, who was one of the company, felt that AE was as natural as at one of his own Sunday night gatherings in Rathgar Avenue.[147] On the next evening he delivered a witty account of his memories of famous Irish writers at the annual dinner of the American Irish Historical Society, and twenty-four hours later the Poetry Society heard him regret that poetry was now more read than recited. On 1 February, he found himself in company with President Cosgrave at the luncheon of the Foreign Policy Association, and when the Chairman unexpectedly called on him to speak, he had the pleasure of praising the efficiency of Cosgrave's Government. On the 3rd, he addressed the League for Political Education in the Town Hall on the politics and economics of the Free State, and after the luncheon which followed at Hotel Roosevelt he had to listen while a succession of speakers deluged him with praise for two hours. He later told Simone Téry how 'at the sixth speaker I became murderous, but saw a vision of flaring headlines in American papers had I let my homicidal mania loose. "Venerable Irish poet goes to electric chair, having brained the sixth orator, who said what a noble soul he had." '[148] On the 6th, he returned to the Town Hall, and while telling comic stories of Irish authors gave his opinion of James Joyce's great novel:

> I think with horror of that famous book, 'Ulysses,' which is the ultimate boundary of realism, but I also think of it with respect. If Joyce would write a Purgatorio and a Paradiso to the Inferno which is his 'Ulysses,' there would be one of the greatest works in literature.[149]

Even in his own room, AE was not always free from intruders. When Shaemas O'Sheel interviewed him there, he praised the material progress of the Free State and denounced the cruelty of those who regretted the passing of romantic mud cabins. 'Some beauty,' he admitted, 'may be lost awhile, but I remember that in Donegal, where I spent my vacations, there was lamentation thirty years ago when the "picturesque" cabins were replaced by stone houses. Now ivy grows on the stone houses . . .'[150]

Early in February, AE began to travel beyond New York, returning at intervals to recuperate in Judge Campbell's apartment.

He made a series of exhausting journeys to lecture in many cities, snatched a little rest on the train between visits, and found time to enjoy American detective stories. Within a week he had spoken at five universities in the North-east, including the venerable Harvard, where the President led the audience through the snow to the largest hall on the campus.[151] He spent 9 February at Yale with its mellow Oxbridge architecture. Here, after listening to a class on Browning, he passed the afternoon at the home of the professor, William Lyon Phelps, before delivering his own lecture at five o'clock. Phelps entertained him in the evening, too, and for ten hours of that day was fascinated by his talk; even his meals, eaten with his usual indifference, could not interrupt the flow. Afterwards he was horrified to learn how much he had talked – a curious instance of the limits of his self-knowledge.[152]

On subsequent journeys, AE travelled as far as Toronto[153] and Chicago. Comparing Chicago with New York, he found it 'a darker, fiercer, more tumultuous jumble of lofty buildings, and a surging humanity.'[154] It may have been on this visit to the city that he spoke of the model co-operator Patrick Gallagher of Donegal, saying, 'I hope Paddy the Cope will leave his story behind him before he passes away'; reaching Gallagher through a newspaper cutting, the wish bore fruit in a simple yet brilliant autobiography.[155] In a museum at Washington, D.C., AE saw a Chinese landscape which prompted him to write: 'I feel I could have been shut up with that marvellous imagination of earth for a month and would not have exhausted its enchantment.'[156]*

By mid-April, AE was back in New York with all his impressions stored up in his memory and ready to sail for home. He had encountered not only scholars and students in his travels, but citizens of all kinds. 'I have met presidents of steel corporations and railways,' he informed Bergin, 'like boys in their interest in poetry and romance, yet terribly efficient in their business.'[157] But discussing America in a more critical mood, he confessed: 'You will find engineers who can plan and carry out mighty constructional schemes; but if you talk to them as human beings, they are no more advanced than a boy of sixteen.'[158] On the eve of his departure he announced that he had found in the United States the seed of a world consciousness. 'I believe,' he added, 'that American literature of the future will be of the type represented by Emerson and Thoreau. I have talked with many young writers during my visit here. They are beginning to acquire the art of introspection . . .'[159]

---

*It is possible, however, that this incident occurred during AE's second visit to America, in June 1928.

On 21 April, having refused a six-month appointment as a lecturer at Yale, AE embarked on the *Samaria* and was immediately surrounded by a crowd of young autograph hunters. Replying to their questions, he spoke of the Irish immigrants who had flourished in their country, and referred to one of the first of these, William Galway, a sailor on the *Mayflower*.[160]

The return voyage seems to have been the one on which AE's main companion was Dr. Robert Collis, an Irish physician. They played deck tennis together, and AE paced up and down reciting his poems while American passengers tried to get within earshot. His unpatronising insight into the United States surprised and impressed Collis, and when the latter asked him in wonderment, 'AE, is there anybody you can't tolerate?' he replied, with less than justice to himself, 'Only fools.' Collis afterwards asserted that

> this crossing of the Atlantic when I was his companion will ever remain the most wonderful experience of my life. For as he talked I reached back to my childhood and down into myself and found something that answered his call.

'So,' concluded the doctor, 'for ten days I sat at his feet and learned more of heaven and earth than in all the other years of my life.'[161]

Back in Ireland, AE talked volubly to his friends of his astonishment at the beauty of American girls and suggested its purpose was to inspire their men to great achievements, but in the summary of his impressions that appeared in the *Statesman* he stressed most of all his surmise that America would develop and propagate a world consciousness and sense of universal brotherhood.[162]

At this time, when AE's editorial success was indisputable and he was planning to expand and republish a selection of his weekly articles,[163] some anti-liberal Catholics (or so AE believed) tried to destroy the *Irish Statesman*.[164] In November 1927, he had published the respected scholar Dr. Donal O'Sullivan's scathing review of a collection of Irish songs, and the compilers, Mr. and Mrs. Seamus Clandillon, brought a libel action against the reviewer, the editor, and the paper: the enemies of the journal seem to have taken the opportunity to work on Mrs. Clandillon's *amour-propre** to make her persuade her husband to sue.[164a] The action was pending when AE received an invitation to return to America to receive an honorary degree at Yale. On 7 June, he again sailed for New York, having decided to hurry back to Ireland to be on hand when the case opened.[165] On the 20th, two days after he landed, he walked in

*Mr. Denson has traced Mrs. Clandillon's indignant protests against a hostile review of an earlier book she co-authored with her husband (*United Irishman*, 30 April, 1904 and succeeding issues).

procession from the campus through the city to Woolsey Hall. After a prayer had been offered, Professor Phelps introduced the candidates for honorary degrees and was applauded when he announced that Ireland ought to make AE her dictator for life. Together with Claudel and Livingston Lowes, he received the degree of Doctor of Letters. During the next few days he was treated to an exhausting round of dinners, theatres, and night clubs, and when he found himself safely on board ship sailing out of New York harbour, he gazed back at the city and composed the poem 'With these heaven-assailing spires' to acclaim the new race that had outdone the wonders of Babylon.[166] At sea he made friends with Miss Leah Bernstein, a Wellesley College girl on her way to Europe, and delighted in sketching her. He was grateful when she took the trouble to correspond with him afterwards, but rebuked her for her unkindness in cutting her fiancé out of the picture when she sent him a photograph of herself.[167] To his great pleasure, she enclosed the young man's portrait in another letter and he praised it with the zest of a warm-hearted matchmaker.[168]

On his return, AE found that he still had a breathing space before the libel action began. Simone Téry visited Ireland in August and found him occupied with the egregious Censorship Bill, and it may have been during this month that he invited her to dinner together with Frank O'Connor and tried unsuccessfully to draw them together. O'Connor describes amusingly but probably inaccurately how 'he looked at me and said, "Isn't she nice?" and then at Simone and said "Isn't he nice?" and for the rest of the evening we sat and glowered at one another.'[169]

The libel action ran from 29 October to 13 November. In the *Irish Statesman* of 19 November, 1927, Dr. Donal O'Sullivan had assailed Seamus Clandillon and his wife for having produced in *Londubh an Chairn* a collection of Gaelic songs so packed with errors and omissions that it cast a slur on Irish scholarship. How the case brought boredom to the jurors and profit to the lawyers can be understood from AE's contemporary account:

> The libel case is still dragging itself through the courts, where it has been for a fortnight. It is the most astonishing case Dublin has any knowledge of for a generation, in which a day's jury heard the evidence of scholars like Dr. Bergin and Rahilly on the proper construction of Gaelic sentences. Musicians like Sir R. Terry and Herbert Hughes spoke on minute technical points of musical notation. Singers went into the impossibility of singing various consonants. Such unintelligible evidence was supplemented by comments on the morals and politics of the defendants.[170]

Under cross-examination, AE asserted that despite a warning from the printers that the article was 'dangerous,' he and James Good had both thought it within the tradition of honourable journalism; he had not suspected that it implied a charge of plagiarism. 'If,' he said, 'I [had] realised what high explosives were in the word *variant* I should never have allowed it into my paper.'[170a] According to L. A. G. Strong, AE was asked by the Judge whether the book did not contain some portions of merit.

'Certainly, my Lord,' he replied. 'Parts of it were good.'

'In that case, Mr. Russell, why did your paper describe it as a bad book?'

'My Lord, if you had an egg at your breakfast this morning, and parts of it were bad, and parts of it good, I think you would have described it as a bad egg.'[171]

After seven and a half hours of discussion the bewildered jury was unable to agree on a verdict, and the case was dismissed. The plaintiffs fared no better on appeal: this time the defence was not even called. The enemies of the *Statesman,* however, were almost victorious, for the costs, amounting to about £2,500, threatened it with bankruptcy. The Directors investigated the position on 1 December and concluded that the paper would have to shut down at the end of the month;[172] Plunkett, too, was unable to see how it could be saved.[173] In January, a group including among other intellectuals such unimpeachably loyal but liberal Catholics as Professor Michael Tierney and Katharine Tynan formed a committee to gather subscriptions to meet the emergency. As their fund grew, AE tried to make personal plans in case the rescue attempt failed. He wondered whether to take a post at an American university or whether to rely on freelance writing and painting.[174] On 22 February 1929, however, he was able to inform Yeats that thanks to public support the *Statesman* would survive.[175]

For the next fourteen months, AE's life followed its usual routine without any major interruptions. In February he was planning *Song and Its Fountains,* a sequel to *The Candle of Vision* which was to probe the spiritual and psychic origins of the poet's inspiration, and by the next month he had begun to work on the text.[176] During April, he paid his annual visit to the Hibernian Academy and was fascinated by Jack Yeats's startling later paintings, in which a riot of dazzling colour half concealed the figures and objects:[177] his reason wished to reject these works, but their appeal to his imagination was too strong, and before the year was out he acclaimed them as 'the only Irish art in which there is genius.'[178] After encountering Yeats's experiments he seems to have softened towards the Cubists. Admitting that their colour patterns had often pleased him, he hoped that they would not revert to representational work but 'explore further in the psyche and create a purely imaginative art.'[179]

April 1929 marked the centenary of Catholic Emancipation, and AE called on Protestants, too, to join in celebrating the end of government interference with religion in the British Isles. Despite the current outbreak of fanaticism, he could not but be moved at the ubiquitous celebrations bearing witness to faith in the unseen:

> . . . they are evidence that in our modern world, in spite of secular and external activities into which men are sucked, the hard business of life, which seems to demand almost all their attention, there is still underlying all that a widespread allegiance to the Spirit, to the Invisible, the Intangible, to a divine order not present to the sense, but which is apprehended and believed in by reason of some still uncorrupted spiritual atom in the soul . . . now that there is religious freedom, we may hope that the energies which in the past were so absorbed in resistance may become creative, and the spiritual nature may manifest in literature, poetry, music, painting, architecture, as it has done elsewhere . . .[180]

After three years with the *Statesman,* Mr. Diarmuid Russell left his father's office to emigrate to the United States. In May, his place was taken by Miss Irene Haugh, a young poetess just over twenty-one, who had first met AE the previous autumn at Plunkett House when he advised her on her verse. She remembered later how 'that spirituality which always emanated from him made me aware, even at that first meeting, of the invisible world which lies all about us.'[181] During the next year, she delighted in his company. He was grave and gay by turns, speaking of poetry and the soul, telling witty stories, sketching her, or cooking lunch for two. He often teased her, claiming that she was always wanting new hats or finery, perhaps not realising that she was little interested in such things. When she went on holiday to Switzerland, he wrote to her:

> I expect you to come back with a new continental way of arranging your hair, why not let it stream behind you like a meteor on the wind instead of having it blown before you like the tusks of an elephant[.] I hear you grinding your teeth at me.[182]

In retrospect, she felt that, having only sons, he had treated her as his daughter.[183]

Miss Haugh was a dedicated Catholic, though, as she came to realise, somewhat mechanical in her devotion. As AE talked of the spiritual world, illustrating his statements with quotations from the Bible and Christian writers, she came to have a deeper understanding of her own faith, and words that had been for her only abstractions began to represent realities. He persuaded her that as a poet she should master at least one philosophy, and she found she could relish St. Thomas Aquinas as she never had in her student days. In the end, she profoundly regretted that he had not been born a Catholic so that he could have done for all Ireland what he did for her. As she explained:

> He was of the white fire of which saints and founders of religion [*sic*] are made, without vanity or selfishness; without any worldly ambitions, virtuous, patient, kindly, humorous, temperate in all things, independent of luxuries, of inexhaustible wisdom, and even in the most casual encounter prodigal of that wisdom, his own soul always leaping to come in contact with another, but he never became that Founder.[184]

On 2 July, Trinity College, Dublin, followed the example of Yale by making AE an honorary Doctor of Letters. He shared the distinction with Galsworthy, almost as unlikely a partner for him as Claudel. Sir Robert Tate, the Public Orator, speaking in Latin, acclaimed AE for (in the words of Lucretius), 'touching everything with the charm of the Muses' and illuminating 'that truth which we cannot contemplate except with the sight of the mind.' 'We salute,' he added, 'a citizen most devoted to his country, who has taught our farmers to work co-operatively so that while each individual seemed to be serving another's good, he himself became richer and happier; a prophet who (I say) mixed divine inspiration with matters belonging to everyday affairs (two things previously incompatible).'[185] In his reply, 'AE said that he feared he might become a "safe writer." It would be a boomerang, he thought, if, instead of inspiring youth, he would be regarded as a kind of dissecting room for academic anatomists.'[186]

At this period the 'talkies' were superseding the silent films, to which AE had become addicted. A weekly visit to the cinema was part of his routine – Mary Pickford and Charlie Chaplin were among his favourite stars – and for a while he detested the raucous soundtrack that broke in on his enjoyment of the screen.[187] 'To sit through one of these performances,' he protested, 'is like having carbonic gas blown into the soul to bring about its dissolution. In the silent films every now and then there was imagination and art to reward the visitor.'[188]

AE's companion at the cinema was Osborn Bergin, with whom he also shared his delight in detective stories. It gave him great pleasure to invent a plot for a tale of crime in which Bergin would be among the suspects. Telling and retelling long stories was one of his greatest joys and he could never resist rehearsing to his friends once again the plot of *The Three Musketeers,* waving his arms wildly when his emotion swept him away.[189]

In February 1930, AE was horror-stricken by reports of religious persecution in the Soviet Union. 'The tales of a Communist war,' he admitted, 'upon the very idea of God has [*sic*] united all the churches, and if they are true they might justify a crusade.' A week later, however, he counselled in a calmer spirit that such a crusade would be 'one of the most terrible wars in history' and might even create a permanent hatred of religion in the most spiritual minds.[190]

During the same month, writing to Judge Campbell about the still uncertain finances of the paper, AE mentioned his wish to retire and visit America again before settling down to write some books in Ireland. Though ready to continue as a duty if the money were forthcoming, he explained that the *Statesman* had already done its work:

> It helped to stabilize opinion at the start of the Free State and I think Ministers realize the help it gave and were [*sic*] grateful. It was at first the only paper which gave the Free State a reasoned support. Now the press has come round and what ministers want is a strong party organ to back them up right or wrong. I could not do that.[191]

In the number for 22 March, AE issued what turned out to be a valedictory warning to the world. Alluding to the parable of the king who gathered guests from the highways when those he had invited refused to attend the marriage feast, he prophesied:

> That being interpreted as applied to the nations suggests, we believe, that if [the] nations of the world do not create a brotherhood among themselves the Divine Will will find a way, a dreadful and terrible way, and will inspire some great Power to the overlordship of the planet – the stars in their courses will fight for that great Power, which will make one people and one nation out of the many nations whose rivalries kept the world in wars and commotion.[192]

In the same number of the *Statesman,* AE reviewed Richard Eberhart's *A Bravery of Earth* and found himself face to face at last with an American poet who seemed to have taken up the Emersonian tradition. His confidence that Emerson and Whitman would have successors in this century has been amply justified in the age of William Carlos Williams, Theodore Roethke, and Gary Snyder.

A week later each subscriber to the *Statesman* found in his copy of the journal a mimeographed sheet informing him that the paper

> as is the case with practically every weekly review of the kind, did not pay its way, and it depended on the generosity of some American friends of Ireland who subscribed the original capital and for some years since supplemented it by an annual subsidy. Some of these friends have died, and as it is impossible to continue publication without such aid as was given in the past, the Directors

have decided that the publication of the paper must cease on the 12th April.

In fact, the most important reason for the reduction of American support was that a number of the guarantors had suffered heavy losses in the stock-market crash of the previous year.[193] Even without this misfortune, AE would soon have had to retire as he had begun to suffer from headaches every time he started to write an article.[194]

Before the last number was issued, there was one more flurry of political excitement. On 28 March, the Government fell. With his usual optimism, AE asserted that the ruling party would hold on 'until the opposition realises that the country does not want the Treaty upset,' but he was frightened enough to ask whether de Valera's party, if they should lose the referendum they promised to hold before breaking the agreement, would 'take that as final for this generation.'[195] On 2 April, however, after a nine-hour debate in the Dail, Cosgrave was re-elected as President of the Executive Council and for the moment the position was saved.

The time had now come for AE to vacate his office and remove the mounds of books and papers from his desk. Miss Irene Haugh noted in her diary how they set to work together:

Yesterday 'AE' started clearing away the debris that the *Statesman* and *Homestead* had collected on his shelves for twenty-five years. It is an occupation full of wistful adventures. Interesting papers and books, long forgotten or mislaid, are being revealed, one on top of the other, and everything he offers to me which is not of personal value to himself... Often when he discovers a poet with something of interest in him, the work of clearing away is suspended and he reads aloud for me.[196]

Laments at the demise of the *Statesman* poured in from all quarters: Mr. Hogan, the modern-minded Minister of Agriculture, attributed much of his success to the paper's support, and Yeats melodramatically claimed: 'it leaves us "sheep without a shepherd when the snow shuts out the day." '[197] AE was touched that others felt his efforts had been more effective than he had believed. 'I have had many letters,' he wrote to Eglinton, 'which make me feel my work was not altogether wasted.'[198] Though he must have have been partly aware of how successfully he had infused into the *Statesman* the richness of his own personality, he never realised how much better he wrote when pouring out his thoughts spontaneously than when conscientiously trying to polish his style. His account of how he aimed in *The Candle of Vision* at a musical prose made resonant with assonance and alliteration[199] goes far to explain this. His inevitable regrets at the closing of his paper were tempered by the knowledge that he could not have continued for long, and his retirement brought him positive consolations. The hills of Donegal had lost none of their glamour, the fascination of America had become hard to resist, and his ambition to write more books, which had come to include his memoirs and an imaginative account of a soul's journey from the corpse to the Heaven-world,[200] had survived seven years of arduous journalism.

Towards the Free State, AE's feelings were now mixed. Hogan's reform of the dairy industry would prove, he still hoped, to be the beginning 'of a second wave in agricultural organisation,' a sequel to the one which 'at its crest was broken up by our internal troubles.'[201] But by now he had realised that the co-operative communities, counterparts of ancient city states, could not be created in the few years he had envisaged. 'When I began,' he admitted to an American professor of political science, 'I thought it might be done fairly swiftly but knew at the end that things are of slow growth and the associations we have started in Ireland will probably need forty or fifty years before they reach their full development . . .'[202] His hopes for a spiritual rebirth had likewise, as he explained to Eglinton, to be postponed to the distant future:

> The Ireland which was so poetic and imaginative twenty five years ago is quite bourgeoise [*sic*], squat and stolid. Only the hills and clouds and lakes still carry the old enchantment and will no doubt provoke some other generation to make life approximate more to their beauty.[203]

It was nevertheless in the life of the spirit that he still placed his deepest hopes, and as he turned his thoughts towards Donegal and rest, he confided to his readers that he 'would like to be remembered for this, that he was the friend of the Irish poets, those who make the soul of the nation.'[204]

VIII

The Loosening of the Bonds (1930–1935)

The last five years of AE's life were occupied with a continuous battle against mental exhaustion, physical illness, and social unease. As he struggled against the blunting of his faculties and the collapse of his hopes, the genius that had captivated so many would disencumber itself and flash out to astonish new friends; despite the burden of many sorrows, it was never extinguished.

By the late 1920's Mrs. Russell, afflicted with cancer, had become an invalid,[1] and on his retirement AE withdrew to Donegal to restore his energy before embarking on a second and much longer lecture tour in America to earn money for her treatment.[2] His holiday proved to be a memorable one, for he struck up a friendship with the renowned American art historian Kingsley Porter, who had rented Marble Hill, the home of his old friends the Laws. Porter, a tall, quiet, widely-travelled scholar with inexhaustible energy for research, fell under the spell of AE's many-faceted monologues, which fences, streams, and peat-holes failed to interrupt as he escorted his guest home through the starlight after their first and only dinner together at Marble Hill. Subsequently, AE preferred to come for afternoon tea in order to spend less time indoors, but even then he proved a most unsatisfactory visitor, for his talk continued into the evening until the meal was on the table, and when he refused an invitation to share it Porter had to save the situation by walking away with him.[3]

During the summer Mrs. Mary Rumsey, an associate of Franklin Roosevelt, and James Pond of the Pond Lecture Bureau in New York arranged the formidable schedule for AE's visit. Mrs. Rumsey wrote to him of the enthusiasm with which he was awaited all over the country: Mr. Leland Olds, the son of a college president, had sacrificed an entire year to work for the programme and accompany him on his journey.[4]

Before leaving Ireland, AE attended a ceremony at Plunkett House. Some of his friends and admirers had started a fund to honour him and on 3 September, 1930, the Governor-General, James McNeill, presented him with a cheque for £800. Father Finlay praised him as '[a] great man – a man of rare gifts,' and one who never made an enemy, and in his reply he said that everything he had done in his life he had done because he liked doing it, and nothing had given him more joy than his work for the Irish Agricultural Organisation Society. All his public spirit he ascribed to the influence of Sir Horace Plunkett, Father Finlay, and R. A. Anderson.[5]

On 13 September, AE sailed from Liverpool aboard the *Cedric*, arriving ten days later in New York, where he made his headquarters in rooms lent to him by Mrs. Rumsey. At this time America had already been suffering from a ruinous depression for nearly a year, and two of its causes, the rural exodus and the modern excess of producing over consuming power, had long been among his preoccupations. The printed text of his speech on 28 October, when he was guest of honour for Farmers' Week at Columbia, Missouri, goes far to explain his appeal to American audiences in this time of economic disaster. Summarising his philosophy evolved over two decades, he ranged from the life of Patrick Gallagher of Donegal to the glorified human forms of Phidias and Michelangelo as he sketched his vision of a rural civilisation which could redeem human life and human nature.[6] An account of his lecture 'An Artist and Poet Considers Dreams' as delivered on 7 March, 1931, in Savannah, Georgia, reflects his genius for drawing others into his own spiritual world:

> Those who responded most deeply to the hystical quality running through his speech felt almost as if he were surrounded by an invisible emanation which changed him before their eyes. For the time, they lived in another world, a serene world of beauty and high desires, into which he lifted them on his wings. When he described the land, like Plato's 'many-coloured land,' that he had created in imagination for himself as a youth, desiring escape from the world of business into the which he was forced, they saw with him this beautiful world, 'self-shining, shining from within by its own light,' with its birds in blazing colours, among the blazing leaves of the trees. This was poetry of the purest, most glorious sort, uttered in memorable prose. He led his audience into the poet's vision of the rosa mystica.
>
> He told of the pity and sorrow with which he had walked in the dark hours of night through the lowest street of Dublin, seeing poverty, brawling, drunkenness and bestiality, and of how there had suddenly come to him consciousness of the immortality which lifts man out of such depths into the godlike, and the audience shared his compassion and his exaltation, feeling in both something divine.
>
> A sort of glory hung about him while he talked. He was poet and prophet. When he stopped, the mantle dropped from him for a moment. He stood hesitant, a simple, kindly, gentle man, a little

bewildered by the applause, and the audience woke too from the dream.[6a]

During his stay in the United States, AE renewed his acquaintance with Henry Wallace, whom he had met long before, in 1912, when the future Vice-President had called on him at Plunkett House and had been much impressed with his idealism.[7] Twenty years younger than AE, Wallace had much in common with him, for he was not only a practical agricultural scientist but an unconventional idealistic politician whose life was deeply rooted in religious faith. As he listened to the visitor lecturing all over the Mid-West and delivering his monologues to small gatherings on Sunday afternoons, he realised that here was a man who, despite his meagre technical knowledge of agricultural economics,[8] could persuade Americans that co-operation should be not merely a mode of business but a way of life.[9]

AE's trip began with an exhausting week in New York. Asked on arrival about the *Irish Statesman,* he quipped: 'There was great need after the revolution for a medium of placidity, and I edited the publication, making it more placid and more placid until finally everyone who read it was placid.'[10] He broadcast over a national network and was filmed talking to the President of Columbia University and to the Irish-American politician Al Smith, who firmly endorsed his appeal for a rural civilisation to keep the countryman attached to the soil: his wife wrote to him that the interview with Smith had been screened in Dublin.[11]

The first stage of AE's tour lasted three months. Rushing westwards from city to city, he repeated three or four prepared talks before university audiences, literary societies, and, to his amusement, Chambers of Commerce, switching easily from an impassioned disquisition on the rural exodus and the co-operative community to his lighthearted memories of Irish authors or his autobiographical exploration of dreams. Several of his talks were broadcast. The strain of travelling by night and lecturing by day – often he was hurried straight from his engagement to the railway station – took its toll on his sixty-three-year-old frame, and as the vastness of the continent opened out before him he thought wistfully of compact, leisurely Ireland, now so remote, and used spare moments to write to his friends at home. 'Is there anything happening in Ireland?' he asked Joseph O'Neill from the remoteness of Grand Forks, North Dakota, and went on to describe his sensations:

> The size of this country is appalling. You start on a ride and the fields go away to infinity and the sense of vastness is impressive. The western folk are very eager and energetic and full of hope and

> imagination about their country. Their power of organisation is stupendous.[12]

At Chicago, AE had enjoyed the interlude of a pleasant reunion with his younger son. As he reached the far West, he was regaled with 'an odd day or two rushing off to see national parks and glaciers and forests and canyons, all inconceivably vast.'[13] The overwhelming heights and depths of the Rocky Mountains and the nearby cactus deserts reminded him of his old delight in cowboy stories, and he found it hard to conceive that the immense city of Seattle on the Pacific coast was only a few decades old. 'It is,' he explained to O'Neill, 'because the farms and houses are well built and attractive and the roads everywhere broad and well laid that the new country even seems to have centuries behind it.'[14] In November he travelled south to California and his imagination was stirred by San Francisco as it had been by New York:

> When I first came to it across the ferry the city rose at night like a city out of the Arabian Nights all glittering with rose and golden and silvery lights, and I said I am getting into Paradise. Then as I came closer I knew the jewelled lights were passionate appeals to smoke particular brands of cigarettes or to eat particular brands of tinned fruits. But there is a romance about the city in spite of that.[15]

Staying in Los Angeles from the 17th to the 19th, AE was able to call on James Pryse, who had been his revered teacher in 1895. Each evening from eight o'clock, they talked together for nearly four hours,[16] and a few days later he wrote to him from San Francisco anticipating their relationship in a future incarnation:

> You have always been one of the transparencies through which one could see the spirit . . . I am certain we will meet again, and I hope I will be better material for you to work on when I return. I have been toughened by my work and will not be so shy and timid as I was when I started this life.[17]

Lecturing at the California Institute of Technology near Los Angeles, AE met and admired the Nobel prize-winning physicist R. A. Millikan. He felt that science was moving in the direction he had envisaged in *The Interpreters,* and he expressed his hopes to O'Neill:

> It is curious that Eddington, Jeans, Einstein[,] Whitney the greatest American chemist are all becoming mystics, and I think we are in for an era of mysticism as a reaction from the solid materialistic science of my boyhood. Jeans states his belief in a divine mind like Eddington and Whitney says all his science is

only an educated man's way of stating something which really exists only because we live and move and have our being in infinite deity . . .[18]

Despite his exhaustion and his longing to take refuge in a hermitage, he found temptation and delight in the semi-tropical vegetation of California and the gracious Spanish architecture of Santa Barbara. Writing of 'sea sunshine palms eucalyptuses gardens palaces in the Spanish fashion,' he told O'Neill: 'You would love this country at first sight and then feel if you did not get out of it you would rot your soul with idleness and beauty.'[19] Before he left the state, he spent a day with the poet Robinson Jeffers, who turned out to be as ruggedly impressive as his verse.

On 29 November, AE found himself on board a train moving towards Arizona. Referring to lovers of the desert through which he was passing, he claimed, 'I am not of their class,' but once across the state boundary he succumbed utterly to 'magical Arizona with its rose amethyst mountains and its cactus covered deserts where a man might live and meditate happily if he had no concern about rattlesnakes.'[20] After this Texas seemed dull, but at Baton Rouge, Louisiana, he was touched and depressed by the poverty-stricken whites and Negroes, indolent, diseased and without hope amidst the ruins of a once beautiful, though slave-based civilisation.

A day or two before Christmas, AE returned to New York for a short rest before setting out early in January on the second half of his tour.[21] He dreamed now of Arizona as well as of Ireland, and looked back with pleasure on the open-mindedness of the Catholic priests in this new civilisation. They had flocked to hear him speak at Seattle and San Francisco and had asked him to autograph even his 'heretical' *Candle of Vision*. 'The Church here,' he reported to Irene Haugh, 'realises I am on the side of the angels.'[22] On 27 December, he gathered up enough energy to address an audience of scientists, actors, artists, and reformers associated with the Pond Lecture Bureau. Wittily blaming the popularity of Longfellow's summons to action in his 'Psalm of Life' for America's over-production problem, he announced: 'Your President and Congress ought to gather on the steps of the White House and formally extract that poem from Longfellow's works and burn it, and then erect a statue to idleness.'[23] This recommendation started good-humoured controversies in newspapers from coast to coast. When he was made an honorary director of the local Irish Theatre at its rooms in the Barbizon Hotel, he noticed prominent Free Staters and Republicans in the audience and treated them to a brief talk on the 'pagan Irish doctrine as outlined in the old sagas that one should love one's enemies.'[23a]

In the new year, 1931, he resumed his hectic travels, and it must have been with some relief that he accepted the hospitality of Kingsley Porter in Cambridge, Massachusetts, where Mrs. Porter noticed how anxious he was to be scrupulously punctual for the lectures which were to pay for his wife's medical treatment.[24] At the end of January, he found himself enjoying the snow and the sub-zero temperatures of Montreal, and after a packed programme in the Great Lakes region during the first half of February, he headed south to Virginia, the Carolinas, Georgia, and Alabama. Like many Europeans he felt at home in the hierarchical, Old World society of the South, and appreciated the spacious grandeur of the pillared colonial architecture. 'I understand the Confederate point of view now,' he admitted, 'as I never did before and I rather like the Southern passion for a rural life and culture against the machine civilisation of the New England industrialists. They are such nice human beings these Southern folk.'[25]

During his travels, AE somehow found time to compile another book of verse, which was published in London on 3 March, before he returned. As the title indicates, he expected it to be his last. Pervaded by a soft melancholy, it is clearly the work of an aging man. The reader is invited to follow the poet's emotions as he looks enviously yet philosophically on the gaiety of the young, and seeks to understand the fate that determines the course of a man's life. He searches for answers in his memories of infancy, in his recollections of the Household of the 1890's, even in the sight of children playing on the Donegal sands. He dares to question anew lifelong beliefs, and persistently touches on his now favourite theme of the child within himself: three times he introduces the phrase 'ancient with youth,'[26] a condensation of the line 'Ancient with glad eternal youth' which he had written before the Household broke up.[27]

Vale, though emotionally less rich, recalls AE's other bitter-sweet volume, *The Divine Vision.* Significantly, he returns in half a dozen poems to the plaintive alexandrine that he had employed as frequently in that collection of 1904, though he had rarely used it between 1913 and 1925. While he retains the largely modernised idiom of *Voices of the Stones,* his imperfect technique still comes between the emotion and the reader. The blank verse which he adopts for several of his meditations has the Wordsworthian plainness without the Wordsworthian inspiration, so that 'How?' is more interesting as autobiography than as poetry, and 'Dark Weeping' almost lapses at times into a prose rhythm. Too often, as in *Homeward* and *The Earth Breath,* forces undoubtedly real to the poet remain unreal to the reader. The powers of nature are softened into sentimentality in 'Sibyl'; in 'Gifts of Heaven' there is no horror in the phrase 'blindness of chaos, tempest and thunder,' nor is there awe in the prophecy of 'The Cities':

> Faery shall dance in
> The streets of the town,
> And from sky headlands
> The gods looking down.

In this stanza 'city' is reduced to 'town' for the sake of the rhyme. While the dancing tetrameters of 'Midsummer Eve' impart a light, even gay air to the versification of AE's thoughts on the spiritual quest, there are too many incongruous intrusions: the old imagery of star and King rubs shoulders with classical nymphs and with the Yeatsian idiom of the line 'Toss dice betwixt the fool and wise?'

In some poems, on the other hand, AE happily matches style to subject. Whereas the technique of repetition in 'Enchantment,' in which he tries to evoke a picture of children playing, is no substitute for the precise visual detail caught in a neat phrase, the light rhythm of 'Earth-bound,' enhanced by skilful assonance and alliteration, exactly conveys the frivolity he sees in earthly gaiety: in this lyric concrete detail would be out of place. The sweeping lines of 'Dark Rapture' are farthest of all from cliché. The baffled mystic, feeling himself outcast from the heavens, is filled with wonder on meeting a drunkard who seems to be rapt in ecstasy. Is he wrong, he asks himself, in his lifelong conviction that drug-induced bliss is spurned by the divine powers? His doubt – for once real and not rhetorical – is intensely moving. The poem is imperfect – 'nigher' and 'ere' are intrusive archaisms, the image of the stars as 'fiery-footed watchers' is uninspired – but the combination of alternately rhyming alexandrines with sentences modelled as in blank verse creates a lively tension between division and continuity. Moreover in a fine simplicity ('I heard him cry GOD in amazement') AE captures the ambiguity of the drunkard's outburst: is it blasphemy or prayer?

The most beautiful poem in the collection is 'Germinal,' in which AE's characteristic lyric delicacy is stiffened with a core of strength. The theme, the determination of character in infancy, is illustrated by the three examples of Dante, Caesar, and Judas Iscariot arranged in a logical order of moral decline. The alternation of tetrameters and dimeters underlines the contrast between the weakness of childhood and the awesome power of fate, and the poet evokes a shiver of horror as he divines behind the crime of Judas a childhood error.

> Call not thy wanderer home as yet
> Though it be late.

Now is his first assailing of
  The invisible gate.
Be still through that light knocking. The hour
  Is thronged with fate.

To that first tapping at the invisible door
  Fate answereth.
What shining image or voice, what sigh
  Or honied breath,
Comes forth, shall be the master of life
  Even to death.

Satyrs may follow after. Seraphs
  On crystal wing
May blaze. But the delicate first comer
  It shall be King.
They shall obey, even the mightiest,
  That gentle thing.

All the strong powers of Dante were bowed
  To a child's mild eyes,
That wrought within him that travail
  From depths up to skies,
Inferno, Purgatorio
  And Paradise.

Amid the soul's grave councillors
  A petulant boy
Laughs under the laurels and purples, the elf
  Who snatched at his joy,
Ordering Caesar's legions to bring him
  The world for his toy.

In ancient shadows and twilights
  Where childhood had strayed,
The world's great sorrows were born
  And its heroes were made.
In the lost boyhood of Judas
  Christ was betrayed.

Let thy young wanderer dream on:
  Call him not home.
A door opens, a breath, a voice
  From the ancient room,

Speaks to him now. Be it dark or bright
He is knit with his doom.

A small group of lyrics, none of them among the best, originate in AE's American experience. 'Atlantic' testifies to his discovery of the ocean as yet another of nature's wonders; 'Blight,' a graceful protest against the New World freedom in love-making, echoes too closely the rhythm of Wordsworth's 'A slumber did my spirit seal.' The book ends with 'Fugitive,' a declaration of faith in the soul's certain transcendence of relative good and evil.

It was not until May 1931 that AE left the United States.[28] He travelled first to London where he called on George Moore, who had shunned him ever since 1916, holding him responsible for Susan Mitchell's witty attack. Describing the reunion to Eglinton, Moore told how he had eventually cut short AE's opening twenty-minute monologue on America with the remark 'And now, Russell, shall we have a little chat?' According to another friend, New World hospitality had even seduced AE into appreciating wine and food, though this new interest was short-lived.[29]

After a brief stay in Dublin, AE went on to Donegal where he spent most of June and July recovering from the effects of his tour. Writing to the American poet Vachel Lindsay, he said:

> I amuse myself painting. I had eight months in your country, and feel empty after talking all the time, and came here to fill the empty psyche . . . I see nobody. I read nothing. I eat griddle bread, drink buttermilk, sit by a turf fire, and walk over hills and sands, and try to empty my mind so that Mother Earth may come into it and talk to me a little.[30]

One day Kingsley Porter and his wife arrived at his cottage near Sheep Haven and carried him off in a motor car across the bleak heather moors to stay with them in Glenveagh Castle. Porter had so fallen in love with Donegal – even with its rain and mud – that he had bought this lakeside mansion as a summer home. When AE asked, 'But where can I throw matches on the floor and not have them picked up?' his hosts good humouredly found him an empty room for his studio. At night the whole party gathered in the library, which was situated in the tower overlooking the lake. For hours after the water had ceased to gleam in the sunset, AE would continue talking in front of the turf fire, and when Mrs. Porter finally induced her guests to retire, he would hold a candle up to the bookshelves and search for something to read in bed. His favourite was Mardrus and Mathers' admirable translation of *The Arabian Nights,* whose treasures he liked to speak of next morning at breakfast. When it was fine, he delighted in rising early to walk outdoors while everyone else was still in bed.[31]

Back in Dublin, AE settled down to work through a depressing accumulation of correspondence, tried to relax over his paintings, and continued *Song and Its Fountains* while taking pleasure in other men's publications. Although he was disappointed to find that his headaches persisted, he managed to oblige Hugh MacDiarmid by writing a preface for his *First Hymn to Lenin*, and he was made so happy by the success of Frank O'Connor's first book of short stories, which he had recommended to his own publisher, that he referred to him privately as a genius.[32] Receiving a copy of *The Crosses and Culture of Ireland*, the product of Kingsley Porter's recent researches, he belatedly discovered that St. Patrick had not put an end to Gaelic art. With some reluctance he confessed:

> I started my study of Christianity in Ireland at the wrong end, that is, in my own time when it produced neither art nor literature and was so sterile that I could hardly imagine any period of fertility.[33]

In the *Statesman*, he had more than once pleaded with the clergy to raise the standard of ecclesiastical art.[34]

Some weeks after AE's return from Donegal, he and Yeats spent a few days at Coole discussing with Lady Gregory the establishment of an Irish Academy of Letters. Back in Dublin, finding that his wife's illness was worse and they could no longer take their evening walk together, he tried to soothe his distress by transferring to canvas his memory of the beautiful lake at Coole.[35] Before the end of October, he received an invitation to meet Mahatma Gandhi, who had read *The National Being* and *The Candle of Vision*, and who was then in England for the Round Table Conference. He longed to talk to the Mahatma, who had put into practice the theory of non-violent power that he himself had advocated in *The Interpreters*,[36] but Mrs. Russell was taken into the Adelaide Hospital for an operation and he felt unable to leave Ireland. Characteristically, he consoled himself with the theory of spiritual gravitation, as he confided to Yeats: '. . . I believe in Karma as Gandhi probably does and if I really belong to him and he to me we must meet . . .'[37]

The end of 1931 was a time of great sorrow for AE. By mid-December he had completed *Song and Its Fountains*, which he dedicated to his wife and younger son. Immediately he tried to resume work on *The Avatars*, the spiritual romance laid aside eight years before, but his mind was too overcast by grief to allow him to work with any regularity, and he refused Yeats's request that he edit the autobiography of Shri Purohit Swami, an Indian monk who claimed to have seen one of the Theosophical Masters.[38] He was in daily attendance at the Hospital, where he sat at his wife's bedside holding her hand.[39] On the 15th he wrote to Mrs. Kingsley Porter: 'I see her every afternoon and stay there for a couple of hours. She cannot talk much but I think she likes me to be in her room.'[40] Mr. Orr, the hospital chaplain, enjoyed visiting her and observed her debt to eastern teachings.[41]

On the 20th AE, haggard from strain, opened the door of his home at Rathgar Avenue to confront a tramp-like figure who had just walked fifty-five miles from his home in County Monaghan. For a moment, as the traveller later recalled, he was taken aback at the sight of AE:

> I was afraid of that man. He looked like a man who had awakened from a dark trance. His eyes stared at me like two nightmare eyes from which there was no escape.[42]

On hearing that his visitor was Patrick Kavanagh, an uneducated farm labourer a few of whose poems he had published in the *Statesman* two years before, AE invited him into the lonely house. Never noticing that the youth was hungry, he talked of ideas and read aloud from Emerson and Whitman; before they parted, he bestowed a pile of books on Kavanagh, including two of Dostoyevsky's novels for which he was ever after grateful. He was the last of the long line of poets whom AE discovered.

Eight days later, Mrs. Russell came home, but her doctors felt that she would not recover and might linger on in her suffering for several months. AE wrote to Mrs. Porter:

> You will understand that I am depressed and unable to write or think of anything. They operated to discover the cause of the trouble which was going on for many years . . . But they are not hopeful. So you will understand how I feel with so much in my life slipping away from me.[43]

A friend who seems to have seen an advance copy of *Song and Its Fountains* called on Mrs. Russell, who asked: 'Do go into the next room and tell my husband how much you like his new book. It will cheer him immensely and take his mind off, for a time from his grief about my illness.'[44] On 3 February, 1932, she passed away almost without pain, and AE had the consolation that she was spared further suffering. To one of her friends he wrote:

> She was a most faithful and unselfish companion, and she had for the last eight or nine years been more or less an invalid . . . She had great courage and could endure suffering better than any I have met.[45]

The funeral took place at Mount Jerome Cemetery. Mr. Orr read the service and then escorted AE back to his home and listened to him talk over tea of Yeats, Plunkett, and his American travels. When they discussed St. Paul, AE claimed that the latter's reference to the Third Heaven and his teaching on the Holy Ghost showed

Indian influence while Mr. Orr imputed them to Jewish speculation.[46]

Almost immediately, AE withdrew to London to spend a week alone in the great rooms of the Euston Hotel in an attempt, as he put it, to 'break away from the heaviness of heart which comes on us while we watch the slowly dying when we seem in sympathy to be dying ourselves.'[47] Returning to Dublin, he tried to settle down in his empty house with only a maid to look after him, and to fend off the spectre of solitude with the help of his dog and cat and such companions as remained. Bergin, O'Connor, and the O'Neills were among the stalwarts, and every Sunday afternoon[48] he spent at Seumas O'Sullivan's, where he sometimes played croquet.[49] He wrote to Eglinton of the loss of his wife adding, 'I am lonely though I have still many friends but they can never be quite like the friends who have been with us for the greater part of our lives.'[50] As soon as he could sufficiently pull himself together, he resumed work fitfully on *The Avatars,* and he began to contribute poems to Seumas O'Sullivan's *Dublin Magazine*.

On 16 February, *Song and Its Fountains* was published and AE was somewhat surprised at its favourable reception by the critics.[51] Knowing that his distress had disturbed his concentration while he was writing it, he thought of preparing a larger revised edition.[52] The book is devoted to his theory of poetic inspiration, but its peculiar charm derives from its autobiographical basis. From the vantage point of old age he ranges widely, even nostalgically, over visions and incidents associated with the writing of his poems, and leads the reader at a leisurely pace by way of many curious anecdotes to metaphysical ideas. While closely related in content to *The Candle of Vision, Song and Its Fountains* is less fiery, passionate and rhetorical, and much farther removed from the proselytizing Theosophical zeal of the 1890's: the urge to persuade others to follow the mystical path has given way to a desire for intellectual understanding of his experiences. Though the vigour of his editorial prose is absent and there are still trite poetic phrases, the mellow tone, the autobiographical flavour, and the earnestness of the enquiry combine to make this one of its author's most attractive works.

During the months that followed, much occurred to increase AE's uneasiness and to tempt him to emigrate. On 9 March, de Valera formed his first government, and his plans to challenge Britain's rights under the Treaty endangered the achievements of the Free State. At the same time a programme was being drawn up for the International Eucharistic Congress to be held in Dublin during the summer, and AE regarded this event, which was to bring hundreds of thousands of pilgrims to Ireland, as an unctuous display of mass servility to the ecclesiastical authorities. To make matters worse, Sir Horace Plunkett died a few days before the end of the month.

AE was doggedly pressing on with *The Avatars,* hoping to broadcast enough heresies to keep Ireland's soul alive, when Yeats publicly announced on 3 April his plan for an Academy. Sceptical of its value and unwilling to be drawn away from his book, AE wrote to him:

> There is nothing to interest me in a nation run by louts, and your Academy of Letters will not have the slightest effect in a country where all the papers are united in fears of clerical denunciation. I may think differently later on, but just now I feel alien to everything except the earth itself and if it was not for that love I would leave Ireland.[53]

AE soon began, however, to hope that the proposed institution would fight the censorship and nourish the new genius that Ireland needed, so he drafted the rules for Yeats and took the trouble to have them officially registered.

Late in May, another link with the past was severed with the death of Lady Gregory. Trying to console Yeats, AE could not hold back the bitterness of his disillusion. 'The Anglo-Irish,' he wrote, 'were the best Irish but I can see very little future for them as the present belongs to that half crazy Gaeldom which is growing dominant about us.'[54] Nevertheless, two days later he informed Kingsley Porter: 'I am not really melancholy. I find myself in deep peace inside only outwardly I rage and gesticulate and curse the fools who run my country.'[55]

The much heralded Eucharistic Congress was held in the fourth week of June, and at the climax the Papal Legate celebrated Mass before an unprecedented congregation of about a million people stretching for a mile in every direction from the altar in Phoenix Park. Unable to endure such a spectacle, AE fled to Glengariff to spend the week with Bergin and O'Connor, and according to the latter he denounced the Congress to a newspaper reporter on the way and arrived in a lighthearted mood. Sitting on a rock while the other two were swimming, he heard thunder in the distance and called out, 'Oh, come on, come on, Mananan! You can do better than that. All I want you to do is to wash out those damned Christian idolators.'[56] He amused O'Connor by the jovial abuse he showered on the latter's drawing and rowing, and he enjoyed making up limericks about both his friends.[57] In a different mood he anathematized de Valera, though O'Connor may exaggerate in making him say, 'I curse that man as generations of Irishmen to come will curse him – the man who destroyed our country!'[58]

During July, AE's fears about the new Government began to be realised. De Valera withheld the Land Annuities – the interest on the sums loaned long ago to tenants to enable them to buy their holdings – from the British Treasury, and when Britain imposed punitive duties on Irish exports he retaliated in kind. In the middle of the month, AE left for another holiday with the Porters at Glenveagh Castle. To his surprise, three poems – 'Distraction,' 'Incarnation,' and 'Lost Talisman' – came to him spontaneously while he was by the lakeside,[59] and when he went out on the water he momentarily held a fishing rod and a fish attached itself to it. In the guest book he wrote, 'Caught three poems and one fish. "Good hunting."' He had not long returned home when a tumultuous thunderstorm struck Ulster, and he observed in a letter to Porter:

> whole villages sat up all night saying their prayers, telling their beads and other magical practices to control the elements. I would like to teach them the real philosophy of magic. But if I went to any pious Catholic village and said, 'You folks, I hear you believe in magic, you have been practising incantations against thunder and lightning. Now the real way to work the thing is this.' I would be stoned as a pagan . . .[60]

After his holiday, AE found it difficult at first to concentrate on *The Avatars*. On 12 September, his efforts to have the Rules of Yeats's Academy officially registered were finally successful, and, anxious to secure an illustrious membership, he seriously set about his work as Honorary Secretary. Attacks appeared in the press, and in November he rose to the Academy's defence in the columns of the *Irish Times*, arguing with his old editorial skill and angry wit against the charge that its members were 'artists of the cesspool' and that the people, not a chosen few, were the guardians of literature. In his third and most forceful letter, he struck at what he believed to be the roots of the matter – race and religion. He was, he said, 'content, even proud,' to be of mixed descent: there were not more than two or three hundred thousand pure Gaels in the nation and they tended to be 'half-wits – the kind of people we meet in the West, their minds a clotted mass of superstition and ignorance, animated by a half-crazy energy.' Denouncing the impossible but now widespread ideal of a culturally isolated Celtic civilisation, he asked:

> What has our self-concentrated nationality given to the world? Even in religion have we produced a single theologian of whom the world has heard? . . . Have we saints like Thomas Aquinas, St. Teresa, St. Francis – a single spiritual figure risen out of our pious mass whose words are a consolation to the troubled soul? We have not produced such figures, because even in religion we were isolated, and confined ourselves to mere pieties rather than

> to the lofty athletics of philosophy. We can, of course, with our talent for organisation, get a million people on their knees before an altar in the Park; but did there come out of all that piety a single vision, a song, a music, any visible sign that the sacrifice was accepted and the fiery tongues had descended?[61]

Mr. Alan Denson has made the plausible suggestion that such tirades as this, with its wholly uncharacteristic insult to the Western Gaels, resulted from the cancer which, unknown to himself, was slowly killing him.[62] About this time, he asked that his fierce 'Open Letter to Mr. Rudyard Kipling' be excluded from an anthology of English prose, since he held all anger to be wrong.[63] This blindness to his own inconsistency was accompanied by other symptoms of decline. The gaiety which had made him such a delightful companion was becoming rarer, and he often seemed unaware of other people as individuals,[64] while his letters to Kingsley Porter show how easily he lapsed into the drowsiness of old age. His intellectual powers, too, were reduced, and he constantly complained of 'the fog in his brain.'[65] Writing to Yeats of Indian thought, he admitted: 'I think now that the essence of that philosophy is to get the sense of oneness of being with the nature around us . . . I have long ceased to worry about the intricacies of Brahmanical psychology knowing that they are only avenues leading to forgetfulness of themselves.'[66] Such a confession shows that he had allowed his adherence to western nature-worship to cloud his understanding of eastern metaphysics.

One evening during the winter, AE called on Frank O'Connor and announced that he had had a premonition that his death was approaching. 'I wasn't told how soon,' he said. 'I dare say it could be a month or a year.' O'Connor, despite his imperfect understanding of his friend, could see that he did not fear death, but only the helpless decrepitude of age.[67] In a letter to Charles Weekes, AE expounded the Theosophical view of the after-life, and explained his disappointment that he had not attained the high spiritual state that would have enabled him to control by willpower the time of his departure:

> I feel my own death will be unworthy because I will go out through the falling in of walls of clay whereas I should by the will have before this been able to find a secret radiant gateway into the spirit and gone out of my own will and not been forced out.[68]

During the early months of 1933, AE continued to work for the Academy, but he was detaching his emotions more and more from the political future of the Free State. In January, he wrote to one of his correspondents:

> I am really more interested in what is going to happen in U.S.A.

> than in what is going to happen in Ireland. I have stepped somehow into having the wide disinterested view of a planetary citizen and I don't think Ireland at present has much to give the world.[69]

In March, he was pleased by an article which Sean O'Faolain published about his work, one of the very few serious analyses, he felt, to appear in Ireland,[70] but his mood of disillusion persisted and in April he declared: 'One's country or one's nation is a brute to be kicked in the ribs. But one's friends are different, one holds to them.'[71] He felt too old, he explained, to go abroad and seek new companions.[72]

At the end of March, he sent the completed manuscript of *The Avatars* to Macmillan, but when the proofs arrived his artistic conscience told him that he had released it prematurely.[73] He decided to dedicate it:

> To
> W. B. Yeats,
> my oldest friend and enemy[74]

but in the end his nerve failed him and he deleted the telling third line.

A passage in the text of *The Avatars* reveals an ambivalence in AE's feeling towards George Moore. The creeping disease in his body seems to have inflamed a long smouldering spark of hostility towards the novelist's leering sensuality, and in a ferocious attack, apparently composed about the time of Moore's death in January, he goes so far as to rank him with the infernal powers.[75] He must have been embarrassed by Colonel Moore's request, made while the book was in the press, that he deliver a funeral speech at the interment of the ashes in May, and instead of attending the ceremony himself he asked Dr. Best to read what he had written. His words combined a fitting tribute to Moore's dedication to his art with sly insinuations about his ostentatious non-conformities, and concluded with the warning: 'If any would condemn him for creed of theirs he had assailed let them first be certain that they laboured for their ideals as faithfully as he did for his.'[76] 'The oration,' he admitted privately, 'was, as Yeats said, a masterpiece of double meaning. Moore would have admired it.'[77] He had paid him back for the string of insults in *Vale*.

The Avatars was rooted in AE's memories of the Dublin Lodge, and on 8 May he took another backward glance when he addressed an assembly gathered together to honour Madame Blavatsky's memory, and spoke of the great debt which the Irish literary movement owed to her.[78] About this time, meeting a stranger named Captain Bowen, he greeted him with the words, 'Ah, a very old friend, I think.' Bowen, a Theosophist, was soon satisfied that AE's conviction that they had met in a former life was based on more than fancy, and he rapidly placed himself in the relation of a disciple to him.[79] AE was still conducting the meetings of the Hermetic Society and teaching from *The Secret Doctrine*. Miss Dorothy Emerson, visiting the group at this period, was especially impressed by his exposition of the Beatitudes in a way she felt to be beyond the reach of any clergyman. Bowen told her that AE had warned him not to become as fluent a speaker as himself.[80]

By the early summer, AE's sense of isolation had become so acute that he determined to leave Ireland for a time. In June, while he was painting at Glenveagh Castle, he and Porter spent the evenings vying with each other in cheerfully composing masterpieces of gloomy prophecy about their homelands,[81] but his mood was bitter when he told O'Connor, 'I have to get out of this country before it drives me mad.'[82] Discussing his plans with his old friend Constantine Curran, he spoke of visiting Daniel Dunlop – once a member of the Household – and Charles Weekes in London, of staying with his younger son in the United States, and of sailing round the world and seeing India. They tried to plan a route which would allow for AE's intolerance to heat.[83] He was thinking at this time of the third of the four stages of the classic Hindu life – the phases of student and householder are followed by a period when the bonds of possession and worldly ties are broken as a preparation for the final role, that of a religious hermit – and he started a poem on the theme.[84] Early in July he sold his house, 17 Rathgar Avenue, and divested himself of property except for a few books, pictures, and clothes. Most of his more personal belongings he gave to friends, and Frank O'Connor, believing him to be hiding deep grief behind a mask of indifference as he gave away cherished possessions, could not bring himself to call for his share. Eventually F. R. Higgins, equally distraught with pity, came to fetch him insisting, 'AE will be hurt if you don't come, and the man is hurt enough,' and indignantly describing the vultures in the old poet's home, he exclaimed: 'You should see the greed in those fellows' eyes.'[85]

While he was selling his house, AE wrote to Weekes for advice as to how he could most comfortably and economically establish himself in London for a year or more, but first he intended to take another holiday at Glenveagh Castle. On 7 July, he wrote in a merry mood to thank Higgins and his wife for a gift of ties, especially a red one which he looked forward to wearing at Kingsley Porter's to arouse suspicion that he had become a Communist.[86] The following night he stood on the Donegal coast beside the Porters' chauffeur waiting for his friends to return from the island of Inish Bofin, where they had built a small cottage. The boat, rowed by a local oarsman, came into sight bearing a single passenger, and Mrs. Porter stepped ashore alone, a woman stunned with grief. As they began the drive to Glenveagh Castle, she broke the news: her husband had been drowned earlier in the day.

AE set himself to spend his holiday comforting the widow, and she afterwards felt that no one else on earth could have taken his place. His infinite tenderness surprised her less than his competence at filling in forms and making practical arrangements. In the evenings she lay on a settee in front of the fire, while he tried to soothe her to sleep by reading from an advance copy of *The Avatars*.[87]

After some days, AE returned to Dublin to make the final arrangements for his departure. At the end of July, he resigned from the Academy, as he expected to be away from Ireland for about a year.[88] He entrusted the leadership of the Hermetic Society to Captain Bowen, to whom he wrote of his own work as a teacher, 'I had no private doctrine, nothing but H. P. B[lavatsky], W. Q. J[udge], the *Bhagavad-Gita, Upanishads, Patanjali,* and one or two other scriptures.' In a different letter to Bowen he explained: 'H. P. B[lavatsky] indicated that there would be a new Teacher in the latter end of the present century; and the main thing is to keep a familiarity with her teaching as widely spread as possible until the new Messenger appears.'[89] He also charged Bowen with the duty of writing an account intelligible to the layman of the path of self-development taught in ancient and modern schools of the Mysteries,[90] but the resultant volume, *The Occult Way*, turned out to be totally lacking in the impassioned conviction of *The Candle of Vision*.

On 2 August, AE arrived in London and took possession of the lodgings that Weekes had obtained for him at 41 Sussex Gardens. The same evening he wrote sadly to Bergin: 'Here I am looking out over trees down a long street after a day of trying to find a way through this prodigious jungle of a city . . .'[91] His energy was quickly sapped by the current heatwave, so that it was several days before he could begin the preface he had undertaken to write for Gogarty's *Selected Poems*.[92]

AE told his friends that he had come to London without informing anyone but Weekes in order to test his belief that his natural companions would be drawn to him by spiritual gravitation. His experiment, however, was perfunctory in the extreme: one of his acquaintances pointed out to Dr. Gibbon that a single dinner invitation was sufficient to advertise his presence to a large circle.[93]

It was not long before the heat abated, and AE settled into a pleasant enough routine, reading in the Times Book Club, visiting the art galleries, and meeting a variety of friends. 'I am rejoicing at present in being a wanderer,' he wrote to Sean O'Faolain, 'the cries of my race no longer touching me, the lights of love and home long behind me, and drowned in hazes of sunken years.'[94] Besides Weekes and Dunlop, his friends included the artist Sir William Rothenstein, the poet Herbert Palmer, the scholar Helen Waddell, and his old admirer Clifford Bax. One day in October, as they sat on a bench in Leicester Square Garden surrounded by tramps, he talked to Bax of the early days of the Theosophical Society.[95] Even mystics were not wanting in London, for he was able to relish the company of Paul Brunton,[96] a journalist turned Yogi, and every Wednesday afternoon he met A. R. Orage for long discussions on literature and Indian philosophy. By the time that Orage died early in November 1934, he felt that he had come to understand him deeply for the first time, and that his finest wisdom had eluded his pen.[97] Philip Mairet, a friend of Orage, tried to bring AE and T. S. Eliot together; both men were looking forward to the meeting, but owing to an error over a telephone message it never took place.[98]

On 3 October, *The Avatars* was published by Macmillan, who commissioned AE shortly after to write the memoirs he had already begun. He had come to London intending to work on these, but he made little progress as the abundance of company left him less time for thought than he had anticipated.[99]

In *The Avatars: a Futurist Fantasy,* AE seeks to recapture the excitement, the romance, and the faith of the summer of 1896 when he and his friends had prepared for the coming of a great Incarnation. Realising that he cannot now relive even in imagination the ardour of those months, he mentions in a prefatory note that the friends who shared his interests are dead or far away, and this is reflected in the fact that the major characters are all aspects of himself. The only speaking voice is his own, and much of the text reads like an anthology of passages from his earlier writings. At one point[100] he summarises three poems of 1896 recounting the spiritual adventures of the children Rory and Aileen, whom he introduces as characters; he describes how the band of artists awaiting the Incarnation know one another's thoughts without speech and project images into each other's minds[101] – a memory of the Household; and he incorporates a piece of rhetoric from his pamphlet of 1897 *Priest or Hero?*[102] In this work of fiction the Avatars actually do appear as their counterpart in life had not, but there is a failure to match language to conception and the story makes pleasant rather than compelling reading.

Living in alien surroundings and well aware of the shortcomings of his book, AE was much cheered by letters from friends telling him how much they had enjoyed it. Such comfort was welcome indeed, for despite his pleasures he was at bottom ill at ease in England. 'It is really a dead country,' he wrote to O'Connor, 'but there are very nice people among the dead, and if they were only alive they would be the best people in the world.'[103] He was in no sense settled and was still thinking of visiting his son in America,[104] but he suffered so much from the London heatwave that he virtually gave up the idea of sailing round the world.[105] Often he longed for Sheep Haven, and when F. R. Higgins sent him his latest work he commented: 'Your Cuala book brought back to me the lights and colours and dusks of Ireland, and as I read I was cursing myself that I had not gone to Donegal rather than to this huge city where I spend a great part of my time brooding over little lakes and hills and patches of woods.'[106]

On occasion AE was able to escape from London, and in mid-November, when the fogs were beginning to descend on the city, he remembered his recent pleasure in the wild moorland of Hardy's country and the solitary wooded landscape he had found in Sussex.[107] It may have been at this stage of his residence in the capital that he travelled to Dorset and stayed for three days with A. G. B. Russell, the Lancaster Herald of Arms, with whom he shared an interest in Blake. They exchanged visits with Monk Gibbon, who was delighted to find AE in his best form, telling comic stories of Yeats's proposal to Katharine Tynan and Fitzpatrick's theory that Shakespeare was Christ reborn. When Gibbon remarked how he always managed to irritate the great poet of Ireland, AE exclaimed, 'I can't understand how you annoy Yeats so much. You are the only person in Dublin who argues with him and he ought to be grateful to you!'[108] Serious discussion ranged from arid modern criticism to the Greek Mysteries, and the host afterwards said of AE, referring to the time when he had known him as an immature youth: 'He had shed all that was fantastic and a little unreal in the interval. I realised in a moment or two that I was talking to a very great man.'[109]

At Christmas AE made a brief excursion to Dublin, where he stayed with Seumas O'Sullivan and busied himself seeing Yeats, Higgins, Captain Bowen and other friends before returning to fog-filled London.[110] During a spare hour he wrote a short, kindly preface for a book of poems by Irene Haugh, and in January he undertook a major literary project. In writing the eleventh chapter of *Song and Its Fountains,* he had recalled how often he had reproached himself for abandoning a blank verse narrative on which he had worked from 1899 to 1904, when he had published a fragment of it under the title 'Dana.' After thirty years he now resumed this epic based on his unforgettable vision of the Irish gods ruled by Nuada of the Silver Hand.* At the same time he was writing lyrics, and soon he planned to add them to the longer work to make up yet another collection of verse. By March he had decided that the London atmosphere was depleting his inspiration, and he arranged to put his books and pictures into storage and take a long holiday in Donegal to finish the volume. 'I have had enough of London mists and fogs,' he wrote to Mrs. Porter, 'to satisfy my taste for these things.' Echoing T. S. Eliot's *Hollow Men,* he complained that the people, though kind and friendly, seemed 'As if they were once alive in some real world and had died there and were living on in this the world of the shades and did not know it.' 'Still,' he admitted, 'I am glad I came here for a year as I met many good and new and old friends . . .'[111]

About the end of April, AE left for Donegal, having leased a cottage near Sheep Haven for three months, after which he hoped to return to Dublin. For holiday reading he took *The Secret of the Golden Flower,*[112] a work of Chinese mysticism, and a twelve-volume translation of the *Mahabharata* imported from India, of which he was soon writing excitedly: 'It is marvellous, a whole literature in itself, cosmic myths, two sacred books, endless stories, treatises on government, magic philosophy and the great epic itself.'[113] Seumas O'Sullivan and other friends visited him, and he felt that he was still enjoying a profound communion with the earth.[114] During his holiday he was asked for advice on the composition of the Senate, and his letter to Mrs. Erskine Childers recommending that it should be a body of experts was passed on to de Valera.[115] His other preoccupations did not keep him from his poems and pictures: it was the last time he was to paint.[116]

The talented English poetess Ruth Pitter, whom he had met in London, came to Donegal with her mother and stayed for about a fortnight. The two poets rambled together over the countryside and on the beach, where AE, still wearing his dark city suit, rolled up his trouser legs and hung his boots round his neck to wade among the shellfish. When Miss Pitter began to boil living prawns and shrimps, he reared up in magnificent fury at such cruelty, and bought her some that had already been cooked. One Sunday morning, they were absorbed in making figures out of wet sand until they suddenly noticed that a silent audience had gathered on the cliff and AE hastily fled. He managed to communicate to his guest his own sense of super-nature all about them, and told her that a stockbroker whom he had taken to the Rosses had spontaneously knelt and poured out a confession. Miss Pitter's mother was a dabbler in the

*See p. 96 above.

occult, and when AE set her a psychic exercise she gave her fancy free rein but he was shrewd enough to be politely sceptical. One night soon after the visitors had left, he saw a vision of Miss Pitter moving about among the Donegal rocks.[117]

In mid-June AE had nearly finished his own book of verse, when a copy of Hugh MacDiarmid's *Stony Limits* arrived. He read his friend's poems on the beach one by one, and wrote appreciatively, 'All your scientific things faded out for me but the pure poetry glowed as it had a right to with other elemental things . . .'[118] About this time he was meditating on the sands when a long poem in the form of a monologue by the Dark Lady of Shakespeare's *Sonnets* spontaneously entered his mind. It had been conceived a year before when, as he recorded, 'I had practised a "Yoga" meditation on The Dark Lady and seemed in deep sleep to have been near her soul, a most wonderful experience . . .'[119] but by the next morning it had vanished from his memory. Now, on recovering it, he read the *Sonnets,* in part for the first time, and believed he found evidence to support its thesis.[120]

In mid-July, AE was looking for new accommodation so that he could stay on in Donegal after his lease on the cottage expired at the end of the month, but by the 24th he had changed his plans. Having just agreed to write his memoirs for Macmillan, he was anxious to find city lodgings so that he could take the books he needed out of storage. He spent the first week of August at a hotel in Dublin, where he would have stayed had he been able to secure permanent quarters.[121] Instead he crossed to London and took rooms at 1 Brunswick Square,[122] where he at least had the pleasure of looking out over trees.[123]

AE now settled down to correct the proofs of his forthcoming collection of poems, *The House of the Titans,*[124] and to work on his autobiography to be called *The Sunset of Fantasy.* He described himself in a letter as 'a wanderer between London and Ireland,'[125] though he hoped to return to Dublin permanently when lodgings became available.[126]

A few years before, AE had read Constance Sitwell's *Flowers and Elephants,* an account of travels in India, and had felt a spiritual affinity with the author. Now, meeting her in London, he found himself talking to her as though she were an old friend.[127] In the presence of this sensitive, gracious lady, he shed the burden of age and recovered all the magic of his personality. 'He is the only person I have ever met,' she declares, 'who made one feel ready to give up all one possessed and follow him everywhere, should he have demanded it.'[128] An invitation to visit her at her home in Northumberland now offered him the chance of a holiday from

London, and he arrived at Barmoor Castle, Lowick, on 8 October. It took him about a day to cast off the fetters of the city atmosphere and radiate his natural merriment and joy. He spent the mornings drawing and smoking by himself in a clump of trees, and in the afternoons Mrs. Sitwell drove him to the coast and round the countryside. She remembered 'the great happy being' he was on an excursion to Norham on the Tweed, where he rapidly sketched the castle, and he especially loved the vast, lonely moors, observing how they resembled those of Donegal. Some stones with ancient markings caught his attention, but he said he had not time to psychometrize them. In the evenings he made up conversations in which Cuchulain and St. Patrick traded insults, and laughed delightedly over memories of his Dublin friends. One of his jokes involved 'his plan of chaining each American to a separate rock till they began to delve down to their own centres.' Mrs. Sitwell writes of his anxiety to be punctual and give no one any trouble, and, on another level, of 'his rich rolling Irish voice, and the sense he gave of going deeper and further and more truthfully into life than anyone else, and being, indeed, built on a different scale to the rest of us.' Describing how they walked on the shore on his last day, she records:

> . . . there was a bank of violet cloud, deep in colour, lying over the sea with a line of the clearest lemon light along the horizon above the green water. He seemed possessed by joy, and said it was the most beautiful colour he had seen out of Ireland. We walked along the shore talking; I never knew anyone who gave me the feeling of such deep happiness, golden wells of it seemed to be springing up.

He returned to London on the 13th, having told his hostess: 'I can't teach you anything, because you have it in yourself; otherwise one wouldn't recognise or learn.'[129]

Six days later, *The House of the Titans and Other Poems* was published. In this, AE's last collection, the blank verse he already favoured in *Vale* is dominant. Most ambitiously, he employs the measure in the title poem, a short epic whose hero, Nuada, is the deified human will. In versifying the story outlined in *Song and Its Fountains,* he tries to exploit such devices as the formal heroic speech and the beginning *in medias res* of classical epic, and to imitate the luminous images gleaming in the darkness of Milton's Hell, as well as to incorporate his knowledge of Celtic and Greek mythology, Indian philosophy, and the cruel Druidism of Blake's prophetic books. Writing of the gods who made the Promethean and Christ-like sacrifice to redeem the fallen world and succumbed to its temptations, he constructs a rapid enough narrative moving from the spiritual oblivion of the present to the forgotten glories of the past and the vain descent into the darkness. To make clear the cosmic dimensions of his myth, AE looks back (without introducing Indian names) to the dawn of Brahma's Day and forward to its evening when all things will be redeemed. However, as he had anticipated in *Song and Its Fountains,* he failed to raise his idiom to an heroic level: the language ranges from the mild pedestrianism of

> It was so very long ago
> It might be but a dream, and thus it ran . . .

to the poetic triteness of

> With sheeny silver, lustrous pearl, pale gold . . .

Moreover, to those unfamiliar with AE's other works much in 'The House of the Titans' must remain unintelligible. Like *The Avatars,* it recapitulates doctrines presented in his earlier writings, and repeats the very words of such pieces as 'The Man to the Angel' and the story 'The Dream of Angus Oge.'

Next to 'The House of the Titans' in length is 'The Dark Lady,' a Browningesque monologue stripped of a convincing concrete setting. 'I loathe Freud,' AE writes in connection with this poem. 'I hate the homosexual . . .'[130] Ignoring such evidence as that of Sonnet 20, which implies that Shakespeare, however infatuated, was not in fact an invert, he allows the lady to tell how she became the mistress both of the poet and the Friend in order to ward them off from 'an unnatural love, The kind that marred the Grecian genius . . .' Though a certain intensity enters her tale, AE is not able to imbue his blank verse with the emotional violence of passion. He handles the form more successfully in 'Wood Ways,' a succinct account of a visionary experience of nature, which moves from concept to concept with satisfying speed. In this poem typical images like 'The air, A flying girl, flame-limbed' are effectively juxtaposed with such straightforward expressions as 'O, the hyacinths!' and 'On moss I lie,' and the worn-out 'Magician of the Beautiful' becomes 'the laughing king, the magic-maker.'

The shorter poems are much concerned with the theme of age. A number of graceful but very slight lyrics record the author's struggle to retain or recapture his ecstatic youthful communion with nature. The jogging octameter couplets of 'The River,' more appropriate to a ballad, fail to render the intensity of a moment of identity with the Spirit, but there is unusual force in the soul's bitter rebuke to the body that plaintively laments its own decay in 'Two Voices.' In 'Growth,' AE interestingly announces his belief that in his next incarnation he will not again experience the joys of 'The arts that once were sweet,' for he has developed spiritually beyond them. The finest poem in the book, however, is the last. Entitled 'A Farewell,' this brief lyric, serene, simple, and yet subtle, distinguishes between the poet's superficial intellectual ignorance and his deep spiritual awareness of his destiny after death:

> I look on wood and hill and sky,
> Yet without any tears
> To the warm earth I bid good-bye
> For what unnumbered years.
>
> So many times my spirit went
> This dark transfiguring way,
> Nor ever knew what dying meant,
> Deep night or a new day.
>
> So many times it went and came,
> Deeper than thought it knows
> Unto what majesty of flame
> In what wide heaven it goes.

About this time AE heard Sir Oswald Mosley shouted down in Hyde Park,[131] and during November, while hampered by a severe cold, he wrote a foreword for Joseph O'Neill's novel *Land Under England*,[132] in which he attacked Nazism, analysing the spiritual temptation to surrender one's freewill to an adored leader. Early in the month, Orage died, making London even less congenial, and he wrote to O'Neill that he wished he were lying naked on the desert sand of Arizona or New Mexico.[133] He had begun to plan his return to Dublin[134] when he received a series of cables from the ailing Mrs. Mary Rumsey asking him to travel to Washington, D.C., as her guest to give advice on rural reorganisation. Torn between a sense of obligation and a deep reluctance to undertake such a demanding task, he left it to Judge Campbell to decide whether he could really be of use. 'Remember,' he warned him, 'I am four years older and out of harness, not yet senile, but at best "a come-back" who are generally a failure in pugilism, if not in politics or economics.'[135] While the decision was still pending, he lunched with Paul Brunton and Monk Gibbon, and the latter noticed how the air of melancholy and diffidence which had descended on him only lifted after they became absorbed in talk.[136] Eventually he consented to go, consoling himself with the thought of resuming permanent residence in Ireland on his return if he could find rooms he could afford in Dublin.[137]

On 13 December, he sailed from Southampton on the *Aurania*, and during the voyage he enjoyed meeting a variety of fellow passengers, especially an aerial photographer who told intriguing stories of geological discoveries he had made while working over the wilds of Canada. Being immune to sea sickness, AE was not troubled when a violent storm arose, but was able to enjoy the sublimity of the ocean in a typically romantic spirit. The *Aurania* eventually had to change course to join other liners going to the rescue of a foundering Scandinavian ship, and he was an onlooker at the bizarre night-time scene where the stricken vessel sank under the play of searchlights.[138] After disembarking at Halifax, Nova Scotia, he reached New York on the 27th and was shocked to learn that Mrs. Rumsey, to whom he was much attached, had died while he was at sea.[139]

AE's return to the United States came two years after Franklin Roosevelt had assumed the Presidency at the height of the depression pledged to push through his New Deal. About twenty million unemployed were said to be on relief, and politicians and officials were desperately seeking economic medicines. In his own eyes, AE was a tired and largely worn out man, but stimulated by America and his American friends, he became again the great bearded prophet casting his spell on officials and administrators, and imbuing them with his own faith that their work had a place in the divine plan for the universe. In New York, Judge Campbell spoke to him of Roosevelt's programme and gradually restored his confidence in his ability to do what was required. 'I soon found,' Campbell observed, '. . . that his mind had lost none of its sweep and that he was as mentally and physically alive and vigorous as ever.'[140]

After a few days, AE went on to Washington, where he addressed groups of eager listeners daily and worked up so much enthusiasm that the demand for conferences with him grew, and he felt inclined to accede to a request from M. L. Wilson, Under Secretary of Agriculture, that he should remain in America for a few months. He lunched with President Roosevelt on 5 January, 1935, and two days later reported to Campbell, 'He seems a creature of abundant energy of mind unoppressed by the load of responsibility, bearing it as Atlas bore the world in the myth.'[141] The leading figure AE most admired was, however, his friend Henry Wallace, now Secretary of Agriculture, whom he described as 'the strong man of the administration, a man with depths below depths in him,'[142] and he took especial pride in having picked him out five years before as having 'the best mind in the States.'[143]

A few days after his lunch with Roosevelt, AE left for Chicago to visit his son and to meet his daughter-in-law for the first time. Reading two of Wallace's recent books on the train, he was delighted to find him 'tracing back to spiritual fountains the economic and political movements,' and he wrote:

> I see some of that universalism or planetary consciousness in you which I think I told you was to be the root idea in the Spenglerian sense in this country and your wish for a religious mood which would embrace Buddhists, Christians and the rest is an expression of that planetary consciousness coming out in thought . . .[144]

AE's reunion with his son delighted him. 'I . . . found him well,' he reported happily, 'with an enchanting American girl, his wife, who looks like a fairy princess and is as kind and good and natural as she could be.'[145]

On the 18th, he returned to Washington and was given accommodation at the Cosmos Club, where he felt at home among the artists, authors, economists, and administrators who constituted most of the membership.[146] Though full of admiration for the ministers who were trying to implement the New Deal, he felt uncertain whether their efforts would avert revolution.[147] 'The Americans,' he nevertheless wrote to Higgins early in February, 'are reeking with suppressed idealism, starved for beauty and if they had a great writer with the vision of Emerson and more of an open appeal he could revolutionise their culture.' In the same letter he described his activities:

> I am having a very exciting time over here meeting groups of officials in the departments dealing with rural life and trying to bring about a unity of policy between them relating to the farmer. They are very human beings these scientists and economists and officials, and my simplifications of their problems are I believe appreciated.[148]

AE had been asked to visit the Indians of New Mexico and Arizona to advise them on forming co-operatives. Certain officials believed that as a fellow pantheist he would understand their minds, and he wrote enthusiastically to Higgins of their 'Earth worship which is lost among the whites except in a few people like Emerson, Thoreau or Whitman occasionally.'[149] Doubtless he remembered Pryse's experiences among American Indians when he declared to O'Neill: '. . . my age cries out against it while something in me longs for the adventure as the most romantic in my life.'[150] During February, however, he found that his energy was seeping away, and dreading illness in a strange and expensive city[151] he decided to return home in haste to finish his memoirs. When it became clear that he was suffering from a serious intestinal ailment, he resolved to go to London in the first instance to be treated by his friend Dr. Hector Munro.[152] Before leaving Washington, he called on the Albanian Minister, Faik Konitza, for a brief visit, but was so intrigued to find that an

Albanian had read the *Irish Statesman* that he stayed more than two hours. When offered a sherry, he asked for 'the national drink of America' and explained that he meant iced water, the refreshment enjoyed by all classes.[153]

AE spent his last few days in the United States in New York, where he saw a good deal of Judge Campbell to whom he expounded his views on the country's future. He maintained that for the average American who was not an intellectual, Christianity formed the sole and indispensable contact with spiritual reality, and, wrote the Judge, 'he agreed entirely with the economist who said the other day that it was a national calamity to lose faith in the immortality of the soul.'[154] AE spoke also of the best method of funding relief expenditures and of the movement from the eighteenth century, a period of ideas, to the current age of power dominated by the conception of the state stemming from Fichte and Hegel.

Campbell, Wilson, and Wallace wished AE to return within a few months: despite the sickness ticking away his life like a time bomb, he had made an overwhelming impression. Louis Taber, an officer of the National Grange from Columbus, Ohio, claimed: 'George Russell's story of agricultural organization in Ireland, which combined matter and spirit, reads like a chapter from the Old Testament.'[155] The Commissioner for Indian Affairs, John Collier, wrote in a parallel vein:

> Not in our race, but in another race, I have known men like George Russell. Two aged Ute Indians visited me recently. Utterly released, utterly aware, they sat; time did not control them, they controlled time. They discussed heavy and dubious tribal concerns, but merriment was at the verge, and often it broke into laughter. They moved in a tide that was more than their personal beings and they drew me into the tide, and all last night the tide flowed on.
>
> . . . [AE and I] talked about Indians a good deal. AE knew all they represented.[156]

On 1 March, AE sailed back from New York on the vessel that had carried him out two and a half months earlier. Before she left the harbour, he met Fred Henderson, who was to be his constant companion during the thirteen days of storm-filled voyage to London. Although AE was suffering quite severely,[157] their discussions ranged over a vast field, and Henderson was astonished by his companion's serene and confident optimism in the future of humanity, an optimism 'based on a profound philosophy and knowledge of the deeper things stirring in the world's life "under the measureless grossness and the slag." ' Referring to 'the elemental natural movement of wild sea and sky which he loved,' Henderson mused after AE's death:

I wonder whether if now he knows the word which we spent an hour trying to discover one afternoon when a great sunburst, with a hundred shafts of light moving with the movement of the scattering clouds, turned the welter of the mountainous seas into a wild glory, and we flung line after attempted line at one another in the effort to picture it and express its movement, and found it inexpressible.[158]

Arriving in England on the 13th,[159] he returned to London, took new lodgings at 14 Tavistock Place, and hastened to consult his doctor, who diagnosed colitis. Ordered to stay indoors, except for brief walks, and to take only milk, junket, barley water and other unsubstantial foods, he felt enervated and bored and was constantly shivering. He had changed in appearance, having reverted to the thinness of his youth. In letter after letter he complained of his insipid diet and he was quite unable to continue his book,[160] though for a while he found some consolation in the belief that he would recover in a few months and return to Ireland. He even asked Mrs. Hugh Law to book accommodation for him near Sheep Haven.[161]

Long, listless hours were relieved by visits from friends, during which his old self seemed to come to life again. He wrote many letters, referring constantly to his longing for Donegal, and during March he prepared his *Selected Poems* for Macmillan. As his books were still in storage, he had to ask Charles Weekes for copies of *Homeward* and *The Earth Breath*. 'If I should be remembered,' he wrote in a miniature preface, 'I would like it to be for the verses in this book,' and he dedicated the selection to his daughter-in-law, who had so delighted him in Chicago. He requested the publisher to have the new volume 'bound in dark blue which is my colour.'[162] This hue, the colour of the god Mananan whom AE believed to be the Celtic Logos, stands in Theosophy for concentrated abstract thought – thought refined and exalted to the point at which it can apprehend the highest realities. In poetic language, this is sometimes represented by a deep blue, star-irradiated sky, a symbol which appears in *The Avatars*.[163]

Early in April, Gibbon called on AE and heard him talk with all his old enthusiasm. 'Look at Monk Gibbon,' he said. 'He smells of the sun and the soil and wild places.'[164] Constance Sitwell was with him on one of her frequent visits. She used to marvel at the way his talk conjured up scenes of beauty in that 'colourless, rather dark, room with its faded walls and ugly furniture.' He spoke to her of his past lives, of Pryse's teachings, which had supported him all his life and were doing so even now, of Rhine's experiments in parapsychology at Duke University, and of the exciting adventure of death. 'Metaphysics,' he said, 'is just organised common-sense, after all . . . nothing makes a whole except from a metaphysical standpoint.' To Mrs. Sitwell, 'his thought seemed so luminous, so deep, that it was as though one's ordinary dense mind was dissolved and beyond them [*sic*] shone a profounder mode of being . . .'[165]

One night AE was well enough to dine out, together with Dr. Munro, at the home of his friend Mrs. Alexander Whyte. Here he met C. F. Andrews, the English missionary who was the intimate companion of Tagore and Mahatma Gandhi, and who had so absorbed the tolerance of India that he had come to appreciate both the riches of Hinduism and the worth of Christian churches other than his own. Relaxing in the luxury of so much company, AE talked for hours telling humorous stories and ranging over many topics. Andrews noticed that though he mispronounced the terms of Indian philosophy, he had a remarkable insight into their significance, and he remembered him as 'a great and noble personality who had retained the heart of a child in his old age.'[166]

In mid-April, F. R. Higgins wrote that Yeats was in London, but AE replied: 'I have not come across him nor do I really want to see him. He and I have known each other so long that we have nothing new to say to each other and are bored internally when we meet.'[167] Towards the end of the month he seemed to be recovering and found himself able to sleep well. He watched the preparations for King George V's Jubilee and observed, 'But royalty does mean something over here.'[168]

When more weeks passed without his hopes of recovery being realised, he consulted a specialist, who prescribed another form of treatment. On 30 May, Daniel Dunlop died, but after the loss of so many old friends and of his wife, AE was no longer able to grieve deeply.[169] Feeling that his own end was approaching, on 14 June he made his will.

On 21 June, accompanied by Charles Weekes and Hector Munro, he travelled on the railway to Bournemouth to spend a fortnight at a nursing home named 'Havenhurst.' It proved to be most beautiful, and he sat in a deck chair under the shade of trees within sight of the sea gleaming in the sunshine. Even in his sickness he was loth to make work for others by staying in bed for breakfast. He rejoiced to renew his acquaintance with John Eglinton, and other friends arrived to visit him, including the young poetess Miss Pamela Travers, who appointed herself his devoted nurse. He still enjoyed reciting poetry and talking of Ireland and spiritual topics; when he was asked, 'What will be the next form of religion?' he replied, 'A religion of ethics.'[170] The news that the Irish Academy had awarded him the Gregory Medal gave him keen pleasure, and in a last letter to his son he suggested that Monk Gibbon take up his old project of editing a selection of his contributions to the *Irish Statesman*.[171]

At the beginning of July, AE's doctor advised him to remain in Bournemouth.[172] By the 5th, though the physicians told him otherwise, his intuition warned him that he was dying, and he wrote to Judge Campbell:

> I feel that I am coming to the end of my work in this world and I have no fears or regrets . . . I lie and doze or sleep on a couch nearly all day long. So you will understand, dear Dick, that I cannot write long or lively letters and have the feeling that the world is receding from me [–] the world where I had so many good friends and which I once thought in my vanity I could move in the direction of the heavenly city.[173]

Eglinton wrote to Yeats of AE's condition,[174] and every day the latter asked anxiously whether his oldest friend had replied, but no answer came.[175] On the 9th his doctors confided to him that his disease was not colitis but cancer and that he had only about a year to live, and his serenity in the face of this announcement made the surgeon, a stranger to him, break down.[176] 'Don't think I feel anything melancholy,' he observed, passing the news on to James Stephens. 'I hold to the spiritual verities I have believed all my life and indeed would be glad and more cheerful if my time was shorter.'[177] He consented to have an abdominal operation to ease his suffering, and next day, after the arrival of Dr. Munro, it was performed at Stagsden Nursing Home in Bournemouth, where he remained. On the 11th, he dictated to his nurse a letter to F. R. Higgins asking him to telephone Yeats.[178] Still there was silence. Four days later, having had his best night's sleep since the operation, he summoned up enough energy to dictate to Pamela Travers a series of brief farewell letters.[179] To Higgins he wished a long and successful life as a poet and entrusted a last message for Frank O'Connor.[180] Wallace he addressed as a kindred soul:

> To you, dear Henry, as to myself, death does not make much matter. There is an eternal pilgrimage and a return and we understand each other.[181]

Turning to his long co-operative labours, he asked Eleanor Skipworth of the I.A.O.S.: 'Will you say goodbye for me to all my dear friends of Plunkett House. I look back upon my years spent with them as the best years of my life.'[182]

Next day Constantine Curran arrived with the news that the Irish Academy intended to recommend him for the Nobel prize for literature. 'I mentioned some dates,' writes Mr. Curran, 'and he smilingly said it would be of little use to a dead man.'[183] His mind was greatly eased when Yeats finally sent a telegram on the 17th, a day when Weekes and other friends were present. In the afternoon Gogarty arrived. 'I was very fortunate,' noted the latter,

> in finding that Russell had a moment's consciousness a few hours before his death. He recognised me and said, 'How delightful of you to come.' I asked him if he were in pain, and if he were breathing easily. He said, 'Yes, I am not in pain.' I brought him messages of affection from friends in Ireland. He said very calmly and slowly, 'I have realized all my ambitions. I have had an astounding interest in life. I have great friends. What more can a man want?'[184]

Gogarty was irresistibly reminded of the death of Socrates:

> His calm fortitude, his lovableness, made even his surgeon, whose skill must defend itself against sentimentality, turn away for a moment in tears . . . His friends were broken-hearted, but he was unmoved. The change in his countenance was remarkable, and the way the mind threw off the veils of death to deepen the great blue light in the eyes as he rejoiced at seeing for a moment a friend's face was something to impress the memory for ever. The hero in the man looked out, and it was his friends who had to brace themselves against life with its loss.[185]

The events of these hours were described next day in a letter by Miss Travers:

> Yesterday he slept most of the time and after being given morphia was partly unconscious. But, as usual, at the service of his friends, he woke up about four o'clock and was able to see Senator Gogarty, an old friend who had rushed over hoping to be in time. He was delighted to see him and spoke calmly and happily for a few minutes, asked for a drink and even was able to move his pillow into a more comfortable position. He slept after that and did not wake. About eleven o'clock last night he fell into a deep calm even sleep and soon after that he died. The night was very clear and luminous; the full moon, that always affected him so strongly, shining over the sea and up in a lofty sky the planets bright and large. Just the kind of night he would have wished for his setting out.
>
> He was very beautiful in death. The grey of his beard golded and his face light and clear and uplifted as though in greeting.[186]

Next morning, while AE's body was still at the Stagsden Nursing Home, Mr. Sean O'Sullivan called to make three sketches of his face. As he worked, the artist was assailed by an overwhelming sense of some strange vitality present in the room, and although it was cool he perspired freely. The circumstance was unique in his experience.[187]

During the day Mlle. Téry, unsummoned but alerted by a premonition, arrived from France to be told by Mr. Curran that she had come too late. On the 19th, James Stephens and other friends accompanied the coffin back to Ireland, and when the ferry reached Dublin Bay, three aeroplanes swooped down in a formal salute organised by Lady Heath. For a day the flower-draped coffin stood in the hallway of Plunkett House, where mourners gathered to pay their last respects while Yeats insisted on sitting in a room by himself, brooding in solitary dejection.[188] To add to his despondency, a fanatical woman nationalist wanted to cover the coffin with the Irish tricolour, and the responsibility for preventing this fell on him.[189] The funeral took place on Saturday the 20th. Starting from the stately Georgian House in Merrion Square, the procession passed through the suburb of Rathmines to Mount Jerome Cemetery; it was described in the *Irish Times* as more than a mile long. AE's elder son, Mr. Brian Russell, was the leading mourner, and Yeats emerged from his lonely gloom to follow the hearse with upright bearing into the cemetery.[190] AE's old political foe Mr. de Valera was magnanimous enough to attend, and he and his rival Cosgrave stood side by side.[191] The Rev. C. C. Duggan read the burial service of the Church of Ireland adding as a well deserved tribute the first fifteen verses of the forty-fourth chapter of Ecclesiasticus:

> Let us now praise famous men, and our fathers that begat us. The Lord hath wrought great glory by them through his great power from the beginning. Such as did bear rule in their kingdoms, men renowned for their power, giving counsel by their understanding, and declaring prophecies . . . Such as found out musical tunes, and recited verses in writing . . . The people will tell of their wisdom, and the congregation will show forth their praise.

Standing by the graveside in front of Yeats and opposite de Valera, Frank O'Connor delivered a final oration. Rather awkwardly, he tried to adopt the viewpoint of the man he had loved and misunderstood:

> The greatest service AE did for Ireland was to help in the creation of new modes of life, to stand apart as the symbol of a more complex and comprehensive existence, to represent through a lifetime the Ireland in the heart, the empire in the womb of time.[192]

A woman obviously of modest means placed an extravagant offering of flowers on the grave. She had been a servant in his household during the early days of his marriage and had 'got into trouble,' but instead of being turned away had been cared for. On being questioned about the costliness of her gift, she declared: 'I would have died for him.'[193]

Of the men who struggled to create an Irish state and civilisation in the early decades of the century, the nation now mourned not the greatest but the best. An editorial in the *Irish Times* proclaimed:

> . . . his views on religion hardly would be acceptable to any of the Churches. Yet, if ever Ireland bred a man whose life exemplified the teachings of the Sermon on the Mount, that man was A.E.[194]

In private, Mrs. Yeats told her husband: 'AE was the nearest to a saint you or I will ever meet. You are a better poet but no saint.'[195] In tribute to his dead friend, the unsaintly poet served as President of the A.E. Memorial Committee, which sought to perpetuate AE's service to Irish literature by offering prizes to native writers beneath the age of thirty-five. John Eglinton tried to erect a small monument of his own by compiling his *Memoir of AE,* but though it preserved much valuable information it was marred by a patronising tone. With a truer appreciation of the man, Dr. Gibbon compiled *The Living Torch,* an anthology of long and short extracts from his prose writings in the *Irish Statesman* and elsewhere. Ranging over nearly the whole field of his interests, this volume is so skilfully edited that it may be regarded as AE's literary masterpiece.

AE's achievements during a life of sixty-eight years were many and various. They embraced a career of service to Ireland and her farmers, the blueprint of the co-operative parish as a modern equivalent to the pre-industrial village, the fostering of generations of Irish writers and of an Irish theatre, a handful of fine poems, a moving record of mystical experiences, the vigorous and flexible prose of his periodical writing, and the creation of a personality of rare perfection that won the devotion of friends and disciples. Above all, AE was a spiritual genius, and though the genius was flawed and incomplete, he found the razor's edge of that love which is all but universal yet mysteriously does not exclude ardent affection for individuals. Even in the sickness and disappointment of age, the storms that racked the surface of his mind never subdued for long the radiance of the underlying spirit, and at the end he faced death with awe and excitement as a crowning adventure.

In the present state of human knowledge, it is impossible to make a definitive pronouncement on the nature of the mysticism that made AE the man he was, but those who cannot accept the Theosophy in which he believed may consider two alternatives. From childhood to old age his outlook on life was moulded by the romantic bent of his imagination. His love for the heroes of boys' stories was succeeded by a lifelong fascination with Dumas' musketeers, and his idealising of O'Grady's rough warriors led him to seek their civilised counterparts among his contemporaries. The airships of his visions filled him with longing for a remote and beautiful past, and when he saw in 1910 the graceful flight of modern aeroplanes he acclaimed them as 'the lordliest thing . . . Ireland has seen since the days of the Tuatha de Danaan.'[196] Eight years later, having spent an afternoon with a distinguished scientist learning how the bacteria that plagued dairy products could be traced to their lair, he wrote delightedly of this Sherlock Holmes of the laboratory and the exquisite pleasure he found in his detective quest.[197] Only a few weeks before his death, he astonishingly praised *The Secret Doctrine* as, on its lowest level, one of the most exciting romances of modern times[198] – so intense was his joy in studying Madame Blavatsky's crabbed exposition of the underlying unity of all religions. Exploring this aspect of his mind, Professor Howarth has shown in *The Irish Writers* how he never abandoned his quest for an avatar, a great man who would lead a whole people forward to a new destiny. If the imaginative impulse is regarded as the fundamental element in his character, it is possible to see him as a romantic with an idealised conception of man, a conception sustained by hallucinatory visions and by the Theosophy which enabled him, despite the modern fragmentation of the pre-scientific world-view, to see economics, politics, arts, sciences, and domestic life as parts of a gigantic whole. With the recent publication of C. G. Jung's autobiography, however, another and a more elevated interpretation of his character has become possible.

When Jung, in old age, collaborated with an editor to produce *Memories, Dreams, Reflections,* he insisted that it be excluded from his *Collected Works* since he did not regard it as a scientific book. In the light of this volume, nevertheless, it may be claimed that for the first time some of the classical mystical experiences have been undergone in their full intensity by a man whose scientific commitment was such that he was in some moods able to stand back in his detachment and question their objective reality. AE, who complained that psychologists tried to analyse mental phenomena alien to their own minds,[199] would have welcomed the autobiography with intellectual delight. Like the Irish seer, Jung sensed in early youth the presence of an unknown, aged self within him, and encountered mental images which he was certain were not of his own creation. In later years, he saw several visions and was impelled by an inner urge to write fantasies, to paint, and to carve stone. Eventually, as an old man, he sometimes felt that he was himself present in the natural objects that surrounded him. He had, too, psychic experiences involving telepathy, a vision of a scene from the past, and the projection of mental energy to split furniture, break metal, and ring bells. Once, in Ravenna, he and a friend examined with deep interest ancient mosaics on the wall of a church; he afterwards found that the mosaics did not exist and concluded that, though visible to his companion, they had been projected by his unconscious mind. While he regarded his personal convictions as irrelevant to his scientific work, he came to believe in the possibility of an afterlife, of a metaphysical reality underlying the psyche, and of a region of the unconscious functioning outside the limits of time and space. His psychology includes the theory that what a man normally thinks of as himself, his limited consciousness with the 'ego' as its centre, may through the stupendous though prosaically named process of individuation be transcended and superseded by the totality of the conscious and unconscious welded into a single entity of which the 'self' is both the centre and the whole: this presents an exact parallel to the fundamental assumption of mysticism, the existence of a higher self to be realised by the sacrifice of the egocentric natural man. Should Jung's beliefs be valid, it would seem probable that AE's visions – occasionally seen by others – were projections from his own psyche, that his mystical exploration was a descent into the unconscious, and that his spiritual search was at least in part the quest for individuation. Such an account leaves fundamental philosophical questions untouched: Jung's statement that the very term 'the unconscious' is a confession of our ignorance points towards that Upanishadic pursuit of truth which inspired AE's life.

NOTES

Chapter One

1. Allan Wade, ed. *The Letters of W. B. Yeats* (London, 1954), p. 477 (henceforward referred to as Yeats, *Letters*).
2. Monk Gibbon, 'The Childhood and Early Youth of AE,' *Dublin Magazine*, XXXI (April and July 1955), pp. 6-14 and 8-17.
3. 'Childhood and Early Youth,' I, pp. 9–10.
4. Unp. ltr. to Lady Gregory, 16 June 1902.
5. N.W., *Irish Homestead*, 15 October 1910, p. 849 (henceforward referred to as *I.H.*).
6. 'The Folk Mind in Politics,' *Irish Statesman*, 21 July 1928, pp. 385–6 (henceforward referred to as *I.S.*).
7. John Eglinton, *A Memoir of AE: George William Russell* (London, 1937), pp. 2–3 (henceforward referred to as *Memoir*).
8. Charles-Marie Garnier, 'Tagore et George Russell (A.E.),' *Revue Anglo-Américaine*, VII (December 1929), pp. 97–112.
9. National Library of Ireland Ms. 9967–69, 'Letters from George William Russell (AE), Selected, Transcribed and Edited by Alan Denson.' Mr. Denson's permission should be obtained before application is made to examine it. Henceforward referred to as D. Ms. This abbreviation is followed by the number of the letter, the name of the addressee, and the date – here 358, to John Quinn, 12 March 1920.
10. C. C. Coates, *Some Less-known Chapters in the Life of A.E. (George Russell)* (Dublin: privately printed, 1939), p. 3.
11. Unp. ltr. to Mrs. James Stephens, n.d.
12. N.W., *I.H.*, 9 December 1905, p.885.
13. N.W., *I.H.*, 8 May 1909, p. 370.
14. N.W., *I.H.*, 10 October 1908, p. 816.
15. A.E., *Song and Its Fountains* (London, 1932), pp. 3–4 (henceforward referred to as *Song and Its Fountains*); Sean O Faolain, 'The Humanity of AE,' *Inisfail*, I (March 1933), pp. 38–43.
16. *Song and Its Fountains*, pp. 7–8.
17. Partly unp. ltr. to Frank Harris, 12 July 1921.

18. Alan Denson, ed. *Letters from AE* (London, New York, and Toronto, 1961), p. 277 (henceforward referred to as *Letters*).
19. *Memoir*, p. 4.
20. George Moore, *Ave* reissued (London, 1947), p. 121; *Song and Its Fountains*, p. 90.
21. *Song and Its Fountains*, p. 5.
22. Katharine Tynan, *Twenty-five Years: Reminiscences* (London 1913), p. 248; Gibbon, 'Childhood and Early Youth,' I, p. 13.
23. A.E., *The Living Torch* (London, 1937), p. 45 (henceforward referred to as *Living Torch*); *Memoir*, p. 7.
24. Hugh MacDiarmid, *At the Sign of the Thistle* (London, 1934), p. 101.
25. Partly unp. ltr. to Frank Harris, 12 July 1921.
26. Darrell Figgis, *AE (George W. Russell): a Study of a Man and a Nation* (Dublin and London, 1916), p. 12.
27. Partly unp. ltr. to Frank Harris, 12 July 1921.
28. Alan Denson, *Printed Writings by George W. Russell (AE): a Bibliography* (Evanston, Illinois, 1961), pp. 198–199 (henceforward referred to as *Bibliography*); Gibbon, 'Childhood and Early Youth,' II, pp. 10–11.
29. Partly unp. ltr. to E.H.W. Meyerstein, 7 Feb. 1920; unp. ltr to James Pryse, 3 June 1925; Shaemas O'Sheel, 'AE – Poet and Irishman,' *Commonweal*, VII (22 Feb. 1928), pp. 1092–93.
30. 'Childhood and Early Youth,' II, p. 10.
31. *Memoir*, p.6.
32. Gibbon, 'Childhood and Early Youth,' II, pp. 13–16.
33. *Song and Its Fountains*, p. 15.
34. Lucy Kingsley Porter, ed. *AE's Letters to Mínanlábáin* (New York, 1937), p. 44 (henceforward referred to as Porter, ed. *Mínanlábáin*).
35. N.W., *I.H.*, 21 November 1908, p. 951.
36. L.A., *I.H.*, 16 January 1909, p. 41.
37. N.W., *I.H.*, 31 May 1919, p. 387.
38. *Memoir*, p. 9.
39. A.E., *The Candle of Vision* (London, 1918), p. 74 (henceforward referred to as *Candle of Vision*).
40. 'The Secret Tradition in Alchemy,' *I.S.*, 7 August 1926, pp. 609–610.
41. *Memoir*, p. 10.
42. D. Ms. 1–11 and 15–18.
43. *Letters*, p. 278.
44. Unp. ltr. to F. R. Higgins, 30 March 1935.
45. Partly unp. ltr. to Frank Harris, 12 July 1921. Cf. *Memoir*, pp. 60–61.

46. *Memoir,* pp. 264–265; Monk Gibbon, 'AE. The Years of Mystery,' *Dublin Magazine,* XXXI (January 1956), pp. 8–21.
47. D. Ms. 14, [July 1890].
48. D. Ms. 10, to Carrie Rea, [December 1887 or early 1888].
49. D. Ms. 7, to Carrie Rea, [summer 1887].
50. Richard Ellmann, *Yeats: the Man and the Masks* (London, 1949), p. 32; Kathleen M. O'Brennan, ' "AE" At Home and in the Art Gallery,' *Irish Packet,* VIII (7 September 1907), pp. 713-714.
51. Unp. draft of AE's 'The Sunset of Fantasy' (henceforward referred to as Draft of 'Sunset'); Monk Gibbon's unp. thesis 'The Early Years of George Russell (AE) and his Connection with the Theosophical Movement' (Dublin, 1947–1948), pp. 66-67 (henceforward referred to as Gibbon, 'Thesis').
52. Joseph Hone, *W. B. Yeats 1865–1939,* 2nd ed. (London, 1962), p. 43ff.
53. *Song and Its Fountains,* pp. 9-11.
54. Gibbon, 'Years of Mystery,' p. 15.
55. J. B. Yeats, *Letters to His Son W. B. Yeats and Others 1869–1922* (New York, 1946), pp. 232-233.
56. Katharine Tynan, *Twenty-five Years,* p. 248; *Memoir,* p. 10.
57. W. B. Yeats, *Autobiographies* (London, 1955), pp. 80, 240-241.
58. 'The Illustrators of the Sixties,' *I.S.,* 3 November 1928, pp. 171-172; Richard J. Finneran, 'Two Unpublished Letters from AE,' *Papers on Language and Literature,* III (Summer 1967), pp. 220-228.
59. Yeats, *Autobiographies,* p. 468.
60. D. Ms. 6, to Carrie Rea, [September 1887].
61. AE, 'The Sunset of Fantasy,' *Dublin Magazine,* XIII (January 1938), pp. 6-11 (henceforward referred to as 'Sunset of Fantasy').
62. *Report by the Committee of Enquiry into the Work Carried on by the Royal Hibernian Academy, and the Metropolitan School of Art, Dublin,* Parliamentary Papers, Commons, 13 October 1905, para. 1223.
63. *Ibid.,* para. 1243.
64. *Letters,* p. 280; Figgis, *AE,* pp. 16-17; *Candle of Vision,* pp. 4, 73.
65. *Candle of Vision,* p. 4.
66. *Ibid.,* p. 75.
67. *Song and Its Fountains,* pp. 8-9, 15-17, 25.
68. *Candle of Vision,* pp. 5-6.
69. Tynan, *Twenty-five Years,* p. 250.

70. 'A Dublin Literary Coterie,' *Evening Telegraph* (Dublin), 14 January 1888, reproduced Gibbon, 'Thesis,' pp. 392-395.
71. *Living Torch,* p. 12.
72. Gibbon, 'Years of Mystery,' p. 15.
73. Yeats, *Autobiographies,* p. 240; *Song and Its Fountains,* p. 52.
74. D. Ms. 7, to Carrie Rea, [summer 1887].
75. *Candle of Vision,* p. 9. Cf. *Song and Its Fountains,* p. 7, and W. Y. Evans-Wentz, *The Fairy Faith in Celtic Countries* (London, 1911), p. 61. Evans-Wentz's anonymous informant is AE (*Letters,* p. 222 n.1).
76. Gibbon, 'Childhood and Early Youth,' I, p. 10.
77. D. Ms. 3, to Carrie Rea, [December 1886].
78. *Candle of Vision,* pp. 71-75.
79. D. Ms. 7, to Carrie Rea, [summer 1887]. Punctuation amended. Cf. *Candle of Vision,* p. 117, and see Taittiriya Upanishad II.i.3.
80. D. Ms. 2, to Carrie Rea, [early 1887].
81. *Candle of Vision,* pp. 130-131.
82. *Readers and Writers (1917–1921)* (New York, 1922), pp. 103-105.
83. *Candle of Vision,* pp. 16, 117; 'Sunset of Fantasy,' p. 8.
84. Charles Johnston, *From the Upanishads* (Dublin, 1896), pp. vii–xi.
85. *Dublin University Review,* I (July 1885), p. 155.
86. Unp. ltr. to Ernest Boyd, 7 February 1915.
87. *Dublin University Review,* I (August 1885), p. 66.
88. Unp. ltr. to Lady Gregory, 9 May 1900.
89. *Letters,* p. 6. Confirmed A. C. Bose, *Three Mystic Poets* (Kolhapur, 1945), p. 52, and P. G. Bowen, 'AE and Theosophy,' *Aryan Path,* VI (December 1935), pp. 722-726. 'The Speech of the Gods,' *Theosophist*, IX (December 1887), pp. 171-176, is signed by Johnston and Russell; the former but not the latter appends the letters 'F.T.S.' (Fellow of the Theosophical Society) to his name.
90. D. Ms. 6, to Carrie Rea, [September 1887].
91. *Letters,* p. 48.
92. Johnston, *From the Upanishads,* pp. vii-viii.
93. D. Ms. 10, to Carrie Rea, [December 1887 or early 1888].
94. *Ibid.*; D. Ms. 7, to Carrie Rea, [summer 1887].
95. D. Ms. 6, to Carrie Rea, [September 1887].
96. D. Ms. 5, to Carrie Rea, [summer 1887].
97. 'Sunset of Fantasy,' p. 8.
98. 'The Poetry of Philip Francis Little,' *I.S.,* 18 December 1926, pp. 355-356.

99. Draft of 'Sunset.'
100. D. Ms. 4, [late spring or early summer 1887].
101. Yeats, *Letters,* p. 76.
102. N.W., *I.H.,* 13 September 1913, p. 762. Russell quotes I John iv.20.
103. *Letters,* p. 277.
104. Typescript of C. C. Coates, *Some Less-known Chapters.*
105. C. C. Coates, *Some Less-known Chapters,* p. 4.
106. D. Ms. 8, 31 October 1887.
107. D. Ms. 22. [? July 1892].
108. D. Ms. 5, [summer 1887].
109. *Ibid.*
110. D. Ms. 6, [September 1887].
111. D. Ms. 5, [summer 1887].
112. D. Ms. 4, [late spring or early summer 1887].
113. *Candle of Vision,* pp. 67-69.
114. Unp. ltr. to Israel Regardie, 18 August 1932.
115. *Living Torch,* p. 41.
116. Partly unp. ltr. to Frank Harris, 12 July 1921.
117. D. Ms. 3, to Carrie Rea, [December 1886].
118. D. Ms. 2, [early 1887].
119. D. Ms. 3, to Carrie Rea, [December 1886].
120. *Ibid.*
121. *Letters,* p. 5; D. Ms. 5, to Carrie Rea, [summer 1887].
122. D. Ms. 2, to Carrie Rea, [early 1887].
123. D. Ms. 4, [late spring or early summer 1887].
124. D. Ms. 5, to Carrie Rea, [summer 1887].
125. *Ibid.*
126. H. P. Blavatsky, *The Secret Doctrine: The Synthesis of Science, Religion, and Philosophy* (Pasadena, California, 1963), I, pp. 151-152 (henceforward referred to as *Secret Doctrine).*
127. D. Ms. 8, to Carrie Rea, 31 October 1887.
128. There is no absolute proof that the letter in question ('Lodges of Magic,' *Lucifer,* III [15 December 1888], pp. 339-341) is Russell's. It is signed with the initials 'A.E'.
129. D. Ms. 5, to Carrie Rea, [summer 1887].
130. D. Ms. 6, [September 1887].
131. Richard J. Finneran, 'Two Unpublished Letters from AE,' *Papers on Language and Literature,* III (Summer 1967). pp. 220-228.
132. D. Ms. 8, to Carrie Rea, 31 October 1887.
133. D. Ms. 10, [December 1887 or early 1888]. Cf. 'Sunset of Fantasy,' p. 9.

134. *Memoir*, p. 6.
135. *Letters*, p. 4.
136. 1886 not 1887 as stated in Katharine Tynan's *Twenty-five Years* (D. Ms. 3, to Carrie Rea, [December 1886], confirmed by a letter from Mr. Alan Denson to the author, 19 July 1967.)
137. *Letters*, pp. 5-6.
138. Porter, ed. *Mínanlábáin*, p. 54.
139. Yeats, *Letters*, p. 91.
140. D. Ms. 10, to Carrie Rea, [? January 1888]; *Bibliography*, p. 219.
141. D. Ms. 4, to Carrie Rea, [late spring or early summer 1887].
142. H. P. Blavatsky, *Collected Writings 1888–1889* (Madras, 1964), p. xxvi.
143. Monk Gibbon, 'AE and the Early Days of Theosophy in Dublin,' *Dublin Magazine*, XXXIII (July 1957), pp. 25-37.
144. *Living Torch*, p. 12.
145. J. M. Pryse, 'George William Russell, Poet of the Inner Life,' *Canadian Theosophist*, XVI (August 1935), pp. 164-166.
146. P. G. Bowen, 'AE and Theosophy,' *Aryan Path*, VI (December 1935), pp. 722-726.
147. 'Years of Mystery,' p. 18.
148. D. Ms. 5, to Carrie Rea, [summer 1887].
149. *Letters*, p. 28; Yeats, *Letters*, p. 112.
150. Eight years before 1897 according to Lady Gregory's *Seventy Years* (Gerrards Cross 1974), p. 311.
151. W. B. Yeats, 'A Visionary,' *Mythologies* (New York, 1959), pp. 11-14.
152. D. Ms. 14, to Carrie Rea, [August 1890].

Chapter Two

1. Gibbon, 'AE and the Early Days of Theosophy in Dublin,' p. 31.
2. P. 15.
3. James Morgan Pryse, *A New Presentation of the Prometheus Bound of Aischylos* (Los Angeles and London, 1925), p. 3.
4. Lady Gregory, *Seventy Years*, p. 311.
5. James H. Cousins, 'AE: Poet of the Spirit,' *Theosophist*, LVI (September 1935), p. 596.
6. *Letters*, p. 222. AE quotes this essay D. Ms. 19, to Carrie Rea, [? May 1891].
7. D. Ms. 15, to Carrie Rea, [early September 1890].

8. D. Ms. 16, to Carrie Rea, 22 September 1890, and 17, to the same, [? February 1891].
9. *Candle of Vision,* p. 10; R. M. Fox, 'A Great Irishman: Recalling AE,' *Aryan Path,* XXXIII (May 1962), pp. 224-225.
10. D. Ms. 17, to Carrie Rea, [February 1891].
11. *The Middle Years* (Boston and New York, 1917), p. 26.
12. Draft of 'Sunset.'
13. *Candle of Vision,* p. 12; *Memoir,* pp. 14-16, 18; partly unp. ltr. from Mrs. M. F. Talbot to Eglinton, 24 November 1935.
14. Draft of 'Sunset.'
15. Unp. ltr. from AE to William O'Leary Curtis, n.d.
16. N.W., *I.H.,* 11 March 1911, p. 184.
17. Partly unp. ltr. to Frank Harris, 12 July 1921.
18. Draft of 'Sunset.'
19. Gibbon, 'Thesis,' pp. 358-359, quoting H. F. Norman.
20. Draft of 'Sunset.' See Patanjali's *Yoga Aphorisms,* III, 23 (in some editions III, p. 24).
21. *Memoir,* p. 17.
21a. O'Leary Curtis, 'A Night with Dublin Theosophists,' *Weekly Irish Times,* 17 June 1893.
22. Yeats, *Autobiographies,* pp. 237-238, 244-245. The latter incident is confirmed in draft of 'Sunset.'
23. Draft of 'Sunset'; N.W., *I.H.,* 22 July 1911, p. 566. Quotation from the latter.
24. Katharine Tynan, *The Years of the Shadow* (London, 1919), p. 96.
25. *Irish Theosophist,* II (15 February 1894), p. 72 (henceforward referred to as *I.T.*).
26. Gibbon, 'Thesis,' p. 264, quoting Miss Mary Scarlett.
27. Ella Young, *Flowering Dusk: Things Remembered Accurately and Inaccurately* (New York, 1945), p. 30.
28. Gibbon, 'Thesis,' p. 81.
29. *I.T.,* I (15 January 1893), p. 35.
30. *I.T.,* V (15 September 1897), p. 240.
31. P. E. Jackson, 'Recollections of the Old Dublin Lodge, Ely Place, in the Years 1891–2–3–4,' *Theosophy in Ireland,* XVII (July and October 1938), pp. 22-25 and 21-25, and XIX (January and March 1940), pp. 15-18 and 20-24.
32. D. Ms. 25, to Carrie Rea, 5 May 1893.
33. *Memoir,* pp. 16-17.
34. Miss Jameson's unp. thesis, 'Mysticism in AE and Yeats in Relation to Oriental and American Thought' (Ohio, 1932), p. 68. Cf. *Bibliography,* pp. 177-181, and *Letters,* p. 57.
35. Gibbon, 'Thesis,' p. 205 n.

36. Draft of 'Sunset.'
37. Ranjee G. Shahani, 'Some Recent English Poets,' *Asiatic Review,* XXXI (April 1935), pp. 379-389.
38. D. Ms. 17, [? February 1891], and 20, 8 May 1892.
39. *Bibliography,* p. 219, citing *Path,* VII (September 1892), p. 202.
40. W. B. Yeats, 'AE's Poems,' *Sketch,* 6 April 1898.
40a. Curtis, 'A Night with Dublin Theosophists.'
41. Jackson, 'Recollections of the Old Dublin Lodge,' III, pp. 15-16.
42. *Ibid.,* II, pp. 21-25.
43. *Letters,* pp. 273-275; D. Ms. 564, to Charles Weekes, 23 December 1932; John Eglinton, 'Charles Weekes,' *Dublin Magazine,* XXI (April 1946), pp. 36-40; *Memoir,* pp. 21-26; John Eglinton, *Irish Literary Portraits* (London, 1935), p. 45.
43a. Curtis, 'A Night with Dublin Theosophists.'
44. Yeats, *Autobiographies*, p. 250; Oliver St. J. Gogarty, *As I was Going Down Sackville Street* (London, 1937), p. 179.
45. *Letters,* p. 262; AE, 'Comfort,' *Collected Poems,* 2nd ed. reprinted (London, 1935), pp. 91-92 (henceforward referred to as *Collected Poems);* Abinash Chandra Bose, *Three Mystic Poets* (Kolhapur, 1945), p. 99. Plunkett's opinion of Norman is given in his unp. Diary, 16 February 1930.
46. 'In Memoriam AE,' *Dublin Magazine,* X (October 1935), pp. 2-7.
47. *Living Torch,* p. 72; draft of 'Sunset'; unp. typescript of AE's lecture 'The Sunset of Fantasy.'
48. Forrest Reid, *Private Road* (London, 1940), p. 133; *Candle of Vision,* p. 56 ff.
49. Unp. ltr. to Israel Regardie, 14 November 1932.
50. *W. B. Yeats 1865–1939,* 2nd ed. (London, 1962), p. 72.
51. Unp. ltrs. to Ernest Boyd, 12 October 1914 and 7 February 1915.
52. Draft of 'Sunset.'
52a. Reid, *Private Road,* pp. 133-134.
53. E.g. D. Ms. 88, to W. B. Yeats, [? June 1901].
54. *Letters,* pp. 149-150; H. T. Hunt Grubb, 'AE, Poet, Painter and Mystic,' *Poetry Review,* January 1938, pp. 39-53.
55. *Letters,* p. 31.
56. D. Ms. 184, to Clifford Bax, [postmark 13 August 1910].
57. 'Myth and Folk Tale,' *I.S.,* 22 November 1924, pp. 334-335.
58. Unp. ltr. to Walter Muir Whitehill, 14 September 1933.
59. AE alludes to the Masters, *Candle of Vision,* pp. 171-172.
60. *I.T.,* I (15 August 1893), p. 118. See *Letters,* p. 175, for a late (1927) reference to the sub-races into which each Root-Race

is divided.

61. James Stephens, *James, Seumas and Jacques* (London, 1964), p. 113.
62. D. Ms. 469, to W. B. Yeats, 6 February 1929.
63. D. Ms. 23, to Carrie Rea, 8 January 1893.
64. Diarmuid Russell, 'AE, George William Russell,' *Modern Reading No. 10* (London, 1944), pp. 23-34.
65. 'Self-reliance,' *I.T.*, IV (15 May 1896), pp. 150-152.
66. D. Ms. 24, to Carrie Rea, 29 March 1893.
67. Russell, 'AE,' p. 27. Cf. Stephens, *James, Seumas and Jacques*, p. 119.
68. *Candle of Vision*, p. 28. See also p. 139.
69. AE, 'The Element Language,' V, *I.T.*, I (15 September 1893), pp. 125-127; Russell, 'AE,' p. 28.
70. *To the Fellows of the Theosophical Society* (Dublin, 1894), reprinted *Theosophical Movement*, VIII (17 March 1938), pp. 66-68.
71. *Song and Its Fountains*, p. 78.
72. *Candle of Vision*, p. 24.
73. 'Shadow and Substance,' *I.T.*, IV (15 January 1896), pp. 62-64.
74. AE, 'The Legends of Ancient Eire,' II, *I.T.*, III (15 April 1895), pp. 119-122.
75. Cf. H. T. Hunt Grubb, 'The Philosophy of AE,' *Occult Review*, July 1936, pp. 162-172.
76. Cf. AE, *Imaginations and Reveries* (Dublin and London, 1915), p. 199 (henceforward referred to as *Imaginations and Reveries*).
77. *Candle of Vision*, p. 140.
78. *Ibid.*, p. 55.
79. Henry W. Nevinson, *Last Changes Last Chances* (New York, 1929), p. 169.
80. *Candle of Vision*, p. 141.
81. Stephens, *James, Seumas and Jacques*, p. 111.
82. *Song and Its Fountains*, pp. 1-2; L. A. G. Strong, ' "AE" – a Practical Mystic,' *Listener*, LIII (10 March 1955), pp. 427-428; Russell, 'AE,' pp. 28, 31-32.
83. D. Ms. 5, [summer 1887].
84. *Some Passages from the Letters of AE to W. B. Yeats* (Dublin, 1936), p. 52 (henceforward referred to as *Some Passages*).
85. E.g. unp. ltr. to Mrs. Mary Colum, 20 January 1917.
86. D. Ms. 26, to Carrie Rea, [May 1893].
87. *Song and Its Fountains*, pp. 2, 128-132; H. T. Hunt Grubb, 'Philosophy of AE,' p. 167; Clifford Bax, *Ideas and People* (London, 1936), pp. 238-239; *Some Passages*, p. 55; *Letters*,

p. 20; *Memoir,* pp. 272-273; unp. ltr. to Mrs. Florence M. Wilson, 4 December 1933.

88. *Candle of Vision,* pp. 94-95. See also *ibid.,* pp. 57-63; Katharine Tynan, *The Years of the Shadow* (London, 1919), p. 23; Yeats, *Autobiographies,* p. 243.
89. *Song and Its Fountains,* pp. 34-36; 'At the Dawn of the Kaliyuga,' *I.T.,* II (15 October 1893), pp. 4-6.
90. *Song and Its Fountains,* pp. 27-29; 'A Talk by the Euphrates,' *I.T.,* II (15 December 1893), pp. 33-35.
91. *Candle of Vision,* pp. 50-51; Russell, 'AE,' p. 27; Yeats, *Autobiographies,* p. 243.
92. *Memoir,* p. 131; 'Night,' *Collected Poems,* p. 11; *Song and Its Fountains,* pp. 37-43.
93. D. Ms. 24, 29 March 1893.
94. 'Yes and Hope,' *I.T.,* III (15 August 1895), pp. 189-192.
95. 'The Element Language,' I, *I.T.,* I (15 May 1893), pp. 78-79.
96. 'The Mask of Apollo,' I (15 April 1893), pp. 67-68.
97. 'The Man to the Angel,' *Collected Poems,* pp. 84-85. Cf. *Secret Doctrine,* II, pp. 81, 421.
98. 'The Hero in Man,' *Internationalist,* I (15 November 1897), pp. 24-26; 'Duality,' *I.T.,* V (15 March 1897), p. 108. Cf. *Secret Doctrine,* II, pp. 36, 411-422.
99. 'A Word Upon the Objects of the Theosophical Society,' *I.T.,* I (15 November 1892), pp. 9-10.
100. 'A Thought Along the Road,' *I.T.* V (15 July 1897), pp. 181-185; AE, *The Interpreters* (London, 1922), pp. 93-94 (henceforward referred to as *Interpreters).* Cf. *Secret Doctrine,* I, p. 433.
101. D. Ms. 25, to Carrie Rea, 5 May 1893.
102. *I.T.,* IV (15 April 1896), pp. 122-123.
103. *I.T.,* III (15 July 1895), pp. 184-188.
104. III (15 August 1895), p. 207.
105. *Memoir,* p. 25.
106. Gibbon, 'Thesis,' p. 278, citing letter from Weekes, 24 July 1945.
107. Two unp. ltrs. to William O'Leary Curtis, n.d.
108. D. Ms. 17, to Carrie Rea, [? February 1891]; *Memoir,* p. 30; 1917 statement – Richard J. Finneran, 'Two Unpublished Letters from AE,' *Papers on Language and Literature,* III (Summer 1967), pp. 220-228.
109. *Some Passages,* p. 51.
110. *Memoir,* pp. 171-172; AE, *Selected Poems* (London, 1952), p. vii.
111. Russell, 'AE,' p. 31.

112. pp. 8, 11, 25-26.
113. Stephen Gwynn, *Experiences of a Literary Man* (London, [1926]), p. 200.
114. Unp. ltr. to F. R. Higgins, 27 November 1933.
115. 'Dusk,' *Homeward*, p. 13.
116. Unp. ltr, 23 September 1934.
117. Ltr. to Dilip Kumar Roy, 6 January 1932, published in the recipient's *Sri Aurobindo Came to Me* (Pondicherry, 1952), pp. 91-94.
118. Unp. ltr. to T. Fisher Unwin, [12 September 1901].

Chapter Three

1. Aodh de Blacam, 'Talks with AE,' *Irish Bookman*, I (February 1947), pp. 13–19.
2. 'Review,' *I.T.*, III (15 June 1895), pp. 165–166.
3. 'Alexandre Dumas,' *I.S.*, 11 May 1929, pp. 192–193.
4. *Memoir*, pp. 41–42.
5. D. Ms. 131, to John Quinn, [spring 1904].
6. Draft of 'Sunset.'
7. *Ibid.* See also AE, 'Standish O'Grady,' *I.S.*, 26 May 1928, p. 231.
8. *Memoir*, pp. 33–34; Yeats, *Autobiographies*, p. 237; Magee's opinion – Gibbon, 'Thesis,' p. 291.
9. James Morgan Pryse, 'George William Russell, Poet of the Inner Life,' *Canadian Theosophist*, XVI (August 1935), pp. 164–166; *I.T.*, III (15 February 1895), p. 88.
10. D. Ms. 36, to W. B. Yeats, [? February 1896].
11. Y.O. [another pseudonym of AE], 'The Christ,' *Path*, I (February 1911), pp. 155-157.
12. Unp. ltrs. to James Pryse, 3 June 1925 and 1 November 1930.
13. Pryse, 'George William Russell,' p. 164.
14. D. Ms. 36, to W. B. Yeats, [? February 1896].
15. D. Ms. 56, to T. P. Gill, [27 February 1898].
16. *Song and Its Fountains*, p. 52.
17. Unp. ltr. to James Pryse, 24 November 1930.
18. Partly unp. ltr. to E. H. W. Meyerstein, 7 February 1920.
19. AE, 'A Strange Awakening,' II, *I.T.*, II (15 April 1894), pp. 96–99; 'Dark Weeping,' *Collected Poems*, pp. 395–398; *Candle of Vision*, p. 137; James Morgan Pryse, *The Restored New Testament*, 4th ed. (Los Angeles and London, c. 1914), p. 292.

20. For the Lamp of the World see 'The Message of John,' *The Earth Breath and Other Poems* (New York and London, 1897), pp. 74–79 (henceforward referred to as *Earth Breath*), *Imaginations and Reveries,* p. 154, Pryse, *The Apocalypse Unsealed,* 4th ed. (Los Angeles and London, 1931), pp. 9–10, and Pryse, *Restored New Testament,* p. 242; for the Ancestral Self, note 100 to Chapter Two above; for the Magician of the Beautiful, *Candle of Vision,* p. 173; for Brahma and the Shepherd of the Ages, AE, 'At the Dawn of the Kaliyuga,' *I.T.,* II (15 October 1893), pp. 4–6, 'A Vision of Beauty,' *Collected Poems,* pp. 86–88, and *Secret Doctrine,* I, p. 9; for the Light of Lights, 'Day' and 'The Fountain of Shadowy Beauty,' *Collected Poems,* pp. 13, 200–208, and *Secret Doctrine,* I, p. 571. AE greatly admired Pryse's *Apocalypse* (unp. ltr. to Pryse, 16 October 1923).
21. *Secret Doctrine,* I, p. 430; Pryse, *Apocalypse Unsealed,* pp. 9–10.
22. *Candle of Vision,* pp. 160–161.
23. 'By the Margin of the Great Deep' and 'The Great Breath,' *Collected Poems,* pp. 3–4, 9; *ibid.,* p. 429. See *Secret Doctrine,* I, p. 353.
24. *Candle of Vision,* pp. 30, 32, 172; *Interpreters,* pp. 47–51. Cf. *Secret Doctrine,* I, pp. 277–278, and II, p. 552.
25. Cf. P. G. Bowen, *The Occult Way* (London, n.d.), p. 21.
26. J. L. Davidge, 'Symbolic Murals in Dublin,' *Theosophist,* LXII (July 1942), pp. 283–288.
26a. O'Leary Curtis, 'A Night with Dublin Theosophists,' *Weekly Irish Times,* 17 June 1893.
27. *Candle of Vision,* p. 11.
28. AE, 'The Children of Lir,' *United Irishman,* 8 March and 15 March 1902; A. R. Orage, *Readers and Writers (1917–1921)* (New York, 1922), p. 107; *Letters,* p. 35.
29. Stephen Gwynn, *Experiences of a Literary Man* (London, [1926]), p. 201.
30. *Imaginations and Reveries,* pp. 195–201; *Candle of Vision,* pp. 35, 157, 168. Cf. *Secret Doctrine,* I, 541, and Plato, *The Republic,* 508-509.
31. D. Ms. 5, to Carrie Rea, [summer 1887].
32. Clifford Bax, *Rosemary for Remembrance* (London, 1948), p. 59.
33. H. F. Norman, 'The Theosophy of George Russell ("AE"),' *'Theosophical Forum,'* VIII (February 1936), pp. 92–99.
34. *Candle of Vision,* pp. 34–35. See also W. Y. Evans Wentz, *The Fairy Faith in Celtic Countries* (London, 1911), pp. 59–66

(Wentz's informant is AE – see *Letters,* p. 222 n. 1).

35. Evans Wentz, *Fairy Faith,* pp. 59–66. Cf. Bhagavadgita vii, 23.
36. D. Ms. 564, to Charles Weekes, 23 December 1932.
36a. Curtis, 'A Night with Dublin Theosophists.'
37. Davidge, 'Symbolic Murals,' pp. 284–285; Gibbon, 'Thesis,' p. 240.
37a. H. T. Hunt Grubb, 'The Philosophy of AE,' *Occult Review,* July 1936, pp. 162–172.
38. D. Ms. 36, [? February 1896].
39. 'The Fountain of Shadowy Beauty,' *Collected Poems,* pp. 200–208. Cf. *Candle of Vision,* pp. 34, 39, and *Song and Its Fountains,* pp. 129–130.
40. *Candle of Vision,* p. 32, quoting Plato's *Phaedo* 111b.
41. E.g. D. Ms. 50, to W. B. Yeats, [? June 1897], and 52, to the same, 9 August 1897.
42. H. Summerfield, ed. 'Unpublished letters from AE to John Eglinton,' *Malahat Review,* April 1970, pp. 84–107.
43. *I.T.,* III (15 March 1895), p. 108; *Memoir,* pp. 23–24.
44. Gibbon, 'Thesis,' p. 243. Confirmed Curtis, 'A Night with Dublin Theosophists.'
45. Philippians iii, 21.
46. *Candle of Vision,* p. 166; Evans Wentz, *Fairy Faith*, p. 64; Pryse, *Apocalypse Unsealed,* p. 12.
47. pp. 172–173.
48. M. K. Gandhi, *My God* (Ahmedabad, 1962), pp. 30–31. References to *Candle of Vision,* pp. 84, 87, 95–96, 102–111.
49. James Morgan Pryse, 'George William Russell, Poet of the Inner Life,' *Canadian Theosophist,* XVI (August 1935), pp. 164–166.
50. 'A Letter from AE,' *Canadian Theosophist,* XVI (August 1935), p. 166. See also Constance Sitwell, *Conversations with Six Friends* (London: privately printed, 1959), p. 54, and *Song and Its Fountains,* pp. 47–48, 84, 107.
51. Cf. *Candle of Vision,* pp. 62–63.
52. *Song and Its Fountains,* pp. 101–102. See also pp. 107, 110. Cf. Plato, *Phaedrus,* 250c. AE quotes I Corinthians xiii, 12.
53. 'Shadow and Substance,' *I.T.,* IV (15 January 1896), pp. 62–64. See also *Candle of Vision,* pp. 35–37, 65.
54. Unp. Diary, 18 July, 9 and 12 December 1895, 17 May 1896.
55. *Candle of Vision,* p. 30; 'The Press Reports,' *Canadian Theosophist,* XVI (August 1935), pp. 170–174.
56. Unp. Diary, 7 June 1896.
57. Pryse, *Restored New Testament,* pp. 34–35.

58. Unp. ltrs. to James Pryse, 2 March 1924 and 24 November 1930.
59. 'Self-reliance,' *I.T.,* IV (15 May 1896), pp. 150–152. See also 'W.Q.J.,' *I.T.,* IV (15 April 1896), p. 121 ff.
60. Gibbon, 'Thesis,' p. 359. Information supplied by H. F. Norman.
61. *I.T.,* IV (15 August 1896), pp. 218–223.
62. Pryse, *Restored New Testament,* p. 24.
63. 'Janus,' *Earth Breath,* p. 48.
64. 'The Chiefs of the Air,' *I.T.,* IV (15 August 1896), pp. 210–212.
65. 'The Dream of the Children,' *Earth Breath,* pp. 30–32. See Pryse, *Restored New Testament,* pp. 47, 395.
66. 'A New World,' *Earth Breath,* pp. 55–56.
67. 'The Message of John,' *Earth Breath,* pp. 74–79. See Pryse, *Restored New Testament,* p. 113.
68. 'When twilight flutters the mountains over,' *The Divine Vision and Other Poems* (London, 1904), p. ix (henceforward referred to as *Divine Vision*).
69. 'The Mid-World,' *Earth Breath,* p. 85. Cf. AE, 'The Fountains of Youth,' *I.T.,* V (15 September 1897), pp. 221–225, *Song and Its Fountains,* p. 104, and Pryse, *Apocalypse Unsealed,* pp. 140–142.
70. ' "Yes, and Hope," ' *I.T.,* III (15 August 1895), pp. 189–192. AE is quoting Isaiah x1.3 and Psalms xxiv.7.
71. 'The Enchantment of Cuchullain,' published serially from November 1895 to March 1896.
72. Entry for 9 [error for 10] May 1896.
73. *Secret Doctrine,* I, pp. xliii–xliv.
74. 'The Wandering Eye,' *Path,* IV (May 1889), p. 49.
75. See *Letters,* pp. 17–18.
76. *Candle of Vision,* pp. 98–101. See also Katharine Tynan, *The Years of the Shadow* (London, 1919), pp. 22–23, and E. R. Dodds, ed. *Journal and Letters of Stephen MacKenna* (London, 1936), p. 141.
77. Unp. Diary. Cf. *Candle of Vision,* p. 144.
78. Unp. Diary, 17 and 31 May 1896.
79. D. Ms. 36, to W. B. Yeats, [? February 1896].
80. *Letters,* pp. 17–18.
81. 'Works and Days,' *I.T.,* IV (15 June 1896), pp. 169–171.
82. *I.T.,* IV (15 August 1896), p. 222.
83. D. Ms. 50, to W. B. Yeats, [? June 1897].
84. p. 101.
85. Unp. Diary, 27 [error for 28] July 1896.
86. *I.T.,* V (15 October and 15 November 1896), pp. 20, 40.

87. Elizabeth A. Sharp, *William Sharp (Fiona Macleod). A Memoir* (London, 1910), p. 287.
88. *Some Passages,* pp. 1–9. Mr. Denson dates one of these extracts (pp. 4–6) early April 1896 (D. Ms. 37).
89. D. Ms. 46, to Sarah Purser, 27 January 1897.
90. W. B. Yeats, Introduction to 'Mandookya Upanishad,' *Criterion,* XIV (July 1935), p. 548.
91. *Some Passages,* pp. 8–9.
92. D. Ms. 439, to Charles Weekes, 30 November 1926. See also AE, 'Twenty-five Years of Irish Nationality,' *Foreign Affairs,* VII (January 1929), pp. 204–220.
93. D. Ms. 39, to William Sharp, [? April 1896].
94. *Letters,* pp. 10–11, 12–13.
95. Frank O'Connor, 'Two Friends: Yeats and AE,' *Yale Review,* XXIX (September 1939), pp. 60–88.
96. *Letters,* pp. 18–23.
97. *Bibliography*, p. 175.
98. Gibbon, 'Thesis,' pp. 330–331, 336.
99. D. Ms. 50, to W. B. Yeats, [? June 1897].
100. AE's unp. Diary, 13 and 17 May 1896, and D. Ms. 51, to W. B. Yeats, [early August 1897].
101. Ella Young, *Flowering Dusk: Things Remembered Accurately and Inaccurately* (New York, 1945), pp. 31–32. Miss North's smoking confirmed, Gibbon, 'Thesis,' pp. 331–332.
102. *Song and Its Fountains,* pp. 52–57. Last statement confirmed Constance Sitwell, *Conversations with Six Friends* (London: privately printed, 1959), p. 57.
103. 'Duality,' *Collected Poems,* p. 132, first published *I.T.,* V (15 March 1897), p. 108.
104. *Letters,* p. 22.
105. 'Illusion,' *Collected Poems,* p. 175.
106. 'Ordeal,' *The Divine Vision,* p. 78.
107. Ltr. to Helen Waddell, published William Rothenstein, *Since Fifty. Men and Memories, 1922–1938* (London, 1939), pp. 121–122.
108. 'Mistrust,' *Divine Vision,* p. 61.
109. Draft of 'Sunset.' Reference to health – *Living Torch,* p. 29.
110. Yeats, *Letters,* p. 291.
111. Lady Gregory *Seventy Years,* p. 311.
     Based on Yeats's account of Mr. Pim's praise of AE.
112. Yeats, *Letters,* p. 292.
113. Plunkett's unp. Diary, 19 November 1897, not 11 November as stated *Letters,* p. 229.

114. *Secret Doctrine,* I, p. 450. AE employs the phrase *Candle of Vision,* p. 143.

Chapter Four

1. Margaret Digby, *Horace Plunkett. An Anglo-American Irishman* (Oxford, 1949), p. 65.
2. Horace Plunkett, *Help for Self-Help in Ireland* (Dublin, 1898), p. 9.
3. Elizabeth, Countess of Fingall, *Seventy Years Young* (London, 1937), p. 242.
4. George Moore, *Salve,* reissued (London, 1947), p. 63.
5. *Letters,* pp. 23–24.
6. Unp. ltr. to W. B. Yeats, [mid-January 1898].
7. N.W., *I.H.,* 9 January 1909, p. 23.
8. *I.H.,* 8 January 1898, p. 916. See also Geo. W. Russell, 'Co-operative Banks,' *I.H.,* 15 January 1898, pp. 54–55.
9. D. Ms. 56, to T. P. Gill, [27 February 1898]. AE here mentions he is sending a report of the Rossmuck meeting to the *Homestead* (printed 12 March 1898, p. 235).
10. *I.H.,* 15 January 1898, p. 62.
11. *I.H.,* 22 January 1898, pp. 84–85.
12. *Ibid.,* p. 84. See also *Letters,* pp. 24–25.
13. Unp. ltr. to W. B. Yeats, [mid-January 1898].
14. Yeats, *Letters,* pp. 294–295; unp. ltr. from Yeats to Lady Gregory, 23 January 1898.
15. *Internationalist,* I (15 February 1898), p. 100.
16. *I.H.,* 12 February 1898, p. 146. See also *ibid.,* 5 February 1898, p. 127.
17. *Ibid.,* 19 February 1898, p. 172.
18. Unp. ltr., 7 February 1898.
19. *Letters,* pp. 24–26; unp. typescript of AE's lecture 'The Sunset of Fantasy.'
20. Unp. ltr. to Lady Gregory, 7 February 1898.
21. H. Summerfield, ed. 'Unpublished Letters from AE to John Eglinton,' *Malahat Review,* April 1970, pp. 84–107.
22. *I.H.,* 12 March 1898, p. 235.
23. Unp. ltr. to Lady Gregory, 31 January 1898; Summerfield, ed. 'Letters from AE to Eglinton,' p. 93.
24. 'Transformations,' *Internationalist,* I (15 February 1898), pp. 91–93.
25. N.W., *I.H.,* 5 March 1910, p. 185.

26. Gibbon, 'Thesis,' p. 359.
27. H. F. Norman, 'The Theosophy of George Russell ("AE"),' *Theosophical Forum,* VIII (February 1936), pp. 92–99.
28. *Report to the Select Committee on Money Lending,* Parliamentary Papers, Commons, 31 March 1898, para. 2228.
29. Summerfield, ed. 'Letters from AE to Eglinton,' p. 94.
30. *Report to the Select Committee,* p. xxvi; *I.H.,* 16 April 1898, p. 336.
31. *I.H.,* 30 April 1898, p. 385.
32. *I.H.,* 2 April 1898, p. 302.
33. N.W., *I.H.,* 17 July 1909, p. 574.
34. *Letters,* pp. 28–29.
35. *Ibid.,* pp. 36–37.
36. Plunkett's unp. Diary, 28 and 29 May and 3 June 1898.
37. Digby, *Plunkett,* p. 103.
38. Unp. ltr. from Plunkett to Lady Gregory, 24 February [1898 – postmark].
39. Unp. ltr.
40. Gibbon, 'Thesis,' p. 360. Information supplied by H. F. Norman.
41. *Memoir,* p. 45.
42. D. Ms. 62, to W. B. Yeats, [29 October 1898].
43. Unp. ltr. to Padraic Colum, 18 January 1918.
44. Diarmuid Russell, 'AE, George William Russell,' *Modern Reading No. 10* (London, 1944), pp. 23–34.
45. Interview with Mr. Diarmuid Russell.
46. Unp. ltr. to Lady Gregory, 16 July 1898.
47. Lady Gregory, *Seventy Years,* pp. 311–312.
48. Arnold Harvey, 'Memories of Coole,' *Irish Times,* 23 November 1959, p. 5.
49. Unp. ltr. to W. B. Yeats, [summer 1899].
50. *Memoir,* p. 62.
51. *Letters,* p. 30.
52. *Letters,* p. 254; *Memoir,* p. 178.
53. *Song and Its Fountains,* pp. 101–110. Spiritual story – unp. ltr. to Lady Gregory, 16 July 1898.
54. D. Ms. 75, to W. B. Yeats, [November 1899].
55. D. Ms. 86, to Thomas Mosher, 4 February 1901.
56. D. Ms. 129, to Charles Weekes, [late January or February 1904].
57. Unp. ltr. to Lady Gregory, 22 July 1898.
58. AE, 'Art in Ireland' and 'The Spiritual Influence of Art,' *Daily Express,* 10 September 1898, p. 3, and 22 April 1899, p. 3; Yeats, *Letters,* p. 307; *Report by the Committee of*

Enquiry into the Work Carried on by the Royal Hibernian Academy, and the Metropolitan School of Art, Dublin, Parliamentary Papers, Commons, 13 October 1905, para 1254.

59. Unp. ltr. to Lady Gregory, 24 May 1900.
60. Countess of Fingall, *Seventy Years Young,* pp. 242–243; Yeats, *Letters,* p. 306.
61. Unp. ltr. to Lady Gregory, 1 May 1899.
62. 3 June 1899, pp. 392–393. Authorship – unp. ltr. to Lady Gregory, 26 June 1899.
63. 'Tolstoy on the Russian Peasantry,' *I.H.,* 7 January 1899, pp. 7–8. Authorship – unp. ltr. to Lady Gregory, 10 January 1899.
64. Unp. ltr. to Lady Gregory, 26 September 1900.
65. All the articles were reprinted in *Literary Ideals in Ireland* (Dublin, 1899).
66. AE, 'The Sunset of Fantasy,' *Dublin Magazine,* XIII (January 1938), pp. 6–11.
67. *All Ireland Review,* I (21 July 1900), p. 2.
68. Unp. ltr. to Lady Gregory, 8 August 1900.
69. 'Irish Ideals and Fiona MacLeod,' *All Ireland Review,* I (18 August 1900), p. 1.
70. D.Ms. 93, to Thomas Mosher, 26 October 1901.
71. *All Ireland Review,* I (28 April and 5 May 1900), pp. 3 and 1.
72. Unp. ltr. to Lady Gregory, 1 August 1898.
73. Unp. ltr. to Lady Gregory, 10 September 1898.
74. E.g. *Letters,* p. 42.
75. D. Ms. 131, to John Quinn, [spring 1904].
76. 'In Memoriam AE,' *Dublin Magazine,* X (October 1935), pp. 2–7.
77. Unp. ltr. to Lady Gregory, 26 June 1899.
78. R. A. Anderson, *With Horace Plunkett in Ireland* (London, 1935), pp. 102–103.
79. Lady Gregory, *Seventy Years,* p. 322.
80. *I.H.,* 3 September 1898, p. 736, and 4 August 1900, p. 498.
81. Oliver St. J. Gogarty, *Mourning Became Mrs. Spendlove* (New York, 1948), pp. 106–107.
82. N.W., *I.H.,* 19 October 1912, p. 843.
83. 'The United Irishwomen,' *I.H.,* 21 August 1915, pp. 546–547.
84. N.W., *I.H.,* 17 July 1909, p. 571; D. Ms. 337, to James Stephens, [26 June 1918].
85. N.W., *I.H.,* 23 May 1914, p. 403.
86. N.W., *I.H.,* 20 November 1909, p. 939.
87. Yeats, *Letters,* pp. 306, 317–318; Geo. W. Russell, 'The

Application of Co-operation in the Congested Districts,' *Journal of the Statistical and Social Inquiry Society of Ireland,* X (August 1900), pp. 517–527; Geo. W. Russell, letter to the editor, *Irish People,* I (18 November 1899), p. 3.

88. 'In Memoriam AE,' Dublin Magazine, X (October 1935), pp. 2–7.
89. P. G. Bowen, ' "AE": Theosophist,' *Canadian Theosophist,* XVI (August 1935), pp. 162–164.
90. L.A., *I.H.,* 10 September 1910, p. 748.
91. Gogarty, *Mourning Became Mrs. Spendlove,* pp. 116–121. Confirmed 'Memoirs of George Roberts,' I, *Irish Times,* 13 July 1955, p. 5.
92. Unp. ltr. to Lady Gregory, 21 February 1898.
93. L.A., *I.H.,* 4 September 1909, p. 716.
94. *I.H.,* 26 March 1898, p. 276.
95. Russell, 'Co-operation in the Congested Districts,' p. 518; *Department of Agriculture and Technical Instruction (Ireland): Departmental Committee of Enquiry,* Parliamentary Papers, Commons, 31 October 1906, paras. 14457, 14467, 14481.
96. *I.H.,* 21 May 1898, p. 444.
97. 'The Irish Cottage,' *I.H.,* 29 April 1899, p. 311. Authorship – unp. ltr. to Lady Gregory, [postmark 22 April 1899].
98. Russell, 'Co-operation in the Congested Districts,' p. 519; *Letters,* p. 27.
99. N.W., *I.H.,* 4 March 1911, p. 166.
100. 'Agricultural Banks in Ireland,' *I.H.,* Special Anniversary Issue, 1902, pp. 16–17.
101. *Letters,* p. 41.
102. Unp. ltr. to Lady Gregory, [postmark 5 August 1900]; grotesque elemental, – *ibid.,* [postmark 4 July 1900].
103. Unp. ltr. to Lady Gregory, [postmark 13 August 1900].
104. Shaemas O'Sheel, 'AE – Poet and Irishman,' *Commonweal* VIII (22 February 1928), pp. 1092–1093. Knowledge of Gaelic confirmed unp. ltr. to James Pryse, 3 June 1925.
105. Unp. ltrs. to Lady Gregory, [postmarks 5 July and 14 August 1901]; Alice Milligan's contribution to 'In Memoriam AE,' *Dublin Magazine,* X (October 1935), pp. 2–7.
106. Unp. notebook in the County Museum, Armagh.
107. Maire Nic Shiubhlaigh, *The Splendid Years* (Dublin, 1955), pp. 28–29.
108. Unp. ltr. from Dudley Digges to Richard Campbell, 13 August 1935.
109. Stephen Gwynn, *Irish Literature and Drama* (New York, 1936), p. 136.

110. Francis Merchant, *AE: An Irish Promethean* (Columbia, S. Carolina, 1954), p. 189.
111. George Moore, *Ave* (London, 1947), p. 120.
112. *I.H.*, 8 September 1900, p. 589. Authorship – unp. ltr. to Lady Gregory, 24 August 1900.
113. Hone, *The Life of George Moore* (London, 1936), p. 237.
114. Unp. ltr., [late 1900].
115. *Ibid.*
116. George Moore, *Letters to Lady Cunard 1895–1933* (London, 1957), p. 30.
117. Susan L. Mitchell, *George Moore* (Dublin, 1916), p. 113.
118. J. H. and M. E. Cousins, *We Two Together* (Madras, 1950), pp. 33–43; 'Memoirs of George Roberts,' I, *Irish Times*, 13 July 1955, p. 5.
119. *Imaginations and Reveries*, p. 33.
120. D. Ms. 548, to W. B. Yeats, [late April 1902].
121. Unp. ltr. to Padraic Colum, 27 December 1916.
122. John Brennan, 'Dublin Fifty Years Ago,' III, *Irish Weekly Independent*, 19 May 1951, p. 4.
123. D. Ms. 251, to Edward MacLysaght, [November 1914].
124. Ulick O'Connor, *The Times I've Seen: Oliver St. John Gogarty* (New York, 1963), pp. 49–50; AE, Preface to Oliver St. John Gogarty, *Others to Adorn* (London, 1938), pp. xi–xvi.
125. Richard Ellmann, *James Joyce* (New York, 1959), pp. 102–104; quotation from L. A. G. Strong, ' "AE" – a Practical Mystic,' *Listener*, LIII (10 March 1955), pp. 427–428.
126. Unp. ltr. to Lady Gregory, [August 1902].
127. Ellmann, *Joyce*, pp. 113, 168–169, 179–180; Richard Ellmann, ed. *Letters of James Joyce*, II (London, 1966), p. 28; Stanislaus Joyce, 'Early Memories of James Joyce,' *Listener*, XLI (26 May 1949), pp. 896–897; *Letters*, pp. 43–44, 55–56.
128. Unp. ltr. to Lady Gregory, 27 August 1900.
129. Ella Young, *Flowering Dusk: Things Remembered Accurately and Inaccurately* (New York, 1945), p. 90.
130. Seumas O'Sullivan, *The Rose and the Bottle* (Dublin, 1946), p. 25.
131. D. Ms. 79, to W. B. Yeats, [May 1900].
132. Moore, *Salve*, p. 276; Young, *Flowering Dusk*, pp. 34–35; interview with Mr. Padraic Colum; Larminie's visits – unp. ltr. to Ernest Boyd, [c. 1915].
133. The much corrected autograph ms. of this poem is in the Houghton Library, Harvard.
134. D. Ms. 137, [? March 1904].
135. George Moore, *Vale*, reissued (London, 1947), p. 167.

136. D. Ms. 235, to James Stephens, [29 December 1913].
137. Henry Wallace, 'An Appreciation of One of Ireland's Greatest Writers,' *Ireland American Review,* Book IV (n.d.), pp. 16–38.
138. *Living Torch,* p. 45.
139. Reference to St. John and Origen – unp. ltr. to Ernest Boyd, [c. 1915].
140. E.g. *I.S.,* 21 January 1926, pp. 529–530.
141. *Song and Its Fountains,* p. 92.
142. 'The Children of Lir,' I, *United Irishman,* 8 March 1902, p. 3.
143. Maurice Joy, 'Some Essays by AE,' *United Irishman,* 3 March 1906, p. 2.
144. Unp. ltr. to Lady Gregory, 4 June 1900.
145. Unp. ltr. to Lady Gregory, 15 February 1900.
146. 'In Memoriam AE,' *Dublin Magazine,* X (October 1935), pp. 2–7.
147. Ann Saddlemyer, ' "Worn Out With Dreams," ' *The World of W. B. Yeats,* ed. Ann Saddlemyer and Robin Skelton (Dublin, 1965), pp. 104–132.
148. 'Memoirs of George Roberts,' I, *Irish Times,* 13 July 1955, p. 5; J. H. and M. E. Cousins, *We Two Together*, p. 66.
149. J. H. and M. E. Cousins, *We Two Together*, p. 70.
150. *Letters,* p. 38; Robert Hogan and Michael J. O'Neill, ed. *Joseph Holloway's Abbey Theatre* (Carbondale and Edwardsville, Illinois, 1967), pp. 16–17.
151. Unp. ltr. from Dudley Digges to Richard Campbell, 13 August 1935.
152. Unp. ltr. from W. B. Yeats to AE, [January 1902].
153. Unp. ltr. to Ella Young, 3 April 1902.
154. *Letters,* p. 41; Yeats, *Letters,* pp. 368–369; W. B. Yeats, 'Notes,' *Samhain*, October 1902, pp. 3–10; quotation from Padraic Colum, 'Early Days of the Irish Theatre,' *Dublin Magazine,* XXV (January 1950), pp. 18–25.
155. *Imaginations and Reveries,* pp. 7–12.
156. *Letters,* pp. 41–42.
157. Unp. ltr. to Lady Gregory, 29 April 1902.
158. D. Ms. 104, to W. B. Yeats, [24 May 1902].
159. Unp. ltr. to Lady Gregory, [c. October 1902].
160. Unp. ltr. from Dudley Digges to Richard Campbell, 13 August 1935.
161. Unp. ltr., [postmark 5 July 1901].
162. Unp. ltrs., [postmark 10 June 1902] and 16 June 1902.
163. Unp. ltr. to Lady Gregory, 16 June 1902.
164. *Some Passages,* pp. 31–33; W. B. Yeats, 'Speaking to the

Psaltery,' *Essays and Introductions* (London, 1961), pp. 13–27.

165. *Vale*, p. 169.
166. D. Ms. 141, [? 23 April 1904]. This account is also based on *Some Passages*, pp. 42–50, and unp. ltrs. from W. B. Yeats to AE, 21 February 1903, [17 June 1903], [17 July 1903].
167. Maire Nic Shiubhlaigh, *The Splendid Years*, p. 29. See also pp. 69–73. This narrative is also based on the following additional sources: *Letters*, pp. 52–54 [September 1905], 66; unp ltr. to Lady Gregory, [? autumn 1908]; several unp. ltrs. to W. B. Yeats, [August and September 1905]; several unp. ltrs. from W. B. Yeats to AE dated August and September [1905] and one dated Wednesday 9 [August 1905].
168. *Letters*, pp. 43, 56.
169. D. Ms. 101, to Stephen Gwynn, 29 April 1902, and 107, to W. B. Yeats, 7 July 1902.
170. *Letters*, p. 46.
171. *Some Passages*, p. 44; *Memoir*, pp. 61–64; *Bibliography*, p. 220.
172. Unp. ltrs. to Lady Gregory, 16 May 1904, 5 July 1904, and [? 2 September 1904].
173. Diarmuid Russell, 'AE, George William Russell,' *Modern Reading No. 10* (London, 1944), pp. 23–34; Katharine Tynan, *The Years of the Shadow* (London, 1919), p. 30; *Bibliography*, pp. 220–224.
174. Anne Marreco, *The Rebel Countess: The Life and Times of Constance Markievicz* (London, 1967), p. 98. The 'mysterious' catalogue mentioned on p. 88 of this book was printed for the art exhibition which opened on Monday, 11 October 1909.
175. L.A., *I.H.*, 24 August 1912, p. 677.
176. D. Ms. 130, to John Quinn, 20 January 1904.
177. Interview with Mr. Agloe of Dunfanaghy.
178. Interview with Mrs. Stewart of Dunfanaghy.
179. N.W., *I.H.*, 13 July 1912, p. 559.
180. Interview with Mrs. Stewart of Dunfanaghy.
181. B. L. Reid, *The Man from New York: John Quinn and His Friends* (New York, 1968), p. 45.
182. Unp. ltr., [early August 1905].
183. N.W., *I.H.*, 20 August 1910, p. 689. See also *Memoir*, p. 113; *Letters*, pp. 51–52, 235, 258; Oliver St. John Gogarty, 'An Angelic Anarchist,' *Colby Library Quarterly*, IV (May 1955), pp. 24–28.
184. Interview at Marble Hill with the family of the late Hugh Law.
185. Unp. ltr. to Frank Harris, 29 April 1921.
186. Y.O. [AE], 'True Dreams,' *I.S.*, 8 June 1929, pp. 271–272.

187. D. Ms. 389, to Cecil French, 29 June 1922.
188. *Memoir,* pp. 57–68.
189. 'Memoirs of George Roberts,' III, *Irish Times,* 19 July 1955, p. 5.
190. Kathleen M. O'Brennan, ' "AE" At Home and in the Art Gallery,' *Irish Packet,* VIII (7 September 1907), pp. 713–714.
191. B. L. Reid, *The Man from New York,* p. 22.
192. See Patrick Gallagher, *My Story* (Dungloe, n.d.), *passim.*
193. *Imaginations and Reveries,* p. 119.
194. D. Ms. 131, to John Quinn, [spring 1904].
195. D. Ms. 143, to Thomas Mosher, 23 January 1905.
196. *Salve,* pp. 73–75.

Chapter Five

1. Typewritten draft of Lady Gregory's 'Memoirs,' fol. 16, p. 8.
2. 'The Heroes,' *Collected Poems,* pp. 79–81.
3. N.W., *I.H.,* 8 February 1908, p. 103; *I.H.,* 12 December 1914, p. 882.
4. Unp. ltr. to Ernest Boyd, 6 July 1915.
5. N.W., *I.H.,* 21 August 1909, p. 671.
6. N.W., *I.H.,* 14 November 1908, p. 919.
7. E.g. L.A., *I.H.,* 27 January 1917, p. 49.
8. George W. Russell (AE), *Co-operation and Nationality: a Guide for Rural Reformers from This to the Next Generation* (Dublin, 1912), p. 28 (henceforward referred to as *Co-operation and Nationality*).
9. N.W., *I.H.,* 27 May 1911, p. 407.
10. N.W., *I.H.,* 2 May 1908, p. 347.
11. N.W., *I.H.,* 9 May 1908, p. 366.
12. N.W., *I.H.,* 5 January 1907, p. 3.
13. L.A., *I.H.,* 11 August 1906, p. 645.
14. D. Ms. 399, to St. John Ervine, 12 March 1923.
15. D. Ms. 338, to St. John Ervine, [? July 1918].
16. Lady Cynthia Asquith, *Diaries 1915–1918* (London, 1968), p. 62.
17. Moore, *Vale,* p. 166.
18. Robert Hogan and Michael J. O'Neill, ed. *Joseph Holloway's Abbey Theatre* (Carbondale and Edwardsville, Illinois, 1967), pp. 201–202.
19. Russell, 'AE,' p. 29.
20. Unp. ltr. to Séan O'Faolain, [c. 1926].

21. Ernest Boyd, *Portraits: Real and Imaginary* (New York, 1924), pp. 257–258; *Living Torch,* p. 22; Frank O'Connor, *My Father's Son* (London, 1968), p. 31.
22. Russell, 'AE,' pp. 23, 34.
23. N.W., *I.H.,* 27 July 1912, p. 601.
24. N.W., *I.H.,* 9 August 1913, p. 651.
25. Interview with Miss Irene Haugh.
26. Partly unp. ltr. to Frank Harris, 12 July 1921.
27. Unp. ltr. to W. T. H. Howe, 9 January 1929.
28. Clifford Bax, *Some I Knew Well* (London, 1951), p. 80.
29. D. Ms. 548, to W. B. Yeats, [late April 1932].
30. Unp. ltr. to E. H. W. Meyerstein, 7 February 1920.
31. D. Ms. 358, to John Quinn, 12 March 1920.
32. Francis Merchant, *AE: An Irish Promethean* (Columbia, S. Carolina, 1954), p. 204.
33. John Brennan, 'Dublin Fifty Years Ago,' III, *Irish Weekly Independent,* 19 May 1951, p. 4.
34. *Imaginations and Reveries,* p. 42.
35. Unp. ltr. to Miss A. W. Denijs, 10 September [1929].
36. D. Ms. 380, to James Stephens, [4 January 1922].
37. *James, Seumas and Jacques* (London, 1964), p. 114.
38. *Letters,* p. 64; *Memoir,* pp. 105–106.
39. D. Ms. 399, to St. John Ervine, 12 March 1923.
40. N.W., *I.H.,* 1 June 1912, p. 442.
41. D. Ms. 377, to W. B. Yeats, [? September 1921].
42. Unp. ltr. to Bernard Shaw, 30 June 1921.
43. G. B. Shaw, 'How Shaw and Russell Met,' *Pearson's Magazine,* XLVII (July 1921), p. 5.
44. Unp. ltr. to Ernest Boyd, [c. 1915].
45. Unp. ltr. to Israel Regardie, [c. December 1932].
46. Interview with Mr. Diarmuid Russell.
47. Clifford Bax, *Inland Far* (London, 1925), p. 142.
48. J. H. and M. E. Cousins, *We Two Together* (Madras, 1950), p. 245.
49. Arthur Power, *From the Old Waterford House* (Waterford and Dublin, 1940), pp. 29, 52.
50. 'The Selected Poems of AE,' *Poetry Review,* XXVII (January 1936), pp. 51–63; 'AE, Poet, Painter and Mystic,' *Poetry Review,* XXIX (January 1938), pp. 39–53; 'The Philosophy of AE,' *Occult Review,* July 1936, pp. 162–172; 'George W. Russell – Mystic,' ' "AE's" Religious Philosophy,' 'Mind Behind Organic Nature,' ' "AE's" Cosmic Philosophy,' 'AE and Origins of Religion,' 'The Philosophies of "AE",' *Light,* 3 June, 10 June, 17 June, 1 July, 22 July and 29 July,

1937, pp. 341, 357, 374, 410, 454, 469.
51. Hunt Grubb, ' "AE's" Cosmic Philosophy.'
52. D. Ms. 199, to Thomas Mosher, [June 1911].
53. 'On the Degeneration of the Drama,' *Sinn Fein*, 16 February 1907, p. 3.
54. AE, 'In Memoriam,' *Bean na h-Eireann*, II (February 1911), p. 11.
55. *Collected Poems*, pp. 229–230.
56. L.A., *I.H.*, 11 June 1910, p. 479.
57. *I.H.*, 25 June 1910, p. 525.
58. *I.H.*, 28 May 1910, p. 445.
59. N.W., *I.H.*, 28 May 1910, p. 440.
60. N.W., *I.H.*, 13 August 1910, p. 670.
61. N.W., *I.H.*, 21 February 1920, p. 122.
62. L.A., *I.H.*, 31 December 1910, p. 1085.
63. R. A. Anderson, *With Horace Plunkett in Ireland* (London, 1935), p. 175.
64. Cf. Porter, ed. *Mínanlábáin*, p. 29.
65. pp. 44, 94.
66. N.W., *I.H.*, 15 June 1907, p. 467.
67. L.A., *I.H.*, 28 April 1906, p. 333
68. E.g. 'Back to the Ten Commandments,' *I.S.*, 29 March 1924, pp. 70–71.
69. Unp. ltr., [summer 1916].
70. *I.H.*, 2 May 1908, p. 346.
71. N.W., *I.H.*, 7 December 1912, p. 995.
72. N.W., *I.H.*, 2 April 1910, p. 271.
73. N.W., *I.H.*, 23 November 1912, p. 943.
74. L.A., *I.H.*, 2 November 1912, p. 881; N.W., *I.H.*, 23 November 1912, p. 945.
75. L.A., *I.H.*, 1 August 1908, p. 605.
76. D. Ms. 165, 12 March 1909.
77. Unp. ltr. from Henry Wallace to Prof. Richard Cary, 22 April 1961.
78. *Song and Its Fountains*, p. 94.
79. N.W., *I.H.*, 21 September 1907, p. 747.
80. N.W., *I.H.*, 5 March 1910, p. 183.
81. L.A., *I.H.*, 7 August 1909, p. 629.
82. L.A., *I.H.*, 19 February 1910, p. 142.
83. N.W., *I.H.*, 1 May 1909, p. 352.
84. N.W., *I.H.*, 26 March 1910, p. 252.
85. Gibbon, 'Thesis,' p. 25.
86. N.W., *I.H.*, 9 April 1910, p. 291; N.W., *I.H.*, 28 May 1910, p. 441.

87. L.A., *I.H.,* 25 November 1911, p. 933.
88. N.W., *I.H.,* 29 February 1908, p. 165.
89. L.A. and N.W., *I.H.,* 22 February 1908, pp. 141, 144.
90. L.A., *I.H.,* 1 August 1914, p. 613.
91. *Co-operation and Nationality,* p. 35.
92. L.A., *I.H.,* 21 August 1909, p. 669.
93. N.W., *I.H.,* 12 December 1908, p. 993.
94. L.A., *I.H.,* 6 September 1913, p. 737.
95. N.W., *I.H.,* 11 January 1913, p. 26.
96. N.W., *I.H.,* 21 December 1918, p. 830.
97. L.A., *I.H.,* 11 May 1907, p. 366.
98. *Letters,* pp. 68–69.
99. N.W., *I.H.,* 24 October 1908, p. 859.
100. *Co-operation and Nationality,* p. 92.
101. N.W., *I.H.,* 13 March 1909, p. 203.
102. N.W., *I.H.,* 13 July 1907, p. 547.
103. L.A., *I.H.,* 27 November 1915, p. 777.
104. Unp. ltr. to Frank Harris, 18 May 1921.
105. L.A., *I.H.,* 2 September 1911, p. 685.
106. *I.H.,* 24 April 1909, p. 323.
107. George W. Russell, 'The Department and the I.A.O.S.,' *Freeman's Journal,* 14 November 1911, p. 10.
108. L.A., *I.H.,* 8 August 1914, p. 633.
109. N.W., *I.H.,* 28 January 1911, p. 65.
110. N.W., *I.H.,* 20 September 1913, p. 780.
111. N.W., *I.H.,* 7 January 1911, p. 5.
112. D. Ms. 201, to Charles Weekes, [? 1 December 1911].
113. D. Ms. 174, [postmark 14 November 1909].
114. D. Ms. 213, to Thomas Mosher, 8 February 1913.
115. Unp. ltr. to Padraic Colum, 27 December 1916.
116. L.A., *I.H.,* 30 September 1916, p. 613.
117. Plunkett's unp. Diary, 9 January 1910. The operation – D. Ms. 176, to Charles Weekes, 27 January 1910.
118. D. Ms. 180, to Charles Weekes, [? 21 April 1910].
119. Plunkett's unp. Diary, 8 November 1912.
120. *Letters,* pp. 72–73.
121. D. Ms. 213, to Thomas Mosher, 8 February 1913.
122. L. A. G. Strong, 'William Butler Yeats,' *Scattering Branches: Tributes to the Memory of W. B. Yeats,* ed. S. L. Gwynn (New York, 1940), pp. 183–229; L. A. G. Strong, 'Yeats at His Ease,' *London Magazine,* II (March 1955), pp. 56–65.
123. Unp. ltr. to Ernest Boyd, 14 March 1913 [error for 1914].
124. *Letters,* p. 96.
125. AE, ' "Twenty-five Years," ' *I.H.,* 25 April 1914, p. 326.

126. Frank Harris, *Latest Contemporary Portraits* (New York, 1927), pp. 78–79.
127. *I.H.*, 14 October 1916, p. 649.
128. Arnold Bax, *Farewell My Youth* (London, 1943), p. 97.
129. 'Sunset of Fantasy,' p. 7.
130. Padraic Colum, 'A Poet's Impression of AE, Ireland's Sage,' *World Review*, VI (19 March 1928), pp. 117, 121.
131. Warre B. Wells, *Irish Indiscretions* (London, [1922]), p. 201; Padraic Colum, 'The Faith and Works of AE,' *New Republic*, XCIV (30 March 1938), pp. 228–229.
132. *James, Seumas and Jacques* (London, 1964), p. 119.
133. G. K. Chesterton, *Irish Impressions* (New York, 1920), p. 140.
134. *Letters*, p. 65.
135. *Living Torch*, p. 8.
136. N.W., *I.H.*, 20 October 1906, p. 851.
137. *Letters*, p. 179.
138. *Ibid.*, p. 65.
139. *Twenty-five Years: Reminiscences* (London, 1913), pp. 248–249.
140. 'AE, George William Russell,' *Modern Reading No. 10* (London, 1944), pp. 23–34.
141. Constantine P. Curran, 'George Russell (AE) 1867–1935,' *Studies*, XXIV (September 1935), pp. 366–378.
142. E. R. Dodds, ed. *Journal and Letters of Stephen MacKenna* (London, 1936), pp. 162–164.
143. Prelude to AE, *The Hèro in Man* (London, 1909), pp. 3–8.
144. C. C. Coates, *Some Less-known Chapters in the Life of AE (George Russell)* (Dublin: privately printed, 1939), p. 4.
145. Interview with Mr. Colum.
146. 'Ireland's Modern Mystic,' *New York Herald Tribune*, 6 February 1938, section ix, p. 4.
147. 'AE,' p. 29. See also p. 32.
148. D. Ms. 399, to St. John Ervine, 12 March 1923.
149. Unp. ltr., 3 June 1925.
150. L. S. Amery, *My Political Life* (London, 1953), I, p. 398.
151. *Letters*, pp. 82–83, 112. On p. 82 'last week' is AE's error for 'last month.'
152. D. Ms. 162, 215, 217, 218, all to Charles Weekes, [3 March 1909], [12 May 1913], [15 May 1913], [15 May 1913].
153. D. Ms. 216, 344, both to Sir Frederick Macmillan, [May 1913], 15 January 1919.
154. Unp. ltr. to AE, 18 October 1913.
155. Cornelius Weygandt, *Irish Plays and Playwrights* (Boston and New York, 1913), pp. 119–120.

156. Printed A. C. Bose, *Three Mystic Poets* (Kolhapur, 1945), p. 95.
157. *I.H.*, 19 July 1913, p. 597.
158. Plunkett's unp. Diary, 15 July 1913.
159. D. Ms. 220, to Charles Weekes, 14 July 1913.
160. Ltr. to Ernest Boyd, n.d., quoted *Colby Library Quarterly*, IV (May 1955), p. 40.
161. N.W., *I.H.*, 9 August 1913, p. 654.
162. N.W., *I.H.*, 23 August 1913, p. 692.
163. N.W., *I.H.*, 16 September 1911, p. 728.
164. L.A., *I.H.*, 10 February 1912, p. 104.
165. J. Dunsmore Clarkson, *Labour and Nationalism in Ireland* (New York, 1925), pp. 10–11, 215.
166. Katharine Tynan, *The Years of the Shadow* (London, 1919), p. 307.
167. Unp. ltr. to Ernest Boyd, 12 April 1915.
168. L.A., *I.H.*, 6 September 1913, p. 737.
169. Darrell Figgis, *AE (George W. Russell): a Study of a Man and a Nation* (Dublin and London, 1916), p. 97.
170. Unp. ltr. to Ernest Boyd, 12 April 1915.
171. Lennox Robinson, ed. *Lady Gregory's Journals 1916–1930* (New York, 1947), p. 97.
172. L.A., *I.H.*, 4 October 1913, p. 817.
173. E. R. Dodds, ed. *Journal and Letters of Stephen MacKenna* (London, 1936), p. 141.
174. *Letters*, pp. 85–88.
174a. H. M. Tomlinson, 'Memories of "AE",' *Observer*, 28 July 1935.
175. George Russell, 'The Crime and the Punishment,' *Irish Worker*, 1 November 1913, p. 3.
176. R. M. Fox, *Jim Larkin: the Rise of the Underman* (London, 1957), p. 105.
177. 'AE' (George W. Russell), *The Dublin Strike* (London, 1913), pp. 1–4. See also *Letters*, pp. 90–91.
178. N.W., *I.H.*, 15 November 1913, p. 943.
179. D. Ms. 230, to Sir John Squire, [7 November 1913].
180. *Letters*, pp. 91–94.
181. Emmet Larkin, *James Larkin* (Cambridge, Massachusetts, 1965), p. 168.
182. *Letters*, p. 91.
183. *Memoir*, p. 112.
184. Draft of 'Sunset.'
185. Douglas Goldring, *The Nineteen Twenties* (London, 1945), p. 117.

186. Unp. ltr. to Ernest Boyd, 14 March 1913 [error for 1914].
187. N.W., *I.H.*, 16 May 1914, p. 384.
188. *Letters*, p. 96.
189. Unp. ltr. to Upton Sinclair, 2 October 1914.

Chapter Six

1. L.A., *I.H.*, 3 January 1914, p. 1.
2. N.W., *I.H.*, 21 February 1914, p. 145.
3. L.A., *I.H.*, 2 May 1914, p. 341.
4. *Letters*, p. 97.
5. N.W., *I.H.*, 4 April 1914, p. 263; L.A., *I.H.*, 9 May 1914, p. 360.
6. G.W.R., 'Peace or War?' *Pioneer*, I (March 1911), pp. 75–76.
7. L.A., *I.H.*, 18 April 1914, p. 301.
8. D. Ms. 336, to James Stephens, [10 May 1918].
9. B. L. Reid, *The Man from New York: John Quinn and His Friends* (New York, 1968), pp. 184–185.
10. N.W., *I.H.*, 18 July 1914, p. 574.
11. L.A., *I.H.*, 1 August 1914, p. 613.
12. D. Ms. 256, to Thomas Mosher, 2 January 1915.
13. W. B. Yeats, *Tribute to Thomas Davis* (Oxford, 1947), pp. 20–22.
14. G. B. Shaw, *The Matter with Ireland* (London, 1962), pp. 86–87.
15. Lloyd Morris, *A Threshold in the Sun* (New York, 1943), pp. 151–157.
16. Katharine Tynan, *The Years of the Shadow* (London, 1919), p. 96.
17. *Letters*, p. 214 n. 3.
18. D. Ms. 519, to Osborn Bergin, 19 December 1930.
19. *Bibliography*, p. 180.
20. *Letters*, p. 98; *Memoir*, pp. 114–115.
21. D. Ms. 256, to Thomas Mosher, 2 January 1915.
22. *Letters*, pp. 99–100; *Bibliography*, pp. 223–224.
23. *Letters*, p. 100.
24. *Collected Poems*, pp. 236–238.
25. *Letters*, p. 99.
26. N.W., *I.H.*, 10 April 1915, p. 232.
27. N.W., *I.H.*, 15 August 1914, p. 656.
28. H. T. Hunt Grubb, ' "AE's" Religious Philosophy,' *Light*, LVII (10 June 1937), p. 357.

29. N.W., *I.H.*, 19 September 1914, p. 719.
30. L.A., *I.H.*, 21 November 1914, p. 833.
31. 'Statesmen,' *Gods of War* (Dublin: privately printed, 1915), pp. 14–15.
32. 'The Spiritual Conflict,' *Imaginations and Reveries*, pp. 86–92.
33. *Letters*, p. 102.
34. *Ibid.*, p. 103. See also p. 105.
35. D. Ms. 270, [? 12 July 1915].
36. D. Ms. 358, 12 March 1920.
37. N.W., *I.H.*, 5 December 1914, p. 864.
38. D. Ms. 269, to St. John Ervine, 31 May 1915.
39. N.W., *I.H.*, 20 March 1915, p. 184.
40. D. Ms. 276, to Charles Weekes, 17 September 1915.
41. Reid, *The Man from New York*, p. 240.
42. D. Ms. 261, to Mrs. St. John Ervine, 5 March 1915.
43. L.A., *I.H.*, 23 October 1915, p. 697.
44. N.W., *I.H.*, 5 February 1916, p. 84.
45. N.W., *I.H.*, 3 August 1907, p. 609.
46. L.A., *I.H.*, 29 May 1915, p. 353; L.A., *I.H.*, 13 November 1915, p. 745.
47. N.W., *I.H.*, 22 August 1914, p. 667.
48. *Memoir*, pp. 115–116; *Letters*, p. 110.
49. D. Ms. 322, to Mabel O'Brien, [25 December 1917].
50. N.W., *I.H.*, 29 April, 6–13 May 1916, p. 286.
51. D. Ms. 293, to John Quinn, 1 September 1916.
52. AE's Foreword to Vane's *Agin the Governments* (London, [1929]), p. vii.
53. D. Ms. 322, to Mabel O'Brien, [25 December 1917].
54. N.W., *I.H.*, 31 May 1913, p. 450; AE 'Standish O'Grady,' *I.S.*, 26 May 1928, p. 231.
55. 'Prose and Poetry of AE,' *Times Literary Supplement*, 23 October 1937, pp. 765–766.
56. Unp. ltrs. to Bernard Shaw, 24 May and 13 June 191[6].
57. 'Address to the Thirtieth Annual Dinner,' *Journal of the American-Irish Historical Society*, XXVII (1928), pp. 367–380.
58. L.A., *I.H.*, 29 April, 6–13 May 1916, p. 285.
59. Quoted Reid, *The Man from New York*, p. 187.
60. D. Ms. 293, to John Quinn, 1 September 1916.
61. *Letters*, pp. 112–114.
62. *Ibid.*, p. 111.
63. *Ibid.*, p. 115.
64. Unp. ltr. to Bernard Shaw, [summer 1916].
65. D. Ms. 293, 1 September 1916.

66. Unp. ltr. to Padraic Colum, 27 December 1916.
67. *Ibid.*
68. N.W., *I.H.,* 7 October 1916, p. 632.
69. Unp. ltr. to Padraic Colum, 7 August 1923.
70. 'Sackville Street, 1917,' *Dublin Magazine,* I (December 1923), p. 367. See also 'Twenty-five Years of Irish Nationality,' *Foreign Affairs,* VII (January 1929), pp. 204–220.
71. *Candle of Vision,* p. 151.
72. D. Ms. 316, to John Quinn, 28 July 1917.
73. Austin Clarke, *A Penny in the Clouds* (London, 1968), pp. 51–56.
74. Ltr. to Miss Grace Emily Jameson, 10 May 1932, quoted in the recipient's unp. thesis, 'Mysticism in AE and Yeats in Relation to Oriental and American Thought' (Ohio, 1932), p. 83.
75. *Living Torch,* pp. 39–40.
76. *Letters,* p. 231; Richard J. Finneran, 'Two Unpublished Letters from AE,' *Papers on Language and Literature,* III (Summer 1967), pp. 220–228.
77. *Letters,* pp. 121–123.
78. Unp. ltr. to Padraic Colum, 6 July 1917.
79. Unp. ltrs. to Lady Gregory, Saturday [26 May] and 28 May 1917.
80. D. Ms. 311, [June 1917].
81. Unp. ltr. to Padraic Colum, 6 July, 1917.
82. N.W., *I.H.,* 7 July 1917, p. 506.
83. D. Ms. 316, to John Quinn, 28 July 1917.
84. *Letters,* p. 129.
85. *Ibid.,* p. 125.
86. D. Ms. 316, to John Quinn, 28 July 1917.
87. *The Economics of Ireland and the Policy of the British Government* (New York, 1920), pp. 11-12.
88. Sir Horace Plunkett, *The Irish Convention. Confidential Report to His Majesty the King,* paras. 36-37.
89. Plunkett, *Confidential Report,* para. 135.
90. *Letters,* p. 134.
91. Plunkett, *Confidential Report,* paras. 141-142.
92. *Letters,* p. 136.
93. *Ibid.,* p. 138.
94. *Ibid.,* pp. 138-140.
95. *Imaginations and Reveries,* 2nd ed., pp. 152-160.
96. *Letters,* p. 132.
97. D. Ms. 333, to John Quinn, 11 February 1918.
98. N.W., *I.H.,* 18 August 1917, p. 623; L.A., *I.H.,* 22 February

1919, p. 115.
99. N.W., *I.H.,* 24 October 1914, p. 780.
100. L.A., *I.H.,* 27 October 1917, p. 789; N.W., *I.H.,* 3 November 1917, p. 807.
101. L.A., *I.H.,* 20 April 1918, p. 269.
102. *Letters,* pp. 141-144.
103. *Memoir;* p. 128 D. Ms. 338, [? July 1918].
104. D. Ms. 337, to James Stephens, [26 June 1918].
105. Margaret I. Cole, ed. *Beatrice Webb's Diaries 1912–1924* (London, 1952), pp. 131-132.
106. N.W., *I.H.,* 24 February 1917, p. 128.
107. Unp. ltr. to James Pryse, 24 July 1919.
108. Reid, *The Man from New York,* p. 317.
109. *Living Torch,* p. 46.
110. *Candle of Vision,* p. 48. See also p. 31.
111. N.W., *I.H.,* 16 November 1918, p. 750.
112. N.W., *I.H.,* 21 July 1917, p. 544.
113. N.W., *I.H.,* 17 November 1917, p. 839.
114. *Letters,* pp. 145-148.
115. L.A., *I.H.,* 7 June 1919, p. 405.
116. Yeats, *Letters,* p. 656.
117. N.W., *I.H.,* 16 October 1920, pp. 758, 760.
118. N.W., *I.H.,* 4 January 1919, p. 3.
119. N.W., *I.H.,* 21 May 1921, p. 349.
120. N.W., *I.H.,* 20 September 1919, p. 700.
121. L.A., *I.H.,* 29 November 1919, p. 867.
122. N.W., *I.H.,* 31 January 1920, p. 71.
123. Unp. ltr. to Douglas Goldring, 26 March 1919.
124. N.W., *I.H.,* 22 November 1919, p. 856.
125. N.W., *I.H.,* 8 May 1920, p. 337.
126. D. Ms. 439. to Charles Weekes. 30 November 1926.
127. D. Ms. 347, to Charles Weekes, [7 February 1919].
128. *Song and Its Fountains,* pp. 58-59.
129. D. Ms. 355. to Joanna Fortune. [postmark 27 January 1920].
130. D. Ms. 358. to John Quinn. 12 March 1920.
131. Francis Merchant, *A.E.: An Irish Promethean* (Columbia, S. Carolina, 1954), p. 237.
132. D. Ms. 440. [6 December 1926].
133. Unp. ltr. to Mr. Hackett.
134. *I.H.,* 18 December 1920, p. 901.
135. N.W., *I.H.,* 13 November 1920, p. 821; L.A., *I.H.,* 27 November 1920, p. 851.
136. N.W., *I.H.,* 23 April 1921, p. 280. See also N.W., *I.H.,* 12 March 1921, p. 169.

137. N.W., *I.H.*, 28 June 1913, p. 532; N.W., *I.H.*, 25 December 1920, p. 918.
138. N.W., *I.H.*, 4 February 1922, pp. 68, 70.
139. *I.S.*, 30 March 1929, p. 75.
140. Unp. ltr. to Frank Harris, 29 April 1921.
141. N.W., *I.H.*, 6 November 1920, p. 805.
142. Unp. ltr., 25 August 1920.
143. 'A Prisoner,' *Collected Poems*, pp. 354-355.
144. *Bibliography*, p. 155.
145. N.W., *I.H.*, 10 September 1921, p. 622.
146. Vera Watson, 'AE to E. H. W. Meyerstein,' *English*, XII (Autumn 1959), pp. 220-225.
147. Frank Harris, *Latest Contemporary Portraits* (New York, 1927), pp. 80-81.
148. *Memoir*, p. 138.
149. Unp. ltr. to E. H. W. Meyerstein, [postmark 8 December 1920].
150. *Some Passages*, p. 54.
151. A.E., 'Twenty-five Years of Irish Nationality,' *Foreign Affairs*, VII (January 1929), pp. 204-220.
152. L.A., p. 915.
153. Mary Devenport O'Neill, 'A.E. is Dead,' *Irish Times*, 23 July 1935, p. 6.
154. Unp. ltr. to E. H. W. Meyerstein, [postmark 8 December 1920].
155. Partly unp. ltr. to Sir William Rothenstein, 13 January 1921.
156. Yeats, *Letters*, pp. 665-671; *Some Passages*, pp. 50-51, 54.
157. O'Neill, 'A.E. is Dead.'
158. Unp. ltr., 29 March 1921.
159. N.W., *I.H.*, 6 November 1920, p. 805.
160. Henry W. Nevinson, 'AE: The Mystical Farmer,' *Week-end Review*, II (13 September 1930), pp. 340-341.
161. Desmond MacCarthy, 'Memories of "AE",' *Sunday Times*, 28 July 1935, p. 6.
162. Mary Colum, 'AE,' *Saturday Review of Literature*, XII (27 July 1935), pp. 11-12.
163. *Living Torch*, p. 57.
164. Warre B. Wells, *Irish Indiscretions* (London, [1922]), pp. 142-143.
165. 'Looking Back,' *I.S.*, 22 November 1924, pp. 327-328.
166. *Memoir*, p. 136.
167. D. Ms. 439, to Charles Weekes, 30 November 1926.
168. 'Farewell to A.E.,' a broadcast talk by Campbell, 23 July 1935.
169. Frank Gallagher, *The Anglo-Irish Treaty*

(London, 1965), p. 28.

170. Unp. ltr. to L. A. G. Strong, n.d.
171. Harris, *Latest Contemporary Portraits,* p. 94.
172. Unp. ltrs. to Frank Harris, 29 March and 29 April 1921.
173. Unp. ltr. to Lady Gregory, 1 June 1921.
174. D. Ms. 369, to W. B. Yeats, 10 March 1921.
175. Partly unp. ltr. to E. H. W. Meyerstein, 25 May 1921.
176. Unp. ltr. to Frank Harris, 10 June 1921.
177. N.W., *I.H.,* 16 July 1921, p. 486.
178. Henry W. Nevinson, *Last Changes Last Chances* (New York, 1929), pp. 193, 197.
179. L.A., *I.H.,* 20 August 1921, p. 571.
180. Lennox Robinson, ed. *Lady Gregory's Journals 1916-1930* (New York, 1947), p. 158.
181. N.W., *I.H.,* 3 February 1923, p. 64.
182. Edgar DeWitt Jones, 'An Evening with AE,' *Christian Century,* LV (20 April 1938), pp. 491-493.
183. Unp. ltr. to Padraic Colum, 16 May 1923.
184. Unp. ltr. to T. J. Kiernan, 21 August 1923.
185. AE's unp. report 'Ulster and Irish Trade Policy.'
186. E. R. Dodds, ed. *Journal and Letters of Stephen MacKenna* (London, 1936), p. 208; Nevinson, *Last Changes Last Chances,* p. 186.
187. Unp. ltr. to Bernard Shaw, 8 September 1923.
188. 'Irish Anticipations,' *Survey,* XLVII (26 November 1921), pp. 291-294.
189. *Memoir,* pp. 142-143.
190. Harold Speakman, *Here's Ireland,* 4th printing (New York, 1927), p. 202.
191. Partly unp. ltr. to Sir Henry Lawson, 28 December 1921.
192. L.A., *I.H.,* 31 December 1921, p. 873.
193. D. Ms. 381, to W. B. Yeats, 16 January 1922. See also Robinson, ed. *Lady Gregory's Journals,* p. 162, and M. J. MacManus, *Eamon de Valera* (Dublin and Cork, 1945), p. 182.
194. L.A., *I.H.,* 17 December 1921, p. 841.
195. N.W., *I.H.,* 11 February 1922, p. 83.
196. N.W., *I.H.,* 18 February 1922, p. 98; N.W., *I.H.,* 28 January 1922, p. 50.
197. Unp. ltr. from W. B. Yeats to AE, [12 January 1922].
198. D. Ms. 381, 16 January 1922.
199. George Russell (A.E.), *Ireland Past and Future* (London 1922), p. 17.
200. D. Ms. 383 and 384, to W. B. Yeats, 21 and 30 March 1922, and unp. ltr. from Yeats to AE, 30 March [1922].

201. Unp. ltr. from Mrs. Padraic Colum to AE, [1922], and unp. ltr. to Mrs. Padraic Colum, 5 April 1922.
202. Robinson, ed. *Lady Gregory's Journals,* p. 173.
203. D. Ms. 386, 9 May 1922.
204. L.A., *I.H.,* 18 February 1922, p. 97.
205. N.W., *I.H.,* 27 May 1922, p. 330.
206. Speakman, *Here's Ireland,* pp. 54-57. See also *Colby Library Quarterly,* IV (May 1955), p. 43.
207. Robinson, ed. *Lady Gregory's Journals,* p. 184.
208. Oliver St. John Gogarty, *It Isn't This Time of Year at All* (London, 1954), pp. 183-184.
209. L.A., *I.H.,* 30 September 1922, p. 581.
210. L.A., *I.H.,* 23 September 1922, p. 569.
211. D. Ms. 391, to St John Ervine, 31 July [1922].
212. Robinson, ed. *Lady Gregory's Journals,* p. 180.
213. L.A., *I.H.,* 2 September 1922, p. 533.
214. Unp. ltr., 20 December 1922.
215. Unp. ltr. to E. H. W. Meyerstein, 26 August 1922.
216. H. Summerfield, ed. 'Unpublished Letters from AE to John Eglinton,' *Malahat Review,* April 1970, pp. 84-107.
217. Unp. ltr. to James Pryse, 2 March 1924.
218. P. 38.
219. L.A., *I.H.,* 14 October 1922, p. 605.
220. N.W., *I.H.,* 21 October 1922, p. 618.
221. Unp. ltr. to Lady Gregory, 20 December 1922.
222. Unp. ltr. to Lady Gregory, 3 January 1923.
223. Unp. ltr. to Padraic Colum, 16 May 1923.
224. 'Lessons of Revolution,' *Studies,* XII (March 1923), pp. 1-6.
225. L.A., *I.H.,* 27 January 1923, p. 45.
226. L.A., *I.H.,* 17 February 1923, p. 85.
227. N.W., *I.H.,* 18 August 1923, p. 523.
228. D.Ms. 401, 10 May [19] 23.
229. Plunkett's unp. Diary, 2 June 1923.
230. Unp. ltr., 16 May 1923.
231. *Colby Library Quarterly,* IV (May 1955), p. 43.
232. Unp. ltr., 25 August 1923.
233. N.W., *I.H.,* 15 January 1921, p. 38.
234. N.W., *I.H.,* 6 January 1917, p. 4; N.W., *I.H.,* 6 July 1918, p. 447; L.A., *I.H.,* 2 September 1916, p. 549.
235. A.E., 'The Leaders of Indian Nationalism,' *I.S.,* 4 October 1924, pp. 111-112.
236. William Lyon Phelps, *Autobiography with Letters* (New York, London, Toronto, 1939), p. 828.

Chapter Seven

1. 'An Evening with AE,' *Christian Century,* LV (20 April 1938), pp. 491–493.
2. *Living Torch,* p. 63.
3. Unp. ltr.. 16 October 1923.
4. H. Summerfield, ed. 'Unpublished Letters from AE to John Eglinton,' *Malahat Review,* April 1970, pp. 84–107.
5. Unp. ltr. to James Pryse, 2 March 1924.

5a. *Irish Literary Portraits . . . W. R. Rodgers's Broadcast Conversations* (London, 1972), p. 190. See also Y.O., 'Art Exhibitions,' *I.S.,* 21 November 1925, p. 337.

6. H. T. Hunt Grubb, 'AE, Poet, Painter and Mystic,' *Poetry Review,* XXIX (January 1938), pp. 39–53.
7. Unp. ltr. to James Pryse, 2 March 1924.
8. Unp. ltr. to James Pryse, 29 November 1923.
9. Unp. ltr. from James Pryse to AE, 19 February 1925.
10. *Living Torch,* pp. 23–24.
11. Monk Gibbon, *The Masterpiece and the Man: Yeats as I Knew Him* (London, 1959), pp. 47, 85.
12. Simone Téry, *L'île des bardes* (Paris, 1925), pp. 99–139.
13. D. Ms. 598, from Simone Téry to AE, 29 October 1933.
14. Translated from Téry, *L'île des bardes,* p. 106.
15. B. L. Reid, *The Man from New York: John Quinn and His Friends* (New York, 1968), p. 528.
16. L. A. G. Strong, *Green Memory* (London, 1961), p. 304.
17. Gibbon, *The Masterpiece and the Man,* p. 56. See also pp. 48, 107.
18. 'A Modern Equivalent to the Sagas,' *I.S.,* 24 August 1929, pp. 490–491.
19. Unp. ltr. to James Pryse, 9 October 1924.
20. Interview with Miss Irene Haugh.
21. *I.S.,* 14 January 1928, p. 438.
22. Interview with Miss Irene Haugh.
23. Unp. ltr. to James Stephens, 1 May 1925.
24. 'A Letter from AE,' *Canadian Theosophist,* XVI (August 1935), p. 166.
25. Unp. ltr. to Bernard Shaw, 17 August 1923.
26. N.C., *I.S.,* 24 November 1928, pp. 224–225; N.C., *I.S.,* 20 February 1926, p. 734.
27. 'Greater Dublin,' *I.S.,* 29 December 1923, pp. 487–488.
28. *I.S.,* 20 September 1924, pp. 43–44.
29. *I.S.,* 19 September 1925, pp. 47–48.
30. N.C. *I.S.,* 6 December 1924. p. 387
31. 'The Army and the Nation,' *I.S.,* 12 January 1924, pp. 550–

551.
32. N.W., *I.H.*, 19 August 1922, p. 507.
33. N.C., *I.S.*, 22 January 1927, p. 468.
34. 'The Making of a Fascist State,' *I.S.*, 20 April 1929, pp. 132–133.
35. E.g. N.C., *I.S.*, 7 November 1925, p. 261.
36. 'A Confession of Faith,' *I.S.*, 15 September 1923, pp. 3–5.
37. *I.S.*, 9 August 1924, pp. 702, 704; N.C., *I.S.*, 12 September 1925, p. 6.
38. *I.S.*, 27 December 1924, pp. 504–505.
39. *I.S.*, 12 September 1925, pp. 20, 22.
40. N.C., *I.S.*, 3 November 1923, pp. 228–229.
41. 'Art, Science and Civilisation,' *I.S.*, 15 March 1924, pp. 15–16.
42. 'From Peasant to Scientist,' *I.S.*, 7 February 1925, pp. 692, 694.
43. *I.S.*, 19 October 1929, p. 128.
44. 'Is Literature in a Blind Alley?' *I.S.*, 9 February 1924, pp. 685–686.
45. *I.S.*, 24 December 1927, pp. 377–378.
46. 'Magazines,' *I.S.*, 20 October 1928, p. 138.
47. *I.S.*, 21 November 1925, p. 346.
48. N.C., *I.S.*, 8 August 1925, pp. 679–680.
49. N.C., *I.S.*, 14 March 1925, p. 4, *et al.*; N.C., *I.S.*, 23 May 1925, p. 324.
50. *I.H.*, 15 February 1913, p. 125.
51. N.W., *I.H.*, 17 May 1913, p. 408.
52. *Letters*, pp. 163–164.
53. *I.S.*, 15 December 1923, pp. 436, 438.
54. 'The Essays of W. B. Yeats,' *I.S.*, 7 June 1924, pp. 397–398.
55. 'Leonardo, the Florentine,' *I.S.*, 12 November 1927, pp. 227–228.
56. 'Poetical Prose,' *I.S.*, 17 December 1927, pp. 350–351.
57. *I.S.*, 25 July 1925, p. 628; *I.S.*, 26 September 1925, p. 89.
58. N.W., *I.H.*, 15 September 1917, p. 692. See also 'A Gold Standard for Literature,' *I.S.*, 2 March 1929, pp. 516–517.
59. 'Is Literature in a Blind Alley?' *I.S.*, 9 February 1924, pp. 685–686.
60. 'The Squandering of National Feeling,' *I.S.*, 27 October 1923, pp. 197–199.
61. N.C., *I.S.*, 10 November 1923, pp. 262–263; Lennox Robinson, ed. *Lady Gregory's Journals 1916–1930* (New York, 1947), pp. 194–195.
62. N.C., *I.S.*, 10 July 1926, p. 479.
63. 'The Lane Pictures,' *I.S.*, 17 July 1926, pp. 510–511.

64. 'An Honourable Agreement,' *I.S.,* 12 December 1925, pp. 422–423.
65. Robinson, ed. *Lady Gregory's Journals,* p. 319.
66. 'AE As I Knew Him,' *Irish Monthly,* CXLIV (September 1935), pp. 606–613.
67. N.C., *I.S.,* 28 February 1925, p. 776.
68. Unp. ltr. to Bernard Shaw, 21 February 1929.
69. N.W., *I.H.,* 19 May 1923, p. 295.
70. N.C., *I.S.,* 15 December 1928, p. 288.
71. *Bibliography,* p. 37.
72. R. M. Fox, ' "AE" Speaks of Ireland's Future,' *New Leader,* 5 June 1925, pp. 10–11.
73. 'The Beggar Within Our Gates,' *I.S.,* 5 September 1925, pp. 810–811.
74. N.C., *I.S.,* 5 June 1926, p. 343.
75. *Letters,* p. 166.
76. Unp. ltr. to Theodore Spicer Simson, 28 July 1922.
77. Harold Speakman, *Here's Ireland,* 4th printing (New York, 1927), p. 288.
78. *Song and Its Fountains,* pp. 76–77, 84.
79. Unp. ltr. to James Pryse, 4 September 1925.
80. Robert Hogan and Michael J. O'Neill, ed. *Joseph Holloway's Irish Theatre* (Dixon, California, 1968), I, p. 16.
81. Unp. ltr. to Herbert Palmer, 29 December 1925.
82. Robinson, ed. *Lady Gregory's Journals,* pp. 277–279.
83. Unp. ltr. to James Stephens, 1 May 1925.
84. L. A. G. Strong, *Green Memory* (London, 1961), p. 306.
85. L. A. G. Strong, ' "AE" – a Practical Mystic,' *Listener,* LIII (10 March 1955), pp. 427–428.
86. Quoted *Living Torch,* pp. 20–21.
87. Strong, *Green Memory,* p. 303.
88. *I.S.,* 7 March 1925, pp. 822, 824.
89. 'The Silver Tassie,' *I.S.,* 21 July 1928, pp. 391–392.
90. *I.S.,* 18 January 1930, p. 394.
91. Frank O'Connor, *My Father's Son* (London, 1968), pp. 82, 84.
92. E.g. D. Ms. 444 and 574, to Sean O'Faolain, 25 January 1927 and 11 April 1933.
93. D. Ms. 316, to John Quinn, 28 July 1917.
94. *I.S.,* 8 December 1928, pp. 279–280.
95. *I.S.,* 9 January 1926, pp. 564, 566.
96. *I.S.,* 5 October 1929, p. 98.
97. D. Ms. 619, to Ruth Pitter, 16 August 1934.
98. Introductory Essay to Hugh MacDiarmid, *First Hymn to*

Lenin and Other Poems (London, 1931), pp. 1–6.

99. B. L. Reid, *The Man from New York: John Quinn and His Friends* (New York, 1968), pp. 355, 530.
100. Porter, ed. *Mínanlábáin,* p. 38.
101. 'A Study of American Culture,' *I.S.,* 19 February 1927, pp. 573–574, 576.
102. 'Adventures in Style,' *I.S.,* 16 April 1927, pp. 136–138.
103. *I.S.,* 29 December 1928, p. 339.
104. 'Magazines,' *I.S.,* 16 March 1929, pp. 38–39.
105. 'The Youth of a Poet,' *I.S.,* 17 October 1925, pp. 176–177.
106. N.W., *I.H.,* 7 January 1922, p. 4.
107. Reid, *The Man from New York,* p. 386.
108. 'The Essays of W. B. Yeats,' *I.S.,* 7 June 1924, pp. 397–398.
109. Monk Gibbon, *The Masterpiece and the Man: Yeats as I Knew Him* (London, 1959), pp. 82–83.
110. 'A Vision,' *I.S.,* 13 February 1926, pp. 714–716.
111. 'The Winding Stair,' *I.S.,* 1 February 1930, pp. 436–437.
112. 'Metrical Experiments,' *I.S.,* 10 September 1927, pp. 12–13.
113. *I.S.,* 2 February 1929, pp. 437–438.
114. Unp. ltr., 20 April 1926.
115. Unp. ltr., 10 March 1926.
116. Unp. ltr. to Cornelius J. Sullivan, 12 May 1926.
117. *Memoir,* p. 184; *Letters,* p. 170.
118. Frank O'Connor, 'Two Friends: Yeats and AE,' *Yale Review,* XXIX (September 1939), pp. 60–88. Confirmed in interview with Mr. Padraic Colum.
119. *I.S.,* 24 December 1927, pp. 380–381.
120. *Letters,* p. 184.
121. Strong, '"AE" – a Practical Mystic,' p. 428.
122. *Living Torch,* p. 37.
123. Interview with Miss Irene Haugh.
124. 'Myth and Folk Tale,' *I.S.,* 22 November 1924, pp. 334–335; *Living Torch,* p. 38.
125. Diarmuid Russell, 'AE, George William Russell,' *Modern Reading,* No. 10 (London, 1944), pp. 23–34.
126. *Ibid.,* p. 24.
127. Unp. ltr., 19 November 1934.
128. *Letters,* p. 173.
129. *I.S.,* 8 January 1927, p. 436.
130. *Memoir,* pp. 184–188.
131. 'The Revival of Prophecy,' *I.S.,* 11 September 1926, pp. 13–14.
132. *Memoir,* p. 158.
133. H. Summerfield, ed. 'Unpublished Letters from AE to John Eglinton,' *Malahat Review,* April 1970, pp. 84–107.

134. *Letters,* p. 175.
135. N.C., *I.S.,* 21 May 1927, p. 248.
136. N.C., *I.S.,* 28 July 1927, p. 463.
137. N.C., *I.S.,* 20 August 1927, p. 559.
138. N.C., *I.S.,* 10 September 1927, p. 5.
139. N.W., *I.H.,* 30 January 1915, p. 67.
140. 'A Study of American Culture,' *I.S.,* 19 February 1927, pp. 573–574, 576.
141. Summerfield, ed. 'Letters from AE to Eglinton,' p. 100.
142. 'An Impression of America,' *I.S.,* 26 May 1928, pp. 227–229.
143. *New York Times,* 26 January 1928, p. 15.
144. 'An Impression of America,' p. 227.
145. Claude Bragdon, *Merely Players* (New York, 1929), p. 177.
146. *Letters,* p. 181.
147. *Memoir,* pp. 193–194.
148. Simone Téry, 'As Others See Us,' *I.S.,* 10 November 1928, pp. 188–189.
149. *New York Times,* 7 February 1928, p. 12. See also *ibid.,* 29 January 1928, p. 3; 30 January 1928, p. 8; 2 February 1928, p. 25; 4 February 1928, p. 7.
150. Shaemas O'Sheel, 'Two Irishmen,' *New Republic,* LIV (22 February 1928), pp. 14–16.
151. D. Ms. 454, to Osborn Bergin, 11 February 1928.
152. William Lyon Phelps, *Autobiography with Letters* (New York, London, Toronto, 1939), pp. 828–832.
153. 'Dean DeLury Pays Tribute,' *Canadian Theosophist,* XVI (August 1935), p. 167.
154. 'An Impression of America,' p. 227.
155. Patrick Gallagher, *My Story* (Dungloe, Donegal, n.d.), p. 321.
156. 'The Reading of Poetry,' *I.S.,* 9 November 1929, pp. 191–192.
157. D. Ms. 454, 11 February 1928.
158. 'Is America Dollar-bound?' *Forum and Century,* LXXXIII (January 1930), pp. 32–36.
159. *New York Times,* 21 April 1928, p. 20.
160. *Ibid.,* 22 April 1928, p. 31.
161. Robert Collis, *The Silver Fleece: an Autobiography* (New York, 1937), pp. 270–278.
162. 'An Impression of America,' pp. 228–229.
163. D. Ms. 459, to Monk Gibbon, 13 July 1928.
164. Implied in an unp. ltr. to Bernard Shaw, 21 February 1929. See also L. A. G. Strong, ' "AE" – a Practical Mystic,' *Listener,* LIII (10 March 1955), pp. 427–428; Francis Hackett, letter to the Editor, *Listener* LIII (24 March 1955), pp. 523, 525.

164a. D. Ms. 467, to Sir John and Lady Lavery, 2 January 1929.
165. *New York Times,* 27 May 1928, III, p. 3.
166. 'Is America Dollar-bound?' p. 36.
167. *Letters,* pp. 177–178, 180.
168. D. Ms. 498a, to Leah Bernstein, 5 May 1930.
169. Frank O'Connor, *My Father's Son* (London, 1968), pp. 79–80.
170. *Letters,* pp. 179–180. See also *Memoir,* pp. 200–201.
170a. 'The Clandillon Libel Action,' *Irish Times,* 9 and 13 November 1928, p. 11 and p. 3.
171. L. A. G. Strong, *Green Memory* (London, 1961), p. 310.
172. *Some Passages,* pp. 59–60.
173. Unp. Diary, summary for 1928.
174. Unp. ltr. to Bernard Shaw, 12 February 1929.
175. *Some Passages,* p. 60.
176. Unp. ltr. to W. T. H. Howe, 19 February 1929; D. Ms. 473, to James Stephens, 8 March 1929.
177. 'The Hibernian Academy,' *I.S.,* 13 April 1929, pp. 106–107.
178. 'Paintings by Jack B. Yeats at the Engineers' Hall,' *I.S.,* 5 October 1929, p. 95.
179. 'Cubist Paintings,' *I.S.,* 1 June 1929, p. 254.
180. N.C., *I.S.,* 29 June 1929, p. 323. See also N.C., *I.S.,* 20 April 1929, p. 123.
181. Irene Haugh, 'A Study of "AE" (George William Russell),' *Ireland-American Review,* I (September 1938), pp. 36–49.
182. D. Ms. 487, [August 1929].
183. Interview with Miss Irene Haugh.
184. Haugh, 'A Study of "AE",' p. 36.
185. Sir Robert William Tate, *Orationes et Epistolae Dublinenses (1914–40)* (Dublin, 1941), p. 95. Kindly translated by Mr. Roger Beck.
186. *New York Times,* 18 July 1935, p. 19.
187. Interview with Miss Irene Haugh; liking for Chaplin – *New York Times,* 27 January 1928, p. 44. See also 'The Los Angelesation of Ireland,' *I.S.,* 15 January 1927, pp. 446–447.
188. N.C., *I.S.,* 4 January 1930, p. 350.
189. O'Connor, *My Father's Son,* p. 93; Mary Devenport O'Neill, 'AE is Dead,' *Irish Times,* 23 July 1935, p. 6.
190. N.C., *I.S.,* 22 February 1930, pp. 487–488; N.C., *I.S.,* 1 March 1930, p. 508.
191. D. Ms. 496, 20 February 1930.
192. 'The Naval Conference,' pp. 45–46.
193. Interview with Miss Irene Haugh.
194. Unp. ltr. to Lady Gregory, 5 April [1930 – postmark].
195. N.C., *I.S.,* 5 April 1930, pp. 83–84.

196. Haugh, 'A Study of "AE",' p. 47.
197. *I.S.,* 12 April 1930, pp. 111–112; Yeats, *Letters,* p. 774.
198. Summerfield, ed. 'Letters from AE to Eglinton,' p. 101.
199. Unp. ltr. to Miss Piercy, 25 February 1929.
200. 'Interview with "AE",' *Observer,* 7 September 1930, p. 12; Charles-Marie Garnier, 'George Russell, AE, Poète du Sommeil,' *Etudes Anglaises,* III (1939), pp. 225–233.
201. N.C., *I.S.,* 5 April 1930, p. 84.
202. Unp. ltr. to John M. Gaus, 12 March 1929.
203. Summerfield, ed. 'Letters from AE to Eglinton,' p. 101.
204. N.C., *I.S.,* 12 April 1930, p. 105.

Chapter Eight

1. Unp. ltr. to Bernard Shaw, 12 February 1929.
2. Porter, ed. *Mínanlábáin,* p. 9.
3. *Ibid.,* pp. 2-3.
4. Unp. ltr. from Mary Rumsey to AE, 12 June 1930.
5. 'National Tribute Paid to Mr. George W. Russell,' *Irish Independent,* 4 September 1930; *Irish Times,* 18 July 1935, p. 7.
6. 'The Philosophy of Rural Civilisation,' *Bulletin of the State Board of Agriculture,* Jefferson City, Missouri, XXVIII (November 1930), pp. 4-13.

6a. Jane Judge, 'AE Appears as Artist, Poet and Prophet,' *Savannah News,* 15 March 1931. See also issue of this newspaper for 8 March 1931.

7. Henry A. Wallace, 'AE: a Prophet Out of an Ancient Age,' *Colby Library Quarterly,* IV (May 1955), pp. 28-31.
8. Unp. ltr. from Henry Wallace to Prof. Richard Cary, 22 April 1961.
9. Henry A. Wallace, 'An Appreciation of One of Ireland's Greatest Writers,' *Ireland American Review,* Book IV (n.d.), pp. 16-38.
10. *New York Times,* 24 September 1930, p. 25.
11. *Ibid.,* 25 September 1930, p. 29; *Memoir,* pp. 207, 217.
12. D. Ms. 510, 13 October 1930.
13. *Letters,* p. 191.
14. D. Ms. 512, 12 November 1930.
15. *Letters,* pp. 190-191.
16. James Morgan Pryse, 'George William Russell, Poet of the Inner Life,' *Canadian Theosophist,* XVI (August 1935), pp. 164-166.

17. Unp. ltr. to James Pryse, 24 November 1930.
18. D. Ms. 518, 12 December 1930.
19. D. Ms. 513, 19 November 1930.
20. D. Ms. 516, to Joseph O'Neill, 29 November 1930; D. Ms. 518 to Joseph O'Neill, 12 December 1930.
21. Unp. ltr. to Stephen MacKenna, 2 January 1931; D. Ms. 520, to Irene Haugh, 23 December 1930.
22. D. Ms. 520, 23 December 1930.
23. *New York Times,* 28 December 1930, p. 19.
23a. *New York Times,* 12 January 1931.
24. Porter, ed. *Mínanlábáin,* pp. 8-9.
25. D. Ms. 524, to Joseph O'Neill, 12 March 1931.
26. Pp. 10, 23, 42.
27. *Earth Breath,* p. 36.
28. William Lyon Phelps, *Autobiography with Letters* (New York, London, Toronto, 1939), p. 833.
29. *Memoir,* pp. 230-231.
30. *Ibid.,* pp. 231-232.
31. Porter, ed. *Mínanlábáin,* pp. 9-14.
32. Unp. ltr. to L. A. G. Strong, 24 October 1931.
33. Porter, ed. *Mínanlábáin,* p. 29.
34. E.g. 'Ecclesiastical Art in Ireland,' *I.S.,* 14 September 1929, pp. 26-27.
35. Unp. ltr. to Lady Gregory, [23 October 1931].
36. Unp. ltr. to L. A. G. Strong, [c. December 1931].
37. D. Ms. 535, [early December 1931].
38. Unp. ltr. from Yeats to AE, 29 October [1931]; D. Ms. 535, to W. B. Yeats, [early December 1931].
39. Gibbon, 'Thesis,' p. 26.
40. Porter, ed. *Mínanlábáin,* p. 34.
41. Gibbon, 'Thesis,' p. 376.
42. Patrick Kavanagh, *The Green Fool* (London, 1938), p. 300.
43. Porter, ed. *Mínanlábáin,* p. 36.
44. Phelps, *Autobiography with Letters,* p. 834.
45. Unp. ltr. to Edith Linnett, 29 April 1932.
46. Gibbon, 'Thesis,' p. 376.
47. Vera Watson, 'AE to E. H. W. Meyerstein,' *English,* XII (Autumn 1959), pp. 220-225.
48. Interview with Miss Irene Haugh.
49. *Bibliography,* p. 175.
50. H. Summerfield, ed. 'Unpublished Letters from AE to John Eglinton,' *Malahat Review,* April 1970, pp. 84-107.
51. Porter, ed. *Mínanlábáin,* pp. 36, 40.
52. Summerfield, ed. 'Letters from AE to Eglinton,' p. 103.

53. D. Ms. 545. [5 April 1932].
54. *Letters,* p. 197.
55. Porter, ed. *Mínanlábáin,* pp. 49-50.
56. Frank O'Connor, *My Father's Son* (London 1968), pp. 111-112.
57. Frank O'Connor, 'Two Friends: Yeats and AE,' *Yale Review,* XXIX (September 1939), pp. 60-88.
58. *My Father's Son,* p. 113.
59. Autograph ms. of the poems.
60. Porter, ed. *Mínanlábáin,* pp. 14, 53.
61. *Irish Times,* 13 December 1932, p. 8.
62. D. Ms. 598, n. 2.
63. *Bibliography,* p. 142.
64. Mary Colum, 'A.E.,' *Saturday Review of Literature,* XII (27 July 1935), pp. 11-12; Clifford Bax, *Ideas and People* (London 1936), p. 233.
65. Frank O'Connor, 'Two Friends,' p. 66.
66. D. Ms. 584, [after 22 July 1933].
67. O'Connor, *My Father's Son,* p. 113.
68. D. Ms. 564, 23 December 1932. Cf. *Avatars,* p. 181.
69. Unp. ltr. to Mr. Ratcliffe, 11 January 1933.
70. D. Ms. 572, to Sean O'Faolain, 5 April 1933.
71. D. Ms. 571, to St. John Ervine, 5 April 1933.
72. *Ibid.*
73. William Rothenstein, *Since Fifty. Men and Memories, 1922-1938* (London, 1939), p. 122.
74. *Letters,* p. 201.
75. Pp. 169-172.
76. *Letters,* pp. 202-203.
77. *Colby Library Quarterly,* IV (May 1955), p. 45.
78. H. F. Norman, 'The Theosophy of George Russell ('AE'),' *Theosophical Forum,* VIII (February 1936), pp. 92-99.
79. P. G. Bowen, ' "AE": Theosophist,' *Canadian Theosophist,* XVI (August 1935), pp. 162-164.
80. Interview with Miss Dorothy Emerson.
81. Unp. ltr. to W. T. H. Howe, 5 June 1933.
82. O'Connor, *My Father's Son,* p. 115.
83. D. Ms. 624, n.l.
84. *Memoir,* pp. 259-260. Verse fragment in notebook at University of Texas.
85. O'Connor, *My Father's Son,* p. 115.
86. Unp. ltr. to Mrs. F. R. Higgins.
87. Porter, ed. *Mínanlábáin,* pp. 15-19.
88. Unp. ltr. to F. R. Higgins, 28 July 1933.

89. P. G. Bowen, 'AE and Theosophy,' *Aryan Path,* VI (December 1935), pp. 722-726.
90. P. G. Bowen, *The Occult Way* (London, n.d.), pp. v, 222-223.
91. *Letters,* p. 205.
92. D. Ms. 587, to Oliver St. John Gogarty, 8 August 1933.
93. Gibbon, 'Thesis,' p. 378n.
94. D. Ms. 596, [? October 1933].
95. Bax, *Ideas and People,* pp. 236-237.
96. D. Ms. 634, to Joseph O'Neill, 29 October 1934.
97. Philip Mairet, *A. R. Orage, A Memoir* (London, 1936), p. 118; 'Orage: Memories,' *New English Weekly,* VI (15 November 1934), pp. 97-100.
98. Unp. ltr. from Philip Mairet to John Eglinton, 10 November 1935.
99. Porter, ed. *Mínanlábáin,* p. 89.
100. Pp. 81-83.
101. Pp. 105-106.
102. P. 132.
103. *Letters,* p. 209.
104. Unp. ltr. to Sir Michael ?, [27 October 1933].
105. Summerfield, ed. 'Letters from AE to Eglinton,' p. 105.
106. Unp. ltr., 27 November 1933.
107. Porter, ed. *Mínanlábáin,* p. 92.
108. Monk Gibbon, *The Masterpiece and the Man: Yeats as I knew Him* (London, 1959), pp. 206-207. See also p. 31.
109. *Living Torch,* pp. 71-73.
110. Unp. ltr. to Seumas O'Sullivan, [late December 1933 or early January 1934]; D. Ms. 601, to Irene Haugh, 1 January 1934.
111. Porter, ed. *Mínanlábáin,* pp. 94-95.
112. Unp. ltr. to Mrs. Fiske Warren, 16 March 1934.
113. D. Ms. 610, to Van Wyck Brooks, 29 May 1934.
114. *Letters,* p. 212.
115. *Memoir,* p. 270.
116. D. Ms. 687, to Eleanor Skipworth, 2 May 1935.
117. *Letters,* pp. 212-214, 239-240.
118. D. Ms. 613, to Hugh MacDiarmid, 19 June 1934.
119. D. Ms. 636, to Monk Gibbon, 1 November 1934.
120. D. Ms. 630, to Osborn Bergin, [? 19 October 1934].
121. D. Ms. 633, to Osborn Bergin, 25 October 1934.
122. Porter, ed. *Mínanlábáin,* pp. 97-98.
123. D. Ms. 619, to Ruth Pitter, 16 August 1934.
124. Unp. ltr. to Seumas O'Sullivan, n.d.
125. Ernest Rhys, *Letters from Limbo* (London, 1936), p. 130.
126. Porter, ed. *Mínanlábáin,* p. 98.

127. D. Ms. 643, to Van Wyck Brooks, 19 November 1934.
128. Raynor C. Johnson, *The Light and the Gate* (London, 1964), p. 16.
129. Constance Sitwell, *Conversations with Six Friends* (London: privately printed, 1959), pp. 46-51.
130. Unp. ltr. to Bernard Shaw, 26 September 1934.
131. D. Ms. 634, to Joseph O'Neill, 29 October 1934.
132. D. Ms. 645 and 646, to Joseph O'Neill, [both late November 1934].
133. D. Ms. 637, [5 November 1934].
134. C. P. Curran, letter to the Editor, *Sunday Times,* 4 August 1935, p. 8.
135. Henry A. Wallace, 'An Appreciation of One of Ireland's Greatest Writers,' *Ireland American Review,* Book IV (n.d.), pp. 16-38.
136. *Living Torch,* p. 76.
137. D. Ms. 649, to Eleanor Skipworth, 9 December 1934.
138. *Memoir,* pp. 274-275.
139. 'Last Letters of AE in Washington,' *Oriel Review,* I (April 1943), pp. 86-103.
140. *Ibid.,* p. 89.
141. *Colby Library Quarterly,* IV (May 1955), p. 46.
142. Unp. ltr. to F. R. Higgins, 6 February 1935.
143. D. Ms. 660, to Charles Weekes, 20 January 1935.
144. Wallace, 'An Appreciation,' p. 26.
145. D. Ms. 664, to Charles Weekes, 29 January 1935.
146. D. Ms. 659, to Joseph O'Neill, 18 January 1935; D. Ms. 667, to Charles Weekes, 6 February 1935.
147. Unp. ltr. to F. R. Higgins, 1 February 1935.
148. Unp. ltr., 6 February 1935.
149. *Ibid.*
150. D. Ms. 662, 26 January 1935.
151. D. Ms. 686, to Joseph O'Neill, 26 April 1935.
152. 'Last Letters of AE in Washington,' p. 96.
153. Faik Konitza, 'Recollections of AE,' *New York Times,* 26 July 1935, p. 14.
154. 'Last Letters of AE in Washington,' p. 97.
155. M. L. Wilson, 'My Impressions of George Russell – AE – the Seer,' *Oriel Review,* I (April 1943), pp. 66-67.
156. John Collier, 'With the Poet of the Celtic Twilight in Washington,' *Oriel Review,* I (April 1943), pp. 70-71.
157. D. Ms. 675, to Joseph O'Neill, 18 March 1935.
158. Fred Henderson, ' "A.E." An Appreciation and a Remembrance,' *Eastern Daily Press* (Norwich), 19 July 1935, p. 8.

159. *Letters,* p. 218.
160. Unp. ltr. to F. R. Higgins, 16 April 1935.
161. Hugh A. Law, letter to the Editor, *Sunday Times,* 18 August 1935, p. 10.
162. D. Ms. 684, to Daniel Macmillan, 17 April 1935.
163. Pp. 57-58. Cf. *Imaginations and Reveries,* p. 253.
164. *Living Torch.* p. 78.
165. Sitwell, *Conversations with Six Friends,* pp. 52-57.
166. C. F. Andrews, 'An Evening with "A.E.",' *Visva-Bharati Quarterly,* I (August 1935), pp. 91-92.
167. Unp. ltr. to F. R. Higgins, 16 April 1935.
168. D. Ms. 686, to Joseph O'Neill, 26 April 1935.
169. Unp. ltr. to Charles Weekes, 1 June 1935.
170. *Living Torch,* pp. 80-81.
171. *Ibid.,* p. 66.
172. D. Ms. 704, to Ruth Pitter, [postmark 3 July 1935].
173. *Colby Library Quarterly,* IV (May 1955), p. 56.
174. Unp. ltr. to F. R. Higgins, 11 July [1935].
175. Gibbon, *The Masterpiece and the Man,* p. 188.
176. Wallace, 'An Appreciation,' p. 28.
177. *Letters,* p. 223.
178. Unp. ltr., 11 July [1935].
179. Unp. ltr. from Pamela Travers to F. R. Higgins, 15 July 1935.
180. Unp. ltr., 15 July 1935.
181. Wallace, 'An Appreciation,' p. 27.
182. *Letters,* p. 225.
183. *Ibid.*
184. 'The Press Reports,' *Canadian Theosophist,* XVI (August 1935), pp. 170-174. Corrected from *Irish Times,* 18 July 1935, p. 7.
185. Gogarty, 'An Appreciation,' *Irish Times,* 18 July 1935, p. 7.
186. Wallace, 'An Appreciation,' p. 28.
187. *Bibliography*, p. 252.
188. Joseph Hone, *W. B. Yeats 1865-1939,* 2nd ed. (London, 1962), p. 442.
189. Yeats, *Letters,* p. 838.
190. Hone, *Yeats,* p. 442.
191. 'The Funeral of "A.E.",' *Observer,* 21 July 1935, p. 15.
192. 'Interment of George Russell,' *Canadian Theosophist,* XVI (September 1935), pp. 221-222.
193. *Memoir,* pp. 284-285.
194. 18 July 1935, p. 6.
195. Yeats, *Letters,* p. 838.
196. N.W., *I.H.,* 3 September 1910, p. 731.

197. L.A., *I.H.*, 10 August 1918, p. 525; L.A., *I.H.*, 6 August 1921, p. 531.
198. *Memoir*, pp. 164-165.
199. *Candle of Vision*, p. 44; *Song and Its Fountains*, p. 131.

ABBREVIATIONS USED IN THE NOTES

Bibliography. Alan Denson, *Printed Writings by George W. Russell (AE)*, Northwestern University Press and Faber (1961).

Draft of 'Sunset'. Unpublished draft of AE's fragmentary memoir 'The Sunset of Fantasy'.

Gibbon, 'Thesis'. Monk Gibbon's unpublished Thesis.

I.H. Irish Homestead.

I.S. Irish Statesman.

I.T. Irish Theosophist.

L.A. Leading article.

Letters. Alan Denson, ed. *Letters from AE.*

Living Torch. A.E., *The Living Torch* ed. Monk Gibbon.

Memoir. John Eglinton, *A Memoir of AE.*

N.C. 'Notes and Comments'.

N.W. 'Notes of the Week'.

Porter, ed. *Minanlábáin*. Lucy Kingsley Porter, ed. *AE's Letters to Minanlábáin.*

Secret Doctrine. H. P. Blavatsky, *The Secret Doctrine* (California, 1963).

Some Passages. *Some Passages from the letters of AE to W. B. Yeats.*

Unpublished material cited in the text and notes is located as follows:

Armagh County Museum, Northern Ireland
  Letters from AE to Ella Young
  AE's notebook containing account of a dream, December 1906
Berg Collection, New York Public Library
  Letters from AE to Mr. and Mrs. Padraic Colum, Lady Gregory (except letter postmarked 4 July 1900), W. T. H. Howe, Joseph Kiernan, E. H. W. Meyerstein, James Pryse, Mrs. James Stephens, T. Fisher Unwin, W. B. Yeats
  Letters from Sir Horace Plunkett and W. B. Yeats to Lady Gregory
  Typescript of Lady Gregory's 'Memoirs'
British Museum
  Letters and a telegram from AE to George Bernard Shaw
Colby College Library, Maine
  Transcripts of letters from AE to Van Wyck Brooks, William O'Leary Curtis, Miss A. W. Denijs, St. John Ervine, John M. Gaus, Monk Gibbon, Sir Henry Lawson, Edith Linnett, Sean O'Faolain, Herbert Palmer, Israel Regardie, Theodore Spicer Simson, Mrs. Fiske Warren, Walter Muir Whitehill
  Letters from Philip Mairet and Mrs. M. F. Talbot to W. K. Magee ('John Eglinton')
  Letter from Henry Wallace to Prof. Richard Cary
  Ms. of an unfinished poem about Apollo.
Collection of Major R. G. Gregory of Devon
  Letter from AE to Lady Gregory postmarked 4 July 1900
Collection of Mr. James A. Healy of New York
  Letters from AE to Ernest Boyd
  Letter from Dudley Digges to Richard Campbell
Houghton Library, Harvard University
  Letters from AE to Sir William Rothenstein
  Mss. of the poems 'I've no exotic deity,' 'Distraction,' 'Incarnation,' and 'Lost Talisman'
Lilly Library, University of Indiana
  Letters from AE to Upton Sinclair, James Stephens, Cornelius J. Sullivan
  Letters to AE from Mrs. Padraic Colum, James Pryse, Mary Rumsey, James Stephens, W. B. Yeats
  AE's lecture 'The Sunset of Fantasy'
  AE's report 'Ulster and Irish Trade Policy'
  AE's Theosophical Diary, 1895-1896
National Library of Ireland, Dublin
  Mr. Alan Denson's transcript of a collection of letters by AE

see Chapter 1, note 9
Ohio State University
Dr Grace Emily Jameson's Thesis
Plunkett Foundation Library, Oxford
Letters from Sir Horace Plunkett to Richard Campbell
Sir Horace Plunkett's Diary
Trinity College Library, Dublin
Dr. Monk Gibbon's Thesis
University of Texas Library
Letters from AE to Mr. E. L. Allhusen, Douglas Goldring, Mr. Hackett, Frank Harris, Mr. and Mrs. F. R. Higgins, Sir Michael Sadleir, Mr. Ratcliffe, James Starkey ('Seumas O'Sullivan'), L. A. G. Strong
Letter from Pamela Travers to F. R. Higgins
AE's play 'Enid'
Draft of AE's 'The Sunset of Fantasy'
University of Victoria Library, British Columbia
Letters from AE to John Eglinton

Abbreviations

Bibliography, Alan Denson, *Printed Writings by George W. Russell (AE): a Bibliography* (Evanston, Illinois, 1961)
Candle of Vision, A.E., *The Candle of Vision* (London, 1918)
Collected Poems, A.E., *Collected Poems,* 2nd ed. reprinted (London, 1935)
Divine Vision, A.E., *The Divine Vision and Other Poems* (London, 1904)
D. Ms. National Library of Ireland Ms. 9967-69 – see Chapter 1, note 9
Draft of 'Sunset' Draft of AE's 'The Sunset of Fantasy'
Earth Breath, A.E. *The Earth Breath and Other Poems* (New York and London, 1897)
Gibbon, 'Thesis', Monk Gibbon's thesis 'The Early Years of George Russell (AE) and his Connection with the Theosophical Movement' (Trinity College, Dublin, 1947-1948)
I.H., Irish Homestead
Imaginations and Reveries, A.E., *Imaginations and Reveries* (Dublin and London, 1915)
Interpreters, A.E., *The Interpreters* (London, 1922)
I.S., Irish Statesman
I.T., Irish Theosophist

L. A., Leading article (number of page on which article begins given)

Letters, Alan Denson, ed. *Letters from AE* (London, New York, and Toronto, 1961)

Living Torch, A.E., *The Living Torch* (London, 1937)

ltr(s). letter(s)

Memoir, John Eglinton, *A Memoir of AE: George William Russell* (London, 1937)

N. C., 'Notes and Comments'

n.d., no date

N.W., 'Notes of the Week' (number of page on which particular passage appears given)

Porter, ed. *Mínanlábáin,* Lucy Kingsley Porter, ed *AE's Letters to Mínanlábáin* (New York, 1937)

Secret Doctrine, H. P. Blavatsky, *The Secret Doctrine: The Synthesis of Science, Religion, and Philosophy,* 2 vols. (Pasadena, California, 1963)

Some Passages, Some Passages from the Letters of AE to W. B. Yeats (Dublin, 1936)

Song and Its Fountains, A.E., *Song and Its Fountains* (London, 1932)

'Sunset of Fantasy', A.E., 'The Sunset of Fantasy,' *Dublin Magazine,* XIII (January 1938), 6-11

unp., unpublished

Yeats, *Letters,* Allan Wade, ed. *The Letters of W. B. Yeats* (London, 1954)

Index

Compiler's note: *The figure shown in brackets following a page reference is to a footnote indice where a quotation has been made without giving the title of the piece from which the extract comes, or the name of the person concerned.*